An Ethical Global Information Society

IFIP – The International Federation for Information Processing

IFIP was founded in 1960 under the auspices of UNESCO, following the First World Computer Congress held in Paris the previous year. An umbrella organization for societies working in information processing, IFIP's aim is two-fold: to support information processing within its member countries and to encourage technology transfer to developing nations. As its mission statement clearly states,

> IFIP's mission is to be the leading, truly international, apolitical organization which encourages and assists in the development, exploitation and application of information technology for the benefit of all people.

IFIP is a non-profitmaking organization, run almost solely by 2500 volunteers. It operates through a number of technical committees, which organize events and publications. IFIP's events range from an international congress to local seminars, but the most important are:

- the IFIP World Computer Congress, held every second year;
- open conferences;
- working conferences.

The flagship event is the IFIP World Computer Congress, at which both invited and contributed papers are presented. Contributed papers are rigorously refereed and the rejection rate is high.

As with the Congress, participation in the open conferences is open to all and papers may be invited or submitted. Again, submitted papers are stringently refereed.

The working conferences are structured differently. They are usually run by a working group and attendance is small and by invitation only. Their purpose is to create an atmosphere conducive to innovation and development. Refereeing is less rigorous and papers are subjected to extensive group discussion.

Publications arising from IFIP events vary. The papers presented at the IFIP World Computer Congress and at open conferences are published as conference proceedings, while the results of the working conferences are often published as collections of selected and edited papers.

Any national society whose primary activity is in information may apply to become a full member of IFIP, although full membership is restricted to one society per country. Full members are entitled to vote at the annual General Assembly, National societies preferring a less committed involvement may apply for associate or corresponding membership. Associate members enjoy the same benefits as full members, but without voting rights. Corresponding members are not represented in IFIP bodies. Affiliated membership is open to non-national societies, and individual and honorary membership schemes are also offered.

An Ethical Global Information Society

Culture and democracy revisited

IFIP TC9 WG 9.2/9.5 International Conference on Culture and Democracy Revisited in the Global Information Society, 8–10 May 1997, Corfu, Greece

Edited by

Jacques Berleur

Computing Science Faculty
University of Namur
Belgium

and

Diane Whitehouse

London Business School
London
United Kingdom

SPRINGER-SCIENCE+BUSINESS MEDIA, B.V.

First edition 1997

Originally published by Chapman & Hall in 1997

ISBN 978-1-4757-5181-9 ISBN 978-0-387-35327-2 (eBook)
DOI 10.1007/978-0-387-35327-2

A catalogue record for this book is available from the British Library

∞ Printed on permanent acid-free text paper, manufactured in accordance with ANSI/NISO Z39.48-1992 and ANSI/NISO Z39.48-1984 (Permanence of Paper).

CONTENTS

PART THREE Cultural Challenges

PART FOUR Democratic Challenges

Jacques Berleur and Diane Whitehouse**, Editors*
** Institut d'Informatique, Facultés Universitaires Notre-Dame de la Paix, Rue Grandgagnage, 21, B-5000 Namur, Belgium*
Phone: +32 81 72 4976, Fax: +32 81 72 4967
Email: jberleur@info.fundp.ac.be
*** PhD Programme London Business School, Regent's Park, London NW1 4SA, United Kingdom*
Tel: +44 171 262 5050 X3646, Fax: +44 171 724 7875
Email: dwhitehouse@lbs.lon.ac.uk

THE 'GLOBAL VILLAGE' OF BABEL?

Babylôn (Greek), *Bâbèl* (Hebrew) is a very old city in southern Mesopotamia where the Israelites were deported in 586 BC. To the Israelites, Babylon was undoubtedly the city opposed to God as well as a permanent reminder of its deprivation. The city of the 'door-of-Gods' (*Bab-ilani*), as the Babylonians called their city, became 'the place to confuse, to muddle' (*bâlal*). Why? What happened?

The biblical text about the myth of Babel is very short: it consists of nine verses (Genesis 11, 1-9). The brief narrative tells how the earliest humans spoke a single language, but an event occurred that explains the subsequent variety of languages spoken among the earth's peoples. Human history takes a decisive turn from a common thread to many strands.

Noah's descendants wandered into Babylonia, where they perfected the techniques for monumental brick architecture. They built a well-known ziggurat, the Tower of Babel, whose top was said to reach the heavens. Building the tower is interpreted as an act of arrogance and an attempt to gain fame while, at the same time, constructing the city is perceived as an endeavour to preserve the unity of humankind. But civilization can become an end in itself; it results in self-defeat.

God descends to Babylon to confuse human speech and to scatter the people all over the earth (Laymon, 1971; Metzger and Coogan, 1993).

The Old Testament explanation of the construction and destruction of the Tower of Babel is written using some very homogeneous lexical categories: construction (building up, city, make, tower, bricks, stones, bitumen as mortar), language (language, name, word, speak, speak to oneself, hear, call), totality (whole, all, one people, all over, all the world, all the earth), uniformity (same language, same words, one name), and so on. Ideas expressed in opposition to each other are also evident: men on earth, Yahweh in heaven, bottom versus top[1].

When we look carefully at the text, we can also discern semantic categories full of significance. At the beginning of the text, we find expressions or reflexive verbs which evoke a kind of rolling-up into oneself: 'the whole world spoke the same language', 'they came upon a valley and settled themselves there', 'they said to one another', 'let us mould bricks', 'let us build ourselves a city and a tower', 'let us make a name for ourselves'. At the end of the text, all the reflexive verbs disappear: 'let us there confuse their language', 'one will not understand what another says', 'that is why it is called Babel', and 'he scattered them all over the earth'[2].

This analysis reveals at least two semantic oppositions: rolling-up on oneself *versus* dispersal, and self-nomination *versus* denomination. The project of building a unique world, a city and a tower that will celebrate its architects, is broken down by another's intervention. The messages of separation and dispersal are the author's way of expressing that the history of mankind cannot be conceived without us receiving a name or being situated by others, and where respect for differences and diversity is the only way to escape being identical. We could also call these opposites 'the self *versus* the other'. This idea of separation is deeply rooted in the thinking of the Old Testament: we also find it clearly expressed in the very beginning of the Bible, the first chapter of Genesis, the myth of creation (Beauchamp, 1969).

Other semantic categories can be found like 'totality *versus* lack of', where the project of 'totality' is contrasted with 'the prohibited'. To quote the act of divine intervention:

> 'If now, while they are one people, all speaking the same language, they have started to do this, nothing will later stop them from doing whatever they presume to do. Let us go down and there confuse their language' (Genesis, 11, 6-7).

What the myth of Babel tells us is that rather than uniformity, uniqueness, settlement, fixation, self-nomination, totality, singularity, and desire for power, real freedom for human beings lies in differentiation, plurality, dispersal, movement, denomination, pluralism, and prohibition. The first grouping of concepts leads human beings - and that was certainly the experience of the Israelites in their deportation - to destruction or to lack of identity in a foreign land.

Each and every society may be tempted to reduce everything to unity and to impose itself in a totalitarian way, abolishing any differences. Official discourse is built as absolute knowledge. Words are identified with reality. Truth becomes a tower constructed of evidence which imposes itself on the world. Similarly, the builders of the Tower of Babel are described as saying: 'Let us dominate the earth and control it, and let our name be known by all and remain for ever' (Genesis 11, 4). It is this kind of world that leads to a regime of identity, repetition, and anonymity; it is a sad, enclosed world, surrounded by solitude. And this world also leads to its own self-destruction.

This one-dimensional world, this chase for a foolish identity, is prohibited by God, who dismantles it, who confuses the languages, by dispersing and separating the people. God speaks in order to subvert the human desire to be everything. Where there is space, we may be born (come to birth), since there is communication, exchange, and mutual recognition between subjects and nations. Because there are differences and diversity, we are enriched by the speech of others, without losing our own identity. 'Therefore is the name of it called Babel; because the Lord did there confuse the language of all the earth' (Genesis 11, 9).

The myth of Babel is all about language, knowledge, communication - culture; building places with materials - economics; and power over or respect for others, domination, control or mutual recognition - democracy. Unity lies ahead of us, but it is not granted: it comes as a result of hard work through respect for other cultures and democracies, and through reconciling diversity.

Recent literature as well as discussions in newsgroups on the global information society remind us that nations, with their particular languages, history, ways of ruling, and cultures are looking for a new place in our time. Most probably, Europe and Europeans could make a contribution to this debate and play a role in the discussion because of their past experiences (Semaines sociales de France, 1997). Would it not be worthwhile reading the philosophical literature on the reconciliation of diversity and respect for different cultures and democracies, for example, Immanuel Kant's *Perpetual peace* and his idea of 'Weltrepublik' (worldwide republic) (Kant, 1983; Ladrière, 1962; Berleur, 1974)?

Building a global village should at least take into account the wisdom of the myth of Babel! In introducing these ideas, we advocate diversity and difference.

THE CONFERENCE AND ITS THEMES

Working Group (WG) 9.2 (Social Accountability) of the International Federation for Information Processing (IFIP), with the support of WG9.5 (Social Implications of Digital Media and Virtual Worlds) organized a working conference in Corfu on May 8-10, 1997. Practitioners and researchers of like minds were invited to join in creating a statement about the future of culture and democracy in an ethical global information society.

The conference was a working conference. This means that papers were intended to present insights and outline issues from which participants would derive various alternatives, solutions, and actions. The conference outcome - a set of recommendations targeting decision-makers, computer scientists and professionals, consumers, and users' associations - is included in the final chapter of this book.

While most of the contributions are papers, students in particular were encouraged to submit essays involving their perceptions and visions of an ethical global information society. The purpose was to create a dialogue about the new visions perceived by younger researchers in relation to democracy and culture in a globalized world. The best essayists received support to attend the conference and their papers are included in this volume.

The conference submissions allowed us to structure the three days into sessions devoted to the main themes: ethics, the global information society, cultural challenges, democratic challenges, and the ancient Greek agora. This framework persists in the arrangement of the papers in this book.

Several contributors whose work is presented here reflect on professional ethics within the range of occupations involved in creating and designing information and communications technology (ICT). But many other papers implicitly include the treatment of ethical questions. The role of ICT professionals and their professional associations - particularly the International Federation for Information Processing (IFIP) - is one which emerges in a number of papers. Perhaps the culmination of these is the charter proposed in this volume by the Australian Computer Society.

ICT professionals need to raise ethical questions at all levels of society - the individual, organizational, regional, national, and international - not simply within their own professional associations. Some authors go further than this, and make proposals for specific legislation relating to ICT while others call for the international harmonization - wherever possible - of any such legislation.

Given the variety of the origins of the conference participants and contributors (among the countries represented were Australia, Belgium, Canada, Denmark, Finland, Greece, Mexico, the Netherlands, Thailand, the United Kingdom, Ukraine, and the United States), it is not surprising that the contributions often emphasize a shift away from a predominantly Anglo-Saxon or North American definition of ethics. They also focus on economic, cultural, and democratic considerations viewed from diverse perspectives around the globe.

Contributors critique the impetus of the global information society, and several question its relevance to their community or society. But no single definition of global information society is used. Among the aspects of a world which is becoming increasingly electronically interconnected, the contributors consider the global village, the new global order, the information society, the information highway or highways, virtual reality, virtual space, and the virtual society. Hence, papers focus not just on the Internet but on other forms of information and communications technology; they examine a range of applications as well as different ways of working and organizing. Clearly, however, the Internet and its effects, its strengths and its weaknesses, are of considerable importance throughout.

While many papers centre our attention on the policy level (probably because so many countries have over the past several years stated so publicly their aspirations to use emerging technologies for their economic development), a large number also explore different societal levels, illustrating both developments in people's everyday lives and in a number of organizational settings. The way we work, conduct commerce, and deal with capital and property are all explored. Covered too are the cultures of large companies, nonprofit organizations, and community and educational networks and their use of information technology.

So many nations have hopes for the global information society, and many have concentrated on the role of commercial partners in this development. The conference participants, in contrast, show more concern for the public availability, affordability, equality or equity, and accessibility of these electronic communications. The authors are concerned with remedying the disparities that exist throughout the world. Certainly, there are still relatively few individuals who are actually able to access the Internet. What kind of democracy will be the result?

The discussions explore the means by which information technology can be made most easily available to all sectors of the populations, including those people least likely to have access. Such a debate is tinged not simply with questions of finance but also by issues related to education, socialization, and the bias of stereotyping. Several articles outline the possibilities offered by electronic services to specific groups of people such as the elderly, or persons with a disability, or both. But even the cohorts of people so favoured by economists should not necessarily be lumped together - there is huge differentiation among people according to their individual needs; indeed, everyone is unique.

A firm commitment is made in many papers and in many of the discussions (see the final paper) to the role of the state in ensuring access. Roles are developed not just for governments but for local governments, and community and citizens' groups.

There is concern too about content. Among the many other aspects of its use, information and communications technology may be involved in changing our sexuality (Turkle, 1996). Adult materials and entertainment on the net and its use by younger people and by children are issues that emerge in a number of papers, though these concerns are expressed with the wide variety of opinion that often arises on this subject (Berger, *et al.*, 1993; Linz and Malamuth, 1993). Diversity of opinion often occurs on such important subjects of debate. Forums for discussion and debate - open spaces like the ancient Greek agora or perhaps, viewed from a certain perspective, today's electronic media - can facilitate such openness.

Because of Working Group 9.2's commitment to the concept of creating spaces for discussion and, because of the particular aptness of the conference location - Corfu - the agora is one of several metaphors that has been applied to the Internet and to the information highway throughout these papers. Other metaphors, some related to ecology and sustainability, some to bookstores and publishing, others to the role of the eighteenth century French café, also emerge. Throughout, the role of language and of rhetoric in building concepts such as the global information society is explored thoroughly and assessed critically.

ETHICS

Ethics is an overriding issue that influences all other questions on the new landscape of the global information society. A civilized community needs to have a set of criteria for its progress and development (Berleur *et al.*, 1990). Hence, we position this topic as the first main section of this book.

Here, various questions are considered from a number of cultural perspectives, enlarging the debate about the universality or the relative particularity of ethics. Ethical concepts can and do differ in various parts of the globe. But this diversity does not inhibit the creation of possible sets of guidelines - charters - that could be used as frameworks for discussions among ICT professionals, lawmakers, and policy-makers. A number of the ethical, social, institutional, and legal dilemmas currently under debate result because technological possibilities run ahead of the legal and regulatory frameworks (Hammond, 1995).

There are common fears, especially in terms of use of the Internet, that particular cultural norms, values, and customs originating in very specific geographic areas will come to dominate assumptions about behaviour in network communications. Some recent legislation attempting to define responsible behaviour on the net has been shown to be inadequately and hastily prepared (as is the case with the Communications Decency Act in the United States). Other countries appear to be moving instinctively to formulate relevant legislation (the European Community generally, and Germany specifically). Yet other analyses indicate that some countries' current legislation covers all aspects of potential illegal behaviour on the net or require few if any alterations (Akdeniz, 1996; Gringas, 1997). There are implications too for self-regulation on the part of a variety of service providers, choices involving labelling and certification of network content, issues related to transborder data flow, and for parallels to be drawn with the certifying and monitoring of other forms of communication (telephone, television, publishing).

Is a charter for citizens likely to provide a solution to the emerging ethical issues in the global information society? We may consider the proposal which France has put forward to the Organization for Economic Co-operation and Development (OECD, 1996). There is also a proposal in this book outlining a set of principles intended as guidelines for lawmakers and decision-makers in government and industry. This charter can be used both as a framework for possible future legislation and as a benchmark for citizens in assessing their own rights and responsibilities. Its format has been chosen precisely because of the difficulties apparent in diverse cultures of establishing a single, universal ethical regime. Among the principal issues of ethical concern outlined are cybercrime, equity of access, rights to privacy, freedom from surveillance, freedom of expression and opinion, democracy, diversity of culture and ideology, equitable distribution of benefits, and ownership of data.

The round table on ethics during the conference also tried to identify the major ethical issues in relation to the Internet.

GLOBAL INFORMATION SOCIETY

The effects of technological change on the global economic structure are creating profound transformations in the ways nations and companies organize production, employ labour, invest capital, and develop new products and processes (Muroyama and Stever, 1988): in turn, these decisions have enormous impacts for the ordinary human beings of this world whether they are located in the first or the third worlds. It is largely this latter perspective - examining the lives of ordinary human beings - which is taken in this selection of papers.

So far, only a small percentage of the world's population is online, and the majority of that number are from affluent countries and have professional backgrounds. In the world's poorest countries, the networking of personal communications looks a remote possibility since even portable radios now lie unused or abandoned through lack of access to batteries (Hammond, 1995; Shields, 1996).

We can all note the immense disparities that are current among regions and countries not only in the first world but also in the third world. Generally the information technology revolution has concentrated production capacities and wealth in the industrialized countries, principally the United States, Japan, and several European countries. Inequality around the globe is likely to grow, and our authors anticipate further homogenization among cultures, altering them in substantial ways that diminish their everyday relevance.

Globalization is happening, seemingly inexorably. A little like a child's kaleidoscope, with every shake of the tube, old ethical, cultural, and democratic patterns merge into new ones that are seemingly unplanned and unpredictable. The trend is both a fact and a process, both technological and human. It has multiple facets: globalization of finance and capital, markets and strategies, technology, research and development, knowledge, ways of living and cultures, perception and conscience, and so on (Group of Lisbon, 1996). Globalization results from the countless, separate actions of innumerable players (Lodge, 1995). There is no single discipline or group of experts that seems competent to explain the forces of globalization. ICT professionals are as involved as any. A call is made here for professionals in the field of ICT to create processes and institutions of reflection and discussion that focus on these momentous developments. There are roles for the members of professional associations like IFIP.

Why continue to increase efficiency? Why continue to increase complexity? Why continue to move online? Will individuals still have homes in the future? Can current and future society be anything more than a mere cocktail party? Can we move beyond a society that simply zaps, surfs or chatters?

Is globalization the 'end of history' (Fukuyama, 1992) or the 'end of geography'? (Virilio, 1997)

CULTURAL CHALLENGES

As the world homogenizes in certain aspects of its culture, a convergence in consumer desires seems to occur. Here are examples from the world of film and entertainment: in 1991, the most popular motion picture in Japan was *Terminator 2* - it brought in five times as much income as its nearest Japanese rival; similarly, Tokyo's Disneyland is the most popular of all the Disney parks and attracts over 16 million visitors a year (Shimbun, 1994; Lodge, 1995). In the years to come, will global electronic communications follow the same path as film, television, and radio or is there some chance of maintaining cultural differentiation? Will mass culture, an Internet culture, eradicate individual differences and create a completely pre-packaged culture? Certainly, it appears likely that there will eventually be a complete merger of many forms of communication, including computers, telecommunications, video, and television.

For instance, while experimentation on television technology first began in the late nineteenth century, most developments have taken place in a seventy-year period since 1926. Television ownership has grown from being limited to a social elite to a high 90+% of households in many industrialized countries. Increasingly too, families in developing countries struggle to buy a television before they buy any other domestic appliance, after saving many, many months' or years' worth of salaries. But in either case, viewers often receive little more than light entertainment and titillation which is frequently the recipient of biting criticism. (Though, from a historical perspective (Johns, 1982), historians, philosophers, and cultural analysts have not always appreciated the precise meanings of the cultural artifacts of previous generations.)

Technologies are socially embedded, and traditional pilot projects show, for example with interactive television services, that audience habits are slow to develop and tend to mirror those of older technologies. The use of computer-related technologies is located in very specific social settings (Shroeder, 1997, p.105). While the information society can stimulate new forms of cultural identity, it can also rekindle and intensify old cultural relations (Held, 1995). So, it is the very same technologies that create the global village as raise awareness of cultural differentiation. It is these cultural differences that may make large, though as yet indeterminate, impact on economic life in the developing global information infrastructure (Fukuyama, 1995).

Among the cultural challenges explored specifically in this section, the authors write of the use of language, whether spoken or written, and how it shapes the way we think. Societies, communities, and individuals are encouraged to question the rhetoric and metaphors handed down to them by policy-makers and politicians. A normative, educational approach offers one means of questioning and counterbalancing such prevailing forces (although other educational institutions may be wholly supportive of their society's commitment to the advances of the global information society).

Several of the cultural challenges covered by our conference participants relate also to the domain of organizations and employment: information technology and its use in different organizational cultures and different cultural forms of systems design and development.

Organizations may be involved with information and communication technology in many different ways. Culturally, it is almost impossible to generalize what use will be made of ICT, and certainly not by employing the model of large business organizations that almost consistently emerges from contemporary business and management literature.

Other authors concentrate on the cultures of not-for-profit organizations, smaller groups and, indeed, communication between individuals.

DEMOCRATIC CHALLENGES

The new information and communication technologies, like many other technologies, have a certain potential for enabling integration and cohesion. But this shift does not necessarily imply as a result societies that are more equal or more democratic. While the governments, public authorities, and even the market, may all potentially act as guarantors of democratic values, it is also the role of ICT professionals and the public at large to keep abreast of challenges to democracy and to fight for human and civil rights.

Cyberspace is not an uncontested terrain; far from it (Shields, 1996). Libertarianism was one of the earliest, most frequently heard, voices describing its aspirations for the Internet. Many views in the early 1980s, even still in the early 1990s, were idealistic and utopian. A perspective of freedom promoted by electronic communications was common. But there are many other stakeholders in contemporary society influencing the development of electronic communications, perhaps the most powerful being market forces.

The freedom provided by electronic communications is one that has been frequently expressed; but it can, in contrast, be viewed as a vast, seductive harvesting machine that delivers bodies, culture, and labour to a virtual irreality that is blind to a sense of geographic place and community (Kroker and Weinstein, 1994). Virtuality may not so much change capitalism and liberalism, as continue to support them (Frissen, 1997).

Among the principle challenges to democracy raised by this collection of papers are opportunities for access to information technology, particularly electronic networks, and the character of present and future content - how dominated it is becoming by commercialism. These too were among the debates taken up vociferously throughout the conference (see the final chapter of this book).

It is likely that among those most affected by lack of access to electronic communications will be individuals on a low income including such groups as women, the elderly, early retirees, and the unemployed as well as people with reduced mobility, with a physical impairment, who have learning difficulties or who are illiterate. This poses a number of questions in relation to both public sector and corporate provision of services.

Among the many social groups whose access to electronic networks may be most limited, as much by economic circumstances as by the prejudices of policy-makers, designers, and manufacturers are elderly people and people with a disability - two groups whose circumstances are explored in this section in some detail. Finally, privacy and the extent to which it may be eroded by technological and legislative advances, is a prime cause of concern.

THE CONCEPT OF THE AGORA

The ancient Greek agora was an open space that served as a meeting place for Greek citizens to conduct their various activities: religious, judicial, political, social and commercial.

Traditionally, WG9.2's conferences have used a story about Greek decision-making related to Thales of Miletus to frame their own deliberations on important themes and emerging ideas (Yngström, *et al.*, 1985). At most of the group's conferences, a system of workshops illuminates emerging suggestions and culminates in a session known as the agora at which the most prominent proposals are debated (see the book's recommendations).

Several of the papers presented at the conference focus attention on the Internet as a form of agora, a public space where citizens may meet to engage in the politics of formal and informal decision-making. Four of the papers in this section explore either implicitly or explicitly the metaphorical relationship between decision-making using the Internet and the agora; a fifth contributes to providing a larger framework of how such metaphors may be interpreted.

There is general scepticism about the terminology commonly used in government and private sector promotion of the information society and particularly the information highway. Interesting, however, a number of the papers in this volume, however tangentially, perhaps even unconsciously, have adopted some of the terminology implicit in the use of the metaphor of an information highway. One author talks of the Oklahoma land rush, another discusses citizens becoming accustomed to using an electronic steering wheel, and yet another paper refers to disabled individuals being free to choose their own mode of automobile transportation/information technology. The rhetorical, aspirational language we hear around us may begin seductively to mould and shape our thoughts and expressions.

Finally, it was one of the conference participants who pointed out that only free men and citizens were allowed to be active in the agora: women were seldom seen there and certainly did not participate in its activities (Keuls, 1993), as did neither slaves, foreigners, or men accused of crimes. None of those authors who used the concept of the agora actively drew attention to the relative lack of democratic involvement of the mass of the people in ancient Greece. Greek democracy in this sense was a brief, historical period that had little direct influence on the practice of modern democratic states.

SAND, SILVER, AND GOLD PLATES

One element of the conference to which all the papers were a contribution was to outline the very latest in academic and intellectual thinking on culture, democracy, and ethics in a global information society. Yet another consideration was, in bringing together a group of academics, practitioners, and policy-makers from a wide variety of countries and cultures, to engage in an active reflection of the state-of-the-art. The intention was to formulate a set of recommendations on the status of the global information society that could be forwarded to decision-makers and might influence them.

This formulation of ideas has its origins in the work of IFIP Working Group 9.2 since the early 1980s (Yngström *et al.*, 1985). The final chapter of this volume therefore describes how, like a band of ancient Greek philosophers, the conference participants wrote on sand, silver, and gold plates, working together in a creative and interactive process, to express a combined set of proposals and recommendations.

The result is outlined in the gold plate which ended the conference. It contains a message which we sincerely hope will be taken on board by policy-makers but will also be taken forward by the conference participants and by all readers of this book who sympathize with its message.

NOTE

For a lengthier appreciation of the papers, the content of the gold plate, and for more information about the activities of IFIP Working Group 9.2 (Computers and Social Accountability), please visit our web site and click on 'Conferences' at URL: http://www.info.fundp.ac.be/~jbl/IFIP/cadresIFIP.html

ACKNOWLEDGEMENTS

In organizing this conference, we would like to acknowledge the sponsorship of the following groups and institutions: IFIP-WG9.2, IFIP-WG9.5, the Greek Computer Society, the Municipality of Corfu Development Company (ANEDK), the Hellenic Evaluation and Technology Assessment Society, the University of Ioannina, the Ionian University, and the Corfu Initiative. Our main supporters were the European Commission, Information Society Project Office (ISPO), the Information Technologies Programme (DG III.F), and Intrasoft S.A. Other helpful contributors were Forthnet (Corfu) and Omega Generation (Bologna, Italy).

We would especially like to thank the organizing committee for its hard work in putting the conference together so impressively: Vassilios Laopodis, Marie Gevers, Christine Leitner, Lone Malmborg, and Christopher Zielinski alongside host country representatives, Sokratis Katsikas, Philippos Drakontaeidis, Dimitris Fotiadis, Vassilis Chryssikopoulos, Anna Karnezi, and Antonis Giallelis.

An especial thanks finally to Colin Beardon, Geoff Busby, Jan Holvast, Leif Bloch Rasmussen, and Marc van Lieshout for their help in reading, reviewing, and selecting papers and in choosing the format of the conference of which this book is the result.

REFERENCES

Akdeniz, Yaman (1996) Computer pornography: a comparative study of the US and UK obscenity laws in relation to the Internet. *International Review of Law, Computers and Technology*, **10** (2), 235-261

Beauchamp, Paul (1969) *Création et séparation. Etude exégétique du chapitre premier de la Genèse*. Paris: Aubier - Cerf - Delachaux et Niestlé, DDB

Berger, R.J., Searles, P. and C.E. Cottle (1993) *Feminism and Pornography*. New York: Praegar Books

Berleur, Jacques (1974) Economique et Politique, *Economies et Sociétés*, Cahiers de l'ISEA, série M, n°28, Paris, 1974, pp. 17-115. (See especially, pp. 62-64.)

Berleur, J., Clement, A., Sizer, R. and D. Whitehouse (1990) *The Information Society: Evolving Landscapes*. New York and North York (Canada): Springer Verlag and Captus University Publications

Fossion, André (1980), *Lire les Ecritures. Théorie et pratique de la lecture structurale*, Bruxelles, Ed. Lumen Vitae, Coll. Ecritures

Frissen, P. (1997) The virtual state. Postmodernisation, informatisation and public administration. In Loader (1997), *op. cit.*, pp. 11-25

Fukuyama, F. (1992) *La fin de l'histoire et le dernier homme*, Flammarion, Paris.

Fukuyama, F. (1995) *Trust: The Social Virtues and the Creation of Prosperity*. London: Hamish Hamilton
Gringas, Clive (1997) *The Laws of the Internet*. London: Butterworths
Group of Lisbon (The) (1996) *Limits to Competition*, MIT Press
Hammond, T. (1995) *Info-Rich, Info-Poor. Access and Exchange in the Global Information Society*. London: Bowker Saur
Held, D. (1995) *Democracy and the Global Order*. Cambridge: Polity Press
Johns, Catherine (1982) *Sex or symbol: Erotic images of Greece and Rome*. London: British Museum Publications Limited
Kant, Immanuel (1983) *Perpetual peace, and other essays on politics, history, and morals*, Translation with introduction by Ted Humphrey, Hackett Indianapolis (Ind.)
Keuls, Eva C. (1993) *The Reign of the Phallus: Sexual Politics in Ancient Greece*. London: University of California Press
Kroker, A. and M.A. Weinstein (1994) *Data Trash. The Theory of the Virtual Class*. New York: St. Martin's Press
Ladrière, Jean (1962) Le concept de communauté mondiale dans la pensée philosophique, in: *Politica*, Tijdschrift voor Staatkunde en Sociologie, Antwerpen, Jan. 1962, n°1, pp. 16-35
Laymon, Charles M. (1971) *The Interpreter's One-Volume Commentary on the Bible*. London and Glasgow: Collins
Linz, D and Malamuth, N. (1993) *Pornography*. Newbury Park, CA: Sage Publications
Loader, B. *The Governance of Cyberspace. Politics, Technology and Global Restructuring*. London and New York: Routledge
Lodge, G.C. (1995) *Managing Globalization in the Age of Interdependence*. Johannesburg: Pfeiffer & Company
Metzger, Bruce M. and Michael D. Coogan (1993) *The Oxford companion to the Bible*. New York and Oxford: Oxford University Press
Muroyama, J. and H.G. Stever (editors) (1988) *Globalization of Technology, International Perspectives*. Proceedings of the Sixth Convocation of the Council of Academies of Engineering and Technological Sciences. Washington, DC: National Academy Press
OECD (Organization for Economic Co-operation and Development), Proposition française présentée à l'OCDE pour une Charte de coopération internationale sur Internet - 23 octobre 1996 - URL: http://www.planete.net/code-internet/Charte.html
Semaines sociales de France (1997) *Entre mondialisation et nations: Quelle Europe?* Paris: Bayard Editions - Centurion
Shields, R. (editor) (1996) *Cultures of Internet. Virtual Spaces, Real Histories, Living Bodies*. London: Sage Publications Limited
Shimbun, A. (1994) *Japan Almanac 1993*. Tokyo: Asahi Shimbun Publishing Company
Shroeder, R. (1997) Virtual worlds and the social realities of cyberspace. In Loader, B. (1997) *op. cit.*, pp. 97-107
Turkle, S. (1996) *Life on the Screen. Identity in the Age of the Internet*. London: Weidenfeld & Nicolson
Virilio, P. (1997) Fin de l'histoire ou fin de la géographie? Un monde surexposé. In *Le Monde Diplomatique*, Paris, N° 521, 44ème année, Août.
Yngström, L, Sizer, R., Berleur, J. and R. Laufer (1985) *Can Information Technology Result in Benevolent Bureaucracy?* Amsterdam: Elsevier Science Publishers BV

---

1 Our comments are inspired by Fossion, André (1980), pp. 72-81. Some notes of the *Traduction œcuménique de la Bible* (Paris, Ed. du Cerf - Les bergers et les mages, 1975) and of the *Dictionnaire des noms propres de la Bible* (Paris, Ed. du Cerf - Desclée De Brouwer, 1978) helped us in specifying etymological and historical questions.

2 Here we follow the text of *The New American Bible*, Catholic Bible Press, Nashville-Atlanta-London-Vancouver, 1987.

Introduction

Introduction

Culture and democracy revisited in the global information society: Summary of a position paper

Jacques Berleur[1]
Programme Committee Chairman
On behalf of IFIP-WG9.2
Institut d'Informatique, Facultés Universitaires Notre-Dame de la Paix, Rue Grandgagnage, 21, B-5000 Namur, Belgium
Phone: +32 81 72 4976, Fax: +32 81 72 4967
Email: jberleur@info.fundp.ac.be

INFORMATION SOCIETY AND GLOBALIZATION

The background to many of today's questions is dominated by what is now called the process of globalization of economy and society. This phenomenon has to be distinguished from the traditional processes of internationalization and multinationalization of businesses, since it includes finance, markets and strategies, technology and its related research and development, lifestyles and consumption patterns with their consequences for culture, regulatory capabilities and governance, as well as political unification of the world[2]. 'Globalization refers to the multiplicity of linkages and interconnections between the states and societies which make up the present world system'[3]. This development is more than an economic or technological process. It gives freedom to capital and labour to move across political boundaries, anywhere in the world. It identifies a global world by playing on intrinsic cultural variables of identity, namely space and time. The so-called global world is most probably not the whole world, but the metaphor has its importance in terms of culture. Delocalization is not recent, it has roots in the past; but what is new, even in the developed countries, is the de-linkage of the poorest regions and countries from the networked and interconnected ones. What also emerges is the penetration of more and more merchandized culture where

An Ethical Global Information Society J. Berleur & D. Whitehouse (Eds.)

culture is identified with cultural goods and services and no longer with the content through which peoples control their own identity and history.

Globalization is ambivalent. Global world, global village sounds nice in terms of linking people together, and allowing them to overcome distance as well as time. But if competitiveness is the guiding principle called to govern visions, strategies, and actions, we are assured that some of today's trends will be accentuated in the future. The scenario of the global world is the scenario of 'winners': expanding monetary speculative movements, growing poverty of some of the world's population, de-linking between rich countries and the rest of the world (the 'triadic alliance'), criminality, drugs, despoliation of common resources, radicalization of fundamentalisms of different kinds, and so on. There is no doubt that this scenario of the global world will lead to a vision which looks more like chaos than utopia.

There is no doubt that information and communication technology has played its part and contributed to this process of globalization: it has made possible such developments as the globalization of financial markets, videoconferencing, telework, telemarketing and teleshopping, just to mention a few. The Internet could be considered an emblematic symbol of this 'unified' world where - it is claimed - everyone has access to any information which they need.

CULTURE

Two words appear frequently when we discuss the future of our societies in a global information society: culture and democracy.

The discussion about the so-called White Book of the Commission of the European Communities on *Employment, Growth and Competitiveness* shows that public policies on information and communication technologies (ICT) networks have to anticipate substantial qualitative societal changes[4]. This is a must if they are to bring the necessary externalities for a real development of a new information society.

Empirical evidence shows that the link between growth and employment is all but obvious, and that new insights have to be provided so that we focus not only on economic activity and income policies, but also on social factors such as social integration and personal identity. 'Growth of the service economy as a component of the information society needs to be related to the political and cultural systems which stand for social cohesion. It is clear that the view prevailing in the media and in the official administrations that cultural and political obstacles must be removed to allow economic growth, needs to be reassessed both for the post-industrial countries and for the developing countries'[5].

From another point of view, no one can forget the clear warning given us by Neil Postman. The problem in the first world today is no longer information scarcity, but information chaos, information without meaning, information without control mechanisms. Postman says: 'The world we live in is very nearly incomprehensible to most of us. There is almost no fact, whether actual or imagined, that will surprise us for very long, since we have no comprehensive and consistent picture of the world that would make the fact appear as an unacceptable contradiction. We believe, because there is no reason not to believe'[6]. While former generations of scientists tended towards positivism, the coming generation of highly specialized experts is, in its conception of the world, tending towards irrationalism and superstition.

What are the intellectual and moral responsibilities of computer scientists and ICT practitioners in making information understandable and comprehensible? Formal mechanisms of information control were traditionally supplied by school and university. The university gave expression to its idea of what constitutes legitimate knowledge and morality. Today, the traditional control mechanisms are breaking down. What should we restore as information control mechanisms, and how? Without real understanding and knowledge, there is no possible control of the development of technology. And that is culture, that is the way we shape our own destiny and make it understandable and practicable through all the institutions, rituals, means, etc., by which we regulate our violence.

New deals require new regulation. People may be upset with present politics, new market trends in the hands of a 'happy few'. Culture remains the way to find new political and economic regulations, according to the genius of nations and particular people.

What is intriguing, in our present age, is the paradoxical claim for both universal and particular, global and local. Maybe the claims are in different mouths. Nevertheless, there is a need for reconciliation between what seem to be extremes. Diversity of cultures is advocated as the only means for personal re-appropriation of what has been 'stolen' by external driving forces. 'The danger of radical breaks in societies, which keep the traditional ignorance against technological development, including the polarized position of complete rejection or uncritical acceptance, lies in severe damages to global cultural diversities: worldwide acting information, communication and media technologies tend to unify the cultural perceptions, leaving little room for regional or national accents and historically grown peculiarities. Sustainable cultural development needs an open debate, and this means before all, it needs sufficient time - time for thought, understanding the challenges, and evaluation, and time for planning, action and correction'[7].

Respect for cultural diversities and differences, need for more precise visions of the future, preservation of culture, information overflow, and capacity of interpretation according to different human perception patterns are necessary to preserve us from the ambivalence of globalization. There is no control out of an understanding space.

DEMOCRACY

When speaking of information society from a 'political' point of view, many people stress different dichotomies: developing and developed nations, women/men, young/old, computer literates/illiterates, rich/poor, able/disabled, minorities/majorities, technophobia/technophilia, etc. Others act to 'empower people'. FreeNets and other Digital Cities are presented as democratic tools for public participation in the building up of the information society and for meeting public needs. Discussions about universal access to information infrastructure are going on all around the world. Personal participation in the civil society is diminishing. Are civil rights not threatened by the integration of formerly separate technologies? Democracy is at stake when contemplating information society development.

The merging of big businesses all around the world, such as between Time Warner and Turner or the two Baby Bells, Bell Atlantic and Nymex, or British Telecom and the Italian Mediaset, one of Berlusconi's holdings, etc., is also felt as domination by a few when it is not a threat against any possible state regulation.

Reactions to the United States' National Information Infrastructure (NII) Agenda for Action, as well as to the G7 Global Information Infrastructure (GII) Project or to the European Bangemann Report highlight the issues at stake in terms of governments' roles, participation of the citizen, protection of nonprofit sectors, etc.

The lack of consensus on the way economics and politics are handled and envisaged reveals opposing visions and ethics and requires closer relationships, and a kind of conviviality, in order to recreate spaces for democratic discussion. The post cold-war period has revealed, if not created, a state of affairs where democracy is on trial[8]. Devolution is in the air. The social fabric has been torn to pieces and has to be woven again by recreating social spaces and social solidarities, in order to restore a common language and build up consensual decision-making. History shows that the weakening of the middle-class - what could be translated in firms in terms of an impoverishment of intermediate positions, especially due to ICT diffusion - results in a totalitarian regime. The development of a nation is due to the strength of its social fabric, its related institutions, and the presence of a well trained middle-class. Fracturing communities and exaggerating self-realization is an anti-democratic process which will most probably lead to the explosion - a chaos? - of societies.

'Democracy in Cyberspace' would at least maintain and develop some specific roles for governments, as was emphasized in the mid-1990s in one of Britain's responses to the information superhighway. Let us mention these proposals: create a coordinated focal point for debate and action; position the information superhighway strategy at the centre of socio-economic policies to ensure it is allocated sufficient priorities and resources; establish effective processes to develop and enact national and international legislation that takes account of the new capabilities of interlinked applications and the speed of technological innovation; ensure government has the authority and resources to assert and monitor the protection of public interests in applications and developments; find suitable mechanisms to support nonprofit 'public interest' applications; seek novel and effective means of encouraging social and organizational innovation in the use of the new ICT; drive innovative applications by using networks to offer a greater range of direct electronic service delivery of public service; and develop appropriate policies for supervising new media regimes, avoiding the growth of multimedia and transnational monopolies[9].

CHALLENGES FOR OUR CONFERENCE

There are many challenges which lie ahead in the development of a global information society. Culture and democracy are two areas which may be under particular threat. It is the proposed role of IFIP-WG9.2 and colleagues to analyze and define the relationships underlying information, globalization, culture and democracy, and to provide to the information society's major decision-makers possible options for future solutions and actions.

*
* *

LET US GO FURTHER ...

This paper was written for the call for papers. It accompanied it to encourage suggestions, comments, and remarks from the different contributors. This means it dates back to when most of the official documents on the global information society were still not well known or even in their infancy. The most important European documents, for instance, date from June 1994 to mid 1996[10]. Is it not worth seeing how important the main themes of our conference were considered to be in the official documents?

PERSPECTIVE OF OFFICIAL DOCUMENTS

What about the information society itself? A document, at our disposal on the official Information Society Project Office (ISPO) site, raises the question 'What exactly is the Information Society?' The answer is given as follows in an attractive box *(We quote 'exactly')*[11]:

- Basic network (physical network + basic functions)
- Generic services (e-mail, data base access, interactive video)
- Applications (telework, telemedicine, telebanking, etc.)

We leave the appreciation of this definition to the reader, but we personally have doubts about the interest of the document's authors in societal questions, when these are spelled out solely in technological terms!

Regarding the interest of officials in democracy and culture, let us have a look at a word count. We know that counting words is not always statistically significant and that ideas or concepts may lie behind other words ... but!

Table 1 is eloquent in itself. Let us stress that, when looking at the market, the Bangemann report underlines what is already explicit in the word count: the report's second chapter is entitled 'A market driven revolution'. We must add that the term culture which seems to be the most important covers expressions such as: culture and leisure activities, cultural traditions and identities, the new information culture and its instruments, multiplicity of cultures and languages, international property rights and wide variety of industrial and cultural sector, without referring at any time to the meaning that we have tried to enlighten. Let us not forget that the European Community is attempting to envisage a *Way to the Information Society.*

Table 1. Word count in official documents

	Bangemann Report	Action Plan	Rolling Action Plan	US - NII Agenda for Action
Democracy, democratic, ...	0	0	2	2
Culture	7	13*	5	0
Language - Linguistics	3			0
Economy, economics	14			
Market	110			

* (five times in titles)

When we look at the actions and policies of the first *European Action Plan* (July 1994), we may wonder how important societal, social, and cultural aspects are! Table 2 shows the number of actions and policies explicitly envisaged, according to four main headings.

Table 2. Number of actions and policies in the *European Action Plan*

Regulatory and legal framework	54
Networks, basic services, applications, and content	27
Social, societal, and cultural aspects	5
Promotion of the information society	11

The later *Rolling Action Plan* (November 1996) changed the classification. The content of Table 3 could seem more satisfactory, since the number of actions regarding 'People at the Centre' has been increased considerably compared to the social actions of the first Action Plan. (Here, we have combined the forthcoming, pending, and ongoing actions.)

Table 3. Number of actions in the *European Rolling Action Plan*

Improving the business environment	47
Investing in the future	13
People at the centre	28
Meeting the global challenge	16

The contents of these tables 2 and 3 should be scrutinized very carefully. Curiously, actions which were classified in the first *Action Plan* under 'regulatory and legal framework' find their place in the *Rolling Action Plan* under 'people at the centre'. The title is nice, but it is not a reason to be rolled like meatballs in flour! It covers so many different items, such as green papers, directives, guidelines, and so on, that it is not very easy to find out what are the main features which will place people at the centre. But the preoccupation must be welcomed.

As recognized in the January 1996 *Report of the High Level Expert Group* (HLEG), 'social policy (...) merits equal if not more weight than economic policy in formulating our approach to the Information Society (IS). We believe that the Commission has paid insufficient attention to these issues so far, ...'[12] 'The Group welcomes the Commission's initiative to provide a major impulse into the broader policy debate surrounding the emerging IS, by setting up the HLEG. So far, the IS policy debate has been dominated by technological issues and more recently the appropriate regulatory economic environment, neglecting by and large, some of the broader issues implicit in the "society" notion'[13].

The first evaluation by the European Commission, which took place in Essen, after the Corfu 1994 endorsement of the Bangemann Report by the European Council, recognized the necessity of looking more carefully at the social, societal, and cultural aspects of the global information society. It was decided to create two new instruments to assist the Commission: the above-mentioned HLEG and the Information Society Forum[14]. Both groups reported in 1996 (in January and June respectively), but there is no evidence that they deeply influenced the *Rolling Action Plan* of November 1996, although the 1995 Essen conclusions proclaimed that they would 'assist the Commission in the preparation of its actions'[15]! The focus, as stated in the same conclusions, was important, but somewhat narrow when it spoke about priority measures mainly in terms of: 'Impact, qualitative and quantitative, of the introduction of new information and communication technologies on employment, and conditions for optimal exploitation of new sources of employment linked to technological progress', or 'Impact of new technologies on work organization (flexible enterprise, teleworking) and potential consequences on social legislation (labour law, social security, including health and safety at work)', etc. All the measures are expressed mainly in terms of adaptation to the consequences of situations which would have happened already, and are surely not expressed in terms of controlling our own future.

ISSUES AT STAKE

The issues at stake are difficult to assess, but certain trends are already there which require our full attention. The world flow of trade in the globalized world is obvious, and the competition is sharp. That cannot be hidden. But what needs to be shown too is the whole picture. In fact, what the figures show is that from 1970 to 1990 in the triadic countries, regional trade flow in terms of manufactured goods (as a percentage of world trade) increased from 60.9% to 73.6%[16]. This means that there are losers, and here they are clearly: Latin America, Africa, the Middle East, central and eastern Europe, and the former USSR. If the same trend continues for the next twenty years, those countries' share of world trade would go down to 5%!

We defined culture in terms of the way we shape our own destiny and make it understandable and practicable through all the institutions, rituals, means, etc., by which we regulate our violence. Does the present information society help culture when the so-called cultural information available on the Internet is mainly 'entertainment'[17]? Or when we are presented with such potential shopping applications as smart cards and interactive kiosks providing information to customers and keeping track of their buying habits so as to adjust inventories and to price and promote products better; intelligent carts organizing customers' shopping through the store's aisles, scanning their shopping lists at the entrance; in-store kiosks, with 'electronic mirrors' with holographic images enabling buyers to see what clothes look like on them without trying anything on; etc.[18]? We know there are more justifiable and defensible applications, but are these also in the mind of our futurologists?

What about democracy? Let us just remind ourselves of the declaration of the Computer Systems Policy Project, a group of chief executive officers of the thirteen largest north American computer companies at its meeting of February 13, 1995, in preparation for the G7 February 25-26, 1995 Information Society Conference in Brussels: 'Let us put the private sector in the driver's seat'[19]. Perhaps this statement is true, but surely democracy is endangered as soon as the public space, which is the key concept of democracy today, is monopolized or captured by a single actor. Policy-makers have reacted immediately, as mentioned already in *Britain's response to the information superhighway* which urges appropriate government roles. The same accents are coming from those who demand global sustainability in the 'development for 8 billion people'[20].

Let us repeat again: 'It is clear that the view prevailing in the media and in the official administrations that *cultural and political obstacles* must be removed to allow economic growth, needs to be reassessed both for the post-industrial countries and for the developing countries' (emphasis added).

CONCLUSION

Globalization, culture and democracy are only words, but they are very important words. This conference aims at clarifying their meaning in the present situation and at seeing where we stand.

That is why, IFIP-WG9.2/9.5 raised in its call for papers some questions which do not have to be answered as such, but which constitute a background to our common questioning:

- How can we cope with the sustainability of society if we are unable to understand and anticipate its cultural, social, political, economic and technological developments?
- What happens to jobs and work-related skills when we face the integration of the different components of ICT unaccompanied by vocational retraining?
- What does it mean for everyone to access information when its diffusion is shaped in a monocultural way?
- How can people stay in control of their development, if it is not deeply rooted in their own culture?
- What is the significance of technological developments that do not meet the needs of society?
- How is democracy affected by the declining power of political discourse resulting from the increasing power of liberal market driving forces?
- Are there specific threats to civil rights from certain technologies and especially from the integration of what were formerly separate technologies?

Corfu is where the *Bangemann Report* was accepted by the European Council summit meeting on June 24-25, 1994. Since then, questions have emerged about the future of the global information society. We could try to remind ourselves of the first steps in moving towards the global information society and revisit them. And make a step forward: From Corfu 1994 to Corfu 1997.

---

1 The author is also a member of the 'Cellule Interfacultaire de Technology Assessment' (CITA) which is financially supported by the Belgian Federal Office for Scientific, Technical, and Cultural Affairs (Interuniversity poles of attraction, Phase IV).

2 The Group of Lisbon, *Limits to Competition*, Gulbenkian Foundation, Lisbon 1993. Published by MIT Press, 1996 (ISBN 0-262-07164-9), 176 p. Translated into French (Ed. La Découverte, Boréal, Labor, 1995), Italian, Portuguese and Swedish (Ordfronts Ferlag, 1996).

3 Anthony G. Grew, Paul Lewis et al., *Globalisation and the Nation States*, Polity Press, Cambridge, 1992, p. 22.

4 Commission of the European Communities, Employment, Growth and Competitiveness, Brussels, December 5th, 1993, COM(93), 700 p final. Published as a book: Jacques Delors, *Pour entrer dans le XXIème siècle.* (Emploi-Croissance et Compétitivité. Le Livre blanc de la Commission des Communautés Européennes), Paris, Michel Lafon - Ramsay, 1994.

5 Gonzales d'Alcantara, Information Overflow - Problem Solving Methodology, in: *Information Processing '94*, vol. III, Linkage and Developing Countries, Karen Duncan and Karl Krueger, Eds., Proceedings of the IFIP 13th World Computer Congress, Hamburg, Germany, 28 August - 2 September, 1994, North-Holland 1994, IFIP Transactions A-53, p. 206.

6 Neil Postman, *Technopoly: The Surrender of Culture to Technology*, New York: Knopf, 1992.

7 Wolfgang Coy, Cultural Stability and Technological Change: The Case of Information, Communication and Media Technology, in: *Information Processing '94*, vol. III, op. cit., p. 217.

8 Jean Bethke Elshtain, *Democracy on Trial*, New York: Basic Books, 1995.

9 The Information Superhighway: Britain's Response, A Forum Discussion, by W. Dutton, J. Blumler, N. Garnham, R. Mansell, J. Cornford and M. Peltu, Paper No. 29, Programme on Information and Communication Technologies, Economic and Social Research Council, Brunel University, UK, December 1994. See also: http://www.isi.gov.uk/isi/dbitis/nat_strat.html

10 Commission of the European Community, *Europe and the Global Information Society - Recommendations to the European Council - The Bangemann Report*, 26 May 1994, CD-84-94-290-EN-C. Commission of the European Community, *Europe's Way to the Information Society. An Action Plan*, Communication from the Commission to the Council and the European Parliament, and the Economic and Social Committee and the Committee of Regions, Brussels, COM(94) 347 final, July 19, 1994. Commission of the European Community, *Europe's Rolling Action Plan for Information Society*, COM(96) 607 final, Brussels, November 27, 1996. *Building the European Information Society for Us All*, First Reflections of the High Level Expert Group on the Social and Societal Aspects of the Information Society, Interim Report, January 1996. Commission of the European Community, *Networks for People and their Communities. Making the most of the Information Society in the European Union*. First annual Report to the European Commission from the Information Society Forum, Luxembourg, Office for Official Publications of the European Communities, CD-96-96-473-EN-C, ISBN 92-827-7805-3.

11 http://www.ispo.cec.be/infosoc/backg/action95.html (April 28, 1995, © ECSC-EC-EAEC, Brussels - Luxembourg, 1995).

12 *Building the European Information Society for Us All*, op. cit., Executive Summary.

13 *ibid*, Introduction, p. 1.

14 The Essen Conclusions (1995). See: http://www.ispo.cec.be/infosoc/backg/essen.html

15 *ibid.*

16 Ugur Muldur, Les formes et les indicateurs de la globalisation, FAST, Commission des Communautés Européennes, 1993. Quoted in: The Group of Lisbon, *Limits to Competition*, op. cit. (French edition, p. 136).

17 See, for instance: (Contents according to Yahoo, on 95.07.23). http://www.cern.ch/CERN/WorldWideWeb/Intro/PresentationsF/General/ContentCategories.html

18 Barrett Seaman, The Future is already there, in *TIME*, Special Issue: Welcome to Cyberspace, Spring 1995.

19 Vigdor Schreibman - FINS (fins@access.digex.net), FINS Special Report, February 21, 1995, Public-Access Computer Systems Forum (pacs-l@uhupvm1.uh.edu).

20 The Common Global Sustainability by Co-Determination and Co-Development. The 47 Major Priority Areas for Science and Technology for the 8 Billion People, CAN-MONITOR Meeting, March 5, 1993, FAST Programme, Theme C: 'Global Perspective 2010: New Tasks for S&T'.

PART ONE

Ethics

1

A charter for citizens of the global information society

Julie Cameron and Karin Geiselhart***
** Info.T.EC Solutions Pty Ltd*
P.O. Box K21 Haymarket, Sydney, NSW 2000, Australia
Phone: +61 2-93269430; Fax +61 2-2181508
Email: cameronj@acslink.aone.net.au
*** Student, University of Canberra,*
Canberra, ACT 2600, Australia
Email: k.geiselhart@student.canberra.edu.au

Abstract

New ethical issues related to the global information society have emerged. Extraterritoriality and legal ambiguity are consequences of the global information society and cyberspace. This discussion paper summarizes key ethical issues that need to be addressed in a charter for citizens of the global information society. For each issue, the main implications for citizens of nations and of cyberspace are discussed and statements of principle are developed. These principles, set out as a charter for citizens, are intended for use as: guidelines by law-makers and decision-makers in government and industry; an ethical framework for possible future international legislation; and as benchmarks for citizens and cybercitizens in assessing their rights and obligations in relation to the global information society and cyberspace.

INTRODUCTION

The power of integrated information and communication technologies to collect, store, combine, manipulate and disseminate data to and from any part of the world now affects every individual, regardless of their personal involvement with cyberspace. Technologies like space-based surveillance, satellite communication,

An Ethical Global Information Society J. Berleur & D. Whitehouse (Eds.)

direct broadcasting and portable equipment allow information collection and flow to transcend national and geographical borders.

High speed computers combined with massive data storage capacity, an unparalleled ability to integrate complex information systems and the power to digitize and analyze data from audio, visual and other media provide the potential for total mastery over the information of all people and all nations. Just as nuclear dominance was the key to coalition leadership in the old era, information dominance will be the key in the information age (Nye and Owens, 1996, p. 27). A global information society affects the balance of power and moves control from within nations.

In this new global information society, cyberspace is defined as the electronic environment established by and/or within the information and communications technologies and infrastructure and associated peripheral equipment. It is a non-specific, fluctuating, separate space where transactions and events occur outside the jurisdiction of the laws of individual nations. Individuals, organizations and governments increasingly engage with this electronic environment and are affected by it directly or indirectly. Indirect effects of cyberspace include unjust denial of access for individuals to finance or employment due to inaccurate electronic data, and threats to physical security and well-being due to activities like net stalking. Interaction in cyberspace may involve citizens and technical infrastructure from numerous nations concurrently. Global laws do not exist. Global mechanisms for governing the cyber realm have not been established. The result is extraterritoriality and legal ambiguity.

In the Oxford Dictionary, society means a social mode of life, the customs and organization of a civilized nation or an association of persons united by a common aim or interest or principle. Therefore cyberspace has citizens - citizens that may be individuals, organizations or governments. And citizenship of a nation and of cyberspace can be concurrent. Rights and obligations relate to roles both as citizens of a particular nation and of cyberspace, with an over-riding responsibility to citizenship of the global society. But, what is cybercitizenship in the global information society? The Oxford Dictionary defines citizen as a freeman of a city or member of a state. Traditionally a citizen is acknowledged by the law of a nation as a member of that particular country and subject to its laws. When citizenship is a local, physical concept the obligations and rights associated with being in a defined geographical area are specified. But in the information society individuals, organizations (including corporations) and governments can act and interact outside geographical constraints. Rights and obligations are not clearly defined either for individuals or collectives. So far it is established only that cybercitizens must pay suppliers of access services, obey the rules of their geographic society related to the Internet and global information and observe netiquette.

Democracy refers to the right of individuals to influence by lawful means issues affecting their lives and well-being. This paper assumes that electronic information and cyberspace should empower citizens and increase opportunities to influence and participate in the government of nations and cyberspace. We need to avoid the creation of cyberslaves - those who use cyberspace but are unaware of the issues and risks (for example, losing money if their cyberbank becomes insolvent) and have no influence on decisions and events that impact on them. Cybercitizens are powerless unless they are able to participate in the governing of the global commons.

Options for setting out the rights and obligations of citizens can be listed in order of enforceability:

- Principles which are generally statements that may provide international guidance, or act as a reference document, or provide a basis for the development of legal instruments in particular jurisdictions (for example, the Organization for Economic Co-operation and Development (OECD) Privacy Principles).
- Public policies that may incorporate aspects of acceptable behaviours, practice and standards.
- Codes of conduct incorporating ethical principles but focusing on behaviours, outputs and quality of service for the interpretation of substantive behaviours. Although they are usually used as standards for self-regulation by industries or professions, they may also be used as guidance in external regulation (for example, by courts assessing what comprises negligent behaviour).
- Guidelines that may be legal within a single jurisdiction and used to provide guidance, legal meaning and relevance, even though they are generally not enforceable.
- Legal instruments which are generally enforceable, provided they are drafted correctly and courts are sufficiently qualified to assess the matters bought before them (Cameron *et al.*, 1992).

Because of problems related to establishing a universal ethical regime in diverse cultures (Berleur and d'Udekem-Gevers, 1996) and the nature of the global information society, the establishment of principles is considered the most appropriate form for setting out the rights and responsibilities of citizens.

The principles set out in this paper are intended to form the basis of a charter for citizens of the global information society. The principles are intended for use as: guidelines by law-makers and decision-makers in government and industry; an ethical framework for possible future international legislation; and as benchmarks for citizens and cybercitizens in assessing their rights and obligations in relation to the global information society and cyberspace.

ASSUMPTIONS AND METHODOLOGY

Principles implicitly and explicitly assume values. The values espoused in these principles reflect the experience of sophisticated users of integrated information and communications technologies and cyberspace. Globalization and transborder data flow has occurred so fast that few nation states have debated and/or understood the consequences. Maritime nations developed laws of the high seas under similar circumstances.

The various declarations of the United Nations and statements like the OECD Principles are based on the premise that some values are universal. International protocols that assume particular actions do not promote international well-being (for example, actions degrading air quality). This paper assumes that all individuals in all societies have the rights set out in the Declaration of Human Rights. The charter aims to enhance the well-being of all citizens throughout the world. The objectives of the principles are to promote a social sustainable development (Berleur and d'Udekem-Gevers, 1996, p. 11). It is acknowledged that despite the precedents for statements of conviction with international relevance, if principles are to be universal and applied internationally, ethical and cultural diversity must be recognized. Situations and circumstances vary. The preamble to the charter therefore provides for justification and exceptions.

This paper was prepared using the following methodology:

- Placement of information about the Corfu conference and an abstract of a proposed conference paper on the Australian Computer Society's World Wide Web (WWW) page with an invitation to participate in writing the paper.
- In order to identify issues and appropriate Principles, the rights and obligations set out in various ethical statements and codes were examined by the principal author. Key source material was published (Berleur, J., this volume; Berleur and Brunnstein, 1996; Australian Privacy Charter Council, 1994, located on the World Wide Web, or distributed electronically, for example, Clarke 1996, WWWa; 1996, WWWb; Durango Declarations, 1995, WWW; Merel 1996, WWW; Kling 1996).
- A general literature search of CD-Rom databases, Internet World Wide Web sites and published journals and books by the principal author. (Material on web sites deleted or moved by 30 November 1996 is excluded.)
- Preparation of a draft paper by the principal author.
- Circulation of the draft paper internationally to 49 key individuals with a known interest in and knowledge of the topic resulted in valuable comments and references.
- Placement of the Draft Paper: Democracy and Cyberspace - A Charter for Citizens by Julie Cameron on a World Wide Web site http://www.-msj.com.au/ELSIC/Corfu97.html in October 1996. The paper was directly linked to the Australian Computer Society web page, and the ELSIC site and comments were invited via email link to the author. No email feedback was received. A count of visits to the paper was not available.
- Amendment of the draft in accordance with electronic material and comments received. All key contributors have been acknowledged and the main contributor is named as co-author.

ISSUES

Justification and Exceptions

In a diverse, complex world it would be unrealistic to establish a set of principles relating to a global information society that apply to all situations and are acceptable to all nations. But in order to protect citizens, any exceptions must be justified and reflect the level of risk to society. 'Exceptions must not interfere with universally accepted human rights. Exceptions to the Principles must be clearly stated, made in accordance with law, proportional to the necessities giving rise to the exception, and compatible with the requirements of a democratic society' (Australian Privacy Charter Council, 1994, Principle 1). Not every law of every nation is a just law. Not every nation is democratic.

Preamble to the Charter: Exceptions to the Principles set out in this Charter must be justified, clearly stated, made in accordance with law, proportional to the necessities giving rise to the exception, and compatible with the requirement to enhance human rights.

Ethics and Protection from Cybercrime

Cyberspace can obviously be used for good or evil. Misuse and abuse of electronic information and cyberspace ranges from unethical behaviours to criminal activities. 'Criminal exploitation is clearly a problem, and there are other concerns too; for example, the norms of human interaction are less likely to be observed in such environments. Electronic violence is in its infancy, but viruses, rumour-mongering, hate-mail and mailbox bombardment are all describable phenomena, and may graduate from art-forms to techniques' (Clarke, 1996 WWWa).

Although it is recognized that currently an international agreement on ethics ... is unachievable (Berleur and d'Udekem-Gevers, 1996, pp. 4-5) the International Federation for Information Processing (IFIP) Ethics Task Group's analysis of 30 codes of member computer societies revealed a consensus on some shared principles (Berleur, 1996b, p. 242). Respect for privacy, accuracy, property and accessibility is required by most codes. To retain the credibility of information, integrity and quality of digital data must be protected by individuals, organizations and governments. Safeguarding the accuracy of information is a core responsibility of individual and collective cybercitizens. False and inaccurate information in the information age can be considered as equivalent to counterfeit currency.

Even though the laws of nations do not keep pace with developments in criminal activity related to the global information society and cyberspace, and the concepts of ethics and instruments designed to deal with cybercrime vary with culture and type of behaviour they are intended to encourage or prevent, cybercitizens are aware of right and wrong. There appears to be a broad consensus that actions that would be crimes outside the electronic environment should be considered as cybercrime (for example, sabotage, forgery, fraud, theft, espionage) (Berleur and Brunnstein, 1996, pp. 260-1). There are well recognized statements of agreement related to information and communications security (such as the OECD Guidelines for the Security of Information Systems). The main risks to cyberspace security relate to insertion of false data; release or insertion of harmful software programs; destruction of valuable data and programs; manipulation and/or disruption of computer and communication systems; and misuse by, for example, information brokers, private detectives, foreign embassies and organized crime. Cybercrime must be punished in the same way as all other criminal activity and be subject to the laws of nations.

In addition to ethics directly related to electronic information and cyberspace, the information technology and communication industries need to consider issues like the environment (like manufacture and disposal of equipment, use of electricity and other resources) and to promote sustainable economic and social development.

Principle 1: Individual and collective cybercitizens must protect the accuracy and integrity of digital information, adhere to all relevant ethical principles, codes and guidelines and uphold the legitimate laws of nations.

Equity of Access to Cyberspace and Electronic Information

Equity of access to cyberspace is of international concern. The information rich and information poor are familiar concepts that apply to individuals, communities, organizations and nations. Access to cyberspace is determined by access to technical infrastructure and electronic information. Even if access to cyberspace is achieved, access to electronic information is not guaranteed.

Access to technical infrastructure and technology

Access to cyberspace depends on the availability and accessibility of technical infrastructure, access to appropriate information and communication technology, and technical skill. Some countries and groups within nations (like rural communities) lack suitable technical infrastructure. Access by some individuals, communities and organizations is limited because of the costs of information technology and communications. Recognizing these facts, the United States Federal-State Board on Universal Service, set up under the Telecommunications Act of 1996, developed draft recommendations to support programs to ensure access to telecommunications for low income consumers and discounts to key community groups (Benton Foundation, 1996, WWW). Verbal accounts of experiments indicate that linking members of disadvantaged groups to the Internet appears to have positive affects on self-esteem.

Discrimination on grounds like sex, age, race, religion or physical disability limits equality of access to cyberspace technology. Equity of access to cyberspace among all citizens should be a goal of education systems. Issues like poverty and illiteracy have obvious relevance to access and realistically other basic human rights may be more significant in some countries (such as freedom from hunger).

Access to electronic information

Information available on the Internet is voluminous, frequently difficult to find, peripatetic, transitory, often fragmented and of varied quality. Equity of access to meaningful electronic information depends on the acquisition and transfer of sophisticated search skills including the ability to discriminate among sources and knowledge of electronic conventions and practices.

There is every danger that pricing information services and placing information and its associated technologies in the market place will ensure the development of an information poor group within society who are unable to capitalize on the benefits of freely available information (Burton, 1992, p. 89). The social impact of any bit tax (a tax on information sent over the Internet) needs to be carefully assessed. Any trend to charging for access to information currently available free of charge in the public domain, via the Internet or published in books that can be accessed free of charge through libraries would exacerbate the disadvantage of those unable to pay.

Governments are major collectors of information. As governments are funded by citizens, '(n)on-personal government information should be freely available unless someone in authority can show it should be restricted. Technology should be used to distribute information to citizens not simply to record information about them' (Burton, 1992, p. 89). But the trend of governments to privatize functions and outsource activities means that information formerly held by government and available publicly is no longer accessible. It is argued that some databases held by private sector organizations should be freely accessible due to the public interest (for example, toxic emissions and chemical hot spots). But the World Intellectual Property Organization (WIPO) has prepared a treaty that proposes new property rights to database owners. If adopted, this treaty may restrict access to information currently available in the public domain (World Intellectual Property Organization, 1996, WWW).

Principle 2: Nations should aim at equity of access to electronic information and cyberspace for all their citizens without discrimination.

Freedom from Surveillance and Rights to Privacy

Principle 3 of the Australian Privacy Charter states that people have a right to privacy and the right to conduct their affairs free from surveillance or fear of surveillance. Rights to privacy are well established in the OECD Privacy Principles, national laws, ethical statements and codes of practice. Surveillance is defined as the systematic observation or recording of one or more people's behaviour, communications or personal information (Australian Privacy Charter Council, 1994). The use of technology for surveillance has three aspects:

a. Surveillance through information.
b. Surveillance of communications in cyberspace.
c. Mass surveillance using information and communication technologies.

Surveillance through information

One stop shopping and integration of data obtained by large entities, including government and commercial conglomerates, encourages merging of information provided for different purposes. Examples include marketing agreements like fly buy schemes and loyalty cards that offer discounts as rewards in return for details of purchases recorded to provide customer profiles. Efficiency benefits may flow from exchange of data and integration of databases but it is essential that the exchange of personal information takes place only with the informed consent of individuals. Individuals must have the option of continuing to deal separately with organizations and business units if they prefer. A key privacy principle is that information should generally not be used for purposes other than those for which it was collected (Australian Privacy Charter Council, 1994, Principle 15). Great care needs to be taken if information is used for secondary purposes (definitions used by various government agencies may differ and data provided by individuals may alter for legitimate reasons). Data-matching schemes have experienced a range of difficulties due to issues like data accuracy, integrity, administrative errors and much lower cost-benefit ratios than claimed at the outset.

Multimedia and convergence of new technologies allow unprecedented opportunities for invasion of individual privacy and surveillance of populations or target groups. When data items held in various formats are combined highly intrusive personal information is easily assembled and disseminated. Even if informed consent is given each time personal data is collected by individual agencies it is unlikely that citizens will be fully informed about or aware of the detailed profiles that can be obtained from combined data (for example, linkages of visual images through photo licences, personal relationships through close circuit television (CCTV), and transactional data - non-anonymous payment of tolls and transport fares with computer records of addresses, health and financial data). Surveillance of individuals through the use of information is not compatible with human rights.

Surveillance of communications in cyberspace

Electronic communications can be monitored electronically using techniques and technology available in the public domain. Software programs can monitor and trigger recording of verbal and electronic communications. Powerful search engines allow Internet searches that monitor activities of individuals including those using news groups. Cookies (small pieces of data that a web server can store with a web browser) allow tracking of Internet users' visits to sites.

There is debate about the right of government and law enforcement agencies to intercept electronic communications and monitor Internet activities. Some enforcement agencies are concerned about the use of electronic money (ecash) and its potential for money laundering and tax evasion; others need to intercept communications among criminal groups. The need to balance law enforcement requirements with rights to privacy and freedom from surveillance is acknowledged, provided the response is commensurate with the level of risk to the community. Law enforcement agencies in most countries already have powers to tap telephone communications of individuals under certain conditions which are usually set out in law and clearly defined. Interception is usually justified during the process of obtaining a warrant or approval from an independent body. Monitoring private communications at random, or in accordance with pre-established automated triggers, is not conducive to freedom or democracy. Interferences with privacy must be justified.

There is debate about the responsibility of Internet service providers to monitor the content of material in cyberspace and to prevent certain transactions (for example, theft of data and risks to security) and transfer of unacceptable material (such as child pornography). It is argued that making Internet providers responsible for content is like making telephone service providers responsible for all voice and data carried on their networks. Will the Internet industry, as a whole, develop meaningful methods of self-regulation which clearly allocate responsibility for content? Will this be acceptable to all governments and to all citizens? A draft Internet Code of Practice prepared by the Internet Industry Association of Australia aims to establish general standards of behaviour for those involved in the Internet industry (Internet Industry Association of Australia, 1996, WWW).

Mass surveillance using information and communication technologies

Mass surveillance incorporates the concept of data capture and storage of information about citizens on a random basis. Mass surveillance creates a culture of fear among citizens. The use of information and communications technology for surveillance of individuals not involved in or suspected of illegal activities should not be permitted. Satellite surveillance of citizens of sovereign countries without approval or justification can be considered as a form of invasion. Video cameras used in public areas without warning and storage of images of citizens obtained without justification should not be permitted. The growing use of CCTV in many countries on the grounds of providing security and protection against crime may tempt operators to store images just in case. Mass surveillance using techniques like automatic streaming through databases is very difficult to justify.

Principle 3: Citizens have the right to privacy and the right to conduct their affairs free from surveillance or fear of surveillance.

Freedom of Expression and Opinion

Cyberspace ignores national boundaries. 'Cyberspace is a place where the denizens are knowledgeable, independent and uppity. Found there is a new type of non-organization. ... cybertribes: like-minded citizens linked electronically by their key interest. They empower one another. They validate one another. Eager to find one another and communicate, they are also eager to influence real events ... (Draper, 1995, p. 30). It is important that cybertribes be permitted to develop. The concept of planet earth requires the free exchange of information, expression and opinion.

Individuals have a moral responsibility to be tolerant and honest in representing their personal views and the opinions of others (Merel, 1996, WWW). Ideally, honest political opinions should be expressed freely, without fear. But this may not be possible in all societies. For this reason the right to anonymous transactions is sometimes advocated particularly to protect whistle blowers and witnesses (Clarke, 1996, WWWa). Freedom of expression and free flow of information are required to support democracy and human rights. (Clarke, 1996, WWWa; Durango Declaration, 1995, WWW; Merel, 1996, WWW; Berleur and Brunnstein, 1996, p. 259). There is, however, a need to balance the right to freedom of expression with the responsibility not to cause harm to other citizens.

Principle 4: Cybercitizens have the right to freedom of expression and opinion and the responsibility to ensure the democratic rights and well-being of all citizens are protected.

Democracy

Cyberspace can be used to facilitate citizens involvement in the government of their own country and to influence world events. The ability to distribute material widely, cheaply and quickly allows issues to be discussed and feedback to be returned to the initiator swiftly. Information and communications technology can be used to facilitate participative democracy within nations and cyberspace. Electronic forms and computer analysis allow the responses of large numbers of citizens to be collated. The Durango Imperatives include calls for designers and applied research to develop infrastructure, architectures and technical interfaces that support democratic participation (Durango, 1995, WWW).

If governments and decision-makers are willing to share power and utilize the Internet to allow direct input by citizens or stakeholders a radical redistribution of power could occur. In the United States, '(a) national initiative and referendum movement already underway will allow people to bypass the Congress, to propose new laws and vote on them directly'. It is predicted that '(w)ith secure lines and positive electronic identification established, ultimately we will see on-line legislative initiatives and electronic voting, a return to direct democracy' (Draper, 1995, p. 730). It is particularly important in a period of significant change that policy development takes place 'in the highest level of participation and (that we) ... avoid the emergence of a two-tier society, (so that) ... the information society addresses the needs of citizens' (Laopodis and Fernandez, 1995, p. 2). Unlike television and mass media, cyberspace is interactive, provided there is no interference to prevent free access and distribution of information. Control of communications and media is frequently an aim of dictatorships. It is important that the unrestrained characteristics and complex matrices of the Internet are protected.

Principle 5: Cyberspace should be used to enhance opportunities for democracy within nations and across national boundaries.

Diversity of Culture and Ideology

Culture, defined as 'the way we shape our own destiny and make it understandable and practicable through all the institutions, rituals, means, etc., by which we regulate our violence' (Berleur, this volume) makes human thinking robust by providing options. Multiculturalism is a way of understanding, respecting and retaining cultural diversity. Cultural diversity is as important as biodiversity. Just as we need access to data from numerous sources to provide perspective and an opportunity to glean our truth, we need diversity in ways of thinking about events.

Technology usage is not neutral. Information and communication technologies can be used not only to control information about physical entities, including economically valuable objects and individuals, it can be used to influence thinking and behaviours. During the Gulf war dissemination/handling of news and access of the media to the military was very different to that during the Vietnam war. Monopolistic ownership and control of electronic information, cyberspace and the associated information and communications technology and infrastructure must be avoided.

Principle 6: Cyberspace should be used to support diversity of culture and ideology.

Equitable Distribution of Benefits

As in the industrial revolution, enormous shifts in economic benefit and distribution of wealth are occurring as the global information society emerges. Obvious impacts include workforce displacement, continued automation of information processing and manufacturing, and creation of a new elite with wealth and power based on ownership of electronic information and information and communications technology and infrastructure. Our new high-tech economy has almost no need for unskilled workers and it is forcing de-massification of the labour force (Draper, 1995, p. 729). To prevent deskilling, equality of access to knowledge about information and communications technology must be available. The total time required from the human workforce to produce a specified quantity of goods and level of services has reduced. In many nations, some people labour longer hours while unemployment increases. Time savings, earning potential and opportunities for leisure need to be shared among all citizens so that wealth and quality of life can be distributed more evenly.

The industrial revolution led to enormous social upheaval in many countries. Social inequalities and denial of access to the benefits of industrial technology destabilized some societies and political systems. We must learn from history. The wealth and benefits of the global information society should be distributed equitably within and among nations.

Principle 7: All participants in the global information society, individual, corporate and government, should aim to distribute the wealth and benefits equitably.

Ownership of Data

Ownership of data in cyberspace relates to issues of copyright and intellectual property, rights to acquire, access and sell data about people, objects and transactions and transborder flows of data.

Copyright and intellectual property.

Ownership of copyright of electronic material and of intellectual property are issues of international concern being addressed currently. Protection and rights in cyberspace should be equivalent to those existing within the country of origin for non-electronic material, publications and broadcasts.

Rights to acquire, access and sell data about people, objects and transactions.

It is argued that computerized data owned by an organization belongs to that organization which has the right to sell or exchange that data, unless prohibited by law. The European Commission Directive related to the processing and movement of personal data (European Directive, 1995) will help protect European Community citizens in some circumstances but it does not address the issue of ownership rights internationally. Money is made from the sale of personal information despite the concern of individuals who believe their privacy has been invaded. If it was clearly stated in law that personal data is the property of the data subject, and this person has the sole right to permit an organization to use that data for authorized purposes, this trade in personal information would at least be reduced and at best cease.

Ownership of information about objects and transactions pertaining to a country is a vexed question. Burton summarizes the issue by asking whether information is a resource or commodity that can be bought and sold on the international market. The treatment of information as a commodity derives from 'the high visibility of IT costs and the increasing degree to which information is created and manipulated by IT systems. ... Third world countries claim that information is a resource which can be used for development and that they have a right to control their individual information resources' (Burton, 1992, p. 59). Rights to acquire, access and sell data about objects and transactions within a nation should be determined by the laws of that country.

Transborder flows of non-personal data.
Transborder flows of non-personal data include:

- Operational data transmitted by multinationals for decision-making, financial purposes and administration.
- Data about a country, its economy, transactions and resources.

' ... Information transfer ... forms a significant part of all the international transactions taking place: it contributes considerably to the operational efficiency of multinationals and to export earnings ...' (Burton, 1992, p. 59). Some information held by private organizations is important to local national governments for understanding their economy. Who owns the data and who benefits?

National sovereignty and resource utilization are affected by transborder collection. (Who owns remotely sensed data relating to physical resources collected by satellite surveillance?) Third world countries argue that they need access to these databases and databanks located primarily in first world countries as a source of expertise and information for economic and social development. 'Systems are in place and are transferring and handling information on an international scale before third world governments (and some of those in the first world) have an opportunity to react: when they are able to consider policy, they are faced with entrenched situations and attitudes which are difficult to change, not least when these attitudes are held by multinational corporations backed overtly or covertly by national governments' (Burton, 1992, p. 58).

It is argued that data about the economy and resources of a country, and data originating in a country, are owned by that nation and continue to be subject to its law. Agreement about transborder collection and use of this data should be negotiated by the collecting/receiving nation or organization. Nations should have the right to access and use data about its economy and resources regardless of where it is stored.

Principle 8: Ownership of personal data resides with the data subject. Rights to acquire, access and sell data about objects and transactions within a nation should be determined by the laws of that country. Agreement about transborder collection and use of data about the natural, economic and social resources of a nation should be negotiated by the collecting/receiving nation or organization. Nations should have the right to access and use data about their economy and resources regardless of where it is stored.

CONCLUSIONS

The global information society is a threat to old social and economic patterns at local and international levels. Langdon Winner told the Durango Conference '... the move to computerize and digitize means that many pre-existing cultural forms have suddenly gone liquid, losing their former shape as they are retailored for computerized expression. As new patterns solidify, both useful artifacts and the texture of human relations that surround them are often much different from what existed previously' (Durango Declarations, 1996, WWW). And at the international level 'the clash between the real and the virtual realities is rendering ineffectual the edifice of national implementations of internationally agreed human rights' (Clarke, 1996, WWWa). The opportunity for reshaping inequitable, dysfunctional social and economic patterns has arrived. Faced with the power of information and communications technology and the political, economic, social and cultural impact of its use, a charter for citizens relevant to the global society and cyberspace is essential.

This charter for citizens of the global information society aims to promote the well-being of all citizens of all nations and of cyberspace. Its principles aim to establish the rights and responsibilities of all citizens and those using electronic information and cyberspace. Although these principles are only a beginning, each is designed to address a key issue arising from the global information society and cyberspace. They require debate, addition and refinement. But they are a beginning.

REFERENCES

Published documents

Australian Privacy Charter Council (1994), Australian Privacy Charter, *Australian Privacy Charter Council,* December 1994

Berleur, J. and Brunnstein, K., Eds (1996) *Ethics of Computing: Codes, Spaces for Discussion and Law*, A Handbook prepared by the IFIP Ethics Task Group, London: Chapman & Hall, 1996

Berleur, J. (this volume), Culture and democracy revisited in the global information society: Summary of a position paper

Berleur, J. (1996a), Final Remarks: Ethics, Self-Regulation and Democracy. *Ethics of Computing: Codes, Spaces for Discussion and Law,* Berleur, J. and Brunnstein, K., Eds (1996), *op. cit.*, pp. 241-253

Berleur, J. and d'Udekem-Gevers, M. (1996) Codes of Ethics Within IFIP and Other Computer Societies. *Ethics of Computing: Codes, Spaces for Discussion and Law,* Berleur, J. and Brunnstein, K., Eds (1996), *op. cit.*, pp. 3-15

Burton, P.F. (1992) *Information Technology & Society* Library Association Publishing, London, 1992

Cameron, J., Clarke, R., Davies, S., Jackson, A., Prentice, M., and Regan, B. (1992) Ethics, Vulnerability & Information Technology. *Information Processing 92 Vol. 11 Education and Society (ed. Aitken, R.) Proceedings of the IFIP 12th World Computer Congress* North Holland, 1992, pp. 344-350

Draper, M. (1995) Beyond Cyberspace: the Real Promise of Virtual Reality. *Vital Speeches of the Day* **61** (23) September 15, 1995, pp. 726-733

European Directive (1995) Directive 95/-/EC of the European Parliament and the Council On the Protection of Individuals with regard to the Processing of Personal Data and On the Free Movement of such Data. 2 February 1995

Laopodis, V. and Fernandez, F. (1995) Enhancing Citizens Participation in an Information Society, *5th Hellenic Conference on Informatics*, December 1995, published by the Greek Computer Society.

Nye, J. S. and Owens, W. A. (1996) America's Information Edge. *Foreign Affairs Journal* **75** (2) March/ April 1996, pp. 23-28

Electronic Sources - World Wide Web Sites and Email Contacts (as at 30 November 1996)

Benton Foundation (1996, WWW) United States Universal Service Provision www.benton.org

Clarke Roger (1996, WWWa) Speech to Victorian Council of Civil Liberties www.anu.edu/people/Roger.Clarke/II/VicCCL.html

Clarke Roger (1996, WWWb) NET-ETHIQUETTE: Mini case studies of dysfunctional human behaviour on the net www.anu.edu/people/Roger.Clarke/II/Netethiquettecases.html

Durango Declarations (1995, WWW) www.lanl.gov/SFC/95/declaration.html

Internet Industry Association of Australia (1996, WWW) Email:conduct@intiaa.asn.au, 1996

Kling, R. (1996) The Information Society: *Letter from Rob Kling for TIS*, **12** (1) Jan-May 1996. Email:kling@binky.ics.uci.edu

Merel, Peter (1996, WWW) The Expectations of Electronic Communities - *A Bill of Electronic Rights and Responsibilities, V0.15* www.usyd.edu.au/~pete/err.html

World Intellectual Property Organization Treaty (1996, WWW) www.public-domain.org/database/database. html

ACKNOWLEDGEMENTS

The authors acknowledge comments, contributions, and assistance from Roger Clarke, Diane Whitehouse, Patsy Segall, Margaret McEvoy, Graham Greenleaf, Philip Argy and Andrew Freeman.

The Charter for Citizens of the Global Information Society

This Charter assumes that all individuals of all societies have the rights set out in the United Nations Declaration of Human Rights. It aims to enhance the well-being of all citizens throughout the world. The objectives of the Charter are to reduce the vulnerability of individuals and societies, and to promote socially sustainable development of the Global Information Society. Exceptions to the Principles set out in this Charter must be justified, clearly stated, made in accordance with law, proportional to the necessities giving rise to the exception, and compatible with the requirement to enhance human rights.

Principle 1 - Individual and collective cybercitizens must protect the accuracy and integrity of digital information, adhere to all relevant ethical principles, codes and guidelines, and uphold the legitimate laws of nations.

Principle 2 - Nations should aim at equity of access to electronic information and cyberspace for all their citizens without discrimination.

Principle 3 - Citizens have the right to privacy and the right to conduct their affairs free from surveillance or fear of surveillance.

Principle 4 - Cybercitizens have the right to freedom of expression and opinion and the responsibility to ensure the democratic rights and well-being of all citizens are protected.

Principle 5 - Cyberspace should be used to enhance opportunities for democracy within nations and across national boundaries.

Principle 6 - Cyberspace should be used to support diversity of culture and ideology.

Principle 7 - All participants in the global information society, individual, corporate and government, should aim to distribute wealth and benefits equitably.

Principle 8 - Ownership of personal data resides with the data subject. Rights to acquire, access and sell data about objects and transactions within a nation should be determined by the laws of that country. Agreement about transborder collection and use of data about the natural, economic and social resources of a nation should be negotiated by the collecting/receiving nation or organization. Nations should have the right to access and use data about their economy and resources regardless of where it is stored.

2

Information technology and ethics

Inger V. Eriksson
Swedish School of Economics and Business Administration
Department of Statistics and Computer Science
Arkadiank. 22, P.O. Box 479, 00101 Helsinki, Finland
Phone: +358 9 4313 3243, Fax: +358 9 4313 3373
Email: eriksson@shh.fi

Abstract

Information technology (IT) exerts a strong influence on people either as individuals, workers or members of society. In this paper, the ethical issues raised by computerization are discussed. IT development is first put into the broader context of technological development in general. Next, ethical issues arising from IT are identified and categorized. Issues which are already the subject of discussion include artificial intelligence and expert systems, work, privacy, social power, computer crime, and intellectual property rights. To this can be added issues which have been recognized but not so much discussed yet, such as artificial and virtual reality technology and its consequences. The paper does not give any simple solutions or answers on how to handle possible ethical issues but rather aims to make the reader aware of them and to stimulate discussion by raising questions. Asking questions is the first step in formulating a solution.

INTRODUCTION

The ethical, legal, and social considerations raised by computerization concern areas such as privacy, crime, health, working conditions, individuality, and employment (O'Brien, 1994, p. 459). Computer monitoring occurs in workplaces. Private information is available through different databases. Well-known examples of computer crimes are the theft of money, services, and information. The computerization of production processes may eliminate jobs. However, while eliminating jobs computerization might also improve the working conditions and job satisfaction of the employees that remain, and make possible the production of higher-quality products at a lower cost to customers.

An Ethical Global Information Society J. Berleur & D. Whitehouse (Eds.)

The following question arises: Do we need to rethink our ethical principles as a consequence of the technical changes or are the new situations which we face reinterpretable based on old and well-established principles – if we have any? The summary of the IFIP WG9.2 position paper (Berleur, this volume) seems to consider a rethink necessary:

> *New deals require new regulation.* People may be upset with present politics, new market trends in the hands of a "happy few". Culture remains the way to find new political and economic regulations, according to the genius of nations and particular people. (Italics added.)

The above point of view finds a resonance in the opinion of Oz in his recent book (1994):

> Information technology revolutionized the way in which we conduct many aspects of our lives. The tremendous technological advancement in the area of computers and related devices created unforeseen situations that necessitate new ethical considerations. Important issues like piracy, free speech, and protection of intellectual property have new meanings in the information age. The ease with which commercial values are transferred from one party to another with the help of computers and computer networks created new crimes. *Ethics have to be modified to accommodate the vast changes brought upon us by the new technology.* (Italics added.)

There is an expressed need in the IT community to develop new ethical codes of conduct (Eriksson, 1996), to identify general ethical attitudes, and to seriously consider users' requirements of information systems. There are particular features of IT which give rise to special ethical problems. Computers often make work abstract. Abstraction makes ethical issues appear neutral. Communication takes place via rather anonymous media. It is easy to monitor employees' work habits, including their use of electronic mail. Such aspects indicate that general and IT ethics cannot be the same, although the basic principles might be.

This situation is not new or unique; technical changes have always caused new problems or accentuated old ones and this is what is happening with the introduction of IT. The new problems just need to be recognized and controlled. Here the IT community's interest in ethics comes in; to be in control of the situation through agreed codes.

But what are the general ethics which should be broadened or reinterpreted to make them contain and explain IT related problems? Teleological and deontological principles represent almost opposing ethical views here. Teleological principles emphasize goals and ends, the good over the right; utilitarianism is one of the well-known theories within this category. Deontological principles on the other hand are based on duty, emphasizing the right over the good. In this category we can find theories such as universalism and Kant's categorical imperative. There are also Christian values and specific Orthodox values. What principles should be considered and to what extent?

Harakas (1983) defines three categories of ethical judgement. Besides good/evil and right/wrong, he also takes in fitting/unfitting or appropriate/inappropriate (p.17). According to Clement and Wagner, what can be considered as 'good' or 'right' is shaped by the context and conditions that characterize a certain social setting (Clement and Wagner, 1996; Piller, 1993). In other words, there are good reasons to assume that people's ideas of 'good' and 'right' differ among social and political cultures. In all likelihood, neither the meaning nor the priorities of ethical concepts are the same in different cultures. Considering the dichotomies fitting/unfitting or appropriate/inappropriate, these pairs of concepts by definition must be culturally defined. Thus, ethics could be considered to be a part of the values, culture, and history in which they have been developed, both on an individual and on a social level. However, computerization and especially the development of communication technology may become a threat to cultural diversity, the result being a monoculture. Defining a common basis for ethics might then be possible - but is it desirable to eliminate this diversity?

TECHNOLOGICAL DEVELOPMENT

One of the issues raised for the conference to consider was understanding technological development. Understanding change can be quite hard but summarizing what has happened, and how and why, is at least one step in that direction, and might give a hint as to where we are heading. In the following sub-section the position of science and technology is discussed in a historical perspective and then the development of information technology is summarized.

Science and Technology

In the classical period, philosophy included all scientific knowledge. Knowledge was a holistic concept. Later specialization split science into different disciplines, the consequence being the fragmentation of knowledge. This splitting-up or specialization continues to this day, e.g., in the field of biology. 'Science' has become to mean natural sciences only.

Nor was technology a separate field of knowledge from the beginning, although the Greek distinguished between three types of knowledge; scientific knowledge in its original and holistic sense (*episteme*), skills (*techne*) and practical wisdom or knowing how to behave correctly in a moral way (*phronesis*). Skills included craftmanship and understanding the nature of the material to be worked upon. Despite the name 'techne' for skills, I presume that technology does not belong there but should be considered part of episteme instead. Technology only gained a more distinct role of its own when mechanics, electromagnetics and, later, electronics became central to the development of products and production methods.

Christianity taught that man was master over his environment and emphasized human superiority over the rest of creation. According to Harakas (1982, p. 161), that led man to study nature (science) and then to control it (technology). Thus, man's dominance over nature permits and requires his knowledge of science as well as his control over technology. Destruction of nature or ecological mismanagement is not acceptable, instead man is expected to assume responsibility and save nature for future generations (Harakas, 1982, p. 162). Several Christian fathers emphasize that ownership amounts to no more than borrowing.

Information Technology

Information technology is a fast-developing field with indisputable influence on our lives. The ways in which we perform our work tasks, make decisions, and communicate have changed. Many of us have become very dependent on computers both in our working and in our private lives.

Computers do not only affect our lives and work but also our behaviour and the way we think of many fundamental concepts. As an example, consider the somewhat unexpected lack of messaging or network etiquette, even among IT professionals, which became evident as a result of general access to email. Human online behaviour seems to be different from face-to-face behaviour.

We can identify three phases or 'paradigm shifts' in IT development from the 1950s to the 1990s (Friedman and Cornford, 1993). The phases go from a focus on the benefits and constraints of computers and system software, to types of applications, and on to the broadening of user categories. This shift of attention is reflected in the characteristics considered most important.

During the first phase, cost-effectiveness was the central characteristic. Computers were used for process control and to automate clerical tasks in offices, and they were certainly effective in this respect. It was rather easy to develop such information systems and make them run fast and effectively, especially since the cost/performance ratio of computers improved remarkably, and seemingly continues to do so.

Computers were fast and cost-effective. This brought requests from users for new information systems, but there were not enough IT professionals to respond to the needs and opportunities available. The so-called software crisis became a reality. During the second phase, this crisis was to be overcome by improved information systems development techniques and tools. Productivity was the major issue. During this phase also, new fields opened up to computerization such as decision support and artificial intelligence applications, offering yet new challenges.

In the 1980s and 1990s, the quality of information systems proved to be the major issue. There were more users than ever and they were from all hierarchical levels in organizations, many of them with no previous training in using computers. They began to understand that they had the right to ask for useful and flexible tools to perform their work tasks. So, new helpful systems were needed.

A further step in this development is represented by the present situation emphasizing information and communication technology (ICT). Easy communication and the availability via the Internet of a huge amount of data and information from around the world present unforeseeable opportunities - and risks. This can lead to democratization as well as to polarization within and between nations. It also has an influence on individuals when they perform their work, utilize the services offered by society, and exercise their political power. The direction in which we are heading depends both on decisions influenced by economic considerations, and on ethics and moral values.

ETHICAL ISSUES RAISED BY INFORMATION TECHNOLOGY

Discussions on ethics are certainly not new - the ancient Greeks specialized in it. For some time, there has also been discussion of what the consequences of the introduction of new technology are on individuals and work, on organizations and their structure, and on society. Even the consequences of introducing information technology have been debated and studied. However, the concept in these discussions has not been 'ethics' but rather 'social issues'. It is pertinent to question why there is now so much debate on 'ethics'. Is there a new awareness that something has been neglected in previous discussions? Does IT pose a major threat which has only been recognized recently? Or is the ethical stage of our society in a crisis of some kind which warrants such an emphasis? Or are there indeed new issues to be taken into account?

The previous sections have stressed the need to consider ethical issues from new perspectives. In the following section, issues which are considered to be ethical are identified, classified, and discussed.

Recognizing the issues

First, the ethical issues raised by information technology have to be recognized, and the variety of topics that can be considered ethical makes some classification necessary. One way to do this is to browse through all literature where the topic is discussed or to use existing bibliographies on the topic. Another way might be to look at empirical studies applying available ethical models as the frame of reference. All approaches have their pros and cons, and I will briefly mention some ideas that appear relevant to me although I have chosen to use the bibliography approach for my study.

Information systems (IS) developed to support work tasks are intended to facilitate work performance, but there are systems which instead control the work, and force users to adapt their way of working to the computer system's way. According to Clement and Wagner (1996), many causes can be identified for such a deficiency, but they can all be traced in some degree to an ethical shortcoming. However, the failure of individuals and organizations to consider the likely effects on people's welfare and to take responsibility for adequate remedial action are key here. Systems development is the activity where the quality of the system to be produced is determined. Clement and Wagner state that this activity represents the obvious stage at which ethical concerns can be brought to bear. However, most attention to ethical issues has focused on IT use, but earlier intervention could help to develop better systems. Research into ethics in information systems development is therefore endorsed. The essential point is the emphasis on prevention instead of adaptation and correction after IS have been implemented.

In a thought-provoking essay, Mason (1986) expressed his concern over people's vulnerability to IT. He studied in what ways users can come to harm either through misuse of IT or by being hindered from exercising their legal rights. For the purpose of analysis, he constructed a framework consisting of four ethical issues: privacy, accuracy, property, and accessibility. This ethical construct, called PAPA, can be applied to identify and to structure ethical problems. For example, the misuse of personal information or use of incorrect data can cause a person harm and violate her privacy. Personal property is protected by law but, for software and data, the concept of property has not been clearly defined. Lately, there have been several legal cases which will form precedents for the future. Not only the protection of, but also access to, a person's property, including intangible property, should be guaranteed. In Mason's study, as in many other studies, ethics and legal rights are mixed. One major merit of Mason's essay is that it initiated discussion on the ethical issues raised by IT.

In my analysis, I have adapted a more pragmatic way of identifying central ethical issues in information systems. Herman Tavani (1995) and his students have put together 'A Computer Ethics Bibliography' made up of over 1,200 entries on the topics of computer ethics and computer and society. This bibliography was published in *Computers and Society*, June-December 1995. The bibliography covers the following major fields: material for teaching computer ethics courses, professional ethics and issues of responsibility for computer professionals, and a section dealing with applied ethics and computing. I have earlier written an article on professional ethics (Eriksson, 1996). In the present article, applied ethics and computing will be discussed. In Tavani's classification these issues cover: artificial intelligence and expert systems, work, privacy, social power, computer crime, and intellectual property rights. They could be categorized as issues primarily dealing with democratic versus cultural aspects, although these categories would not be quite exclusive, which a good categorization should be, but partly overlapping. In the following, however, I will follow such a structure. Another categorization, and maybe a more interesting one, which I apply, is issues under discussion and issues not yet discussed.

Tavani and his students deserve to be acknowledged for the major effort in putting together the bibliography which they are also continuously updating. The latest update was published in *Computers and Society* in September 1996. Of course, it can be questioned whether this classification is the right one, whether it covers all aspects of ethics, whether there are issues which do not necessarily belong to the ethics field but are primarily legal issues, for example - and, no doubt, there is an American bias since most American journals and books are covered but not the European ones. I do not, however, consider these points to be critical. Each researcher using Tavani's bibliography can make his own judgements and utilize the results as best fits his purpose. The American bias, on the other hand, could be balanced by sending Tavani information on European articles discussing the topic which would then certainly be included in the bibliography.

Issues under discussion

Tavani's bibliography includes references to articles and book chapters dealing with ethical issues. Consequently, these are the issues generally under discussion, but there is great variation in the frequency with which a certain topic occurs. Most references are to North American journals and books, and discuss issues which are considered major topics there. It might be that other issues would be more important in Europe or Asia. A similar study of these cultural regions would be interesting.

In the United States, the most important issue is privacy and individuality. Issues not yet so much discussed are artificial and virtual realities. In the following, a brief overview of relevant ethical issues categorized either as democratic or cultural is presented.

Ethical issues with democratic challenges

Computers and work

Computers and work is one of the themes, but I have discussed it earlier in another article (Eriksson, 1994), so I will be very brief here. The discussion concerns the impact of computers on contemporary workplaces and work. There are now less dangerous and monotonous jobs but also a higher rate of unemployment. New jobs require new skills and not all people are able or willing to invest their time and energy in continuous learning. On the other hand, computerization is blamed for deskilling people's proficiency, something the use of expert systems might maintain. The organization of work is also changing, e.g., telework is a rather new concept with varying impact on individuals.

The quality of working life is the other major issue. There are health hazards and medical injuries associated with the workplace, including the electronic office. Stress due to computer monitoring is a reality, although monitoring could also be interpreted as a form of support, all depending on how the information is used.

Communication technology, networks and groupware have an influence on the division of work, also at the global level. There is the opportunity and the risk of an unfair distribution of work to areas where the workforce is cheapest, thus creating and maintaining economic inequality in the world.

All these issues deal with ethics - the rights and responsibilities of employer and employee, work and the family. Hitherto, these have been discussed under the concept of 'social consequences'; but now they can even have global dimensions, and thus we are talking of not only democratic but also of cultural effects.

Computers and privacy

Computers and privacy is the most eagerly discussed topic. There is the 'big brother' issue, the fear of government's attempts at social control. Employers can not only monitor their employees' working but also read their email and monitor their telephone conversations. The use of databases in the commercial sector and the selling of personal information for unintended use has been criticized. The accuracy of data in databases and access to these are also relevant issues in this context.

The security of medical records, public and protected databases as well as electronic fund-transfer and point-of-sale systems, or more generally, security in networks represent issues for both individuals and organizations, also in the ethical dimension. The expanding use of the Internet for both private and business use accentuates the significance of security and the need for protection.

There are the assumptions of individual and personal privacy as aspects of human dignity, and the protection of economic interests which have to be considered. The economic aspects concern both individuals and business. Here an overlap between economic, i.e., legal, aspects and ethics is obvious.

Privacy is a hot topic, especially in the United States, with its accompanying reference to democratic rights. However, as far as I know, there are no such rights enshrined in any legislation. There are other countries where the issue is the reverse, and the government wants to protect itself from the insight of its citizens. There are also countries which do not consider privacy an issue at all. In other words, the democratic issue is certainly culturally flavoured.

Computers and the distribution of social power

Ethical issues under this sub-heading concern computers and equity, computers and gender, computers and education, and computers in the political sector. Three of the issues mentioned above are closely related. It is a fact that there are inequities in opportunities to access computer resources and thus in computer literacy - and computer literacy soon becomes a necessity when competing for places at work. This is both an economic and an attitudinal issue. For example, women are not expected to be interested in technology in general nor in computers, and yet it is mostly women who use computers but for simpler tasks. In an interesting contradiction of this widely-held notion, in 1996, a new course in multimedia at the vocational education level in the Aland Islands (Finland), a region considered rather conservative in many respects, attracted the majority of its applicants from women over the age of 30!

In Finland, the government is making a major investment in computers and teacher training in public schools. This is expected to guarantee students equal opportunities in computer literacy. The Internet provides an opportunity to bring global resources into classrooms -- given the basic resources are available. Computer aided instruction programs (CAI, CAL, etc.) are also becoming more common and widely available and offer new ways of broadening the educational supply.

A major problem in the quest for equality is represented by all those people already in the workforce who have missed out on computerization. They might be passed over if vocational retraining is not organized. If computer literacy becomes a must, in the same way as literacy is, for a person to function and use his social power in the society of tomorrow, then this is one of the critical political and moral issues our society has to solve.

The third world represents a global problem, also in respect of equity for computer resources. Where computers and computer-related knowledge are available together with a cheap labour force for programming, for example, this can be utilized by enterprises in developed countries. The question is whether this will be enough to give developing countries a real chance to improve their own conditions in the future.

From the political point of view, centralization versus decentralization of power is an interesting question and either choice is easily made possible by IT. There are discussions on 'teledemocracy' or 'digital democracy' bringing computer aided voting and political decision-making to the home. The problem of the security and reliability of systems and networks has yet to be solved. The risk of misuse is obvious. And, of course, the infrastructure in society and the resources in the home are needed!

If the distribution of social power is to be considered an ethical issue, then we certainly have many new ethical issues to find solutions for and to study.

Computer crime and abuse

Computers make new ways of committing old crimes possible and that is why one of the topics which has been discussed a lot is computer crime and abuse. Viruses are one of the first issues which come to mind, although this it is not the major problem, albeit an annoying one. Economic crimes are the most central and these are often committed by employees and not by hackers. Industrial espionage is another important issue and the risk of wiretapping, for example, is why some big organizations do not dare to use open networks. Before the security problems of the Internet are solved, electronic commerce with all its potential will probably remain no more than that - potential. Software piracy as well as the illegal copying of software are also central problems to be solved. They concern profits and economic justice, but here different attitudes to intellectual property in different cultures represent a problem.

From the ethical point of view computers do not create very many new types of crimes but mainly legal issues. Computers just make committing some crimes easier and open to new groups of people. Somehow they also make the borderlines between acceptable and non-acceptable behaviour fuzzy.

Intellectual property rights and information ownership

Intellectual property rights and how to extend them to the ownership of electronic information is a crucial point. There is the issue of protecting creativity and ideas, for example a piece of electronic music. According to 'normal copyrights', a piece of electronic music would be the property of its creator, but how can such rights be enforced in an electronic environment? A very special case is the availability of the source code to all home pages on the Internet. Normally, printed material is protected by copyright laws but for 'printed home pages' there is no way, and maybe no point, in insisting on any copyrights. The realization is available to whoever wants to reuse it.

We also have the issue of the ownership of information in electronic form. Who owns it? Is it the person whose data have been collected or the instance that collected it? And, if it has been sold on, can the new owner decide how to use it? What is a fair price for information and who decides it? Answering these questions concerns not only ownership but also privacy, and the Internet will make manifold the problem since collecting data on who visits which web sites is so easy.

With these property issues, we can observe changed practices and changed values. If this reflects changed morals, we probably need new ethical rules or a reinterpretation of old ones to solve the problems experienced.

Ethical issues with cultural challenges

In the previous sub-section, ethical issues primarily related to democratic challenges were discussed, although many of them represent cultural challenges as well. Only one class in Tavani's classification, artificial intelligence and expert systems, fits better under cultural challenges and is discussed below.

Artificial Intelligence and Expert Systems

Artificial intelligence (AI) and expert systems (ES) aim to assist in decision-making. From the outset, the goal was to replace expert knowledge where no experts were available - or to replace expensive expertise by a cheaper labour force.

Such use met with a lot of criticism. Johannessen (1987), among others, pointed out that it might be possible to tap the expert's factual knowledge and include his/her decision rules into a computer program, but it is never possible to tap the expert's judgement based on experience and intuition. Heuristics do not help here either.

The locus of moral responsibility in decisions made with the aid of ES has been questioned, as has the question of whether the goals of AI are proper and ethical. For example, the latest way to make point in a courtroom in the United States is computer animation. Knowing the power of pictures over words and the American habit of watching television, and being aware of the opportunities to build up the situation in a favourable way in a computer animation, would make me at least question the objectivity of the presentation, the protection of justice, and the rights of the people concerned. Clinical judgement and diagnosis is another problematic issue. Correctly used by experts, it can certainly be helpful, but trying to replace non-existing knowledge and trusting suggested solutions too much can be dangerous and risky - an issue of moral responsibility and liability, as I see it.

To this field also belong efforts to try to make computers more humanlike. There are attempts to encourage computers to learn to interpret facial expressions in terms of signalled human emotions. The issue of simulated sex is not far off - and is being discussed. Do we want it?

The major issue about the challenges that AI and ES offer is to what extent the solutions are acceptable. Do they fit our cultural and moral context? And, if not, what should be changed: the ethics, the local culture, or the opportunities the new technological solutions offer? Here I see the need for serious discussion.

Not many of Tavani's categories fitted properly under the sub-title of cultural challenges. Partly, this is due to the fact that the categories are not strictly distinct. The most likely explanation for the small number of topics purely dealing with cultural challenges is, as I see it, that these are the issues that are not yet discussed.

Issues not yet discussed

One topic in Tavani's bibliography which has not yet been widely debated but which is important from the ethical point of view is the use of artificial or virtual reality technology. For many young people in particular this is becoming a reality where they spend a lot of their time. It might be just fun, but it may also be 'addictive' and isolate users from real life. The American film industry has made a comedy about young professional people unable to communicate except via their computers, something which does not seem very likely but is not entirely impossible either (*Denise Calls Up* by Sony Pictures Entertainment) - and, in that case, I would not call it a comedy.

Besides the isolation of people, there is also the ethical issue, as I see it, of what is created or manmade versus our duties, an issue which has been discussed since Aristotle. Now, the borderline between manmade and created just seems to have become quite diffuse.

Manmade versus natural and our moral duties has been considered an ontological issue since Plato and Aristotle, and was a concern of Christian values as well up to the mediaeval period. The thinking, however, changed in 1,500-1,600 when new science evolved (Tyørinoja, 1995).

Aristotle's distinction, in Physics II[1], between natural things and artifacts was that natural things had the principles of movement and change and their own strivings which artifacts lacked. Mediaeval thinkers often based their ideas on Aristotle but they, as theologians, had to address the issues of 'made' or 'created' as well.

Thomas of Aquino (circa 1,225-1,274) wanted to make Aristotle's philosophy the basis for theology and thus make theology a theoretical science, the highest of all sciences, because of its objects of study. The simple principle concerning made versus created was: God created living things, while man made artifacts.

Ockham (circa 1,285-1,347/9) represents later Franciscan theology and new nominalistic thinking which reinterpreted ontological issues into epistemological and logical-semantic issues. Thus, the distinction of natural versus artifact became context-dependent causality.

Ockham's theology gave rise to the question of possible worlds (already discussed by Aristotle) and also to natural philosophy, which had been discussed in England already in the twelfth century. Science, in that respect, was thus established in England by Roger Bacon (circa 1,214-1,292/4), and others.

Renaissance Platonism was followed by neo-Aristotelian philosophy with its discussions about mechanism and its nature, whether it is a theoretical or practical science. This gave rise to the development of technology, I suppose. At this time the discussion about artifacts concerned whether a manmade product could be better than a natural one. Artifacts were considered to be of two types, those which followed their nature and those which were freely designable.

In the sixteenth century, Francis Bacon (1561-1626) no longer accepted any essential difference between natural and manmade things. Descartes (1596-1650) agreed. Descartes had a mechanistic interpretation of all living things; they existed just for the moment without any ultimate purpose; God recreated the world constantly.

In the eighteenth century, Julien Offray de La Mettrie tried to show that human beings are machines, all biological processes are mechanic.

Now, we come to the discussion of virtual and artificial reality - which is so real. Do we have and, in that case what, moral responsibilities to manmade things? Who owns what we create? Who owns what we say in cyberspace? What is play and what is cheating? It is probably time to think of the ethical consequences of living in cyberspace as well as the interpretations. This is a new ethical issue which has not yet been seriously addressed and requires attention.

DISCUSSION

The purpose of the Corfu conference, according to the call for papers (see also Berleur, this volume), is to develop 'a statement about the future of culture and democracy in a global information society' and to present its outcome 'in the form of recommendations targeting decision-makers, computer scientists and professionals, consumers and users' associations, ...'. My approach in contributing to this major task is to try to establish what the issues are, especially from the ethical point of view, which of these are being discussed by IT and management information systems researchers and professionals as well as by researchers in other fields, and which are not. The justification for my approach is that the first step to change is to recognize the need for it, and that means being aware of what the issues are. I think there is hope for a reappraisal, where necessary, of the topics under discussion. Topics which have not yet been discussed represent a more problematic and threatening domain.

Seven broad questions are stated in the beginning of the call for papers. The first question concerns the sustainability of a society whose cultural, social, political, economic, and technological developments we did not understand. Our society is probably much more complex or at least we are better aware of its complexity than ever before. The solution is hardly to be found in IT, but I would not regard IT as being the problem either. It is what makes the global information society possible. We have it and we need it. How to cope with it certainly is an issue and an important one, but I cannot see any other way around the 'problem' than education and individual confidence in oneself. The issues at least are being discussed.

The second question concerns changes in jobs and work-related skills. Computer literacy is a topic where research has been and continues to be done. The threat of AI and ES and their effects on deskilling people has been discussed but perhaps has not been studied very much yet, so here is a field for research.

The third question concerns the monocultural view of information. Western culture seems to dominate today. However, the global society is really opening up through ICT, and many Asian countries at least are taking up the challenge, so monocultural might become multicultural in the near future.

The fourth question also deals with cultural issues, the right to one's own culture in a global society. This topic has been discussed in articles and the issue is thus recognized.

In the fifth question, I think I can recognize the old discussion on technocracy and technological determinism from years back. What is new here now?

The sixth question deals with issues where economic and political interests are in conflict. However, this is not a new issue although it will probably be accentuated when electronic commerce takes off. Such markets will be very hard to regulate since many legal issues are all new. This will certainly be one central field of both research and political action.

The last question concerns the threats to civil rights from IT and especially from IT integration. Democratic rights is a typical topic for American society so the issue is being discussed, and will certainly continue to be, at least in the United States.

To summarize, there are problems, some of them caused by computerization, but computers are essential to our society today. They are necessary for business, government, and individuals. ICT in particular can be considered a threat but an opportunity at the same time.

It is my belief that, by recognizing an issue and starting to discuss it, we are on our way to solving it. The major problem is that in our 'global village', western culture is dominant. I would like to see studies like Tavani's performed in Europe, Asia (the Pacific Rim), and other continents as well. What are the political and cultural, i.e., ethical, issues there? Recognizing these is the first step to making our world a global and democratic information society.

Many of the issues discussed above are a mix of IT and ethical considerations. The fundamental question that arises is what kind of basis for moral judgement is applicable and relevant to IT. The title of my paper might suggest solutions according to different ethical and moral theories. However, I do not think that it is really possible to start analyzing global IT issues before recognizing them - in a global perspective. Next, we have to accept that there are different cultural settings and we should not enforce any general solution as the whole truth. The solutions might have to be context-dependent, even in a global world, if we want to promote variety instead of a monocultural view.

In this article, I asked the question whether it is necessary to rethink ethical issues because of IT, and my answer to this is, yes. There are new issues to consider, old issues have to be seen in a new context, and there are the local-global aspects to consider. Whether we need new ethics or new moral theory is another issue. It may be that the old principles still hold, if only we could agree what the principles are.

REFERENCES

Berleur, J. (this volume), Culture and democracy revisited in the global information society: Summary of a position paper

Clement, A. and Wagner, I. (1996), Ethics and Systems Design. The Politics of Social Responsibility, in *Ethics of Computing: Codes, Spaces for Discussion and Law*, Berleur, J. and Brunnstein, K., Eds. (1996)

Eriksson, I. (1994) Computers as Tools, in J.M. Kizza (ed.), *Ethics in the Computer Age*, Conference Proceedings, Gatlinburg, Tennessee, Nov. 11-13, 1994, ACM-SIGCAS, pp. 86-95.

Eriksson, I. (1996) Computers or Humans: Who are in Control? in J.M. Kizza (ed.), *Social and Ethical Effects of the Computer Revolution*, McFarland & Company, Inc., Publishers, Jefferson, pp. 80-97.

Friedman, A.L. and D.S. Cornford (1989, reprinted 1993), *Computer Systems Development: History, Organization and Implementation*, John Wiley & Sons, Chichester.

Harakas, S.S. (1982), *Contemporary Moral Issues Facing the Orthodox Christian*, Light and Life Publishing Company, Minneapolis, Minnesota.

Harakas, S.S. (1983), *Towards Transfigured Life: The Theoria of Eastern Orthodox Ethics*, Light and Life Publishing Company, Minneapolis, Minnesota.

Johannessen, K. (1987), Ekspert kunnskapen og grensene for dens meddelbarhet, *Humanistiske Data*, June 1987.

Mason, R. (1986), Four Ethical Issues of the Information Age, *MIS Quarterly*, March 1986, pp. 5-12.

O'Brien, J.A. (1994), *Introduction to Information Systems*, Irwin, Burr Ridge, Illinois.

Oz, E. (1994), *Ethics for the Information Age*, Business and Educational Technologies, Wm. C. Brown Communications, Inc., Burr Ridge, Illinois.

Piller, C. (1993), Bosses with X-Ray Eyes: Your Employer May be Using Computers to Keep Tabs on You, *Macworld*, July 1993, pp. 118-123.

Tavani, H. (1995), A Computer Ethics Bibliography, *Computers and Society*, June, September and December 1995.

Tyørinoja, R. (1995), Keinoelæmæ - Kæsitteellinen ristiriitako?, *Keinoelæmæ - Artificial Life*, Publication of the Finnish Artificial Intelligence Society, pp. 42-55.

[1] All the following references on philosophy are indirectly taken from Tyørinoja's work (1995). Unfortunately, I do not understand the original languages.

3

Much ado about nothing: The Internet dream

Joseph M. Kizza
Department of Computer Science and Electrical Engineering
The University of Tennessee, Chattanooga
Chattanooga, TN 37403, USA
Email: jkizza@utcdc01.utc.edu

Abstract

In the last five years the growth of the Internet has gone far beyond the expectations of many. From its humble beginnings as a small communication medium of the privileged few to the global mass communication medium for everyone, the Internet has aroused many dreams and expectations that may never come to be. While it is too early to pass judgement on its achievements, already two camps of opposing philosophies have emerged. Those who think that the Internet is a wonder kid to perform miracles, in one camp, and those who see it as a cancer of our civilization, in the other. Is the Internet an empty promise? This paper surveys many of the visible pitfalls that may make the argument about the pending abyss of the Internet plausible.

INTRODUCTION

Is the Internet broken? Does it need fixing or it is just going through the experiences of growing pains and it is just fine? These are questions whose answers support the two views in the current debate about the state and the future of the Internet. The debate pits two opposing philosophies against each other which for our discussion we will refer to as the 'wonder' and the 'problems in paradise' philosophies.

An Ethical Global Information Society J. Berleur & D. Whitehouse (Eds.)

WONDER

The wonder philosophy, led mostly by the intelligentsia, advocates a market-driven Internet with no central regulating and enforcement authority. Indeed, those in this camp were happy to see what had long been the rudimentary Internet central force - the United States (US)-based National Science Foundation backbone - cease to exist. Since the termination of the backbone, commercial interests in the Internet have skyrocketed and the Internet now resembles the historical American West land rush in Oklahoma, but this time with companies struggling to set up shop on the Internet. The supporters of this philosophy usually paint a very rosy and romantic picture of the future of the Internet drawing from its past and current successes which have changed the cultural and socio-political landscape along the way.

These changes have not only been social and political, but have also been culturally fundamental as the Internet lingo has entered mainstream languages at a higher rate than no other technology before it. For example meaningless symbols like http://www.something.somethingelse/ or ftp://something.somethingelse/ or gopher://something@somewhere.something, and uniform or universal resource locators (URLs) have come to mean something, whatever the meanings are. Cyberspace came to mean something other than fiction; cybercommunities were no longer made up of fictional creatures with funny heads. At the same time, old words picked up new meanings just overnight: the web no longer referred to cobweb; and surfing no longer required a surfing board and water - just a mouse - but not that mouse - a computer mouse.

Beside changing our lingo, the Internet has also had a profound effect on us in a number of other areas. In business and commerce, the Internet is rapidly driving the creation of new technology industries and companies unknown just a few years back, with telecommunications in the lead. On a personal level, the Internet has brought a more personal touch to communication allowing a wide range of personal communication facilities with more freedom. Individual benefits have not only been in communications but also in information gathering in fields like education, research, medicine, the arts, you name it. The Internet brought into reach scarce resources at the click of a mouse. The latest research data can be obtained in a fraction of the time it would have taken to get from the best research centres to the remotest places around the globe. School children can get instant information saving mum and dad a trip to the library.

PROBLEMS IN PARADISE

As expected in a debate, the opposing problems in paradise philosophy believes that, despite the Internet goodies described above and more, the Internet has nevertheless lost its soul - the guiding philosophy and decision-making body to set its agenda, pace, and guide it through the difficult growing pains. There is a litany of problems. Among these are: over-commercialization, poor architectural design, protocol, bandwidth, frequent breakdowns, the content and nature of the user community, censorship, and unfulfilled expectations, all plausible points in the argument.

When the US government relinquished its role in the Internet backbone, on which the Internet has depended for policy and guidance since its inception, commercialization of the Internet started immediately. Big and small companies started vying for control of the Internet and, very soon, a monopoly of one or more companies is likely to emerge with a potential for a cartel. The so-called superhighway has become a dangerous highway cluttered with advertising billboards. What is even more worrying is that this advertising is on the rise. Besides advertising, the Internet is also providing fertile ground for other business vices like the unprecedented rate of information gathering from the public by companies purely for commercial reasons. Many corporate sites now require users to register before they can access the site, thus scooping information like email addresses from unsuspecting users which is used later to build databases either for sale or for their own direct marketing. The result of all this has been a high volume of junk mail, both snail and email. On one discussion group of which I am a member, a user got 5,848 emails in one day, costing the poor fellow several hours of valuable time shifting through and deleting the mail. The downside to this corporate invasion of the Internet is the possible loss of individual privacy as companies cast global nets to get customers in their customer base.

Rapid over-commercialization is not the only problem with the Internet. The poor architectural design of the Internet as a loose network of computers has caught up with the demand. Since 1988, the number of Internet users and services has been doubling every year with email and world wide web in the lead [1]. With this exponential growth of web sites on network computers, and with each site using several links to other sites, the network of computers is now like a giant pot of spaghetti. Searching for information in this pot with its billions of links is becoming more and more a nightmare, contrary to the goals of the Internet. Information search and retrieval is further hampered by the poor Internet protocol itself. The Internet uses a protocol known as the TCP/IP suite, really a combination of two protocols, the Transmission Control Protocol (TCP) and Internet Protocol (IP). Between them, they offer a connection-less packet-switching and a reliable connection-oriented delivery service. In the IP scheme, each computer host in the Internet is assigned a unique 32-bit number known as an IP-address. It is this number that must be used with all network communication with this host. In addition to assigning each network host with a unique IP-address, IP also assigns one or more unique IP addresses to the network routers - computers with multiple network connections or bridging computers. TCP, a major and reliable transportation component in the TCP/IP suite, breaks up each message originating from a network host into packets called an IP datagram. Each IP datagram consists of two parts, the header which contains information about where the packet is from, where it is going, the type of information carried within it, and the body which contains the information itself. Packets are numbered and TCP makes sure that they are delivered error-free at the destination in the same sequence. So, with TCP/IP, any message from one host to another in the network is broken into hundreds of smaller packets before it is sent. On a busy day, there are billions of these small packets floating around in all directions. At peak times, at times of crisis, and at other high profile events, like the 1996 US presidential elections, billions of floating packets become too much for the system to handle and the whole system slows down to a rate that is becoming annoying to many.

Late in 1996, many of the major Internet providers started the flat rate user fee and, at the beginning of 1997, three small US Internet providers started to offer free Internet access in exchange for sending advertisements to their registered customers' screens as long as the customers are logged on to the Internet. If either of these actions or if both of them take root among Internet users and the anticipated growth comes true, there is likely to be gridlock on the Internet. To overcome such a gridlock, the bandwidth must be increased faster than the rate at which users are joining otherwise the whole protocol will be hanged. Although there are already plans dubbed Internet II to increase the bandwidth of the overtaxed Internet, such efforts may not be enough to catch up with the anticipated growth of the Internet and may even be too little too late.

A number of events have in the past tested the strength of the Internet bandwidth to withstand a rapid and unexpected upsurge of usage. Two events in particular are worth mentioning here: the 1996 US presidential elections and the storm that hit the eastern coast of the US in 1994. In both events, the Internet bandwidth was stretched to the limit causing many delays and frustrations. Now the question which many people are asking is whether the Internet can withstand a crisis of a magnitude greater than any of these two events. What about a catastrophic incident? From what we know so far we can probably guess that the potential is there for a complete breakdown of the whole Internet system in the event of a crisis that demands a bandwidth ten to twenty times greater than any of the events experienced so far.

The recent America Online (AOL) problems that resulted after AOL decided to charge a flat monthly fee of $US19.95, created the worst crisis in the Internet's history and resulted in a near breakdown of the whole AOL system, one of the major global Internet providers. This problem, together with frequent breakdowns of major carriers, are episodes of things to come if the growth of the Internet does not abate. These frequent breakdowns by carriers, coupled with the infrastructure of the Internet itself as a loosely connected network of computers which are largely self-regulating, together with an almost chronically poor rate of improvements, service additions that constantly lag behind the rate of people joining the Internet, and poor maintenance, are all symptoms of things yet to come and may offer a good indication of the likelihood of total anarchy that may engulf the Internet community.

OTHER PROBLEMS

Besides structural weaknesses and poor administration, the Internet is a fertile medium for scams and bad content. A study of Internet scams by the Washington-based National Consumer League found widespread use of pyramid scams, bogus Internet-related services, spurious equipment, claims of quality goods while delivering inferior ones (if any), fraudulent business opportunities, and appealing work-at-home offers. The study further noted that Internet scams are on the rise [2]. Whether a scam or not, Internet content is also getting more and more worrisome as more and more users of all shades join the Internet bandwagon with little or no regard to civility. The result has been a decline in the standard of the Internet content to a level that borders on distasteful. Distasteful content takes, among others, the following forms:

(i) Garbage: Though not an evil in itself, but certainly an irritant, the web is starting to become a garbage can where people of all shades post their garbage for the world to see on personal and business home pages. Because of the volume on the web, it is difficult to know where garbage is but it is always there. It is estimated that nearly 50% of the stuff on the web is garbage, the spectrum of which varies from obscenity, at one end, to just bad taste, at the other. Although the web is the third most used Internet service, and is soon becoming only second to email, in a poll of the 7.5 million web users in the US conducted by FIND/SCVP, 75% of the web sites users visited were either not available or had unintelligible messages [3, 7, 8].

(ii) Hate: Hate groups around the globe have seen the Internet as an inexpensive way of disseminating their hate messages and furthering their causes. Some are using the Internet as a recruiting tool. For example, hate groups like the Neo-Nazi Heritage Front, White Power, and the Ku Klux Klan have web pages and home sites to disseminate their message of hate.

(iii) Criminal Acts: The Internet has been used for criminal activities since its inception. The most notable of the criminal activities have been paedophilia, drug trafficking, espionage, child abuse, and many others.

(iv) Bad Taste and Entertainment: The graphic nature of the web has given the pornography industry a boost. The web has become the prime spot for advertising pornography. With no regulating and responsible body to check on sites and, because of the borderlessness of the web, the industry is doing a booming business.

The problem with bad content on the Internet is exacerbated by the structures and nature of the Internet communities and the ability to be anonymous. The Internet community as a whole is a mosaic of different interests, intentions, social and cultural backgrounds, and varying degrees of moral character. Since many of the user communities are clustered around special interests, they spend little time outside these clubs and, therefore, have little interest in, let alone know, what else is carried on the Internet. Those who care to know have little power to influence change because of the way the Internet is structured as a highly individualized and self-controlled medium.

As a mass medium that is geared to serve a diverse audience, the Internet has fallen prey to what all other mass media serving diverse audiences have - all materials are not appropriate to all audiences in different communities, cultures, and countries. This is reflected in the reactions to the Internet's contents from different countries that is, in some cases, total censorship and, in others, a curb in individual freedoms. Reasons for Internet censorship vary depending on historical, cultural, social, and religious grounds. For example in Singapore, one country well known for Internet censorship, the reasons given for censorship are historical and social-political. China's censorship, on the other hand, is political and, in Iran, it is religious. Whatever the reasons, Internet censorship is catching on in unlikely places including Germany and the US.

And, finally, there are unfulfilled public expectations. Contrary to public expectations, every house is not likely to have a computer by the year 2,000. Therefore, Internet use is likely to fall far short of predictions and this may well be the linchpin that will let down the whole success of the Internet. Social expectations of the Internet included enhancing human individualism and adventurism, since both have been the catalysts for the rapid growth of computer technology. While this has happened in some sectors, it has not been widespread. The limitless human exploration of the Internet was hampered by a number of issues including the accessibility of the Internet itself, contrary to public predictions. Computers and computer technology since inception have been and remain in the domain of the haves, those who can afford thousands of disposable dollars to buy, connect, and subscribe to commercial online services. Outside the commercial online services, access can only be obtained through higher education institutions and research institutions, serving but a small sector of any society. The poor have yet to participate fully in the Internet game [4].

CONCLUSION

If the dream is to be held dear for every community user worldwide, the Internet needs to be a lot more than it is currently. It needs to be a decent place where my children and your children can log on, without sparking fear in you as you cross your fingers and hope that little John Mukasa will not stumble on to guess what. Besides the social issues on the Internet, there must be a balance between the commercial interests and other users' interests, like research and personal communication. It would be tragic if the Internet becomes like television, completely taken over by commercial interests and a user has to navigate commercial advertisements in order to surf the net. There is a need for a loose central body to set the philosophy and agenda for the Internet and spearhead it through difficult times with little or no commercial interests. One immediate advantage coming out of such a body is the timely response to the Internet needs, like a quick response to the constantly changing bandwidth and the installation of other timely technologies.

Luckily there is a growing sense and interest in Internet issues and the problem in paradise philosophy is gaining ground. Both governments and the private sector are taking steps to keep the Internet to its intended goal and mission. Governments are passing legislations that will create safe environments for users although many are being challenged in the courts like the US Communications Decency Act. On the private front, community groups and companies are also trying measures to curb illegal activities and bad content; for example, the Platform for Internet Content Selection (PICS) establishes an Internet convention for label formats and distribution methods. PICS labels describe Internet content on several levels. PICS works with selection software to prohibit access according to labels. Parents can use PICS labels to prohibit access to unlabelled Internet documents. Already major companies like IBM, Microsoft, and Microsystems are supporting PICS-compatible products while online companies like AOL, CompuServe, Microsoft Network (MSN), AT&T, and others are providing free blocking software [5, 6].

REFERENCES

[1] Weise, Elizabeth (1996) Some Suggest Internet Poised for a Collapse. *Chattanooga Free Press*, Section O, October 27.
[2] (1996) NewsTrack, *Communications of the ACM*, **39** (12), 10.
[3] (January, 1996) New survey finds Internet use surging. *CNN Interactive*. URL = http://www.cnn.com/
[4] Miller, Michael (January, 1996). A Bad dream Comes true in Cyberspace, *NewsWeek*.
[5] Resnich, Paul and Miller, James (1996) PICS: Internet Control Without Censorship, *Communications of the ACM*, **39**, 10, 87-93.
[6] Lewis, Peter (1996) Blocking Information on the Net is easier said than done, *New York Times*, January 15.
[7] CNN Headline News, January 15, 1996.
[8] Dornin, Rusty. The Internet: Will it last or fade into the past?, *CNN Interactive* URL=http://www.cnn.com/

4

An analysis of ethical awareness related to computers and information technology of people in the Bangkok metropolis

Pateep Methakunavudhi
Associate Professor, Faculty of Education, Chulalongkorn University, Bangkok, 10330 Thailand
Phone: +66 2 2182690; Fax: +66 2 2153558
Email: fedupmt@chulkn.car.chula.ac.th

Abstract

The objectives of this study were to analyze the ethical awareness of people in the Bangkok metropolis in relation to computers and information technology. The people were divided into three groups: computer professionals, customers, and students. Each of the three groups was further divided into three subgroups. Interviews were conducted with 358 people by using ten scenarios covering computer security principles. The study revealed that the ethical awareness among the groups was not different in eight of the ten scenarios. The groups considered the behaviours unethical in all scenarios on the issues of obligation and quality of the professional work; in all the scenarios on the issues of piracy and unauthorized access; in all the scenarios on the issues of intellectual property, contract, and business agreement; and only one scenario on the issues of confidentiality and privacy. However, the average percentages stating unethical behavior were not very high; they varied between 51-79%. Two other scenarios on the issues of confidentiality and privacy were viewed as ethical behaviour, which was confirmed by Thai culture. The students' different educational levels created differences in ethical awareness and their responses. The variations in work experience of the computer professionals did not cause differences in ethical awareness.

An Ethical Global Information Society J. Berleur & D. Whitehouse (Eds.)

SYNTHESIZED VIEW OF THE RESEARCH

Research Rationale

Computer systems raise many potentially serious social and ethical problems. In a society where information is a source of power, it is important to ask questions about who has access and who lacks access to information. To handle this, we need strict controls on who can do what with private information about any individual in the society. Data protection and information privacy are of ever-increasing importance with the advancement of technology in communications. Privacy in information systems requires a different approach from those found among the strictly technically-oriented approaches. Technical professionals often focus largely on improving the stage of technology without considering the ends to which that technology is applied. However, there is a growing interest in understanding the social and ethical implications of technology. Some professional groups have been concerned with these issues and have pointed out that, when we design new technological systems, we should also ask what is ethically desirable as well as what is technically feasible. If codes of ethics and professional conduct in the age of technology are used, technology may be controlled and redirected towards achieving positive human and environmental values.

The concepts of ethical and legal issues in relation to computers vary in different societies and have been very well developed in the western countries. In Thailand, there are few concerns among the people or among public and private organizations about ethics and legislation related to computer and information privacy. However, from a business point of view, there is a need to change attitudes if Thailand wants to become an equal participant in the global world market. Increasing interaction in the world market, international markets such as the European common market and the Organization for Economic Cooperation and Development (OECD), calls for critical concerns and movements in relation to information technology, business, customers, and citizens.

Prior to proposing great changes in any legislation, the positive approach is to convince people. It is a humane way to start with demands from the users and laypeople. Wise and good decisions concerned with information technology cannot be made unless people know and understand reality. Thus, the findings from this research on people's awareness will reveal significant points for future changes in the use of information technology in Thailand.

Objectives

The objectives of this research were as follows:

- to survey people's ethical awareness related to computers and information technology, and
- to analyze people's ethical awareness according to Thai culture and towards the Association for Computing Machinery (ACM) Code of Ethics and Professional Conduct.

Research Framework

In accordance with the research questions specification stated above, the research framework was designed as follows.

Table 1. The Research Framework

Objectives	*Sample and Instruments*	*Analyses*
1. To survey people's ethical awareness related to computer and information technology. 2. To analyze people's ethical awareness according to Thai culture and towards the ACM Code of Ethics and Professional Conduct.	Scenario interviews of three main groups of people: a) computer professionals (3 subgroups) - administrators of computer centres/offices, - instructors on IT programmes, - project leaders/system engineering/system programmers/database administrators/etc. b) consumers as users (3 subgroups) - users with at least a bachelor's degree and whose work related to law, - users with at least a bachelor's degree in any area, - users with secondary and elementary education. c) students as young generations (3 subgroups) - students on bachelor's degree programmes in IT, - students on bachelor's degree programmes in any area, - students in elementary/secondary schools.	1. Comparison of opinions: - within groups - between groups 2. Comparison of opinions with Thai culture and with the ACM Code of Ethics and Professional Conduct

The specific questions were as follows:

1. What was the ethical awareness related to computer and information technology among the groups of people with different backgrounds such as computer professionals, consumers, and students?
2. Did the work experiences of persons who had used computers or any machines related to data or information storage or transmission affect their ethical awareness?
3. Did the levels of education of the young generations (the students) affect their ethical awareness?
4. What was the analysis of the ethical awareness according to Thai culture and towards the ACM Code of Ethics and Professional Conduct?

METHODOLOGY

The Scenarios Development

Reviewing related materials led to the development of scenarios as a research instrument. The scenario method was chosen as a technology assessment analysis which systematizes the nature, importance, impacts, and advantages. This assessment can trace, formulate, and develop socially desirable and useful technological applications (Berleur, 1993). The scenarios were created by using a three-dimensional framework: Dimension 1 - Issues, which included security, privacy, quality of work, use of service and contract; Dimension 2 - Environment, which included academic, business, government, and hospital environments; and Dimension 3 - Object, which included physical property, intellectual property, and financial assets. Firstly, thirty-two scenarios were created. After reviewing the scenarios context, ten scenarios were selected (for the full text of the ten scenarios, see Appendix B) and were classified into a three-dimensional framework.

Table 2. Composition of the Scenarios

Issue	*Scenario*	*Object*	*Scenario*	*Environment*	*Scenario*
Privacy	3	Database	5	Government	3
Confidentiality	2	Software	3	Business	3
Quality of professional work	2	Hardware and software	1	Academic	2
Unauthorized access	1	Intellectual property	1	Independent	2
Use of service	1				
Contract	1				

The Sample of Scenario Interviews

The stratified sample of three groups of people in Bangkok was selected for the scenario interviews by using three criteria showed in summary table as follows:

Table 3. The Sample Groups for the Scenario Interviews

Group of sample	*Subgroup 1*	*Subgroup 2*	*Subgroup 3*
Computer Professionals (N=118)	Administrators of computer centres (50)	Instructors on IT programmes (23)	Project leaders, etc. (45)
Consumers (users) (N=150)	whose work related to law (30)	at least a bachelor's degree (60)	secondary/elementary education (60)
Students (Young generations) (N=90)	bachelor's programmes (IT area) (30)	bachelor's programmes (any area) (30)	secondary/elementary education (30)

In total, the sample in the scenario interviews was 358 persons. The sample in each subgroup was selected by using the following combination:

- Computer professionals, subgroups 1 and 3, were selected from persons in different working areas such as in banks/finance/stocks/insurance companies, hospitals, government/semi-government offices, Social Security Office, Civil Registration Office, and the Office of the Narcotics Control Board. Subgroup 2 consisted of instructors on computer science/IT programmes in public and private universities.
- Consumer subgroup 1 was selected from persons whose work related to law such as police officers, lawyers, judges, senators, representatives, and persons who worked at the Office of the Council of State. Other subgroups were selected from people with different educational backgrounds who were working and who did not work.
- Student subgroups were selected from public and private universities and schools.

The Scenario Analyses

In order to analyze people's awareness from their responses to the scenario interviews according to the stated objectives 1 and 2, three steps were taken: 1) analysis according to the affective domain within 2 levels (level 1- acknowledge, and level 2 - opinion/reaction) (Krathwohl, *et al.*, 1956); 2) analysis according to Thai culture (belief, values, and ways of living); and 3) analysis according to the ACM Code of Ethics and Professional Conduct (ACM, 1993) (see also Appendix A).

RESULTS

Findings of Question No. 1

Table 4. Percentage Comparison of the Responses between Computer Professionals, Consumers, and Students towards the Issue: Obligation and Quality of Professional Work

Group	*Professionals (n=118)*			*Consumers (n=150)*			*Students (n=90)*			*Average (n=358)*		
Scenario	*2*	*5*	*9*	*2*	*5*	*9*	*2*	*5*	*9*	*2*	*5*	*9*
Ethics	51	25	25	48	31	36	43	25	37	47	27	32
Unethics	47	73	74	50	68	64	56	74	63	51	71	67
No Response	2	2	1	2	1	-	1	1	-	2	2	1

More than 50% of the computer professionals considered scenario 2 ethical, but fewer than 50% of the consumers and students considered it was unethical. Reasons for considering it ethical were that the application programs had already been accepted by users as stated in a contract, and the application programs could be implemented even though there were some problems which should be resolved later. The reasons it was considered unethical included that the application programs could not be used according to the users' needs; and the computer company should have taken responsibility for the effective application programs development even though the programs had already been accepted by users.

In scenarios 5 and 9, more than 50% of all groups believed that the persons acted unethically. Scenario 5 dealt with the project leader who implemented the company design but handed in the chief officer's design documents in order to please him. The respondents considered the project leader acted unethically because the documentation did not match the implementation, and because he delivered an unmaintainable system. In Scenario 9, a system programmer who used his office computer to do his personal work during the weekend was considered unethical because he used official resources for personal benefit, and he used them without permission.

Table 5. Percentage Comparison of Responses between Computer Professionals, Consumers, and Students towards the Issue: Piracy and Unauthorized Access

Group	*Professionals (n=118)*			*Consumers (n=150)*			*Students (n=90)*			*Average (n=358)*		
Scenario	*1*	*6*	*7*	*1*	*6*	*7*	*1*	*6*	*7*	*1*	*6*	*7*
Ethics	38	20	43	30	34	36	25	23	37	31	25	34
Unethics	61	79	55	70	66	64	75	77	73	68	74	65
No response	1	1	2	-	-	-	-	1	-	1	1	1

Regarding piracy and unauthorized access (Table 5), the majority of the responses from the three groups considered persons in scenarios 1, 6, and 7 acted unethically. In scenario 1, a system programmer dealt with confidential data concerning an individual with alcohol and drug problems. He brought the data home from work and left it at home. He acted unethically because the data was a confidential government document and disclosure of the data would be dangerous. In scenario 6, the participants considered a scientist's action unethical because he did not give informed consent to subjects and he did not ask for the university's permission to use the data. In scenario 7, a bank was involved in a joint project with a department store involving customers' information. The participants believed the act was unethical because it violated customers' privacy, used personal data for other objectives, and disclosed customers' personal data without permission.

Table 6. Percentage Comparison of Responses between Computer Professionals, Consumers, and Students towards the Issue: Confidentiality and Privacy

Group	*Professionals (n=118)*			*Consumers (n=150)*			*Students (n=90)*			*Average (n=358)*		
Scenario	*3*	*4*	*8*	*3*	*4*	*8*	*3*	*4*	*8*	*3*	*4*	*8*
Ethics	25	48	54	15	51	48	21	53	51	20	51	51
Unethics	74	51	46	84	48	51	79	47	49	79	48	48
No response	1	1	-	1	1	1	-	-	-	1	1	1

On the issue of confidentiality and privacy in scenario 3, as seen in Table 6, every group of participants agreed that a company administrator's behaviour in reading employees' email was unethical. However, their opinions differed in scenario 4, which was about using multimedia in neurosurgery at a teaching hospital. The professional group viewed it as unethical whereas the consumers and the students concurred that the hospital acted ethically. The professionals did not agree very strongly that the hospital violated patients' privacy. The consumers and the students considered the activity was an efficient use of technology for medical education. In scenario 8, only the consumers stated that the life insurance company acted unethically in violating personal privacy by storing HIV/AIDS tests in the customers' database. However, the professionals and the students contended that the company had policies and procedures for data security and that the data were important medical records for life insurance.

As far as intellectual property, contract, and business agreements are concerned (Table 7), a large majority of the participants considered the programmer's behaviour in developing a new application program from an existing product was unethical. Such developments, they insisted, violated copyright law. The programmer had to ask for permission to apply the designs and had to honour the intellectual property of others.

Table 7. Percentage Comparison of Responses between Computer Professionals, Consumers, and Students towards the Issue: Intellectual Property, Contract, and Business Agreement

Group	*Professionals (n=118)*		*Consumers (n=150)*		*Students (n=90)*		*Average (n=358)*	
Scenario	*5*	*10*	*5*	*10*	*5*	*10*	*5*	*10*
Ethics	25	21	31	25	25	15	27	20
Unethics	73	78	68	75	74	85	71	79
No response	2	1	1	-	1	-	2	1

Findings of Question No. 2

The percentage comparison of ethical and unethical acts between computer professionals with experience equal to or more than 5 years (n=10), fewer than 5 years (n=35), and information technology students (n=30) was not much different from the findings to question no. 1 except in scenario 2 where the group of computer professionals who had fewer than 5 years' experience did not judge that the computer company action was ethical or unethical in submitting the inefficient application programs to the customers. They stated that the company acted 50% ethically and 50% unethically. Thus, the findings concluded that the work experiences of persons who had used computers or any machines related to data or information storage or transaction did not affect their ethical awareness.

Findings of Question No. 3

The percentage comparison of ethical or unethical acts between bachelor's degree programme students in information technology (n=30) and in other areas (n=30), and secondary and elementary school students (n=30) was different. The responses to the issues revealed that, in scenario 2, only the secondary and elementary students stated that the computer company acted ethically. They could not determine whether the programmer who accessed all the files and copied them to do work at home (scenario 1) showed ethical or unethical behavior. Their responses were 50% of ethics and unethics. In the confidentiality and privacy issue (scenario 4 and 8), elementary and secondary school students and bachelor's degree students in other areas concurred that the hospital and the insurance company acted ethically. Thus, it might be concluded that their responses showed how they perceived ethical issues of information technology. Their responses, for example, were as follows:

- scenario 1 : ethical behaviour because the programmer did not intend to do it;
- scenario 2 : ethical behaviour because the computer company did nothing wrong;
- scenario 3 : ethical behaviour because the administrator did the right thing;
- scenario 6 : ethical behaviour because the researcher asked his friend to do it; and

- scenario 7 : unethical behaviour because the bank should not attach commercial advertisements.

Thus, the findings could reveal that the educational levels of the young generations did affect their ethical awareness.

A summary table of ethical awareness related to computer and information from the sample groups with different backgrounds; the sample groups with different lengths of experience; and the sample groups with different levels of education are shown in Table 8.

Table 8. Summary of Ethical Awareness Related to Computers and Information Technology of People in the Bangkok Metropolis

Comparison	Issue no.1 ethics	Issue no.1 uneth.	Issue no.2 ethics	Issue no.2 uneth.	Issue no.3 ethics	Issue no.3 uneth.	Issue no.4 ethics	Issue no.4 uneth.
Between Groups	2, 5, 9	-	1, 6, 7	-	3	4, 8	5, 10	-
Within Group								
Comp. professionals	5, 9	2	6, 7	1	3	4, 8	5, 10	-
Consumers	5, 9	2	1	6, 7*	3	4, 8	5, 10	-
Students	5	2, 9*	1, 6, 7	-	3	4, 8	5, 10	-
Experiences	5, 9	2	1, 6, 7	-	3	4*, 8	5, 10	-
Education	5	2, 9	6, 7	1	3	4*, 8	5, 10	-

* Percentage response was 50% of ethical and 50% unethical behaviour

Note:
Issue no.1 : Obligation and Quality of Professional Work
Issue no.2 : Piracy and Unauthorized Access
Issue no.3 : Confidentiality and Privacy
Issue no.4 : Intellectual Property, Contract, and Business Agreement
Ethics/uneth.: Response was ethical or unethical behaviour
Nos. 1-10: The scenario number

Findings of Question No. 4

The analysis of people's ethical awareness according to Thai culture derived from the sample's responses. Normally, Thai culture is very traditional. People are brought up in a traditional way and are very friendly to others. They are taught to respect their ancestors, parents, and leaders. They are grateful and devout. Thus, the group of school students, who did not have much computer or information technology knowledge, reacted ethically or unethically according to tradition as stated in their responses (see Findings of Question No. 3). Generally speaking, Thais are not sensitive to privacy issues. Perhaps this comes from a long tradition of close cooperation which is necessary for rice cultivation. In this way, Thai behaviour has been formed not on the basis of respect for original individuality but for orderly human relations based on community social strata. Behaviour has been formulated according to the relations between subordinate and superior, young and old, husband and wife, parent and child, among colleagues, and among relatives. Such behaviour also remains today in the bureaucratic societies of large companies and administrative organizations. It is also the cause of the ambiguous Thai attitude towards decision-making: for example, Thais do not say no clearly. They do not wish to hurt others by giving a definite no to those who have asked them a question. Since Thais have become more involved internationally and come in contact with other cultures, this kind of communication and way of decision-making has changed. So, it can be said that there are now two types of cultures of people in Thailand: those who are very sensitive to privacy and those who are not. This difference could be seen by the participants' responses to the ethical awareness of scenarios 3, 4, and 8.

The analysis of people's ethical awareness towards the ACM Code of Ethics and Professional Conduct shows that the participants' responses in scenario 1, for example, could be classified according to the principles in the ACM Code, 1.7, 1.8, and 2.8, which were described as respect for the privacy of others, honouring confidentiality, and accessing computing and communication resources only when authorized to do so. Other scenario responses could be classified according to other principles.

CONCLUSIONS AND SUGGESTIONS

Conclusions

1. The ethical awareness related to computer and information technology among the groups of people with backgrounds as computer professionals, consumers, and students was not different in eight of the ten scenarios. The groups considered the behaviour unethical in all scenarios related to issues of obligation and quality of professional work (scenario 2, 5, 9); all scenarios on the issues of piracy and unauthorized access (scenario 1, 6, 7); all scenarios on the issues of intellectual property, contract, and business agreement (scenario 5, 10); and only one scenario in the issue of confidentiality and privacy (scenario 3). For the other scenarios, the responses varied. However, the average percentages stating unethical behaviour were not very high: in scenarios 2, 5, and 9, they were 51%, 71%, and 67%; in scenarios 1, 6, 7, they were 68%, 74%, and 65% respectively; and 79% in scenarios 3 and 10.
2. The variations in work experience of the computer professionals who had used computers or any machines related to data or information storage and transmission for 5 years or more than 5 years, fewer than 5 years, and students did not cause differences in ethical awareness.
3. The different educational levels of students (young generation): IT bachelor's degree programme students; other bachelor's degree programme students; secondary school students; and elementary school students created differences in ethical awareness and their responses.
4. The analysis of sample responses showed different opinions or reasons according to various points of view related to work experience. These did not include the consumer groups who did not work and the elementary and secondary school student groups. The school students used their common

sense in responding to the scenarios. However, most of the sample's opinions were based on Thai culture. One significant finding was that two of the three scenarios (4 and 8), relating to confidentiality and privacy, were viewed as ethical behaviour, which was confirmed by Thai culture.

5. Most of the sample's responses concurred with the ACM Code of Ethics and Professional Conduct. However, there were sample groups mentioned above whose responses were different.

Suggestions

From the findings, there are some suggestions for further development in ethical awareness related to computers and information technology in Thailand:

1. *Computer Ethics Education.* Basic ethical values are learned in the formative years of childhood at home, church, and school. Computer ethics education is made more complicated because there are computer users at all levels throughout the society. Computer ethics education should not indoctrinate the individual with new values but assist individuals in clarifying and applying their ethical values. As technology assumes an integral role in education, institutions in the electronic community of learners should train and support faculty, staff, and students to use information technology effectively. This could include the skills to use the resources, to be aware of the existence of data repositories, and to understand the ethical and legal use of the resources (Connolly, 1993). At any level of curriculum and instruction, there should be an integration of both general and specific approaches to computer ethics and social impact issues. The general approach is to incorporate these concerns across the curriculum and instruction.
2. *Computer Code of Ethics and Professional Conduct.* During the last few years, the International Federation for Information Processing (IFIP) set up an Ethics Task Group. The Ethics Task Group undertook a survey of codes of ethics in four major areas of ethics: individual professional ethics, multinational organizational ethics, international legal informatics ethics, and international public policy ethics. They analyzed codes from the IFIP national societies, IFIP affiliate members (regional societies), and other computer societies. From the survey, the responsibility field is of course the most developed part within the codes. Five main categories appear as regrouping the different wordings adopted by the different societies: respectful general attitude, personal/institutional qualities, promotion of information privacy, production and flow of information, and regulations (Berleur, 1996). This movement should be a sign that there is a need for the computer society in Thailand to work on this issue and propose solutions which will really protect society as well as the public and the computer profession.
3. IFIP recommends treating with care the distinction between Codes of Ethics and Codes of Conduct. It appeared in the analysis and in the comments that the first are more often oriented towards the public and society, while the second seem to be related more to the computing profession. Codes of ethics could be seen as mission statements of computer societies, providing visions and objectives in relation to their public mission and anticipating the issues in a computerized world or in an information society. Codes of Conduct would

have to deal with issues in the specialized fields of the profession (Berleur, 1996).

4. *Computer Laws.* International guidelines may provide statements which act as reference documents or as a basis for the development of legal instruments in particular jurisdictions. Legal instruments are generally the most enforceable, provided they are drafted correctly and the courts are sufficiently qualified to assess the matter brought before them. Ethical principles, codes, guidelines, and policies may anticipate and supplement the law (Berleur and Brunnstein, 1996). In Thailand, the need for international standards of a computer code of ethics and professional conduct and computer laws should be considered for the near future, for example, computer crime laws, privacy law, data protection law, telecommunication law, and electronic data interchange law (Methakunavudhi and Pethsiri, 1996). There is a belief that legislation is the best method of enforcing ethics and also that a code of ethics can enforce a set of rules.
5. *Recommendation for Further Research.* The research recommendation based on the findings of this research is for an analysis of university policies, organizational policies, and public policies regarding codes of ethics in information processing. It is known that other organizations have also stated a process of reassessing their role about ethical issues. The analysis of university policies should include curriculum and instruction analysis. Although some more specific fields seem to be covered by the universities and their policies, an ethical preoccupation does not appear explicitly in the wording at least as a specific statement. The comparison of university policies with computer societies codes could be quite interesting.

REFERENCES

ACM Code of Ethics and Professional Conduct, *Communication of the ACM* 36(2) (February, 1993): 99-105.

Anderson, Ronald E. et al., Using the New ACM Code of Ethics in Decision Making, *Communication of The ACM* 36 (2) (February, 1993): 98-107.

Berleur, Jacques. What is happening now with technology assessment? In: Beardon, Colin and Whitehouse Diane. (Eds.) *Computers and Society.* Oxford: Intellect Books Publishing, 1993.

Berleur, Jacques. International Federation for Information Processing's Framework for Computer Ethics. *Science and Engineering Ethics.* 2 (2), 1996, pp. 155-165.

Berleur, J. and K. Brunnstein. (Ed.), *Ethics of Computing: Codes, Spaces for Discussion and Law.* London: Chapman & Hall, 1996.

Clement, Andrew. Privacy Considerations in CSCW: Report on the CSCW92 Workshop, *SIGCHI BULLETIN* 25 (4) (October, 1993): 34-41.

Connolly, F. W. A Bill of Rights and Responsibilities for Electronic Learners, Published Paper, 1993.

Krathwohl D.R., Bloom, B.S., and Masia, B.B. *Taxonomy of Education Objectives: The Classification of Educational Goals.* Handbook II: Affective Domain New York: David McKay, 1956.

Methakunavudhi, Pateep and Pethsiri, Apirat. *A Guideline for Data Protection and Information Privacy Legislations in Thailand.* The Office of National Research Commission, Thailand 1996.

Oz, Effy. Ethical Standards for Information Systems Professionals: A Case for a Unified Code, *MIS Quarterly* 16 (4) (December 1992): 423-433.

Oz, Effy. When Professional Standards are Lax: The CONFIRM Failure and Its Lessons, *Communications of The ACM* 37 (10) (October 1994): 29-36.

Parker, Don B. *Ethical Conflicts in Information and Computer Science, Technology and Business* Massachusetts : QED Information Science, Inc., 1990.
Schwarz, Heinrich. Multimedia Technology and Privacy: A Case in Neurosurgery, *ACM SIGOIS Bulletin* 4 (1) (July, 1993): 19-20.

APPENDIX A

The Suggested Comparison with the ACM Code of Ethics and Professional Conduct

The ACM code of ethics and professional conduct can be classified in each scenario as follows:

Scenario 1
No. 1.7 Respect the privacy of others.
No. 1.8 Honour confidentiality.
No. 2.8 Access computing and communication resources only when authorized to do so.

Scenario 2
No. 2.1 Strive to achieve the highest quality effectiveness and dignity in both the process and product of professional work.
No. 2.4 Accept and provide appropriate professional review.
No. 3.2 Manage personnel and resources to design and build information systems that enhance the quality of working life.
No. 3.4 Ensure that users and those who will be affected by a system have their needs clearly articulated during the assessment and design of requirements. Later the system must be validated to meet requirements.

Scenario 3
No. 1.7 Respect the privacy of others.
No. 3.2 Manage personnel and resources to design and build information systems that enhance the quality of working life.

Scenario 4
No. 1.2 Avoid harm to others.
No. 1.7 Respect the privacy of others.
No. 1.8 Honour confidentiality.

Scenario 5
No. 1.3 Be honest and trustworthy.
No. 2.5 Give comprehensive and through evaluations of computer systems and their impacts, including analysis of possible risks.
No. 2.6 Honour contracts, agreements and assigned responsibilities.

Scenario 6
No. 1.5 Honour property rights.
No. 2.3 Know and respect existing laws pertaining to professional work.
No. 2.8 Access computer and communication resources only when authorized to do so.

Scenario 7
No. 1.7 Respect the privacy of others.
No. 1.8 Honour confidentiality.
No. 3.3 Acknowledge and support proper and authorized uses of an organization computing and communication resources.
No. 3.5 Articulate and support policies that protect the dignity of users and others affected by a computing system.

Scenario 8
No. 1.2 Avoid harm to others.
No. 1.7 Respect the privacy of others.
No. 3.5 Articulate and support policies that protect the dignity of users and others affected by a computing system.

Scenario 9
No. 1.3 Be honest and trustworthy.
No. 2.3 Know and respect existing laws pertaining to professional work.
No. 2.8 Access computer and communication resources only when authorized to do so.

Scenario 10
No. 1.5 Honour property rights including copyrights and patents.
No. 1.6 Give proper credit for intellectual property.
No. 2.6 Honour contracts, agreements and assigned responsibilities.
No. 2.8 Access computer and communication resources only when authorized to do so.

APPENDIX B

Scenario 1
Thanachai worked in a large state department of alcoholism and drug abuse. The agency administered programmes for individuals with alcohol and drug problems, and maintained a huge database of information on the clients who used their service. Some of the data files contained the names and current addresses of clients. Thanachai had been asked to take a look at the track records of the treatment programmes. He had to put together a report that contained a number of clients seen in each programme and each month for the past five years, with details of the length of the client's treatment, the number of clients who returned after completion of a programme, criminal histories of clients, and so on. In order to put together this report, Thanachai had been given access to all the files in the agency's mainframe computer. After assembling the data into a new'file that included the client names, he downloaded it to the computer in his office. Under pressure to get the report finished by the deadline, Thanachai decided he had to work at home over the weekend in order to finish on time. He copied the information onto several disks and took them home. After finishing the report he left the disks at home and forgot about them. (Adapted from Anderson *et al.*, 1993.) Thanachai's behaviours are ethical or unethical according to professional conduct in computing?

Scenario 2
A computer company was writing the first stage of a more efficient accounting system that would be used by the government. This system would save taxpayers a considerable amount of money every year. A computer professional, who was asked to design the accounting system, assigned different parts of the system to her staff. One person was responsible for developing the reports; another was responsible for the internal processing; and a third for the user interface. The manager was shown the system and agreed that it could do everything in the requirements. The system was installed but the staff found the interface so difficult to use that their complaints were heard by upper-level management. Because of these complaints, upper-level management would not invest any more money in the development of the new accounting system and they went back to using the original, inefficient system. (Adapted from Anderson *et al.*, 1993.) The computer company's behaviours are ethical or unethical according to professional conduct in computing?

Scenario 3
When Ratana arrived for work at a company one morning, she discovered her supervisor reading and printing out electronic mail messages between other employees. As electronic mail administrator, Ratana was appalled. When she had trained employees to use the computerized system, Ratana had told them their mail was private. Now the company manager was violating that trust. When Ratana questioned the practice, she was told to mind her own business. A day later, she was fired for insubordination. She still bristled about the company for the reason that the company administrators did not read people's mail, just as they did not listen to people's phone conversations. However, the administrators disagreed completely. 'If the corporation owns the equipment and pays

for the network, that asset belongs to the company and it has a right to look and see if people are using if for purposes other than running the business,' they said. (Adapted from Clement, 1993.) The company administrators' behaviours are ethical or unethical according to professional conduct in computing?

Scenario 4
Multimedia technology can facilitate communication particularly in situations where people do not share time and space. It does that by taking information out of its original context and presenting it in a different one. Video and audio were used to support neurophysiological monitoring during neurosurgery in a teaching hospital. The video image was the view of the operating field through the microscope. This image was also displayed on a television monitor in the operating room to give other people in the operating room information about the progress of the operation and the surgical activities. The audio comprised everything that was picked up by a small microphone attached to the microscope: sound from the surgical procedures, voice, and other sounds from the room. When video and audio transmission were first introduced, there was little objection. But a year later, when it was going to be used more regularly, criticism about the practice became loud, leading to a wider discussion and open resistance. The reasons for the criticisms were concerns about legal implications, job control issues, impacts on teaching, the flow of conversations, and the patients' privacy. (Adapted from Oz, 1994.) The procedures at the hospital are ethical or unethical according to professional conduct in computing?

Scenario 5
Surapol worked in a computer consultancy and, as a skilful software tester, he had carefully designed a computer system to manage dangerous material for the navy. His design was rejected by a chief officer who was in charge of the project. The chief officer wanted his own design substituted for Surapol's design. Surapol believed that the chief officer's design was untestable. The chief officer said to do it this way or the project would be abandoned. Surapol sought advice but there was a deadline for this project, so he had to make a decision. He went to the chief officer and said that he would implement the chief officer's design. After a few months, the system was completed. The system passed its acceptance tests. The chief officer, with a self-congratulatory tone, told the other officers how he had helped Surapol's design. Surapol too was satisfied. He knew the system would pass the tests because he had implemented the system in the way he had originally designed. Although Surapol's documentation of the system made it look like the chief officer's design had been used, the code did not follow the chief officer's untestable design. The design documentation did not match the implemented code. (Adapted from Clement, 1993.) Surapol's behaviour is ethical or unethical according to professional conduct in computing?

Scenario 6
Nikom was a scientist employed by a university as a researcher. He learned that two different kinds of data on essentially the same subject were contained in two files stored in the university's computer. He believed that there would be significant scientific value in merging the files and reanalyzing the data. Although the subjects' informed consent had been obtained for the earlier studies, their permission for this new use of the data had not been sought. Nikom was aware that it would be desirable to seek permission for use of the data, but he decided not to do so, because it would be time-consuming and would add considerably to the cost of the study he was proposing. He thus asked one of the university's programmers to access the data, merge the files on the same subjects, and analyze the data as he indicated. The programmer did as he requested. (Adapted from Oz, 1992.) Nikom's behaviour is ethical or unethical according to professional conduct in computing?

Scenario 7
A department store cooperated with a bank in arranging a credit card for their customers, and the bank stored the customers' information in their computer. Every month the bank chose some of the current or prospective customers for particular offers of products or services. The use of existing customer information such as name, address, and appending additional data elements of demographic information relating to its customers such as estimated income, dwelling size, propensity to use credit, and so forth, was also done at the bank. The bank submitted the computer tape with this information to outside vendors who had connections with the bank. These were used, in turn, to target customers for various product offerings, either via mail or sometimes using inserts in

customers' bills. The customers began to complain about marketing practices. (Adapted from Parker, 1990.) The bank's behaviour is ethical or unethical according to professional conduct in computing?

Scenario 8
A life insurance underwriting process entailed the gathering of medical information regarding each applicant for life insurance so that, based on the individual's health risk, the application could be accepted or rejected and, if accepted, the appropriate premium could be calculated. When testing for the AIDS virus became available, the life insurance company wished to include those tests in the underwriting process, store the results in the databases, and share the results with other life insurance companies through the Medical Information Bureau. After the life insurance companies began performing AIDS tests, they had to confront the issue of negative public and legislative reaction to the collection of AIDS tests information. (Adapted from Parker, 1990.) The life insurance companies' behaviors are ethical or unethical according to professional conduct in computing?

Scenario 9
Nakorn worked as a systems analyst in a government office. In the workplace, his job was usually not busy, so he could spend some time doing his own extra work. He used the computer service at his workplace early in the morning, after office hours, late at night, and even during the weekend to develop programs. His colleagues, however, explicitly stated that the government office's computer was not to be used for personal benefit and they sent a notice to the administrators. (Adapted from Oz, 1992.) Nakorn's behaviour is ethical or unethical according to professional conduct in computing?

Scenario 10
A system programmer in a computer company, Akachai, was assigned to do a systems design project for a commercial company. While he was working there, he learned that there was an interesting application software which was used in this company and it was not included in his project. He realized that he could produce a new package that would be faster, have greater capacity, and offer additional features. He also concluded that other commercial companies could be users of this package if he could produce it. Then he offered the manager of the commercial company to add to his project by using the program modification. When his work was completed, the manager of the commercial company was satisfied with the package without knowing that Akachai had sold the package to other commercial companies. (Adapted from Oz, 1992.) Akachai's behaviour is ethical or unethical according to professional conduct in computing?

PART TWO

Global Information Society

The global information society: Some reflections on labour and work

Libby Bishop
Institute for Research on Learning, 66 Willow Place,
Menlo Park, CA 94025 USA
Phone: + 1 415 614-7974; Fax: +1 415 614-7957
Email: Libby_Bishop@irl.org

Abstract

The global information society is fundamentally changing many aspects of modern life. One of the areas undergoing the most dramatic change is employment. Important shifts are occurring in the effects of information technologies on production, newly emerging occupational structures, structural unemployment, and so on (Krueger, 1993). Technology changes how we labour. As important as these issues are, there is also a broader question, namely, the implications of this information society for work itself. Here, I am distinguishing labour from work: by labour I mean the conditions under which we act on and with the material world, whereas work means not just what we do to survive, but what we make and create in order to live as humans[1]. I am addressing the question: what does work mean as a social category: for society as a whole, as an entitlement to economic resources, for the self, and the constitution of identity? My claim is, *the consequence of information technology is not merely that we are labouring differently, but rather, the meaning of work is changing*. This paper addresses and reflects on some of the implications for labour and work of an information society.

1 I find Arendt's (1958) distinction between labour and work a useful one, although I am not following her definitions here. Her argument that the only realm for human relations is *vita activa*, I find too limiting. I would argue with Aronowitz and DiFazio (1994) and, drawing on Marx, that work too can be an authentic human activity. Implicit in Arendt's and others' devaluation of work is, I believe, a privileging of mind over body, or contemplation over action, with which I am not comfortable.

An Ethical Global Information Society J. Berleur & D. Whitehouse (Eds.)

WHAT IS NEW ABOUT AN INFORMATION SOCIETY?

Technological change is enabling a shift from a Fordist system of mass production of goods to a postmodern world based predominantly on services and knowledge work (Coriat, 1992; Piore and Sabel, 1984). The key characteristic of this transition is the move from 'fixedness' to flexibility. The ideal type of Fordist work was the assembly line. It was marked by the rigidity of high levels of fixed capital, inflexible labour markets and work rules, very narrow and specialized occupational categories, and significant rigidity in consumption, i.e., mass marketing of standardized goods. Flexible accumulation has challenged this model with downsizing and corporate divestitures creating smaller, allegedly more nimble businesses. On the labour front, firms are attempting to use high percentages of contingent workers (part-time and/or temporary) in order to reduce their wage costs. Production is more often team-based, with broader job categories, flatter organizations, and reduced bureaucratic hierarchy. Finally, marketing has dramatically changed from mass to niche, sometimes even to personalized products (e.g., my Internet-provided *Wall Street Journal Interactive Edition* provides only the stories my 'profile' knows I will like).

Within this complex of changes, probably the most important is the shift from making things to manipulating information or other symbols (Bridges, 1994; Zuboff, 1988). It has disrupted assumptions about time, space and work that had been in place since the Industrial Revolution (Harvey, 1990). The factory system came about, in part, because the existing technologies were best suited to synchronous work, i.e., people had to be working at the same time to coordinate their activities. (In addition to these technical requirements, issues of power and control also shaped these decisions (Marglin, 1974).) Workers had to be spatially collocated, i.e., in the same factory, in order to weave, smelt, etc. Much of the wrenching cultural transformation of the Industrial Revolution concerned making the shift from agrarian to industrial time and from countryside to factory (Thompson, 1966). No less wrenching is our current shift from industrial to Internet time, and from factory to virtual office.

LABOUR, WORK AND CHANGING SPATIAL CONFIGURATIONS

Information technology has greatly altered the spatial and temporal constraints on work. Although many of these technologies remain imperfect, hard to use, and no substitute for face-to-face interaction, some tools such as electronic mail, fax, intranets, etc., do allow much work that had to be collocated and synchronous to be done 'anywhere, anytime'. One of the most visible changes is the physical displacement of work. A 1995 survey by the International Facility Management Association shows that 83% of companies are using alternative office strategies, ranging from innovative layouts to hotelling (no dedicated offices, employees check into non-personal space) and telecommuting. Telecommuting, for example, is used by over one-third of U.S. businesses (with 100 or more employees), and over two million employees telecommute (Gemini Consulting, 1993). What do these new spatial arrangements say about how work is changing?

Before addressing this question directly, it is necessary to step back and look more generally at the complex and interactive effect between the physical environment of work (office, partitions, furniture) and its social relations. They mutually affect each other. The space can shape what kinds of work happens (widely dispersed private offices deter collaboration) and what work needs to get done shapes space (people who do not have space for visitors' chairs improvise with portable stools).

I have recently been engaged in a project studying office environments, collaboration and work practices. In this case, the initial focus was to explore the potential benefits of mobile furniture. The company was in the process of office renovation: from an existing open layout (no offices, low partitions) to a more enclosed, high partition environment. One information systems group decided they did not like the new design. Their primary objection was the height of the new partitions (about 72") that were too high to see over, even when standing up. The members of this group needed to communicate and collaborate extensively, and they feared the high partitions would block that.

As an alternative, a small group agreed to pilot yet a third configuration of furniture and office layout. This new furniture is highly mobile, literally all pieces are on wheels. Also, rather than partitions, there is a mesh scaffolding which offers semi-privacy, and storage devices hang from the scaffold.

The more flexible furniture made the relation between the work done and the environment 'visible' in new ways. Specifically, the mobility of the furniture allowed more detailed aspects of the work practices of the team to become visible. For example, there were a lot of finely-grained adjustments of teams and groups that took place. With the flexible furniture, these adjustments could be accommodated as the furniture could be adjusted to small-scale groupings and regroupings. Under the traditional facilities model, moves happen only when new buildings open, teams relocate, etc. These micro-level adjustments—that occur on a time-scale of hours, days or weeks, not months or years—had not 'appeared' or become visible in the previous, more rigid, physical environment.

This experiment in mobility speaks to issues of both labour and work. It demonstrates in what ways spatial flexibility is showing up in labour. Examples include the open office as embodying flatter organizations; team, not individual, based organizations; and project-based work that requires ongoing adjustments in team membership. While I am not suggesting these are insignificant, they do not address a broader insight about work. *Just as the mobile furniture is making some previously invisible work practices visible, the effect of information technology more generally is to make some aspects of work, namely the changing relationship between employer and employee, more visible as well.*

This process of making visible is revealing in physical forms, the rapidly changing nature of the employment relationship. What is being heralded as the virtual corporation takes on a different meaning when viewed in this light. Hotelling, telecommuting and telecentres are physical embodiments of work-at-a-distance. But what has not received as much attention is that the weaker geographical and physical bonds to the organization are, in many respects, a metaphor for the weaker affective bond as well. Casey (1995) calls the effect a 'decentered workplace'. Work-at-a-distance takes on the figurative, as well as the literal, sense of being distant from the centre of the organization. Just as workers no longer need to be central, similarly work may no longer need to be central for such workers.

If we look at the implications of information technology for work, not just labour, it appears to point to a weakening relationship. It appears that our bonds to the workplace, and hence to work, are weakening. This is being manifested in the business press as the 'new social contract,' 'the end of the job' and 'the new employment rules'. In general, what has changed is that the old contract—employment security in exchange for hard work and loyalty—is no longer in effect. More analytically, issues of commitment and loyalty are being addressed by academic researchers as well (Heckscher, 1995; Kunda, 1992). Information technologies and accompanying spatial reconfigurations are not so much causing this shift as they are creating affordances for the changes in the employment relation to become visible.

LABOUR, WORK AND CHANGING TEMPORAL CONFIGURATIONS

Unlike the Fordist emphasis on the uniformity of the 40-hour week, post-Fordist work models compress and stretch time in new ways. One television advertisement opens with an aerial view of an approaching car. The setting is stunning, something like the Badlands in the United States—glorious red rock hills, winding empty road, a solitary driver. Suddenly the driver stops, gets out of the car to stretch, pulls out a laptop, and sends a fax. Anytime, anywhere. However, the virtual technologies that promise freedom to work any time, ironically, enable us to work all the time. The work week is at an historically record high. The compressing and stretching of time makes the all-too-real work getting done disappear, and become invisible, as we fill our commuter journeys with phone calls and our 'leisure' with self-service work.

After many years of 'time-saving' technologies, work hours are up, not down. The manufacturing work week is still near post-war highs of about 48 hours. The average employed American is working 163 hours—nearly a month—longer per year in 1987, compared to 1969 (Schor, 1992). There are many confirming minor indicators: only 2-4% of those eligible took time off under the United States Family and Medical Leave Act and 90% of lunch breaks are 30 minutes or less. Also, telecommuting hours take place more often in addition to time at the office, not in place of it (Perin, 1991). Rather than saving time, the macro-level data on working hours present a different picture, summarized in *The Overworked American* (Schor, 1992), of people working more for stagnant real wages.

Once again, the labour/work distinction is a useful window into this issue. As with space, the implications of technologies that support work 'anytime' have schizophrenic effects. They afford much greater flexibility and latitude, often relished by those with competing obligations of work and family.

Yet, the reality of flexibility is that it often becomes not working later instead of now, but later *and* now. In this environment of job-churning, downsizing, etc., the indirect pressures to work long hours are nearly irresistible. In 1995, 44% of surveyed workers report workload is excessive, up from 41% in 1991 and 37% in 1988. More specifically, in my own research projects, I have encountered examples of how employees were offered computer-based training in lieu of the 'obligation' to attend classes. The online class was specifically developed to minimize time away from work. But one participant reported spending 10-12 hour regular work days, then having to do his training in the evenings. He was thus unable to lead a normal life with his family. He said he was seriously reconsidering the advantages of a 1-week off-site class where his co-workers would cover for him, and he was less subject to burnout.

Even when the problem is not more total work hours, there are costs as well as benefits to the flexibility of splicing time between work and life. One story captures the feel of this tension:

> 'I work at [my child's] volleyball practice. I took my laptop. I think I was working on a dealer letter about the status of some of our products. I had time in the car with my child on the way to practice and on the way back. As for volleyball practice, I didn't actually have time to watch. It was something about me being there. So I sat in the gym stands and worked on the letter.' (Fishman, 1996)

What is lost? There is an assumption here that we can parse work into ever-finer increments, that all these work/life time units are, somehow, interchangeable.

However, the implications for work, in addition to these effects of 'time-shifting' on labour, are, in the longer view, perhaps even more significant. We miss the broader implications for the meaning of work if we address only the literal level. What are people trying to signify with their overwork? Much time at work is now largely symbolic, and in fact, attempting to compensate for the decline in physical presence. Workers are trying to show loyalty, commitment and so on, through their sunrise meetings and all-night efforts, precisely because their more formal and contractual ties to the organization are fraying (Casey, 1995; Perin, 1991).

As we saw with space, the malleability of time is uncovering and making visible changes in work, specifically in the structure of employment relations. Time-based competition is being extended from manufacturing to managing human resources. Just like industrial plants are supposed to retool overnight for new model production, now humans are also supposed to 'retool', creating several careers in a lifetime. Guaranteed employment is being replaced by 'employability', with the additional requirement that employees willingly engage in continuous learning. And many times, we see one dimension, in this case speed, pushed to ridiculous extremes:

> 'It should be perfectly clear to all of us that speed is a key source of competitive advantage ... Of course, a company can't be fast if its people are slow. It can't rapidly adjust to change if employees resist ... Our mindset should be to think of ourselves as accelerators for the organization. Our job is to bring speed to everything we touch' (Pritchett, 1996).

Many aspects of this new employment relation are attractive: the flexibility of trying many careers, the opportunities for innovation relatively free of traditional hierarchical control, and the occasion to engage in new learning. And yet, despite the long hours spent at work, work no longer provides the same central framework for self-definition and identity. Casey (1995) argues that a fundamental shift has occurred at work, exemplified by continuously reconstituted project teams. As workers become more cross-trained, more flexible, and experienced in aspects of what were formerly multiple careers or jobs, these workers can no longer look to any particular job, career, or occupation as central to who they are. Ironically, corporations have created precisely the autonomous, non-specialized, interchangeable worker-widget they claim to need.

CONCLUSION

The question, which remains as yet unanswered, is whether or not corporations can operate effectively with this 'no commitment, no loyalty' model of employment that is emerging. I will hazard a prediction that such a model of work, based almost exclusively on contractual instrumental relations, will founder for want of the affective and social community aspects of the workplace that make it human as well as productive.

REFERENCES

Arendt, Hannah. *The Human Condition.* Chicago: University of Chicago Press, 1958.

Aronowitz, Stanley and William DiFazio. *The Jobless Future.* Minneapolis: University of Minn. Press, 1994.

Bridges, William. *Job Shift: How to Prosper in a Workplace without Jobs.* Reading, MA: Addison-Wesley Publishing Company, 1994.

Casey, Catherine. *Work, Self and Society: After Industrialism.* London: Routledge, 1995.

Coriat, Benjamin, The revitalization of mass production in the computer age, in Michael Storper and Allen Scott, eds., *Pathways to industrialization and regional development,* pp. 137-156. London: Routledge, 1992.

Fishman, Charles, We've seen the future of work, *Fast Company.* Aug-Sept, 1996, pp. 53-62.

Gemini Consulting, Telecommuting Research and Implications for Silicon Valley, October 1993.

Harvey, David. *The Condition of Postmodernity.* Cambridge, MA: Blackwell, 1990.

Heckscher, Charles. *White-Collar Blues.* New York: Basic Books, 1995.

Krueger, Alan, How computers have changed the wage structure, *Quarterly Journal of Economics,* Feb. 1993, pp. 33.

Kunda, Gideon. *Engineering Culture: Control and commitment in a high-tech corporation.* Philadelphia: Temple University Press, 1992.

Marglin, Stephen, What do bosses do?, *Review of Radical Political Economy,* 6:2, 1974, pp. 60-112.

Perin, Connie, The moral fabric of the office, in S. Bacharach, S. Barley, and P. Tolbert, eds., *Research in the Sociology of Organizations.* Greenwich, CT: Sage, 1991.

Pritchett, Price, Mindshift: The employee handbook for understanding the changing world of work, Dallas, TX: Pritchett and Assoc., Inc., 1996.

Piore, Michael and Charles Sabel. *The Second Industrial Divide.* New York: Basic Books, 1984.

Schor, Juliet. *The Overworked American.* New York: Basic Books, 1992.

Thompson, E.P., *The Making of the English Working Class.* New York: Vintage Books, 1966.

Zuboff, Shoshana. *In the Age of the Smart Machine.* New York: Basic Books, 1988.

6

Global digital commerce: Impacts and risks for developments of global information societies

Klaus Brunnstein and Kathrin Schier
Faculty for Informatics, University of Hamburg
Vogt-Koelln-Str. 30, D - 22527 Hamburg-Stellingen
Phone: +49 40 5494 2406, Fax : +49 40 5494 2226
Email: Brunnstein@rz.informatik.uni-hamburg.d400.de,
schier@informatik.uni-hamburg.de

Abstract

Many regard the Internet as a prototype of an information infrastructure on which a global information society may be built. Some enterprises are trying to take advantage of early applications of digital commerce on the Internet. As the Internet is missing essential features of reliability, functionality and confidentiality which are prerequisites for the fair distribution of risks between market participants, current digital commerce services load all the risks on customers and users. This paper discusses some essential requirements for safe and functionally acceptable information services, and it discusses current problems with actual examples from digital payment systems. The paper concludes that public and legal action is required to release customers and users from their overwhelming share of risks.

INTRODUCTION

Concepts of global information societies depend strongly upon the existence and reliable operation of either a unique global (worldwide) information infrastructure or, if several such concepts or structures exist in limited spatial or organizational contexts (dedicated networks such as SWIFT, regional networks, or intranets), on the global acceptance and implementation of a set of standards which, if enforced, guarantee a minimum degree of interoperability of independent information infrastructures. Besides its required global availability, such infrastructures must also support the distribution of and access to information at any of their single

An Ethical Global Information Society J. Berleur & D. Whitehouse (Eds.)

components. In this context, the meaning of information has deliberately been neither specified nor defined *a priori*. Indeed, only the technical implementations of information, as streams of bits transmitted (communication standards: protocols, name services etc.), files of documents stored (databases) and accessed (agents), prescription for processes (executables), structures (relations, directories, dictionaries etc.) of any kind of agglomeration of bits, must be defined to determine the technical details of such infrastructures. This technology-driven approach leaves maximum freedom to its users (at least to those parties dominating information infrastructure usage) to define the purpose, applications and content within such information infrastructures. This implies that social aspects and user concern play a limited role in present developments.

Many people, from technical experts to interested parties of all kinds (not excluding politicians), regard the Internet (which is not a unique information infrastructure but which acts as a cooperation of independently operated networks using a multitude of platforms) as a prototype of a global information infrastructure. If the Internet were indeed such a prototype, then studies of its design and development, experiences with its present usage and services including incidents and malicious usage as well as observations of public discussions about its benefits, should be instructive to discuss likely developments of societies based on related technologies.

Indeed, there is good reason to analyze likely or potential influences of information and communication technologies on updating present societies into future stages wishfully named information societies. It is not the first time in human history that technologies have shaped the developments of societies. Since ancient times, technical abilities and facilities have contributed to shaping societies; one can study such impact in cultural masterpieces such as the Tower of Babylon, the Egyptian pyramids, Greek temples or mediaeval cathedrals with their respective forms of state organization. More recent (and, in several aspects, more relevant) examples may be the impact of Gutenberg's printing machine, as well as the complex set of industrial machines which supported developments in industrial societies. A retrospective analysis of 230 years of industrial history (starting in 1765 with Watts' basic patent of the vapour-driven machine), especially including its false hopes and real dangers (for example, inhumane workplaces and inadequate consumer protection), may be very helpful in understanding the risks and requirements for future developments, and to support forgotten requirements (such as in developing legal systems to protect users).

As the industrial societies differ so visibly and so strongly from those societies valid at their start in their respective domains (nations, areas, organizations etc.), it might be interesting to analyze historical developments against the technical concepts basically built into the dominant industrial techniques. When some achievements (such as the contemporary understanding of concepts such as work or the market) are related to the basic concepts of their constituent technologies, this analysis may also lead to an *a priori* analysis of likely impacts of present information and communication technologies on future information societies.

Following such thoughts, the paper analyses whether and to what degree (if at all) contemporary information technologies fulfil the basic requirements of global digital commerce. Besides, the general implications of technical concepts (part 2), the developments and risks of electronic payment systems are discussed in some detail (parts 3-4) as one major driving factor of Internet commerce. Finally, some general requirements for improved customer protection in information societies are discussed (part 5).

RISKS CAUSED BY BASIC TECHNICAL PARADIGMS AND CONCEPTS OF THE INTERNET

To measure and predict the side-effects, in both wishful and beneficial but also in possibly hazardous and undesirable directions, of actual information and communication technologies, the following frame of reference is suggested:

In order that any information technology can be regarded as a globally accepted basis for commercial activities, services derived from such technologies must fulfil a set of requirements (R1-4) from the beginning:

R1) Services must be well-defined, reproduced and controlled.

R2) Services must be available when needed, and must work reliably.

R3) Misuse or unauthorized use of services must be excluded.

R4) Proper means must guarantee that customers can trust services even if they do not understand how they work.

It is interesting to analyze whether and to what degree the Internet supports such services on any acceptable level of functionality, safety, and security. The facts may be shocking:

The Internet's basic built-in concepts of communication, especially packet-driven data exchange built on TCP/IP protocols and naming conventions are technically well-defined but in a way that misuse is easy to manage and hard to detect. The following experiences (for example, reports of Computer Emergency Response Teams (CERTs)) are ubiquitous:

- *Spoofing*: it is easy to misuse electronic addresses;
- *Sniffing*: inherent in demands for performance monitoring, it is easy to monitor and store foreign electronic traffic;
- *Hijacking*: it is easy to steal or misuse data streams;
- *Manual or Automated Hacking*: it is easy to access or misuse services or information which should be solely accessible or used from its owner; there are multiple sites on the Internet which offer introductory or assistant material on hacking techniques;
- *Malicious Agents*: it is easy to design malicious software exploiting features or weaknesses of Internet services; such malicious software may even distribute itself through the network, and it will be difficult (if not impossible) to control activities or consequences of such agents;
- *Malicious Documents*: even documents regarded as non-malicious for long times can import unforeseeable malicious side-effects into a single local Internet station.

As the Internet does not fulfil any of the above-mentioned requirements (R1-R4) even on a minimum level of service, the Internet cannot be regarded as a relevant prototype of a global information infrastructure, at least from the point of view of customer protection. Otherwise, an information infrastructure based on contemporary insecure and unsafe technologies will provide such serious risks to digital commerce that related applications can at best work only with severe restrictions. The following examples of digital commerce, namely Internet-based payment systems, show how some services may be conceived to reduce risks somewhat but that there are side-effects, for example, on user privacy that develop even from security mechanisms.

EXAMPLE: INTERNET-BASED PAYMENT SYSTEMS: RISKS AND IMPACTS FOR THE GLOBAL SOCIETY

Information technology provides an important support to many different financial services like various payment mechanisms and remote banking. Industrial developments push the use of electronic payment mechanisms. A huge amount of information technology is already in use or in pilot projects to support Internet-based financial services. People are beginning to use the Internet for widespread applications. Transferring money on a chipcard, buying goods over the net, booking and paying travels via the net, or using remote banking will become more and more common.

The new network technology changes people's everyday life very quickly. In the past, and still somewhere in the present, people had to go outside of their home to work, shop, or manage their banking. These activities were often combined with important social and personal contacts. Especially old and lonely people used the daily walks to the bank or to the shops to get some personal talks and contacts with other people.

Nowadays, and in some foreseeable future, properly equipped people can arrange their daily shopping, banking, and even working, directly from their home. Information technologies like international networks make it possible and viable. The Internet seems to satisfy all commercial needs: it supports the mechanisms to buy goods, information and services and to do remote banking over the net. Today, several different types of electronic payment systems are more or less available and usable.

Internet banking started with the transmission of credit card numbers over the net for paying ordered goods and services; this mode is obviously rather insecure. Now, there are concepts for digital money, digital credit cards, digital cheques and digital coupons at least in test phases which seem to fulfil some security requirements.

Digital payment systems can be seen as the electronic representation of conventional payment schemes. Therefore, all characteristics of conventional schemes have to be implemented in their digital analogies. Indeed, Internet banking overcomes some of the disadvantages of traditional money: digital money can be easily accessed (if an access service is available), stored and transmitted to any remote location, and its exchange into any other currency is done just-in-time (as multiplication with a suitable currency factor). In the following four world-renowned pilot projects, payment mechanisms will be discussed briefly.

Digital Money: Mondex

The concept of digital money proposed by Mondex International [Mondex 96] especially provides the property of transferability of money between private persons. The money is stored on a chipcard; it is more than an Internet payment system because it can also be used in ordinary (not networked) shops. The money on the card can be stored in five different currencies. With an additional device, money can be transferred from one card to another. Both cards have to authenticate each other. A personal identification number can be used to lock the card but no authentication will happen if the card is 'open'. While transferring money, identification data can be stored to prevent unauthorized use. Payment profiles should help to block a card suspected of misuse but, at the same time, risks of misuse of personal data are evident. Pilot projects started in Swindon in Britain and with major banks in Australia.

Digital Money: Ecash

Ecash [Digicash 96] is designed for secure payments from any personal computer to any other workstation over Internet or email. Ecash is one-sided anonymous. When paying with Ecash, the identity of the customer is not revealed automatically. During the payment he/she can identify him/herself, but only when he/she chooses. When clearing a transaction, the merchant is identified by the bank. Before Ecash can be used to purchase products, it must first be withdrawn from the bank. The withdrawal uses a blind signature to prevent the bank from recognizing the coins as having come from a particular account. Customers create the coins at random, hide them in a digital envelope and send them off to the bank. The bank withdraws them from the customer's account and makes them valid using an embossed stamp on the envelope before returning them to the customer's computer. Now, the money can be spent in a shop or between private persons. When merchants receives the money, they automatically send it to the bank and wait for the acceptance before sending the goods to the customer along with a receipt.

Digital Credit Cards: Secure Electronic Transaction (SET)

VISA and MASTERCARD have jointly developed the Secure Electronic Transaction (SET) Protocol as a method for bank-card transactions over open networks [SET 96]. The SET protocol provides a payment gateway, an institution which organizes the transfer of money from the consumer's bank to the merchant's bank. The protocol is divided into two phases, the purchase request and the payment authorization. In the purchase request, the first phase handles the initiation request and response, followed by the second phase where the purchase request and response take place between the consumer and the merchant. The payment authorization will be done by authorization request and response, and it will capture the request and response via the payment gateway. This procedure enforces a certification process producing certificates binding the user's identity to the person's public encryption key. SET uses cryptographic methods to provide confidentiality of information, payment integrity and authentication of consumers and merchants. Here, there are problems with the strength of cryptosystems as well as the legality of their usage.

Digital Coupons: Millicent

In December 1995, the System Research Centre of Digital Equipment Corporation presented the Millicent Protocol for Inexpensive Electronic Commerce [Millicent 96]. It is designed for very small amounts of money, so it should not require high security standards. The idea of this protocol is based on a new currency named *Scrip*. Scrip is comparable with tickets or coupons, therefore it depends on the product and its merchant. The protocol contains three different types concerning security, complexity and secrecy. On the lowest level, one finds Scrip in the clear which is very easy and efficient, and uses no cryptography at all. The Private and Secure type uses encryption and digital signatures to ensure privacy and integrity of the user and the transaction. While using public key algorithms, it is quite slow. A compromise is the Secure without encryption type, which renounces privacy while only using digital signatures.

These four new digital payment systems offer several new payment mechanisms but also introduce huge possibilities for misuse. The Internet is completely insecure and unreliable, and it is not acceptable to provide these financial services without reflecting on the impacts for society and without caring for the security and privacy needs of individual customers. Some concepts have built-in security features. Presently, means of encryption and digital signatures are used to secure electronic transactions over the Internet. It is quite established to use a symmetric algorithm (like Data Encryption Standard (DES)) for quick encryption as well as asymmetric algorithms (like Rivest, Shamir, Adleman (RSA)) for creating digital signatures. One still unresolved problem is the establishment of an international solution for key exchange and certification authorities. Some national or regional suggestions exist to solve this problem but global concepts are missing. The situation is especially complex as relevant national laws and regulations start from different assumptions and are somewhat contradictory.

Another problem is concerned with suggestions for key escrow and regulations for export licenses for symmetric and asymmetric algorithms. Limitations of the key length decrease the security of the algorithms and will not be of any help in detecting criminal actions over the net. A law for depositing a part of the used key will not hinder criminally-oriented people from hiding information in other ways. Several methods, summarized as steganography, allow the hiding of information in texts and pictures, etc. Everyone who has seen pictures treated with steganography knows that it is impossible to detect whether a picture contains any secret information or not. For an example, look at the two pictures of Shakespeare presented on a special webpage: one is hiding information, the other is not [Stegano 96].

Besides these more technical problems, other problems are concerned with legal and social implications. In several countries with a constitutional or regulatory basis of privacy, the fact that data protection cannot be guaranteed when user data are collected during transmission is of major importance. With broader usage of financial services, new threats develop especially when user profiles are collected without proper customer protection.

SPECIAL REQUIREMENTS FOR PROTECTING USERS OF FINANCIAL INTERNET SERVICES

New technical and organizational institutions for trusted key management and new trusted services have to be installed to decide what kind of information or services conforms with the responsible organization's policy. The price for such improved security may be high, as this leads to growingly complex technologies providing a little bit more security within the intrinsically insecure technology of the Internet. In this way, easy handling of these systems is lost, and people need to become experts to ensure a correct and secure usage.

Besides the technical requirements for secure electronic payment systems, a lot of organizational or even social aspects have to be required and specified to support proper implementation. The use of asymmetric cryptographic algorithms enforces a structure for key management. The keys have to be created, issued and administrated by a trusted third party (TTP). This party or another trustworthy organization signs the public keys and gives out certifications of validity and any expiring information. Additional tasks can include consulting and teaching about security issues and how to use security in an effective way. Trusted third parties should also built up trust in new payment systems or should at least inform the users about trustbuilding activities. To realize an effective work of trusted third parties, acceptance studies are necessary to find out what the users really need. Nowadays almost all acceptance studies are product-oriented and not, as they should be, user-oriented. A new approach to the area of acceptance studies is necessary. The general question behind such concepts is : if trusted third parties are at least initially trustworthy, can customers safely assume that they remain trustworthy under any future conditions (for example, after unfriendly take-overs by other parties)? At least, legal prescriptions (which are presently being discussed in several countries including Germany) should allow users to get legal assistance in cases of TTP frauds.

Following traditional security requirements, an essential requirement is that all relevant financial transactions are logged and audited. Audit data can help to detect unauthorized use of systems or even to prevent misuse. As usual, auditing of logfiles is the weakest point, because the logfiles contain very interesting information about the financial behaviour of people. If logfiles are audited in an unauthorized way, the information can be misused for advertising or marketing purposes. It depends on the point of view if this is wanted or not. From the privacy viewpoint, it is very delicate to create profiles about financial behaviour and to sell them to commercial companies. So there has to be a strict regulation of the purposes of auditing and using audit data. The users have to be informed about the use of the information being collected about them. For that reason (and even for others), it is necessary to provide anonymous payment systems for daily use. The electronic form of ordinary payment systems must have at least the same properties as the ordinary ones have. Especially the form of coins has the property of being anonymous. So it has to be required that there is free choice of using anonymous payment systems whenever they are wanted, independent of whether they are in an electronic form or not.

GENERAL REQUIREMENTS FOR PROTECTION OF CUSTOMER INTERESTS AND RIGHTS

The cases given are just very obvious examples of what happens, usually at the expense of customers and users, with the introduction of so-called information infrastructures. Less obvious are other changes, for example, in controlling the growth of the (formerly national, now worldwide) monetary system as well as its misuse in such issues as how to detect and hinder the laundering of digital money. From discussions of other risks, one reaches the following general conclusions:

- *If Internet-like techniques are used, huge risks arise, most of which materialize at the expense of the weakest parties in the game: customers and users!*
- *If present trends in information economies continue, the winners will be the suppliers of those technologies which today determine all the features but which guarantee nothing, thus rendering users, customers and those affected by the technologies with no chance of influencing features essentially structuring such information societies!*

To avoid such perspectives, control of developments must be broadened from supply-side control to include all participants, especially users, customers and those indirectly affected by such developments. This approach may be compared to Ralph Nader's contribution to customer protection in the 1950s. As cars *were* unsafe at any speed in those times, Nader began to fight a long but eventually successful battle to develop customer-friendly legislation, mainly at the expense of car manufacturers. Presently, the situation is similar to the missing qualities of cars in the 1950s: customers have no support when information technology services fail, and the Internet is unsafe at any speed. In order to develop guarantees for the quality of IT products and services, developers and vendors must be forced, for example, by legal action (possibly initiated by customer protest) to change their design, implementation and services accordingly.

One basic prerequisite for such a development will be that politicians and bureaucrats stop painting insecure and unsafe techniques in inadequately beautiful colours. It must become common knowledge that present computer and network techniques (including PCs, the various UNIX systems, Internet and intranets) are not reliable and not functional enough to make future economies and human lives dependent on them. Such insight (though difficult without hands-on experience with crashing personal computers and failing Internet email) may become a starting point for a Ralph Cyber-Nader to fight for customer protection against the disadvantages of digital commerce.

REFERENCES

[Digicash 96]Product information, Digicash (http://www.digicash.nl)
[Millicent 96] Information about Millicent (http://www.research.digital.com/SRC/millicent/)
[Mondex 96] Information about Mondex (http://www.mondex.com/mondex/)
[SET 96] SET specification, Visa and Mastercard 1996, (http://www.visa.com/cgi-bin/vee/sf/set/intro.html)
[Stegano 96] Information about Stegano, 1996, (http://patriot.net/-johnson/html/neil/stegdoc/sec101.html)

7

Going to the future

Bo Dahlbom
Department of Informatics, Göteborg University
PO Box 3147, 411 80 Göteborg, Sweden
Phone: +46(0)31 773 2735; Fax: +46(0)31 773 4754
Email: dahlbom@butler.adb.gu.se

Abstract

Every society has its institutions for reflection. When societies go through major changes those institutions change too. Industrialization brought us science, replacing the religion of traditional societies. Moving into the information society, we may expect a new institution for reflection to replace science. And, looking around, there seems to be such an institution in the making, combining the methods of an archaeology of the future with the more general ideas of a science of the artificial, an institution for reflecting on our social possibility space as part of a more deliberate effort to design our future.

INTRODUCTION

The nineteenth century is often described as a century looking very much into the *past*. After the turmoil of the French Revolution and the Napoleonic wars, the intellectual stage for the new century was set by the Vienna conference in 1815 - it was to begin as a century of restoration. History, as a subject matter, as an emerging academic discipline, and as a general intellectual orientation, dominated intellectual and cultural life. Nations were born seeking their identity in a glorious past. People went looking for their roots. The nineteenth century was a century of Hegelian idealism, romantic nationalism, philology, hermeneutics, historical geology, and theories of evolution and revolution.

One explanation for this preoccupation with the past and with history can, of course, be found in the powerful changes brought about by the beginnings of industrialization. The political and intellectual elite of the nineteenth century mainly feared these changes. It took a century for that elite to be replaced by the moderns, to be replaced by an intellectual and political elite saying yes to industrialization, saying yes to modernization and change. Thus, the twentieth

An Ethical Global Information Society J. Berleur & D. Whitehouse (Eds.)

century is very much a century of the *present*. Historical roots give way to social reform, spiritual values are replaced by material welfare. Hermeneutics and philology make room for social science and structural analysis. The twentieth century is a modern century.

If we continue this somewhat whimsical, broad brush, world historical exercise, what can we do but expect the twenty-first century to be a century of the *future*? Having moved from reactionary avoidance reactions, to industrial change, to a positive preoccupation with the facts and values of modern life, we will move, again, to a future oriented interest in the possibility space of social design. In the beginning of yet another technological revolution, brought on by information technology, the intellectual elite is not responding with rejection but with enthusiasm, and media are filled with speculations about information society and cyberspace. People are beginning to realize that they can just as well look for their identity in the future as in the past. The future is on everybody's lips and there are reasons to believe that this is not just a passing fad. Here, I want to give some of those reasons as well as contribute to a discussion of how that interest in the future ought to be implemented.

THE FUTURE IS NOT A FAD

The nineteenth century interest in history was an interest in the big picture, in world historical trends, mythical pasts, and heroic deeds. It was an interest in history as edifying fiction rather than factual book-keeping. It took an elevated view with ideal, spiritual subjects such as heroes, nations, elites, classes, and cultures as the agents of history. The twentieth century is dominated by a down-to-earth, material interest in facts and figures. History is replaced by science and, instead of elaborating our mythical past, we subject the minutiae of our everyday present to close and careful scrutiny. Historical storytellers have been replaced by statistical bureaucrats.

Our interest in the future is again redirecting our attention from facts to interpretation. Even if that interest began, in the 1960s, with an interest in facts about natural resources, global warming, and the like, and certainly to some extent will continue to focus on such facts, there has been a growing attention to the social changes designated by our entering the era of postindustrialism. Interest in the social changes going on today tends to focus on the role of information technology both in the automation of industrial production and as the dominating technology of postindustrial society.

With advancing automation made possible by information technology, fewer and fewer people will find work in the factories of the industrial era. When this leads to unemployment people begin to worry. Soon they realize that automation ought to make us all richer, of course, since it means that a small percent of us can produce the food and goods for all of us. One farmer today can produce more food than a hundred farmers did a hundred years ago. Industrialization has made us wealthy - at least in the sense of giving us an abundance of material goods.

Industrialization made us focus on the production of goods, and it made the factory a model for social organization. For a while yet, we will continue to focus on material goods, and we will use the resources set free by automation in developing, marketing, and selling goods and in managing the factory organizations. But, as automation continues, our focus will shift, as it once did from farms to factories, from factories to services, and we will begin to think more creatively about the organization of our everyday lives. Instead of modelling services on the way goods are produced in factories, we will begin to experiment with more human-oriented ways of organizing education, care, entertainment, travel, living, and life in general.

Even if industrialization was clearly seen by nineteenth century utopians as a means of achieving paradise on earth, an existence of leisure with machines doing most of the work, unemployment is a nightmare to our politicians today, rather than the reward for a work well done. It takes a while to recognize paradise for what it is. And when we do, we realize, of course, that there is work left to be done. For the hard-working farmer, leisure is the same as paradise, but we moderns would of course get nervous very quickly there on the meadows of heaven - is there nothing to do here? The farmer could not imagine the amount and variety of goods that a modern person would bring on a trip to heaven. Nor could he imagine the amount and variety of services - entertainment - needed in paradise.

The recently growing interest in the future began as a defensive reaction to apocalyptic warnings about atomic wars, chemical pollution, and nuclear meltdowns. Even if this interest has to a large extent been reactionary in the way it has expressed itself, in attempts to stop or abandon certain technologies, it has also led to a more constructive interest in scenarios of the future. Even if 'sustainable growth' is not itself a particularly creative view of the future, the discussion of material resources, uses of technology, and environmental hazards, has slowly turned people's attention to the possibility space of the future.

With information technology this defensive interest to 'save the future' has begun to be combined with a more optimistic interest in how to shape the future. Riding on a wave of interest in information technology, busily trying to contribute to that wave, futurists of all sorts easily make their fortune in media today, predicting and preaching the blessings of information society. Such discussions of trends and details of information society often seem to be interpretations of the use of information technology, reminiscent of the way archaeologists try to reconstruct the past from the artifacts found. I therefore use the term 'future archaeology' to characterize such attempts at investigating the future, and I think it is possible to make that occupation at least as academically respectable as archaeology itself.

ARCHAEOLOGY OF THE FUTURE

Archaeologists have to do their cultural studies solely on the basis of material artifacts, and a haphazard collection of remnants at that. This does not mean that they cannot draw on ethnographical studies of cultures still using those artifacts, in their attempts at interpretation, nor that they cannot make use of experimental methods in actually trying to recreate the details of ancient artifact use. And yet, whatever they are able to say about the cultures they study, they rely on a material conception of what a society is. To archaeology, a society is a technology, a way of organizing the use of that technology, and ideas about, or derived from, the technology and its use. There is a lot speaking in favour of this definition, and it is not as narrow as one might first think.

Like other historical disciplines, archaeology was established in the nineteenth century (Trigger, 1990). In the twentieth century, it has become a major industry, called in to check for ancient dwellings whenever industrialization wants to perform major surgery on the landscape. Sometimes its perspective is applied to the present, as in material culture theory, an approach to social and cultural studies that looks carefully at the material infrastructures of contemporary life. Having moved archaeology from the past to the present, it becomes easier to get used to the idea of an archaeology of the future. Similarly, having moved ethnography from the exotic tropics to our everyday neighbourhood, it will not be too difficult to conceive of an ethnography of the future.

An archaeology of the future is just as scientifically respectable as an archaeology of the past or present. The artifacts that we bring back from the future are really no less, or more, reliable as data than those we dig out of our past. When I hold up the new net computer and begin to expound on the kind of everyday habits of a culture dominated by this sort of technology, I am really in a much better situation that the traditional archaeologist. I cannot tell, until there are more models on the market and the sales are beginning to take off, that the net computer will ever play an important role in shaping our everyday existence. But neither can the traditional archaeologist. Finding an artifact is one thing, determining that it once played an important role is a completely different matter.

Ethnography, except to the extent that it really is archaeology, cannot really claim to study the future in a scientific way. Relying on interviews and detailed behavioural observations, as it does, it finds it difficult to do empirical studies of the future. But that is not really important, I would argue, since nothing says that an interest in the future needs scientific respectability in order to be cognitively interesting. All we need is an understanding of knowledge that is such that it does not reflexively identify knowledge with scientific knowledge - as if most of us did not learn more about life from novels than from the social sciences. Let me quickly give the outlines of such a conception of knowledge.

SCIENCE AND TECHNOLOGY

Information technology is today changing both public debate, business strategies, and political agenda by increasing our interest in the future. This may prove to be a fad, but it is hard to avoid the feeling that, if so, it is a fad that will last for a while. One indication of this is the way information technology has changed the relations between science and the rest of society. Academic research is now becoming integrated with the rest of society in a way reminiscent of the situation in countries at war. Information technology has managed to mobilize the scientific community in a major social change effort. There is no question any longer but that science has to participate actively in designing the future information society. In this way, science changes its fundamental knowledge interest and begins to change into an institution for reflections on the future.

There is a more powerful reason to believe that there is an institution for reflections on the future in the making, however, and that is a reason grounded in the general role and nature of technology. In the industrial age, technology is understood as applied natural science. There are objections to this view, certainly, pointing to the way the evolution of technology, including major technological innovations, tends to go on independently of mainstream natural science research. And yet, with the increasing cognitive content of an increasingly complex technology, the view that technology is applied natural science tends to grow stronger. I believe that this view can explain our strange tendency to take technological evolution as somehow pre-determined.

Ever since natural scientists were geographical discoverers, we have had a view of science as developing by struggling through the jungle of the unknown, collecting facts and charting the territory. Reaching a hill, the view will clear and the mighty scientist will discern another hill, defining new challenges, new problems to be solved. There is no direction to science other than that given by the territory, and the way those hills look when glimpsed from afar. Some scientists may prefer to follow rivers, others to climb mountains, others again to venture out on the oceans, but it is the nature of the terrain that gives true, objective science its direction. When technology is viewed as applied science, as the material spelling out or implementation of scientific findings, then there is no direction to technology either, except that given by the territory of the unknown. So, we will get atom bombs and laser guns, gene-manipulated tomatoes and Formula One automobiles, six-lane highways and cross mountain-bike knee-protection gear, rather than solar energy plants and artificial limbs, ecological cultivation and electric automobiles, meeting places and comfortable shoes, just because those things were there in the terrain and those other things were not.

Rubbish! If anything, science is applied technology rather than the other way around. Technology provides the instruments, the ships, telescopes, thermometers, and computers, needed for the expeditions and the nature of the instruments will give the expeditions their general direction as well as determine what can be discovered. Technology will also provide science with its subject matter, producing in chemical laboratories, accelerators, and on the workbench, the very nature to be investigated. Once it is clearly seen how the evolution of science and technology are human enterprises, it becomes obvious that scientists and innovators can no longer hide behind such a silly view that they only go where the terrain takes them.

When scientists, innovators and engineers begin to really see that they shape the world for all of us to live in, they will of course take an interest in questions concerning what that world should be like. It is a little strange that it has taken them so long to realize this. Humanists, artists, and politicians who have virtually no impact on the shaping of our world worry about its direction, while the engineers who are busily building seem content not to think globally at all. But that is changing now when science and technology are becoming so obviously oriented towards designing an artificial world rather than discovering the natural. One way to describe this is to say, with Herbert Simon (1969), that the natural sciences make way for the sciences of the artificial.

The modern world is an artificial world, Simon says, but modern science is a science of nature. Something is wrong. When we realize that the world we live in is an artificial world, a world of human creation, made up of artifacts of all kinds, becoming ever more complex and intertwined, our attention will shift from studying nature to contributing to the design of artifacts. In the natural sciences we want to find out what the world is like while in the artificial we are interested in what could possibly be and how to make it so. Artifacts inspire us to improvements. Our interest in how they are made is guided by our interest in making them ourselves, and making them better. Rather than turning to the natural sciences for legitimacy and status, disciplines like engineering, economics, and, more generally, the social sciences, should develop their own identity as design-oriented knowledge disciplines (Dahlbom and Mathiassen 1993, 1997).

ARTIFICIAL SCIENCE

Simon's own view of the sciences of the artificial are strangely conservative. With an extremely general notion of design, Simon turns his design-oriented science of the artificial into a general theory of problem-solving, adhering to the values of traditional empirical science, rather than following up on his very radical introduction. My own view of the sciences of the artificial is, in comparison, much more radical, even if I would argue that it only draws out the implications of Simon's initial identification of the nature of the world we live in and how to study it.

The sciences of the artificial are design-oriented. Such disciplines will strike a balance between traditional scientific values such as essential truth, documentation, objectivity, and the use of method, on the one hand, and values of engineering such as complexity, success, engagement, and the use of heuristics, on the other. Exactly how such a compromise between truth and successful implementation will turn out will vary, but the result will be very different from traditional science, or so I would argue.

I imagine a situation in which ideas of design, the difference between usefulness and functionality, and the normativity of research and engineering, are appreciated; a situation in which an essence-oriented and idealizing, objective natural science, to which human beings are human factors, no longer serves as the foundation for engineering, but is replaced by an artificial science with an interest in accidents and achievements, in local design principles as well as general laws, heuristics as well as methods, with an engaged appreciation of the complex, tinkering, interaction between human beings and technology.

The scientific attitude to nature objectifies nature, leaving behind the close interaction between humans and nature typical of life in traditional society. As long as you experience yourself as one with the world when you are engaged in it, your research will be biased by paying particular attention to what is useful. Science becomes possible when you can make a clear distinction between yourself and the object you are investigating. The scientific attitude is one of objective detachment. As a neutral observer of events you minimize the risk of being prejudiced by your interests. Generalizing from science, we have adopted such an objective attitude to our environment, nature and artifacts. We are alienated from them. It is one of the aims of an artificial science to restore the interactive engagement that has only been suppressed, between people and their environment, artifacts and nature.

In the artificial sciences we will also supplement the standard conception of engineering with, what Lévi-Strauss (1966) calls *bricolage*, or tinkering, when it comes to both the production and use of technology. Tinkering is what we do when we interact with artifacts, when we are active rather than passive, tinkering is different from use. As an alternative to functionalistic engineering, to functionalism, tinkering rejects the very simple notion of functioning as an analysis of technology use, in favour of a view of our interaction with technology as complex, changing, and practically unpredictable unless we can assume a substantial cultural homogeneity.

The metaphor of tinkering describes a position that strikes a compromise between the different approaches to the social study of technology. Tinkering expresses well how what we do with an artifact draws on and is supported by our previous experience with artifacts. Technology is a social, cultural phenomenon. The process of technology design is a complex dialectic process involving engineers, users, and artifacts, their backgrounds and culture, negotiating, learning, constructing and reconstructing, designing and cultivating, tinkering and decorating.

FROM SCIENCE TO FICTION

To be a *bricoleur* is to have imagination. Imagination, our capacity to think about what is absent or does not exist and to think what we perceive as being different from or more than what we see, is 'an essential and transcendental condition of consciousness', to speak with Jean-Paul Sartre (1940, chapter 5). It is our capacity to dream of things that never were that makes us human. It both introduces 'negation' and 'lack' into the world - and with lack 'values' - and is the very foundation of human freedom. It is imagination, the capacity to see the world as it is not but as it could be, that makes it possible for us to change the world. Imagination gives us alternatives and makes us see the lack in the world as it is. The world will always be lacking as long as we remain human. Human consciousness is by its very essence an 'unhappy consciousness'. It is from that unhappiness that human beings draw their strength to act, to change the world, to design a better world. And it is that unhappiness that is the *raison d'être* for the sciences of the artificial.

By stressing the importance of imagination, the artificial sciences will make explicit the important role played by fiction in our search for knowledge. For what is it we do when we draw up a design document, be it for an electrical installation, an information infrastructure, an organization, or a research project? We produce fiction. We use our experience and imagination to describe something that does not (yet) exist. The only principal difference between such design fiction and literary fiction is that our ambition normally is to turn our design fiction into fact. Design is future-oriented. And yet much design fiction is produced more in order to examine what is possible than in order to actually have it implemented. Thus, design is an important element in planning, decision -making, learning, and most other cognitive activities.

With an explicit appreciation of the artificial sciences, design will be understood as an important scientific method, but if design is taken seriously enough then this will introduce a new scientific orientation. Our traditional understanding of science can be saved, in the way suggested by Simon, by viewing design as a method to investigate the boundaries of the possible. Thus, the possible is only the other side of the real. But my suggestion is, contrary to Simon, that we take artificial science to aim at examining the possible, in its own right, rather than as a means to determining what is real. Then we are interested in what is within the space of possibilities, rather than in the boundaries of that space, and design will introduce fiction as a major product of science, in addition to truth. But then, perhaps, we will prefer not to call such a design-oriented research, with fiction as its product, *science* after all. Perhaps, we will prefer to reserve the term 'science' for research into facts and truth, rather than into fiction and possibilities. Or, perhaps, we will say it is exactly because artificial science is interested in fiction rather than in truth that we call it 'artificial'? For what are artifacts when compared to nature, if not fictive (products of imagination)?

RELIGION, SCIENCE, AND FUTURE

Art, politics, religion, philosophy, science, sports, and entertainment are examples of ideology producing institutions. Louis Althusser used to expand on Marx's idea that to each major economic system there is a corresponding, dominating ideological institution. Thus, in a feudal society, religion is the institution for reflection, while in industrial capitalism it is science. Using such a simplified account, we might well wonder, as we enter the information age, what will replace science as the dominating institution for reflection. There are, of course, several possibilities.

Institutions of reflection are servants of the institutions of action. In the twentieth century, politicians and business executives, generals and healers, have turned to science for support and advice. But science is severely inadequate in this role. The specialization of the sciences makes it difficult to use their advice in real life, complex situations. The sciences do not help you with a longer perspective on your actions. Science tells you what the world is like, it is up to you to draw the consequences for how to build a new world. As long as this is being done with the ideologies of the nineteenth century, there is a least some general advice on what to do. But when those ideologies lose their applicability and credibility, you really have very little use for science.

The idea of social engineering, particularly the experimental, piecemeal version, advocated by Popper (1961) is the idea of using science as a basis for political reform. But, piecemeal engineering presupposes that the fundamental structure is alright and relatively stable. In a time when the foundation of society is undergoing revolutionary change, piecemeal engineering seems like a waste of time. When industrial society is changing into a service society, when factories cease to be the model for rational, human activity, be it information work, education, care, or entertainment, society will begin to change in so radical a fashion that piecemeal engineering becomes hopelessly inadequate. Instead of scientifically informed, social engineering making sure to have adequate information about the current situation in society, we will have to use methods like future archaeology and the ideas of artificial science to develop a more future-oriented examination of the space of social possibilities.

People have always created institutions for reflection. Farmers have their religion and industrialists have their science. We can understand how these institutions develop and why they do what they do. We can study how reflection in such institutions stagnates and becomes bureaucratic. And, we can see that today it is time to create a new such institution, an institution for reflection on the future, a sort of seminar of the future - but how we best go about creating such an institution is not so easy to see.

When Auguste Comte wanted to turn science into the institution for reflection of modern society, he tried to market science as the new religion, even building a church for it. Perhaps, we should market the future as the new science, as a combination of artificial science and archaeology of the future?

Whatever way we choose, we need to create an institution for discussing the future, and I am not speaking about an institute for future studies at the margin of the scientific community, but about an institution that can take the place of science as we leave industrial society behind. But we have to be careful when criticizing institutions for reflection. Such criticism is often misinterpreted as an attack on reflection, when it is only the subject matter and objective of the reflection that is questioned. Religion gives us comfort and science gives us knowledge - and we need them both. But in a constantly changing society we also need ideas about where to go and how to get there, and such ideas we cannot find in either religion or science (or art for that matter).

Nor does politics seem such a good place for the kind of reflection on the future that I am asking for. In politics, the daily issues dominate, and the administrative competence needed by contemporary politicians does not seem to go well with ability and interest for reflection. The questions about our future are not such that one can answer them once and for all. Instead, they indicate major investigations into what is valuable and what is possible and what it takes to make the valuable possible.

Every day, we spend more time discussing what to have for dinner than discussing what the world should be like in fifty years. But perhaps we could spend at least two hours every Sunday on the future? Spend them in a sort of seminar for the future rather than in mass or in popular scientific lecture? Rather than going to church or a popular lecture on Sunday, we could be going to the 'Future'.

A TAXONOMY OF QUESTIONS

What then will we be doing in the 'Future'? Let me end by giving some examples of big questions about the role of technology in shaping our society, trying to formulate a relatively systematic agenda for an institution for reflections on the future. There are questions about the relations between our form of life and technology, about the role of change and stability in a good society, about the idea of progress, about complexity and an incomprehensible society, about the trade-offs between ethics and technology, about fundamental forms of social organization, about where to live and what to do in an affluent society, and so on. We can make a simple taxonomy to organize these questions into different categories.

General Questions

Some questions concern the more general phenomenon of technology and social change. A fundamental question is that of technology control. If technology is a major social change agent, how do we learn to control it? Technical evolution changes our lives. With machine technology we leave the country and move to the cities, to a life in the factories. With information technology we move again, from the cities to the net. Do we have to go where the technology is taking us? If we have carefully chosen a form of life, acquired habits with which we are happy, constructed institutions and organizations making a good life possible - why would we give them up just because a new technology was beckoning us to move on?

Another aspect of technology control concerns the very way that technology is developed in the midst of our societies. We have no reason to believe that technical evolution will slow down. We can expect further changes in our form of life. Perhaps we could make change itself a form of life? Turning life into an adventure, society into an experiment? But do we really want to live in society which is an online test site for new technology?

Making change itself our form of life would be to let the conditions of technical evolution rule our lives. But, even if we accept the fact that technology is a dominating framework in our form of life, we may still hesitate to fall flat on our faces in front of technology. We use technology for many purposes, but if we look at technology itself, its internal purpose is technical functionality, efficiency. And, it is efficiency that makes possible the amazing productivity of industrial societies. Technology makes us rich. No wonder efficiency becomes such an important value in modern societies. But, do we really want a society in which efficiency is the highest value?

With technical evolution, the world becomes more complex. Evolution is diversification and integration. People feel at home in a simple environment they shape themselves, but the technical evolution makes the world complex and strange. So, why do we continue to increase the complexity of our world? Are we thoughtless children with much too powerful tools? Or is the increasing complexity worth its price?

Such questions are all examples of how to handle the more general phenomenon of technology and social change. As such they presuppose an understanding of the powerful role played by technology as a social change agent, and they invite us to develop institutions for technology control, for democratic, professional, control of the evolution and diffusion of technology. They also invite us to question fundamental values, such as efficiency, complexity, and change, pressed upon us by technology.

Domain Questions

General questions concern the democratic control of technology as a social change agent. Domain questions go into the details in areas that change because of the use of new technology. All aspects of human life can come under the influence of technology, and the change can often be dramatic. To accept the new technology is to accept the change, unless we take explicit measures to restrict the influence of the new technology. Let me give a few examples from different domains.

Information technology gives us unbelievable possibilities for behavioral regulation with technology rather than with social norms. With a widespread use of this technology, we can look forward to a society in which human relations and norms have become technical. But, do we want such a society? Do we really want to substitute respect, solidarity, honesty, compassion, responsibility, and the like, for technology?

Information technology dissolves the boundaries of factories and lets the market into our organizations. Bureaucracies change into networks and marriages become affairs. A society that is like a cocktail party may have its advantages, but there is something to be said for commitments 'for better and for worse' as well. If information technology favours the market alternative that does not necessarily mean that we have to do so.

Just as we once left the farms in the country and moved to the factories of the city, information technology now makes us leave the city and move out on the net (Dahlbom and Janlert, 1995, 1996). In the country we worked on farms. Those farms were our homes, a base that we would always return to, a centre to our lives, providing us with roots. In the cities we work in factories and live in apartments. Even if we have tried to retain a home, apartments eventually become nothing but a place to sleep (and watch television), and no longer play the role of homes. In information land, we become even less dependent on a base, on a home. We can do whatever we want to do wherever we are, as long as we are logged in. So, perhaps we become nomads again, leaning our head on some anonymous pillow when the screen begins to flicker and we are overcome by fatigue. But, maybe we would like to have a home even in the future?

Institutional Questions

When there is a social revolution, the ruling order is questioned. What used to be disparate activities mix and dichotomies lose their power. Leaving the factories of industrial society behind, we begin to mix working hours and leisure, work and entertainment, public and private, children and adults, men and women. Boundaries move and dissolve, new ones come instead. The old order is disappearing, and a new one has to be created. But, even if we want this revolution to come, would it not be a good thing to be a bit better prepared for the different options available? How can we make ourselves prepared?

When we enter service society, working becomes talking. People in talk society want entertainment and variety in an increasingly hectic world. Zapping between stations, surfing on the net, and chatting in the bars, we realize ourselves at a quickening pace. But we seem to have drifted into this lifestyle without much conscious deliberation. Technology has made us rich. We can live in abundance, but we have only rudimentary ideas about how we would like to live, now that we do not really have to work. How could we form such ideas? How could we begin to seriously discuss designing the good life?

Science has nothing to say about the future. But if there is something to be known about the past, the future ought to be equally accessible. In order to turn the design of the future into a rational enterprise, we have to chart it, in order to determine what our possibilities are. We need to develop an institution for studying the future.

A NOTE OF WARNING

Institutions for reflection have their dark sides. Bigotry and nuclear bombs are examples of such ill effects. What will be the ill effects of future? Directing human creativity into the design of possible worlds may end in horror, when experts on the future go on to implement their designs. We have seen some of this in the influence of the Bauhaus school in architecture on the design of the modern city. Creativity is by its very nature irresponsible, and I for one would prefer to live in a boring bureaucracy rather than to participate in the happenings of artists turned world designers.

One might object that such ill effects of possible world-making are encouraged by the choice of name for the new institution of reflection. Why call it 'future', if really what is meant is an institution for reflection on possible artificial worlds? Why talk of an 'archaeology of the future', when an 'archaeology of the possible' would be more apt? Why invite the misunderstanding that it is the future we are investigating, when really we are only trying to determine what our possibilities are? If we want to strike a blow for fiction as distinct from truth, why not choose a name that makes this clear? Why not use the very term 'fiction' when naming the new institution for reflection? From science to science fiction?

The answers to all these questions should be obvious. It is precisely because I want fiction to play an important role in shaping the future, rather than in just being a silly pastime, that I have chosen the name. It is because I want researchers and engineers to become aware of their responsibility that I want to remind them of the fact that they are busy shaping our future. If this has the effect that some of them become megalomaniac, and really get going, it is a price we have to pay, and a problem we have to deal with. Only when those who play such an important role in shaping our future understand that this is what they are doing, will our societies wake up from their technological somnambulism.

ACKNOWLEDGEMENT

I am grateful to the Swedish Council for Planning and Coordination of Research for financial support.

REFERENCES

Dahlbom, B. and Janlert, L.-E. (1995) Life on the Net. In M. Karlsson and L. Sturesson (eds) *The World's Largest Machine*. Almqvist and Wiksell International.

Dahlbom, B. and Janlert, L.-E. (1996) Nomaden im Cyberspace. *Bertelsmann Briefe*, Heft 135, Frühling/Sommer 1996.

Dahlbom, B. and Mathiassen, L. (1993) *Computers in Context. The Philosophy and Practice of Systems Design*. Oxford: Blackwell.

Dahlbom, B. and Mathiassen, L. (1997) The Future of Our Profession. *Communications of the ACM*, **40** (6), June.
Lévi-Strauss, C. (1966) *Savage Thinking*. London: Weidenfeld and Nicolson.
Popper, K. R. (1961) *The Poverty of Historicism*. London: Routledge and Kegan Paul.
Sartre, J.-P. (1940) *L'Imaginaire*. Éditions Gallimard. English trans. *The Psychology of Imagination*. New York: Philosophical Library, 1948.
Simon, H. A. (1969) *The Science of the Artificial*. Cambridge, MA: MIT Press.
Trigger, B. G. (1990) *A History of Archaeological Thought*. Cambridge: Cambridge University Press.

Moving towards the millennium: Will information technology take democracy into the 21st century?

Karin Geiselhart
PhD student, Faculty of Communication,
University of Canberra,
c/o 48 Nangor St, Waramanga ACT 2611, Australia
Email: k.geiselhart@student.canberra.edu.au

Abstract
The impending new millennium offers a rare opportunity to assess the impact that the technological revolution in communication technologies might have on human systems. This essay focuses on their potential role for democratic processes, and the responsibilities for professionals in this field. The economic and political forces shaping the uses of these technologies are outlined.

INTRODUCTION

We are rapidly approaching the turn of the century, and a new millennium. This rare circumstance, which appeals to our particularly human preoccupation with numbers and abstract concepts, will increasingly take up conversational and media space. Like more mundane milestones, it offers an opportunity to look both back and towards the future.

There is no doubt that the world is changing much more rapidly than in the year 999. Most startling to a mediaeval time traveller might be the sheer numbers and extent of human settlement, and our ability to communicate across time and space. What has not changed, perhaps, is that our species is defined by its extremes - an amazing capacity for both creation and destruction.

Will someone looking back on this time, in another century or two, see us as limited by our achievements, too caught up in the dominant paradigms to see the contradictions which bind us? Or will this epochal breakthrough in communication ability, symbolized by our ability to know more and see more

An Ethical Global Information Society J. Berleur & D. Whitehouse (Eds.)

than could ever have been imagined by our ancestors, lead to a new age of harmony and balance?

This essay explores some of the themes outlined in a position paper on culture and democracy prepared by the working group on social accountability in computing (Berleur, this volume), among them the problem of confusion in the midst of knowledge. Here I raise some aspects of responsibility for the path ahead and propose that, many of us here today, and our global community of colleagues in related fields, have the capacity and the duty to direct that path, by focusing on our role as professional communicators, in the fullest sense.

First, I will discuss our current communication tools and factors influencing their structure and control. From there, I argue the need for a normative, global approach. Finally, an outline will be given of how information and communication technology (ICT) professionals can contribute to developing a value-based framework for global ICTs.

KNOWING WHERE WE ARE

The current state of information and communication technologies offers some very good news, which is cause for justified pride. The world is wealthy; neither skill nor cost should prohibit access to the information necessary to achieve almost anything. We can explore the furthest reaches of the universe, and map the codes that create and differentiate life forms. Sending detailed pictures and sound and data around the world is no longer a challenge.

Not just high end scientific and commercial applications benefit from this cornucopia. In the developed countries, many individuals benefit from ready access to information, entertainment, and communication facilities. We keep in touch with friends, talk to distant relatives, see our children reaching out to explore vast oceans electronically. Community networks such as VICNET in Australia help keep citizens informed. Leading projects on electronic democracy in the United States and the United Kingdom encourage citizens to participate in government.

Howard Rheingold's virtual communities seem to fulfil McLuhan's promise of commitment through interactivity.

Clearly, if many cannot take advantage of these wonders, the fault is not with the technologies. As David Lyon has pointed out, it is misleading to talk of the social impact of technology when the technologies are an outcome of existing social and economic structures. There is no point at which society ends and technology begins. On a small scale, examples from studies of computer-mediated communication illustrate this continuum. When email was first introduced to companies, many claims were made for its democratizing effects on organizational structures. By reducing visual and status cues, it was thought to make internal communications less hierarchical and more open. However, it soon became apparent that patterns of email use followed, and were determined by, existing organizational structures.

One hypothesis of my research is that similar technologies combine with similar social structures to create self-organizing fractal patterns of technology use. Problems encountered on one scale will resemble those on other scales. The implication is that we can learn from case studies, and adjust either the technology or the social context to produce the desired outcomes. This assumes, of course, that our concept of desired outcomes is also similar on different scales. This is where a normative framework is necessary, as discussed in the next section.

This audience especially understands the technical structure of ICTs, but we may need to clarify the social, economic and political context which shapes them. This is, partly, the bad news, as there are some dark truths that are seldom highlighted and brought to public attention in the same way as the technical achievements.

The processes of globalization and convergence are not unique to ICTs. Many industries, cultures, and demographics reflect these trends. The spur towards growth has long been a feature of capitalist development, with technological mastery of nature as handmaiden. As Lyon points out, the cultural, military and economic domination of a few highly industrialized nations in Europe and North America extended almost organically to telecommunications and ICTs. Governments geared towards central control and competitive advantage readily turn towards global markets in communications to continue their development.

However, the competitiveness that fostered growth and innovation also encouraged democracy and diversity. This has led to an embarrassment of riches in information, along with internal contradictions and ambiguities. We are now seeing a decline in power for the very nation states whose strength supported the expansion of global industries. We find ourselves not so much lacking in consensus as unable to achieve global public communication beyond the barriers that global control presents. The capitalist parent is eating its child, democracy.

Thus, the collapse of Communist regimes was frequently presented as the end of ideology in the globally structured western press. It could equally have been presented as the end of dialogue about capitalism and social responsibility. Distribution of the world's vast wealth is becoming more concentrated, in a pervasive, global process. It is a fractal outcome of the current self-organizing structures of capital that creates similar process and outcomes on many scales. From it arise many of the contradictions which characterize this period of transition to global control.

On the one hand, we are consistently told of the coming information age, with steady updates and previews of the latest breakthroughs and how they will enhance our lives. On the other, news about the steady advances in the privatization of information and commercialization of ICT pathways is soft-pedalled. This news circulates primarily in the back pages of computer sections in our newspapers or in the self-selected listservs which inform an elite few. The implications of this quiet convergence of control over our communicative futures are not household issues. On smaller scales, workplace implementations of interactive technologies do not generally empower even the professionals most closely associated with them.

The less developed nations may call for a New World Information Order, but only a few in the luckier nations see or speak about the processes that link the disenfranchised everywhere. As with employment, information creates new alliances and patterns of behaviour: some have too much, and are too busy to make sense of it all; others have too little, but lack voices to protest what they are missing.

This subtle transformation of society, not so much because of, but rather with the assistance of ICTs, has been going on longer than most of us realize. It began when the telegraph became the first technology to separate travel from communication. Information flows, unsurprisingly, followed colonial patterns of travel. Today, the development and application of ICTs still reflect not just ownership, but the inherently diverse and turbulent features of the societies that conceived them. This ambiguity of purpose and control is a window of opportunity for those of us who are acutely aware that decisions are being made that will affect many who do not know what is at stake. We are at a crossroads, having realized that competition must give way to collaboration, and growth must acknowledge the need for sustainability.

But the voices calling for new approaches are not the driving forces. They lack power, and are often drowned by the compelling surge of demand which propels the juggernaut of technological advance. Consensus exists, but it is often shallow and ill-informed, oblivious of internal contradictions. Just as classic liberalism helped create representative government but it did not preclude ill treatment of the sick, old or women; likewise, our advances in communication do not of themselves urge on us a concern for those who cannot even eavesdrop on our global conversations. What is missing is a global framework to match the global reach of these developments.

WHAT ARE THE UNIFYING CONCEPTS?

We have demonstrated our ability to bring the world closer and generate wealth through ICTs. Our short-term thinking is very good. Using the same ICTs to reach for broader goals requires a different level of understanding. Again, using the fractal concept, consider Shoshana Zuboff's insightful analysis of the introduction of computerized production. Most managers felt threatened when junior staff gained access to new levels of information. Some took steps to limit understanding and integration of this information to managers. But some realized that their roles, too, had changed, and became more guiding than controlling, more coordinating than deciding. These workplaces tended to integrate the new technologies more effectively. However, these managers were in the minority. On larger scales, the challenge to both industry and government is to make information available, and to use it consciously to clarify and to move towards structures which promote a more balanced dynamic. ICTs are crucial to the creation of 'communicative action', to borrow a term from Habermas - without it there can be no sustainability, social or environmental.

Such action, in turn, requires a value set which transcends economics. Habermas has said that the status of citizenship relies on a kindred background of motives and beliefs that cannot be enforced legally. He recognizes that the legitimacy of the nation-state is not only less appropriate for a globally connected and interdependent world, but that citizens have been reduced to clients by pervasive privatization. Management theorist, Mintzberg, also calls for a return to more normative models of government, reminding us of the crucial differences between citizens, clients, and consumers. McChesney, writing about information policy in the United States, calls for communication scholars and journalists to renew their commitment first and foremost to democratic values, regardless of the corporate consequences. These corporate views now influence university research, as well as media reporting.

A universal charter of democratic rights in cyberspace, such as that developed in the paper for this conference on behalf of the Australian Computer Society (Cameron and Geiselhart, this volume), would articulate these values for ICTs. These rights could eventually assume standing alongside other fundamental rights recognized by the United Nations. To have impact, they would not just be binding on governments, but also on corporations. It would offer a benchmark against which to assess technology proposals, and would act as a recognition of the implicit structures which govern today's world. The fundamental ethical question for ICT professionals is how they can support this process of defining, articulating, and implementing goals to overcome the contradictions of global forces and create meaningful local change.

PLANNING FOR EMPOWERMENT

The previous statement that ICTs cannot of themselves reshape society, but rather that they reflect existing structures, must now be qualified with the element of personal and professional freedom that many of us possess. Within our workplaces, we know what we want and need to function fully and to develop our skills. We seek openness, not just of technical systems, but of pathways to information. On a larger scale, we require our governments and corporations to tell us the truth, to help us make collective decisions free from pressure. For this, we need universal access to the machines, skills, and networks needed to use this information as well as to the content. Increasingly, this information is held by private companies, but it is crucial for public decisions. It must be available, freely, to those who want it. Treaties which seek to privatize information which was previously in the public domain must be challenged. Within the workplace, all decisions relating to the implementation of ICTs must be considered in their political context.

The erosion of social capital cannot be reversed through ICTs, but these technologies can give citizens essential tools for participation and cooperation. There are now many community networks, electronic civic centres and online organizations for electronic democracy: Computer Professionals for Social Responsibility, the Electronic Frontier Foundation, the Benton Foundation, the Electronic Privacy Information Centre, to name just a few. Last year's Internet Society meeting in Montreal, the first to focus on social issues of the Internet, attracted many papers on issues of control and access to the superhighway. Computer professionals are recognizing the importance of the decisions now being made, but are still reluctant to speak out. Government officials, constrained by their formal roles, hesitate to put forward views which may be politically unpopular. Canadian, Peter Heimler, has outlined in familiar detail how hierarchical power structures prevent the implementation of productive information technology systems in the public sector. Politicians, in turn, are notoriously shortsighted, and tend to vanish into obscurity when reckoning is due. Those with influence are often most cautious about pushing an equalizing agenda, and the courageous get no support. Without commitment to clarifying longer-term goals, data systems and information can only be shuffled; they rarely can be called knowledge, and almost never wisdom. As David Lyon points out, wisdom is not a common word any more, and integrity, like other value-laden terms, is interpreted in many postmodern ways.

Models for a democratic global information infrastructure are available. One with that name has been proposed by Vigdor Schreibman. It consists of three interconnected virtual networks funded respectively by public, nonprofit and for profit sources, supported by an authorized use policy which would ensure that use is limited to services which enhance the goals of sustaining democratic government, social equity, and ecological integrity. It would ensure that government information is freely available, and that resources are supplied for collaborative participation in decision-making.

These are the principles which we can apply in our workplaces, and in influencing, in whatever way we can, the development of ICTs. Information relevant to public decisions should be widely accessible, and the process of deciding relevance should itself be open to public debate, with ICT professionals as important contributors. There is a great need to reach beyond our individual specialities to become more broadly informed on issues of privacy, data ownership, universal access, and the implications of new technical proposals for these. We have an obligation to communicate to others who have less understanding about these matters, to build strength by linking together, rather than concentrating on differences.

In conclusion, I cite a quote from Russell Ackoff, Chairman of INTERACT, a firm that facilitates interactive management:

> 'Creative leaps are "discontinuities," qualitative changes. They involve three steps: identification of self-imposed constraints (assumptions); removal of them; and exploring the consequences of their removal. That is why there is always an element of surprise when we are exposed to creative work - it always embodies the denial of something we have taken for granted, usually unconsciously.'

The most significant self-imposed constraint, in relation to the creative and productive use of ICTs for the greatest social good, may well be our own lack of faith in the transformations which are possible. The members of this working group are in a unique position of power, at a unique point in time. Let us work together creatively.

SELECTED REFERENCES

Ackoff, R. (see Schreibman, Victor).

Aikens, S., A History of Minnesota Electronic Democracy, 1994. *Proceedings INET '96*. Annual Conference, Internet Society; Montreal, June, 1996.

Cameron, J. and Geiselhart, K. (this volume) A charter for citizens in the global information society.

Doctor, R., Social Equity and Information Technologies: Moving Toward Information Democracy, *Annual Review of Information Science and Technology (ARIST)* 1992, **27**, 43-95.

Fang, N.-H., *The Internet as a Public Sphere - A Habermasian Approach*, PhD thesis, State University of New York at Buffalo, 1995.

Fulk, J.; Steinfield, C.; Schmitz, J. and Power, G., A social information processing model of media use in organizations, *Communications Research* 1987, **14** (5), 529-552.

Geiselhart, K., Accountability modelling and on-line policy development in the Australian Public Service, *Proceedings INET '96*. Annual Conference, Internet Society; Montreal, June 1996.

Goodfellow, John M., Technology and the Production of Meaning. http://www.wolfenet.com/~jmg/index.html

Habermas, J., Citizenship and National Identity: Some Reflections on the Future of Europe, *Praxis International* 1992, **12**, 1-19.

Ham, C. and Hill, M., *The Policy Process in the Modern Capitalist State*, 2nd Edition; Wheatsheaf Books, Brighton, 1993.

Heimler, P., The Problem of Hierarchy in Government, *1996 International Symposium on Technology and Society, 'Technical Expertise and Public Decisions'*, Princeton, New Jersey, 21-22 June, 1996; IEEE Society.

IEEE Society on Social Implications of Technology. http://www4.ncsu.edu/unity/users/j/jherkert/index.html

Klein, H., Public Access Television and Democratic Empowerment: Lessons for the Internet, *Internet Society Conference: Transforming Society Now*. Montreal, June 1996.

Lyon, D., *The Information Society - Issues and Illusions*. Cambridge, Polity Press, 1988.

Mantovani, G., Is Computer-Mediated Communication Intrinsically Apt to Enhance Democracy in Organizations? *Human Relations* 1994, **47** (1), 45-62.

McChesney, R., The Internet and US Communication Policy-Making in Historical and Critical Perspective, *Journal of Communication* 1996, 98-119.

McLuhan, Marshall, *Understanding Media,* London, Kegan Paul, 1964.

Mintzberg, H., Managing Government - Governing Management, *Harvard Business Review* 1996, 75-83.

Newhagen, J. and Rafaeli, S., Why Communication Researchers Should Study the Internet: A Dialogue, *Journal of Communication* 1996, **46** (1), 4-13.

Peters, G., Contradictions in Public Sector Reform: Reflections on Current Practice, delivered at the *ANU 50th Anniversary Public Lecture Series*, The Australian National University, Canberra, 31 July 1996.

Preissl, Brigitte, Information Technology: A Critical Perspective on its Economic Effects, *Prometheus,* **15** (1), April 1997 (prepublication copy).

Preliminary Report of the Information Management Steering Committee on Information; Management in the Commonwealth Government. *Management of Government Information As a National Strategic Resource*, October 1996. http://www.nla.gov.au/imsc/es.html

Putnam, R., Bowling Alone: America's Declining Social Capital, *Journal of Democracy* 1995, **6** (1), 65-78.
http://muse.jhu.edu/demo/journal_of_democracy/v006/putnam.html

Reinecke, I., Information as a free public good, *Australian Communications and the Public Sphere, Essays in Memory of Bill Bonney*, Edited by Helen Wilson, Macmillan: Sydney and Melbourne, 1989; pp 147-162.

Rheingold, Howard, *The Virtual Community*, Secker and Warburg, London, 1994.

Schreibman, Vigdor: various postings to communet mailing list.

Slade, C., *Regulation and the Public Sphere*, University of Canberra, 1996.

Sproull, L. and Kiesler. S., Reducing social context cues: electronic mail in organizational communication, *Management Science* 1986, 32 (11), 1492-1512

Zuboff, S., *In the Age of the Smart Machine - The Future of Work and Power*, Heinemann Professional Publishing, Oxford, 1988.

Information assets as a platform for economic growth

Ernest Jordan and Janice Burn***
** Macquarie Graduate School of Management, Macquarie University, Sydney, NSW 2109 Australia*
Phone: +61 2 9850 9041; Fax: +61 2 9850 9019
Email: Ernest.Jordan@mq.edu.au
*** Edith Cowan University, Perth, Western Australia*
Email: j.burn@cowan.edu.au

Abstract

The poverty of many third world countries includes the fact that they are poor in information assets. When physical assets are formally recorded they become a negotiable basis for investment, such as in the form of collateral for loans. In this sense, these are increases in information assets. One desperate need in developing countries is for the recognition of formal rights to land. In many societies, land has group ownership without any form of formal title. When properly recorded, this ownership forms the basis of an information asset - whether owned individually or collectively. Land title information systems in the developed world contribute to economic progress by enabling additional investment. The implementation of robust but state-of-the-art land title information systems would form a basis for economic development in the third world.

We further argue that there is a significant role for information technology professionals of the developed world to transfer the knowledge and skills of such, for us, bread-and-butter systems. The transfer does, however, need to be sensitive to the cultural environment of the target country. Suggestions are given about how this may be accomplished.

An Ethical Global Information Society J. Berleur & D. Whitehouse (Eds.)

INTRODUCTION

The contribution of information systems and information technology to an organization are sometimes difficult to measure. Issues of competitive advantage and competitive necessity are widely discussed as are organizational responsiveness and employee productivity. The degree of difficulty of assessing the contribution increases when a community or a nation is considered. It is thus with some risk that we suggest here ways in which the world will benefit from information systems. For a starting point, we are suggesting a win-win scenario with no losers; quite different from the ideas of competitive advantage of organizations or nations, where there are winners and losers. There is the additional perspective here, which is of some concern to the thinking professional, of the responsibility that a professional has to enhancing the community that gives him/her legitimacy.

The developed world, like the Organization for Economic Co-operation and Development (OECD) member countries, has over the last twenty years been investing enormously in information technology and systems built on that technology infrastructure. Proposals for systems are typically justified in advance by cost/benefit analysis or return on investment. After implementation, the systems may be assessed for their efficiency or effectiveness or even simply for meeting the costs and benefits described at initiation. An increasing interest is displayed in the concept of white-collar productivity as a measure of the usefulness or effectiveness of a system. We discuss some of the limitations of this approach and give the case for an increased interest in the concept of the information asset.

Part of the justification for an information system can be its ability to help build an information asset, while the complement is the ability to generate a return on the asset, to put it to productive use. We examine the ability of land title information systems to add wealth to a nation and suggest ways in which the technology for such systems can be transferred to third world nations. We demonstrate a valid contribution to global development that can be made by the information technology and information systems professions.

One may wonder what contribution information technology (IT) could make to a developing economy, when the main emphases of IT are usually cost reduction, reduced employment, and increased productivity. The value of information is more important than the quantity of information. In reality, investments in information technology will only generate improved productivity if this is defined as improved effectiveness in serving internal and external customers (Davis, 1991). We show that the building of information assets is a valuable step in the development of any economy.

INFORMATION ASSET

The term information asset is suggested here as an alternative method of assessing the contribution of information technology to an organization. It will be taken to mean an off balance sheet asset derived from the accumulation of, and power to use, information for the organization's advantage. This is a broad definition that is nevertheless useful.

The nature of information assets

That organizations have information assets can be seen clearly enough through the concern of insurance companies to assess the risk to which they are exposed by the loss of data (Jones, 1993). The literature is overwhelmingly concerned with the safeguarding of an organization's information assets, rather than the need to put these assets to their greatest use or to find ways to increase them (Bacastow and Burns, 1991; Hansen, 1992; Menkus, 1992; Worthen, 1992; Fried, 1993). The term information asset is typically used in such cases to refer to trade secrets, copyright, and patents (Schwartz, 1990), but a wider use is also meaningful (Framel, 1990). The idea of information as an asset derives directly from thinking of information as a resource, an approach that has become widely accepted. Raw inputs to an organization can be seen to be the essential resources of materials, labour, machinery, money, and now information. Information resource management is concerned with the flows of information in organizational processes; that is, it operates at a micro level. Whenever physical resources are stockpiled they are regarded as assets; the same approach is valid for information. Thus a database is an information asset, as would be the organizational programmes and practices that support and use it.

Accountants are familiar with the concept of off balance sheet assets. Brand names and goodwill have been bought and sold, as part and parcel of a business or as assets in their own right. Like goodwill and a brand name, an information asset may need to be drastically revalued if an unforeseen or unfavourable event occurs. If information is found to be systematically incorrect, out-of-date or unreliable, the value of the asset must be written down. On the other hand, writing up the value of an information asset may well be strongly resisted. There can be an attitude that the only news is bad news. Knowing that your organization has a superior information asset to its competitors gives managers a good feeling but accepting that it is an asset, on a par with a brand name or goodwill, is often difficult (Elliott and Jacobson, 1991). At the micro level, it is easier to accept the value of information when, for instance, sales representatives are recruited because of their networks of contacts - their information assets - and will be expected to enhance them.

An organization, such as the freight company DHL, has established an information asset that is valuable. This may not show in the balance sheet but, in some circumstances, it is a more valuable business concept than productivity. The information asset may reveal itself in the price at the stock exchange. A company with rich information assets can attract a high premium on its earnings performance. Sony's purchase of entertainment archives led the way in establishing new, even higher, premiums. If resources can be accumulated and owned, then they become assets. At that point, they must then perform, that is, enable the owner to generate profits. While this is clearly true for organizations, it is also true for governments (Davies, 1992).

Measuring the effectiveness of information systems

The contribution of an information asset to a business is twofold. First, if it is an asset then its place near the balance sheet demonstrates to the stakeholders the value of information. This is, however, very dangerous to declare explicitly. It is similar to goodwill or the value of a brand name. Both of these can disappear in a short time if goodwill becomes bad will or a brand name is exposed to negative publicity. In the same way, an organization's information asset may become inaccurate, out-of-date, unreliable or simply inferior to that of another organization. In some cases it may even be copied. It then needs to be written off just as a bank writes off bad loans (it will perhaps be done just as reluctantly). Second, the asset may generate income, profit or benefit. In this sense an asset needs to be assessed by return on investment. If it is an asset, it should produce profit. If the profit is not up to requirements then the asset may be sold, activated, downgraded or whatever.

The latter aspect is that which is referred to in leveraging the asset (Ulrich, 1990). Putting an asset to work, generating income and profits, enabling more effective competition or simply, allowing an organization to survive while competitors fail, all these are potential benefits of the information asset to an organization.

Leveraging the asset - putting it into practice

The first step has to be awareness, to make the whole organization aware of the information assets that it has and their value to the organization. This is essential in order that maintenance of its accuracy and integrity is seen as a priority. The information asset can disappear rapidly if it is unreliable. There is an increasing awareness in many organizations of the value of their information assets, such as in banks, media and entertainment organizations, travel, insurance, and related industries. The next step is to look for ways of leveraging that information. Clemons (1986) showed that sustainable competitive advantage can reliably be obtained from resources that others could not duplicate. This is most apparent in the information asset. Intimate knowledge of customers, products and transactions can be put to work through creative service development, adding support of innovation to the corporate culture and facilitating try-outs of new ideas.

While we have concentrated on organizations that are rich in information and that have a considerable information asset, there are many organizations and even countries that lack such resources. A first step in the development of such organizations can be the systematic evolution of an information asset.

LAND TITLE SYSTEMS

Land is an asset that is recognized throughout the world. In developed countries, the ability to secure formal title to land is something that we take for granted. Such titles have existed in some communities for centuries and are an inherent part of our capital and asset base. Land title systems are typically small-scale systems developed by city, province or state administrations (rather than national ones).

They record the current owner of the land, its physical location, and any financial restraints on it, such as mortgages. In a world of high-volume, real-time transaction processing, they are not regarded as glamorous systems but very much as the bread-and-butter of local administration.

Market economy and property economy

In a penetrating and illuminating article, Hernando de Soto (1993) exposes the potential for economic development that formal title to land creates. While many politicians and economists claim that a market economy is the key to development, de Soto reveals that even with an effective market in place there is no guarantee of prosperity. In his nation, Peru, gold has been traded for centuries without building great wealth while, in the London Metal Exchange, gold futures may be traded profitably because the market place has been expanded. There is a quantum leap between selling gold nuggets and gold futures. It is this distinction that separates the market and the property economies.

Property economies recognize property rights in assets - land, gold, companies, income streams - and thereby allow instruments to be created to facilitate trade in those rights. For each asset, there is a multiplier effect as the rights generate other assets, for which new rights may be recognized. De Soto traces the most significant developments in the prosperity of nations to the creation of property rights that are formally recorded.

Land title and its uses

A formal recognition of land title shows the location, boundaries, owners and their rights. The *traditional* owner of land then becomes the *rightful* owner of land. This enables loans to be secured. Banks and others will have collateral so that default on repayments is not a complete write-off. Furthermore, there is the potential of the owner to put the asset to work. Although the traditional owner may work the land and produce income from it, there is little incentive to improve the land or to develop the property. On the other hand, an owner with title can invest in the property and multiply the value of the assets. The formal land title thus immediately enhances the asset value of the land. It is the beginning of the creation of wealth. Once the squatter becomes the rightful owner there is the incentive to maintain, invest, and develop. Their view becomes long-term, as when the squatter farmers of Australia in the nineteenth century, after their title became secure, planted trees that would take a hundred years to mature.

Of course, a major impediment to land title and land title systems is an ineffective legal system or structure. Many countries are not accustomed to the rule of law and others have legal institutions that are the playthings of the rich or powerful. Legal aspects are outside the concern of this paper, although in any realistic implementation the role of lawyers and legal institutions is primary. Information systems support and build on these legal rights, and enable the *real* asset to become in addition an *information* asset.

An additional impediment in many countries is the lack of formal maps recording land and its boundaries. The need for survey work and adjudication of rightful ownership are then paramount.

Effects of implementation of land title systems

Land title systems in the developed world today enable administrators, developers, financiers, and owners to carry out transactions at low cost. The transaction cost view of information systems (Ciborra and Olson, 1989) simplifies the analysis of the value of information systems. Without an efficient and effective system there is a high cost of performing transactions such as the examination of rightful title, the querying of boundaries, the collection of land taxes, and so on. This transaction cost acts as a disincentive to the operation of markets. With low transaction costs all of the stakeholders can get on with their core or principal activities rather than spending inordinate amounts of time and money in establishing simple data.

AN AGENDA FOR THE IT INDUSTRY

We now suggest that the IT industry collectively has the opportunity to develop a social contribution agenda. Here the term IT industry is used in a wide sense, particularly to include information systems practitioners. It is also used internationally, to include people and organizations in all the developed world. Many national associations of professionals are affiliated to the International Federation for Information Processing (IFIP) that serves as an umbrella organization for conferences and publications. Members of the American Association for Computing Machinery (ACM), Australian Computer Society (ACS), and others are automatically covered by IFIP. It is to such an audience that this section is addressed.

State of the art

We members of the professional associations in the developed world have the state of the art in IT. We create it and put it into effect. Today's state of the art, even yesterday's, is already adequate to meet the needs of the third world in this area. Personal computers are used effectively in Canada, the United Kingdom, and elsewhere to run land title systems (Fedorko, 1993). The simple local area networks that have been in use for the last five years are quite robust and, to a great extent, debugged. Client server approaches to land title establish databases in a central office that are processed by user workstations in diverse, distributed locations (Morse, 1990; Collicott, 1992).

The experience of the Australian company BHP, now 13 years into a 20-year project in Thailand, suggests that the project management skills to implement an effective manual system may be adequate without computerization (Burns, 1993; Burns *et al.*, 1996).

In the developed countries of the world, source data for the land title systems were manually maintained records, established decades or even centuries ago. These systems are seldom considered remarkable, except when quantum improvements are made such as with the new, open access, system implemented in London (Coltman, 1991; Baker, 1992). Our state of the art in land information systems is now way beyond simply recording ownership. It involves satellite monitoring of physical and environmental conditions, land utilization, and more precise measurement (Welborn, Wagner and Weber, 1990; Dueker and DeLacy, 1990; Forrest, 1991). Recreational sailors are able to monitor their position on the earth's surface to within an accuracy of 50 metres, using an affordable, reliable device. The technology is all here. What is needed is the will, skill, and ingenuity to transfer it. We do not wish to minimize legislative problems and the difficulty of deciding on rightful owners. These are indeed major hurdles, but information systems will help once these implementation tasks are completed.

Technology transfer

It is a commonplace to remark that third world countries have played technology leapfrog, where an entire generation of technology is skipped as the following one is implemented. India proceeded directly to satellite communication systems without first installing cable over the whole country. South American countries have airlines operating to remote regions that are not served by roads. Many developing nation families move directly to television communications without first using radio, or have telephones before newspapers.

We are suggesting here that third world countries can move directly to computerized land title information systems. Qualified agents include IFIP and ACM, and appropriate channels include the World Bank, United Nations agencies and government agencies such as AusAID and USAID. IFIP, ACM, ACS, the British Computer Society (BCS), and others can provide the skills, knowledge, and access to professionals.

The effects in Thailand have been dramatic, with many land transfer transactions taking place and wealth being developed (Burns *et al.*, 1996). Not all projects have been as successful; there are many barriers to success, but success is attainable. Land owners around the third world, with title to their traditional properties will be able to invest, to develop, and to make the land productive. When they borrow money from banks, the banks' own development can continue, and the economic wheels can start to spin. The creation of an information asset can enable this. Productivity with information is of little value to the developing countries where labour costs are generally low. The metaphor for productivity is multiplication but, for asset creation, the metaphor is addition. Productivity increases multiply the small output but it remains small in world terms; asset creation adds wealth. Productivity comes next.

Professionalism and empowerment

The information technology industry has enabled business organizations to change their nature dramatically. The connections to the customer are now much closer, the awareness that organizations are interdependent has grown, and the average worker is more involved in the day-to-day business activity of the organization. The potential for empowerment of workers has been realized to only a limited extent. There has always been the ominous idea that if the system users become too knowledgeable, then our position as experts is under threat. In reality, the users are usually more interested in doing their own job than in taking over those of the systems' professionals.

An extension of this argument applies to the development of skills and knowledge in other countries: if developing countries need information technology, let us go there, sell it to them, and look after it for them. That will establish a new market for our products and services that will add to the bottom line. What is needed instead is the development of professional skills or even just good end user skills in the developing countries. Let us help develop a new generation of professionals around the world, in the same way that the Orbis flying eye hospital travels around the developing nations, passing on skills to the local professionals. We do not need to keep this to ourselves, we can empower. This is true professionalism.

CONCLUSIONS

We have demonstrated the potential for the information technology profession to contribute to the development of the global economy, especially in the third world. International cooperative efforts could help establish land title information systems in developing countries. The injection of technology alone is inadequate; it is essential that there is a simultaneous programme for developing local personnel to support and maintain the systems. It is here that the most significant role is to be found for the information technology professional the training and support of beginning professionals in the target countries.

The effect of creating formal title to traditional lands will be to establish assets for the owners that will create a multiplier effect in the local economies. The information asset recorded in the formal title can be the starting point of a wave of economic development that is beneficial to all. The traditional emphasis of aid to the developing countries has been to assist in food production, health programmes, and infrastructure development. The information resource is one that we, in the rich world, have only recently begun to appreciate. It is one that is needed throughout the world.

REFERENCES

Bacastow, S. and Burns, R. P. (1991). Protecting the banks information asset. *Bank Management*, **67** (4), 44-45.

Baker, M. (1992, September). HM Land Registry - a new approach. *Credit Management*, 31-32.

Burns, A.F. (1993). Land Titling - the big picture paper presented at the Land Titling and Land Administration Regional Workshop, Bali, November 11-12.

Burns, A.F., Eddington, R., Grant, C. and Lloyd, I. (1996). Land Titling in Asia paper presented at the International Conference on Land Tenure and Administration, Orlando, Florida, November 11-14.

Ciborra, C. U. and Olson, M. H. (1989). Encountering electronic work groups: A transaction costs perspective. *Office Technology & People*, **4**, 285-298.

Clemons, E. K. (1986). Information systems for sustainable competitive advantage. *Information & Management*, **11**, 131-136.

Collicott, G. (1992). Top man at BC systems. *Canadian Datasystems*, **24** (4), 36, 38.

Coltman, L. (1991, March). Land registry opens up. *Credit Management*, 42-43.

Davies, K. (1992). Information management in the 90s. *Australian Accountant*, **62** (5), 45-48.

Davis, T. R. (1991). Information technology and white-collar productivity. *Academy of Management Executive*, **5** (1), 55-67.

de Soto, H. (1993, September 11-17). The missing ingredient. *The Economist* [Supplement The Future Surveyed], **328**, 8-12.
Dueker, K. J. and DeLacy, P. B. (1990). GIS in the land development planning process: Balancing the needs of land use planners and real estate developers. *Journal of the American Planning Association*, **56**, 483-491.
Elliott, R. K. and Jacobson, P. D. (1991). U.S. accounting: A national emergency. *Journal of Accountancy*, **172** (5), 54-58.
Fedorko, C. (1993). Easier access to databases, results in greater usage, higher profits. *Computing Canada*, 19 (4), 41, 46.
Forrest, D. (1991). Geomatics needs cooperation. *Computing Canada*, **17** (1), 17.
Framel, J. E. (1990). Managing information costs and technologies as assets. *Journal of Systems Management*, **41** (2), 12-18.
Fried, L. (1993). Distributed information security: Responsibility assignments and costs. *Information Systems Management*, **10** (3), 56-65.
Hansen, M. (1992). Counter-espionage techniques that work. *Security Management*, **36** (9), 44-52.
Jones, D. C. (1993). Computer advances create new data theft exposures. *National Underwriter (PCE)*, **97** (24), 2, 7.
Menkus, B. (1992). Introduction to computer security. *Computers & Security*, **11** (2), 121-127.
Morse, P. (1990). Metro to decentralise LIS. *ComputerData*, **15** (2), 1-2.
Schwartz, M. (1990). Computer security: planning to protect corporate assets. *Journal of Business Strategy*, **11**, 38-41.
Ulrich, W. M. (1990). CASE: Full life-cycle tools from ugly legacies to artistic beauties. *Software Magazine*, **10** (15), 33-45.
Welborn, H., Wagner, J., and Weber, D. (1990). Trends in choosing a geographic information system. *Engineering & Management*, **137** (11), 20-23.
Worthen, J. D. (1992). Protecting LAN-based information assets. *Telecommunications*, **26** (10), 22-24.

10

Technology, economic development, and sustainability: The case of Latin America

Jorge Martínez-Contreras, Raúl Gutiérrez-Lombardo** and Marcela Lombardo-Otero***
** UAM-Iztapalapa, Mexico*
Phone: +52 5 724 47 85, Fax: +52 5 612 56 82
Email: jmc@xanum.uam.mx
*** CEFPSVLT, SEP, Mexico*
Phone: +52 5 661 4987, Fax: +52 5 661 17 87
Email: lombardo@servidor.dgsca.unam.mx

Abstract

This contribution is divided in three parts. The first draws attention to the problem of the new global order and the complex realities lived in the many diverse countries of Latin America. The second part analyzes the problem of identities and culture. We try to answer two fundamental questions: 1) How the question of cultural identity and problems concerning resistance and integration in Latin America arise in the framework of the neo-liberal model? 2) What is the role of the media in the current redefining of new identities and new cultural borders? The third part of the paper refers to the problems of globalization and sustainable growth in the modernity-postmodernity debate in Latin America. In particular, we analyze the preservation and/or conservation ecological question.

THE NEW GLOBAL ORDER

There are numerous authors who agree in asserting that the information revolution which occurred in the last decades and the globalization of the economy are phenomena that are perceived as proofs of the emerging of a seemingly definitive age. This era will be characterized by a homogenization of human societies all over the world, by an increasingly strong embracing of western ways (while peoples

An Ethical Global Information Society J. Berleur & D. Whitehouse (Eds.)

throughout the face of the globe give up old traditions, customs, and heritage) and, more generally, by a disappearance of local cultures. From here on, claims Francis Fukuyama, in his essay on the end of the history, 'everything will be more or less the same, no alternatives to the actual world will exist'[1].

This assertion, as Edgar Samuel Morales pointed out, presupposes that the actual world, the one that really deserves to be called actual, is that of the United States whose citizenship Fukuyama bears. Or maybe it is the world of airports, freeways and malls that follow the American fashion for the urban-suburban in the main European metropoles, some Asian cities, and even a few capital cities in Latin America. They all undeniably resemble each other. The world is constituted, so Fukuyama says, by all those social spaces where the market economy has an absolute rule: those places where a large share of the population sports western-style clothes and where people have access to technological products from the information industry. Thus, Fukayama claims, the world will be like a big global village[2].

Nevertheless, assertions like Fukuyama's stand in absolute contrast to the social, economic and political relations produced in every corner of the world, especially those complex realities lived in the many diverse countries of Latin America. In fact, these suppositions take for granted that, in the west, there is a sort of continuum where everything is free competition, equal access to consumption, homogeneous thinking, and material culture. Now, we all know that, contrary to the above fantasy, in western countries there are strong social disparities and strong economic contrasts between the different social groups in the various populations that arise not just from the fact that these countries have been formed by several strikingly different local groups but also because they have been forced to integrate large masses of population that came from faraway places. Immigrants are a part of their social landscapes[3].

We must not forget that the highly praised globalization of the economy is just the expansion of the most powerful transnational companies. The beneficiaries of the wide circulation of Asian, European and North American commodities are mostly countryless, ill-defined corporations with no clear origins. These financial entities switch their capital from one country to another, causing false economic booms and national bankruptcies in just a few days. In Latin America, the cases of Mexico, Argentina, and Venezuela exemplify pretty well the nasty doings of these fuzzy organisms, which are sometimes linked to obscure interests that set governments and sovereignties at bay. Furthermore, we should point out that there are strong inequalities as a result of the very access to the now-globalized markets. There is no fair and equal opportunity access for all companies. It is a well-known fact that in very specific domestic markets there are always companies that receive favours, preferences, subsidies, and even monopoly entitlements from governments that support so-called neo-liberalism. In addition, we should state that the transnational companies' Big Bang did not happen by fortuitous or miraculous circumstances. Nor did it happen by spontaneous generation. Actually, it had its origins in the centuries-old technological domain which favoured those countries that had previously engaged in conquest wars that endowed them with lands and markets. Another advantage for these countries came from the domination and colonization imposed on peoples of a traditional kind and the ransacking of natural resources in lands subjugated by colonialism. The globalization of the economy, such as it is currently practiced, is nothing but the expansion of large industrial and commercial companies and their technologies that, when applied in their own original countries, ruined micro, small and middle-sized entrepreneurs by forcing them into bankruptcy in an atmosphere of unfair competition. One incentive behind globalization is that big transnational companies move away from their original countries when their workers demand better labour conditions and higher wages, and establish themselves in countries where labour is ten times or more cheaper in spite of initial training expenses. Such deeds cause a continuous loss of hundreds and thousands of jobs even in highly developed countries[4].

The above point is closely tied to the theory proposed by the authors of the report of the Trilateral Commission. This theory, described by Lorenzo Córdova as a consequence of the end of the postwar economic boom, fostered ferocious and harsh criticism of the social regime and democratic achievements entailed in the welfare state of the so-called neo-liberals. Thus, the welfare state was charged with responsibility for the political and economic crises that flooded capitalist countries, especially the United States, in the 1970s.

Aiming to propose feasible solutions to face both the underlying economic recession and the diminished credibility of their political structures and the opposition to them, the First World countries in Europe, America and Asia appointed a task group called the Trilateral Commission. This committee was commanded to do research on the causes that had triggered the crisis. The results of the analysis made by Professors Michael Crozier, Samuel P. Huntington and Joji Watanuki were summarized in the paper, *The Crisis of Democracy: Report on the Governability of Democracies to the Trilateral Commission.*

In the report, the authors reach the generic conclusion that the excess of democracy which characterized the welfare state had generated a situation of ungovernability that could not be solved unless there was a reduction in the social and democratic achievements obtained by means of welfare state policies[5].

Crozier, Huntington and Watanuki imputed the welfare state with the following four charges: a) a delegitimation of authority and mistrust of the rulers' leadership (problems with basic elements of every society; in the authors' view, these troubles were caused by the pursuit of the democratic virtues of individual equality and freedom); b) an overloading of state structures caused by the inefficiency of government aimed at the spread of democracy as a result of political participation, by an uneven increase in government activities, and by an exacerbation of the inflationary tendencies in the economy; and c) intensified political competition. This competition can be considered as a foundation of democratic states but disrupts interests and causes political parties to fracture if it grows uncontrolled. Out-of-hand intensified political competition causes phenomena such as 'ill-pluripartisanism', like that which has characterized Italy's political life where major decisions are not taken by big political parties but are made instead by small political parties. Under these circumstances, small political parties become fundamental elements in the formation of congressional majorities. In this sense, the authors point out, democracies can only be handled on the grounds of consent but they are very hard, if not impossible, to reach in the complex multiparty regimes that define most contemporary democratic societies. Finally, d) there is a parochialism that democratic tendencies in the welfare state have generated in international structures.

Among the features pointed out by the authors of the report, there are two that are most often quoted by neo-liberal writers, namely, the second one (the overloading thesis) and the third one (the exaggerated vitality of the democratic multiparty system)[6].

Accordingly, José Fernández has called attention to the fact that, in the face of governability crises caused by overloading and by state intervention in the economy, neo-liberals have tried to substitute interventionist strategies using privatization as a first remedy. That is, they allow the market to retain its own dynamics without the obstacle of state intervention. A second remedy aimed at diminishing the overload of demands plainly means diminishing democracy[7].

Something similar happens in the so-called technological revolution. There have been huge advances in telecommunications, means of transportation, and especially in informatics, that allow a vertiginous flow of human groups, ideas, fashions, information, and so forth. But this situation has caused several problems. First, not even in the most developed countries does everyone have easy access to advances in informatics or cybernetics. It is true that technological innovations will continue to originate particularly in highly developed countries and it is also true that research on these matters will keep on developing mostly there, but there is no guarantee that people in those countries will have an equal right to goods produced by technological advances. On the other hand, the development of informatics and robotics has given rise to the so-called post-industrial era which, in itself, is turning into a source of unemployment for thousands of workers whose services are rendered unnecessary day after day[8].

This new industrial revolution, the high tech revolution, as it is often called, has had adverse effects on large masses of humankind and severe repercussions on people's development and standards of living.

Once high technology was introduced into the large transnational monopolies, their production rose in an extraordinary way, thus multiplying their power. But, given the magnitude of their production, the combined markets of their own countries and influence zones became insufficient and were rather restricted in fully consuming it. Hence, big monopolies needed to transform the whole earth into a single market. So they needed trade to open up in every country and free trade to be set up. This is how the globalization theory got started.

Globalization is defined as a new productive process on a world scale. Production, technology and commercialization are linked in world-integrated chains of added value. This fact demands liberalization of trade, capital, services, and technology. In turn, the neo-liberal doctrine fulfils its role by introducing reforms inside countries. In this way, state participation in production and services is suppressed and there is a growing tendency to eliminate regulations and controls in the whole area of production. In the first instance, this proceeds to the privatization of public companies with the aim of shifting power from the hands of the state to those of private enterprises.

It is important to take into account the fact that, to compete successfully in the globalizing process, a sound capacity of industrial development and high technology is required. That is why, according to United Nations' reports, ever since this policy was propelled forward at a world level, the main countries that have reinvigorated their industrial development are the United States, Japan and some European powers. On the other hand, the production capacities in those industrialized countries also reached a high rate of concentration when high tech electronic equipment for productive processes is taken into account.

In the above mentioned industrialized countries are concentrated 82.3% of the world's total production capacities, while the rest of the countries, with a heavy leaning towards China and the newly industrialized Asian countries, share only 17.7%. In Latin America is concentrated only 4.8%.

In just ten years' existence of the new world order based on economic globalization and neo-liberalism, this deeply unfair disproportion of the world's distribution of development and industrial capacity has had consequences that could not be more disturbing and severe. Here are some facts:

1. They have broken social cohesion, thus aggravating poverty and unemployment. Not even highly industrialized countries like Germany and the United States have escaped from high unemployment rates but, in the underdeveloped countries, the effects have been stronger.
2. They have concentrated the world's wealth to an utterly monstrous point. Of course, the existence of high concentration rates that benefit a minority can be observed; this is generally associated with large transnational monopolies.

According to data registered with the help of the GINI coefficient technique, we can see that, between the years of 1960 and 1989, there was an increase in inequality between the richest and the poorest countries. That is reflected in a change in this coefficient from 0.44 to 0.55 (the higher the coefficient, the higher the inequality).

Also, inequality has grown as measured in terms of deciles (tenths of the total population). That is, if we take the 20 percent richest and the 20 percent poorest of the population, we find a disparity that grew from 11.1 to 17.1 in the same period.

The 1996 World Report of the United Nations for Industrial Development states that it is possible to foresee that world inequality will grow as a consequence of the globalization process.

IDENTITY AND CULTURAL RESISTANCE

Other writers agree with the thesis that one of the most controversial consequences of the neo-liberal expansion is the awakening of identities. The decade of the 1970s was marked by the abandonment of social classes while the 1980s placed stress on social actors' theories. The big concern of the current decade is a discussion about national, social, and cultural identities.

In order to analyze identity and resistance in Latin America, Marià Nazareth Ferreira states some preliminary remarks[9]. There are two questions that are necessary to locate the problem, namely: 1) How does the question of cultural identity and problems concerning resistance and integration in Latin America arise in the framework of the neo-liberal model? and 2) What is the role of the media in the current transformation that is redefining new identities and new cultural borders?

To answer these questions, it will be necessary to refer to the recent transformations that the world is undergoing, among them, new ways of establishing third world countries in the world economy by means of schemes imposed by neo-liberalism[10].

Defenders of neo-liberal doctrines have characterized the 1980s' decade as lost. However, from the point of view of self-knowledge, it was only during the past fifteen years that Latin America got rid of several simplistic theories that harmed a realistic self-view. A realistic self-view has several advantages over others, namely, it is founded on actual Latin American problems and is developed by domestic intellectuals and scientists. These specialists have been able to reevaluate and overcome old concepts and dichotomies, allowing them to think both about the new geopolitical realities and to understand questions such as those proposed above[11].

Integrated in a downward fashion ever since the time of the discoveries, Latin America today is living under a new form of integration. Nowadays, the integrationist discourse acts by means of a neo-liberal model: the homogenization of markets, culture, and consumption. Participation of the media is required in the formation of consent needed for the acceptance of such a discourse[12].

An avalanche of arguments, laws, agreements, and other figures is directed towards consent, setting up a political and economic scheme that has been moulded from outside. Ulloa[13] refers to this universe as the integration rhetoric, which is constituted by discourses expressed from different positions, that seeks to legitimize the neo-liberal model by creating favourable public opinion and by forming subtle ways of embracing neo-liberal ideas in different parts of society. These rhetorical statements are transcribed and spread by the media. They echo the International Monetary Fund's mermaid songs in attempting to define globally our economic destinies in the twenty-first century.

Changes on the road to globalization, proposed by a new phase in monopolistic accumulation of international capital, have brought harsh consequences for cultural matters, insofar as these are suffering from an unprecedented transnationalization process never before experienced in history. The expansion of cultural industries, the appropriation and privatization of the media, the expansion and homogenization of information networks, the weakening of the nation-state and the blurring of the distinction between public and private are deemed necessary conditions to warrant efficiency and rationality in the markets[14].

Marià Nazareth Ferreira has pointed out that the most important feature is the internationalization of cultural industries which, joined by internationalization of other parts of the economy, is strongly interfering with cultures in every corner of the world by several means, and looking forward to homogenizing cultural goods and markets of symbolic items of every kind.

Thus, the crucial question refers to the system of information and communication. The expression of new technologies related to information illustrates the strategic place of the communication system in the neo-liberal new order, as long as it is no longer a state-run public entity but a commodity that follows market laws[15].

In this sense, the system of communication and information becomes a reproducer of the dominant culture on a world scale, reproducing the system as a whole. Homogenization of cultural items, markets, tastes, and consumption is one of the most significant tasks of this new communication order. Still, social movements and cultural processes that resist the drive to homogenization arise, due to the peculiar nature of these dominating forms that are expressed through an uneven development. Beginning with these resistances, it is possible to evaluate the existence of essential constituents of cultural identities[16].

If the concept of identity, whether national or cultural, started from factors such as land, race, language, and religion, it will be necessary to evaluate how these ingredients have transformed their representations during the past decades. We will need to reset the relationship between the unity and the diversity of ethnic groups, knowledges, lands, and languages, in order to understand and interpret the conformity of new identities (cultural, regional, national, and transnational) in which new sectors of society recognize themselves, and to analyze new symbols and identity models that emerge in different contexts as a result of an unfair match between tradition and modernity and between primitive and postmodern in *mestizo* America[17].

From these considerations, we draw at least one conclusion: there is not a single, unified identity and culture in Latin America but several identities and several cultures: just like all the countries that form it, Latin America is pluricultural[18].

Particularly in relation to the media, one of the effects that have been produced in folk cultures is that all direct forms of social interaction are substituted by mediated forms of a wider communication system, where the new forms constitute a foreign or distant element of that reality. Symbolic markets are reorganized in a fashion that runs contrary to tradition. Traditional folk cultures are reconstituted in accordance with this view. There is a massification of consumption patterns and new industrial techniques are introduced with regard to the production of commodities[19].

Hence, massification does not eliminate traditional cultures but changes them in a substantial way that diminishes their meaning in everyday life. A contradictory position can be seen with regard to the Latin American masses, even under the conditions of fragmentation and multiplicity that characterize Latin American reality. This position tries to gain recognition while attempting to be distinguished as different from other groups in society. But, at the same time, as groups are trying to assimilate into society as a whole, they are trying to develop a sense of belonging. One of the ways that make these processes of self-acknowledgment and self-esteem possible is through everyday life, from a daily construction drawn from experiences, memories, and consciousness of the present, including all its rights and wrongs. 'A whole deal of folk culture has been repression, machismo, an authoritarian way that has been preserved with diverse excuses, hollow rituals, but also a fair share of these cultures has been folk culture, imagination, creativity. Thus, the history of Latin America is also the history of the masses' culture'[20].

GLOBALIZATION AND SUSTAINABLE GROWTH.

Rigoberto Lanz[21]. maintains that, in Latin America, there has been an ongoing, lively debate that unveils some tracks. This debate has likenesses and differences with its European post-capitalistic counterpart. The Latin American debate shows a certain resistance, both attitudinal and theoretical, to assuming all the implications of the modernity-postmodernity debate.

Today, the fuzzy times of crisis have transmuted the language of imperialism, class struggle, national liberation, bourgeois democracy, new man, and dependence into more civilized keywords such as governability, sustainable growth, full democracy, integration, and new economic order. Modern friends, says Lanz, would like to find some ontological ground in identity to refill the void of the portable, fleeting, and ephemeral concept of Latin America. In the face of the theological triad of market, technology, and democracy, contemporary thought in Latin America refers back to Habermas' statement, 'everything within the bounds of the rule of the law'[22].

There is a common background shared by all defenders of modernity: 1) a collective allergy to every sort of irrationalism; 2) a suspicious, epistemic amnesia regarding the hot issue of power; 3) a discreet retreat away from social change topics, now transmuted into governability; 4) a submissive attachment to an Enlightenment *minima moralia* for cloudy times; 5) an unrestrained acritical bent towards technological logic; 6) a marked tendency to empty the crucial debate on democracy of its substantive contents; and 7) an evident difficulty in thinking about economy apart from market terrorism[23].

On the side of postmodern thought, it is possible to track a backdrop that communicates theoretical developments from different writers. In their common background, there is an easily distinguishable screen that reflect some signals: 1) the rise of a new sensitivity that is expressed in every discursive fold of social practices; 2) the deconstructivist dismantling of the main rational pivots of modernity; 3) a strong bent for relativism in all fields; 4) a substantial regaining of multiculturalism; 5) an acrimonious impeachment of every form of centrality, totalism, and hierarchy; 6) the rise of a new vision and sensitivity that keeps its distance from dominating rationality; and 7) a minimalist ethics founded on a new sociality[24].

What is the shared feature of the common background of Latin American postmodernism? Lanz believes that certain provisional characteristics can be singled out, namely: 1) a harsh questioning of tropical "picturesquism" that has been hiding behind the mask of patriotism, naive indigenism, and the several variants of a traumatic identity theory; 2) a breaking away from the dominant epistemological paradigms that have prevailed in academic culture; 3) a huge effort to reinterpret the very concept of Latin America beginning from the theoretical tension generated inside the modes of cultural configuration; 4) a constructive regaining of the anthropologically hybrid character of the area in the face of the inexorable techno-cultural processes of globalization; 5) a full questioning of the traditional agenda of ecology that focuses on technical rationality and the unfeasibility of the reigning "ecopredator" model; 6) a questioning of the development culture so as to start lifting the ideological veil of the different discourses at stake; and 7) a criticism of the neo-conservative instrumentation of postmodern thought[25].

When the ecological question is focused under this view or under what is now called sustainable growth, we cannot help understanding it as part of a crisis that radically questions those values in the western tradition that, ever since the Bible, have held that the world was created for the exclusive benefit of human beings. This crisis also questions, in a particular way, principles and values of the Enlightenment. The Enlightenment valued to the highest degree instrumental rationalism, which held as a paradigmatic principle that progress joined by advances in technology will benefit and change mankind. Such values were never questioned in the nineteenth-century utopias proposed by Hegel, Marx, Engels, Comte, and others in their positivistic and socialist revisions.

With regard to nature, the Enlightenment hoped to apply the scientific revolution of the seventeenth-century. Nature should be tamed for the benefit of men, and purged of noxious or non-productive species. Nature had to be transformed, for man's benefit, into a garden where only useful or beautiful and not-so-dangerous plants and domestic animals existed. Thus, the great philosopher Locke said: 'Land that is left wholly to nature ... is called, as indeed it is, waste.'

Buffon went further in proposing a statement that could be adopted by all destroyers of ecosystems and all land developers as a justification for their actions: 'La Nature brute est hideuse et mourante; c'est Moi, Moi seul qui peut la rendre agréable et vivante: desséchons ces marais, anomons ces eaux mortes en les faisant couler (...) mettons le feu à cette bourre superflue, à ces vieilles forets déjà demi consommées; achevons de détruire avec le fer ce que le feu n'aura pu consommer: bientôt, au lieu du jonc, des nénuphars, dont le crapaud composait son venin, nous verrons paraître la renoncule, le trèfle (...), des troupeaux d'animaux bondissants fouleront cette terre jadis impraticable ...'

We have lost, perhaps for the planet's future benefit, certainties, beliefs, and utopias about the domesticity of the earth. Many thinkers have attributed the origin of many of our cultural evils to the end of teleological utopias. On the contrary, we believe that utopias lead us into believing the existence of those non-existent places, those 'no places' that Moro, who coined the term, told us about.

Nevertheless, there do not seem to exist clear options to instrumental rationalism and to the belief that a continuously supported growth that can be sustained in nature are the only solutions to ease the material evils suffered by the majority of humanity.

In Mexico, talk of sustainability is omnipresent in politics, culture, and especially in fashionable economic theories that attempt to justify the kind of economic development that some are trying to impose on our country. Sustainability has become an ingredient in official speeches as well as in speeches in so-called civil society. But this is just a theoretical advance at best, since the very condition of the national ecosystem shows that Brundtland's formula has not worked in Mexico. The alleged improvement in material conditions for mankind has brought a larger and faster destruction of ecosystems; it has not really improved the living standards of society in general. Pollution in big cities is out of control even when official speeches claim that it can be managed within twenty or thirty years. Desertification of farmlands, destruction of ecosystems, and the irreparable loss of biodiversity are out of real control. On top of this, the Catholic church in Mexico is still encouraging unrestrained demographic growth. This population growth will, by itself, prevent any attempt at sustainable growth.

Hence, we think that the acknowledgment of this problem in political discourse is a useful step because it has opened up a debate on this reality. But the fundamental step, the enactment of protective laws and their strict enforcement, still faces an uncertain future.

Our cultural heritage stems from admiring the beauty of the Parthenon but also from realizing that such a monument was built at the expense of deforesting a whole mountain. This urbanization process, that has been going on for only ten thousand years, a tiny interval in biological terms, has joined with the processes of agriculture and animal, powered to a point of endangering the existence of biodiversity on our planet.

What solutions can be offered? There is no sustainable growth without preservation and conservation. These two concepts are different and opposed. Preserving means that we should have ecosystems with no human participation whereas conserving means that humans ought to contribute to the survival of ecosystems, acting on them in a positive way. Probably, ultimately, conservation and preservation are concepts that are antagonistic to that of sustainability. Thus, sustainable growth can perhaps aspire to or, at the most, slow the pace of the destruction of ecosystems as well as any greater pollution control. Up to a certain point, the sustainability speech is not fully sustainable.

---

1 Quoted in Morales Sales, Edgar Samuel, La cultura latinoamericana en la aldea global, *Cuadernos Americanos*, ano X, vol. 60 (Noviembre-Diciembre 1996), UNAM, Mexico, (pp. 37-44), p.37

2 *Ibid*, p. 37.

3 *Ibid*, p. 38.

4 *Ibid*, pp. 38-39.

5 Córdova Vianello, Lorenzo, Liberalismo, democracia, neoliberalismo e ingobernabilidad, *Revista Mexicana de Sociologia*, ano LVIII, vol. 4 (Octubre- Diciembre, 1996), UNAM, Mexico (pp. 3-35), p. 23.

6 *Ibid*, pp. 25-26.

7 Fernández Santillan, José, *Filosofia politica de la democracia*, Fontamara, S.A., Mexico, 1994, p. 101. (quoted by Córdova, *op. cit.*, p. 27).

8 Morales Sales, *op. cit.*, p. 40.

9 Ferreira, Mara Nazareth, Identidad y resistencia cultural en América Latina: Algunas consideraciones preliminares, *Cuadernos Americanos*, ano X, vol. 60 (Noviembre-Diciembre, 1996), UNAM, México (pp. 45-53), p. 45.

10 *Ibid*, p. 46.

11 Ulloa, S. Alejandro, Identidad cultural e integración en América Latina. Desafos y perspectivas, *En torno a la identidad latinoamericana*, México, 1992 (quoted by Ferreira, *op. cit.*, p. 46).

12 Ferreira, *op. cit.*, p. 47.

13 Ulloa, *op. cit.*, p. 47.

14 Ferreira, *op. cit.*, p. 47.

15 *Ibid*, p. 47.

16 *Ibid*, pp. 47-48.

17 Ulloa, *op.cit.*, p. 106 (quoted by Ferreira, *op.cit.*, pp. 48-49).

18 Ferreira, *op.cit.*, p. 49.

19 *Ibid*, p. 52.

20 Monsiváis, Carlos, interviewed by Martha Elena Montoya Vélez (quoted by Ferreira, *op. cit.*, pp. 52-53).

21 Lanz, Rigoberto, La ventaja de llamarse América Latina, *Cuadernos Americanos*, ano X, vol. 60 (Noviembre-Diciembre, 1996), UNAM, México, pp. 54-62

22 *Ibid*, p. 55.

23 *Ibid*, pp. 54-55.

24 *Ibid*, p. 56.

25 *Ibid*, p. 57.

PART THREE

Cultural Challenges

11

Information society and Greek society: Socio-cultural and political incompatibilities

Demosthenes Agrafiotis
Professor of Sociology, National School of Public Health
196, Alexandras Avenue, Athens, 115 21, Greece
Tel.: +30 1 6466243, Fax: +30 1 6466243
Email: agraf@compulink.gr

Abstract

The term information society is being used in the field of techno-science as well as in politics, cultural studies, journalism, and public discussions; yet, a question arises: is the term pertinent from a scientific point of view or acceptable from the political and socio-cultural perspectives of all modern societies?

The question is not only academically interesting but also of immediate practical concern since the conceptual accuracy and the study of its social perception is indispensable for successful, collective, and organized action. From a societal point of view, the technologies of information and telecommunications embody in an exemplary way the cultural mega-process and political mega-changes of contemporary societies. While it is more and more accepted that the essence of the new technologies is not technological, the fate of new information technologies is connected with the future of many other institutions and the summoning of multiple sources. The establishment and composition of the above-mentioned expression, leads to the hypothesis that the term information society should be used with the utmost care, provided of course that its connotation is recognized. In the case of Greek society, certain conditions and circumstances are not yet present which can render the use of the term/expression information society rather dysfunctional.

The nature of the obstacles that do not permit the use of the expression information society in the Greek case is both socio-cultural and political. On the horizon of the next century, it is urgent to determine which of these obstacles can be removed and by which mechanisms and social actors. It is equally important to

An Ethical Global Information Society J. Berleur & D. Whitehouse (Eds.)

determine which socio-cultural and political particularities of Greek society will permit different social actors or groups to elaborate their presence in a global world.

INTRODUCTORY REMARKS

Many themes/issues of collective life whose nature is compound and intricate are defined by a complex of words or by a theoretical expression: for instance the Aids epidemic is the plague of the century, the prospects for molecular biology and biotechnology are called the kingpin of the twenty-first century, the next millennium is the area of intense religiousness and international political and social upheavals are the end of history.

The above expressions have particularly the ambition to prove clever or inventive and essentially to explore the effectiveness of communication. On the other hand, they seem to take advantage of one aspect so strongly that the complex meaning of the phenomenon they refer to is somehow lost. Thus, although many expressions have been presented in the social context of debates and discourses [1] very few, of course, have succeeded in establishing themselves.

These phrases-expressions remain valid for a certain period only; they are used for communication between individuals and groups and sometimes they are established without previous inspection of their validity or origins. The organization of society as a whole has primarily become a pole of attraction for many denominations and rhetorical expressions. In this spectrum, the industrial society [2] (a sociological term) has also been redefined - named the society of progress, the mature society, the society of abundance, the society of organization etc. Meanwhile the post-industrial [2] society's definitions range from the society of image, the society of knowledge to the postmodern society [3], [4], and so on. Very recently, the complex of the information society is beginning to appear in various areas and places and is being used in a number of social debates and discourses (political, journalistic). In this context, the following questions could be expressed: Is the term information society scientifically pertinent or valid and culturally acceptable? Under what circumstances is its use justifiable? Does it actually lead to a new form of social structure? Under what conditions should its use become acceptable in the case of Greek society? To what degree is the information society considered a pole, an objective of the initiatives of social actors in Greece? How do social actors use, (de)construct or even manipulate the expression Information Society?

THE PROBLEM OF PERTINENCE AND VALIDITY

There are two ways, two routes to be followed in terms of analysis which can be applied in order to specify the interconnections between the elements of the binomial [information-technologies-communication] and [society]. The first would start from the social and cultural changes and upheavals of the years 2,000-2,010 AD and would continue by focusing on how these new social and cultural circumstances determine the development of technological systems and, more specifically, of the socio-communicative strategies and their demands in terms of technical solutions.

The second way would start from the potential and the limitations of every technological system and especially of information technology and telecommunications; it would consequently focus on how these technologies could affect the present and future demands, needs and desires for information and how these technologies could cause change in many levels of the economic and socio-cultural systems. Bearing in mind that the questions explored at the end of the last paragraph have been expressed at a societal level, it is clear that the first way of analysis should be the one to follow. Thus, in order to set the socio-cultural trends of contemporary societies, there should be a comparative presentation of the basic data of the industrial/post-industrial societies according to the contexts outlined by A. Touraine [2], [4].

(i) The industrial societies have kept an eminent place for their major invention, industrial capital; interwoven with labour, it allows a part of the social product to return to the production areas and to change infinitely the conditions of labour. This homeostasis of industrial capital also functions, without a doubt, in the post-industrial societies, but the crucial variables are now the knowledge and information which provide adequate feedback to the production system, and open up new horizons with increasing speed in any action. The industrial societies are allowing new balances to grow, from systemic origins, while the post-industrial societies are allowing other kind of balances to grow: those stemming from the theory of catastrophe or chaos.

(ii) In the last two centuries the dominant production and consumption systems are cultivating a meager universality which is based mainly on the activation of natural resources with, as a target, the international market. The industrial societies are forming a flowing system that weaves its way through the globe; in it, natural resources, money, information, products, machines are circulating creating a time space that decreases in the name of speed and continuous expansion. Traditional societies were looking towards a horizon where geography played an important part, while in industrial societies this horizon became planetary and in the post-industrial societies became global.

(iii) Industrial societies are turning towards the production of machines, appliances, and products. Mass production and productivity along with the standardization of human needs, all add up to the establishment of the total market. In the post-industrial societies this sort of challenge is being transferred to the administration of the system, simply because there is not only the need for production but also for ensuring production by protecting natural resources, the environment, and the quality of life. In traditional societies, survival was the central issue; in the industrial society, it was the massive production of goods and, in post-industrial societies, it is the management of information and material and immaterial systems.

(iv) Compared to traditional or primitive societies, the industrial societies' main characteristic is the continuous diversity of policies and institutions. The systematic and analytical separation of the social continuum goes hand in hand with the abandonment of meta-social references. Society is not the outcome of the will of one super being or of a deity anymore, but of the action taken by social groups in the name of progress, development and of the conquest and the transcendence of all limits - real or imagined. Industrial society seeks unity by continuously negotiating and setting new policies and institutions, by opening up with no *a priori* guarantees. In post-industrial societies, progress dynamics are subsiding, but the search for the new - sustainable or not, politically justifiable or not - is still a dominant cultural model.

(v) Industrial society can also be called a society of strong historicity (*historicité*) [2], because this society has the material infrastructure and the knowledge as well as the cultural standards to intervene in its own mode of existence. The post-industrial society is mainly turning towards its production and not its reproduction. In this mega-process, information is the most crucial constituent, it is the fuel for boosting this whole, collective, and organized action [5]. This aforementioned production of society, however, will become a cultural problem in the context of the post-industrial society since the great challenge will be the invention of an actual meaning representing the huge potential in the production of material and non-material goods [6], [7].

(vi) The new technologies of information and telecommunications will possess the following characteristics: a complex combination of logical schemes, automatization and machines that clearly imitate human intellectual functions or biological systems, globalization, the high production cost of innovation, a significant contribution to scientific and technological research and development in order to shape and diffuse them [8]. On these grounds, we are also allowed to use the term techno-science [7]. The new technologies of information and communication will have direct consequences in the shaping of institutions and organizations, in the division of labour (in mental/manual/male/female etc.), the training of employees, the relations between groups of professionals, the distribution of power in terms of decision-making [8]. Perhaps, the most basic element is the fact that communication, the most fundamental function of the socio-cultural process according to C. Lévi-Strauss, will be supported by these technologically dependent functions. In this context, technology should be classified in the social sciences since it determines both meaning and social interactions: information technologies from a simple instrument tend to become language (*langage*) [1].

(vii) According to studies referring to the future, three scenarios are the most eligible for direct materialization [7]. The first is a two-gear Europe, a dual Europe: its main characteristics are uneven areas, social groups, sexes, the accumulation of environmental problems, and the dominance of economic rationalism. The second is Europe as a fortress (*L'Europe forteresse*) whose basic aim would be to ensure economic growth and the strict control of the flux of population. At the same time, Europe will try to enforce a new Marshall Plan for the nations of the former Soviet Union. The third is a Europe oriented mainly towards the control of inequalities, the search for new forms of mutual support, and the emergence of new shapes that will help us all to live close to nature. The most probable meta-scenario would be that of the co-existence of these three scenarios in different areas of the European continent. In this perspective, the technological systems of information will face the dilemma of the particularity or the universality, of the social control of information [9], [10], of the creation of an electronic illiteracy at a global level, and the possible emergence in power of information highways. Without any doubt, the presentation of these ideas concerning the cultural characteristics of contemporary societies has been positive and epic. Yet, in the societies of progress, the elements that are in contrast to these ideas co-exist as negative consequences with unpredictable side effects; inevitable outcomes include the existence of uniformity in the uncontrollable abundance of society, the establishment of a technocratic elite, the transformation of nature into a repository of sources that calls for exploitation, the lack of participation in fundamental decisions for social evolution, the restriction of alternatives, the social and psychological cost that arises from the establishment of a fast pace of life with little or no time available, and the pursuit of constant changes [11], [12].

The process of pointing out the above-mentioned socio-cultural characteristics, although totally indicative and far from any sense of completion, allows some elements to be outlined in order to answer the questions that arose as far as the scientific pertinence of the term Information Society is concerned. Information will undoubtedly play an important role and checking its basis will be a turning point for the action taken by organizations, institutions, regions and nations [12], [14]. It is also clear that any sort of information requires a certain frame, a dynamic and a whole set of conditions and circumstances whose nature is neither technological nor scientific.

In this sense, the term information society refers to a crucial or prevailing element of modern societies without referring in an obligatory manner to the whole of the socio-cultural dynamic. It does not possess the pertinence to characterize or to predetermine what takes place in contemporary and future societies because the essence of information technology is not technological - as a lot of variables and situations of non-technological nature contributed to its production and consumption (see (i) - (vii) above). Since this expression is not valid enough to act as a denomination, it can be a source of connotations - and, for that matter, very rich ones. This fact leads us to the following wise form of attitude: in order for the term information society to be acceptable there should be convergent assumptions and conditions (examples of conditions are presented in (i)-(vii) above), otherwise there lies the risk of creating confusion and simplifications which in turn are completely opposed to the cultural norm of accurate diagnosis and subsequently of the denomination or specification of reality. That is to say, the expression information society loses its scientific pertinence, social validity and, finally, its cultural legitimacy.

THE GREEK CASE

Every society finds its characteristic mark in the intersection of the readings provided by history and sociology. According to this axiom, these readings are the contribution of cultural sociology and also the instrument for recognizing the special and specific characteristics of the industrial and post-industrial societies in the cultural history of mankind in relation, of course, to the challenge of the new technologies of information and communication. It is therefore essential that this assumption should be checked out and assessed in accordance with Greek society.

It could be said that Greek society is characterized by a continuous lack of correspondence between goals and means, and between orientations and mobilizing or organizing mechanisms, while it has introduced technologies, institutions, data and practices of the industrial society from the dawn of the century, industry changes from development to retrogression - an alternation of industrialization and de-industrialization; autonomous growth seems to be unapproachable. Besides, the co-existence of structures of pre-industrial, industrial and post-industrial characters is intensifying the presence of diversity and variety. The challenges that are directly connected with the application of information technologies imported into Greece will interweave this diverse world of economic and socio-cultural meanings.

In relation to other European societies the challenge for Greek society to direct its socio-cultural trajectory towards the information society is double:

(i) to overcome the socio-cultural deficiencies due to a rapid transformation of traditional Greek society (the dominant form until the Second World War) to industrial and even post-industrial society without having the time for political and cultural institutions to foster their status and role. These uncertainties create a situation of interventions coming too early or too late, an absence of reform cultures and, finally, a confusion between the objective and corresponding actions.

(ii) to define or at least to make visible the Greek version of the information society in a such a way that the actions of social actors can find a relative place in a global and coherent framework. A lot of actors have already implemented (partial) projects but the overall product is poor in synergies. The heterogeneity of socio-cultural conditions is accentuated by the heterogeneity of the initiatives. The information society oscillates between the two extremes: a) a strategic objective for innovative Greek enterprises in the global market; b) ideological, rhetorical devices or poles for apocalyptic (positive or negative) attitudes.

Until now, it is extremely difficult to distinguish the social actor who has the capacity to play the leading role in tracing the pathway towards the information society. The public sector is characterized by its pre-industrial inertia, the private sector has to face questions of scale and poor traditions of major social changes, the political system has not completed the phase of democratization and rationalization, and civil society is characterized by a mixture of over-fascination with the new and confidence that no major upheavals are probable.

Could the threat from the international scene (competitiveness, unemployment, lost autonomy, acculturation) play the role of catalyst? Or have the initiatives to be local and internal in spite of the pressure of planetary evolution?

This development will render the use of the term information society even more difficult and risky from a scientific point of view. In other words, in order to use the term information society (even in its most vaguely scientific version) in Greek society, it is not enough simply to introduce new information technology systems but to adopt and develop institutions and socio-cultural models thoroughly in conjunction with the social part of these systems. Furthermore, there should be an effort to understand and to face a number of future challenges in the interfaces of the whole: Information/Science-Technology/Economy/Society - not only in the Greek context but in European and in international perspectives.

These challenges are of different nature, for example:

a) Epistemological. How to avoid the contradiction related to the *a priori* use of term information society in different socio-cultural contexts? To what degree is this term pertinent, when it permits an investigation of different dimensions of reality or when it can predict its evolution [2], [4]?

b) Scientific. What kind of social research is needed to elucidate the mode of existence of the information society, its evolution, and its internal contradictions? To what degree can comparative studies contribute to this elucidation [15], [16]?

c) Semantic. Why has the term information society been elaborated recently in contemporary societies? What type of social imagery corresponds to it? What variety of meanings can it generate in different segments of the population? How do individuals construct or elaborate discourses and realities in the name of the information society [17], [20]?

It is clear that the ambiguity of the information society is not of a negative character. This ambiguity could be the origin for a fertile and polymorphous questioning. But, of course, the answers presuppose long-term action and research [16].

CONCLUSION

The introduction and use of a term or expression is a complicated procedure which is definitely not impartial to interests, conflicts, and challenges on a national, European or international level. Given the fact that there are ambiguities and multiple meanings in the expression information society, it is necessary to examine its articulations and its complications in order for this expression to become a starting point for analysis and action and not to produce a diagnosis of contradictory perspectives or rejection of alternative social initiatives. If, every time the subject comes up, it is implied that technology and science are the results of a socio-cultural evolution then, the expression information society does make sense; and if this expression encourages the multiple articulation of [Science-Technology] and [Society], then the cultural legitimation of its use is strongly reinforced. In the case of Greek society in order for information society to be accepted as a socio-cultural horizon, a series of incompatibilities of a diverse nature have to be overcome. This means that a systematic and well conceived plan of action has to be implemented at a variety of levels in order to achieve coherence and a convergence of efforts. If this type of effort is not initiated, not implemented, not completed, it renders the use of the term-expression information society rather dysfunctional and socio-culturally unfounded.

REFERENCES

1. D. Agrafiotis, Theoretical Aspects of the Complex: Art and New Technologies, in K. Brunnstein and E. Raubold (Ed.), IFIP, *13th World Congress 94*, Volume 2, Elsevier Science, P.V., 1994, 714-15.
2. A. Touraine, *La production de la société*, Seuil, Paris, 1974.
3. A. Touraine, *Critique de la Modernité*, Fayard, Paris, 1992.
4. D. Agrafiotis, Politistikes idiotypies tis viomihanikis kinonias sto *Viomhaniki Archaiologia - Viomihanikos Politismos*, EIE/Archaiologia (in press).
5. Epistimoniki Ekthesi, *H Epikinonia stin Evropi toy avrio. Pera apo tin technologia*, Tomos 4, Programma FAST II, E.E.K., 7/1988.
6. V. Laopodis (Ed.), *Communicators Across the Research - Society Interface*, Proceedings of the 1st CORSI Meeting, Luxembourg, 19 and 20 May 1994, Interfaces, Science-Technology-Society, E.C. - DGXIII, 1995.
7. D. Agrafiotis, Technologia - Systimata Ygias - Politismos, *Koinoniogramma*, No. 32, 12/1994.
8. Euroabstracts, *Technology and Society: EU Initiatives in Technology Assessment*, No. 33, January, 1995, 3-10.
9. V. Laopodis and D. Gritzalis, Information Services for Assessing the Impact of Technology in an Information Society (in press).
10. V. Laopodis and F. Fernandez, Enhancing Citizens Participation in an Information Society, *5th Hellenic Conference on Informatics*, December 1995, published by the Greek Computer Society.
11. L'évolution des valeurs des Européens, Numéro spécial. *Futuribles*, No 200, 7-8/1995.
12. Report EPTA, *Conference on Information Society*, Rathenau Institute, The Hague, 1996.
13. Report, *The Information Society, Policy Options for the New Telecommunications*, STOA/European Parliament, Luxembourg, 1996.
14. Report, *The Information Society, Information and Communication Technologies for Sustainable Technical Development*, STOA/European Parliament, Luxembourg, 1996.
15. P. Ahonen, Strategies to Elaborate the Information Society: An EE - Finland Comparison, *ESST: A laboratory without walls?*, Athens, Greece, September 13-15, 1996.
16. J. Berleur, Information Highway Belgian Policy Confronted to Different European Utopias, ESST Third Working Conference, *ESST: A laboratory without walls?*, Athens, Greece, September 13-15, 1996.
17. J.F. Lyotard, *La condition post-moderne*, Minuit, 1979.
18. J.F. Lyotard, *Les moralités post-modernes*, Galilée, Paris, 1993.
19. F. Chatelet, J. Derrida, M. Foucault, J.F. Lyotard and M. Serres, *Politiques de la philosophie*, Figures/Grasset, Paris, 1976.
20. G. Fourez, Scientific and Technical Literacy in a Socio-Constructivist Perspective. Third Working Conference, *ESST: A laboratory without walls?* Athens, Greece, 13-15 September, 1996.

Just-in-time open and distant training offers must match market and learners requirements

Michel Arnaud
Researcher, CNED Research Laboratory on Knowledge Industry, Téléport 4, Asterama 2, BP 300
Avenue du Téléport, F-86960 FUTUROSCOPE CEDEX
Tel: +33 5 49493468; fax: +33 5 49490584
Email: michel.arnaud@cned.fr

Abstract

The European project METASA (Multimedia European Experimental Towns with a Social-pull Approach) has sought to involve citizens as partners in the development of the information society and to demonstrate telematics applications for specific domains: administration, employment, education/training, health care and leisure/entertainment. After a careful analysis of citizens' expectations in the four small towns involved, Arnedo (Spain), Parthenay (France), Torgau and Weinstadt (Germany), which was done by a team of social researchers[1], education and training not surprisingly appeared as a priority for citizens to get acquainted with the new communication tools and to meet the challenges of the post-industrial society where everyone has to adapt continuously to the requirements of an ever-evolving job market.

Because patterns of learning are changing, because adults do not have long time periods available for study, and because they may have problems studying alone using communication tools, training processes are to be customized to their special needs: flexibility in schedules, and adaptability in content. Distance training offers have to be designed to reach learners where they are and when they are available, which means taking into account their time constraints, remedying their media-related cognitive hurdles and, in fact, developing a new continuing school paradigm. To build a just-in-time approach satisfying both employers and learners needs, educational content designers must work in a coordinated manner with employers and training administrators to prepare learners through adequate

An Ethical Global Information Society J. Berleur & D. Whitehouse (Eds.)

training so that they can acquire the professional skills and competencies needed for them to apply for and get jobs. Knowledge centres (to accommodate learners' time constraints) and knowledge exchange networks (to compensate for the asynchronous/synchronous difficulties of communication tools' use) are two aspects of the new continuing education set up to meet the challenges of the information society.

INTRODUCTION

For the last twenty years, resource centres for distance learning in France and in Europe have come up short in providing adequate services. One of the reasons for this failure may be that they were not designed according to a bottom-up approach: learners' needs were taken into account only through a typology that reduced them to stereotypes. To define learners' needs requires considering them through a full-scale analysis of learners' life conditions; personal background, history and social setting are important factors shaping reactions to a knowledge transmission and building process.

The METASA project has offered us the opportunity to apply this approach through the study of four small towns and their citizens' needs. The definition of the METASA project came out of a 'political vision - local democracy, underpinned by a theoretical orientation - local particularity combined with general integration, and by an economic purpose - fostering of sustainable development'[2]. The METASA project has sought to develop a 'social-pull' instead of a 'technical-push' approach, by allowing citizens to participate fully in the development of the information society and by aiming to demonstrate applications for economic actors (small-medium enterprises, micro and single-person enterprises, local commerce and crafts). By concentrating totally on users' needs, it has chosen therefore to focus on improving quality of life and on developing specific application domains: employment, education/training, health care, leisure/entertainment and administration.

Although each of the four METASA towns has its own socio-demographic and socio-cultural characteristics, it seems possible to draw from the report on users' needs written by METASA social science researchers, a common hierarchy of expectations linked to the development of local socio-economic systems, based in particular on the analysis of users' socialization and relationship to technology. Education and training not surprisingly appear as a priority for users to get acquainted with the new communication tools. To restrict social exclusion, training offers have to be customized not only for computer-literate users but also for beginners. This approach takes into account the whole population. It is based on a market segmentation, designed first to cater to potential service purchasers' needs but also to include progressively other users. It takes into account their expectations, in order to build extensive and therefore economically and socially viable services.

EDUCATION AND TRAINING REPRESENTED NEEDS

Users understand what is at stake, constraints are correctly perceived as well as opportunities. They see how positive and negative factors may influence their decision to use or not to use these new communication tools: they may start using them if they feel that benefits drawn from their usage compensate for hurdles they encounter when trying to use them. They are afraid that more jobs will be lost because of the information society and that new communications tools will be reserved for the happy few able to pay for them. In order to keep control of local social evolution, a willingness to be informed and to be part of the decision-making process at each project phase is clearly expressed. Students as well as adults ask to be consulted regularly: their remarks must be taken into account, they want a users' group to be part of the METASA steering committee.

The opinion survey undertaken by METASA social science researchers has shown the importance of education and training needs in relation to technology. Although the same pattern appears more or less in the four METASA small towns (Parthenay, Arnedo, Weinstadt, Torgau), we have chosen Parthenay's population as the most significant as far as users' mental representations are concerned. Not surprisingly, the users are aware of structural changes needed in schools and educational institutions in order to match emerging training challenges: new communication tools cannot be used in a traditional classroom, teachers not only have to master them but must change their pedagogy.

Basic training for every learner is a first requirement. In order to help teachers, who are certainly not numerous enough to respond to this global basic training demand, tutors are to be made permanently available as local help in public resource centres. They help to achieve this computer literacy objective, making it possible to improve access to information for all, and therefore to provide efficient public online services. Although the teacher's role seems more than ever crucial for a proper knowledge transmission process, self-training is seen as a means of completing whatever face-to-face contacts with teachers can be secured.

Potential users also stress that distance learning must be developed as well as public resource centre access. In order to facilitate the preparation of exams through distance learning, knowledge exchange networks should be fostered. Youngsters should be trained as a priority, not only to fight against their dropping-out of schools but also to open up new study opportunities through the promotion of foreign language learning, thereby multiplying study options, school networks, and teachers and students at national and international levels. Adults should benefit from the development of professional training tools, bringing enterprises and the educational system closer, with facilitated access to data banks on job markets and information on local and global economic activities. Services development should lead to the setting up of training servers with adapted tools for learning, professional orientation, accreditation of prior learning (APL), and job offers.

THE KNOWLEDGE CENTRE PROJECT

We think that we could avoid the failure of our cooperative concept of knowledge centre by choosing a new approach, taking into account factors which have usually been excluded from needs analysis. Three areas seem of interest to us as potential roadblocks on the path of learning: making time available for study versus constraints such as transportation, family chores, etc., overcoming media-related cognitive hurdles as they exist in distance learning, and getting appropriate training for a specific job.

Three changes are to be implemented in various aspects of a classical resource centre: facilitated access to knowledge centres, appropriate tutoring and knowledge exchange network, customization of learning modules to the requirements of the job market and learners' levels. As we expect problems and resistance, this project action plan has been designed with an integrated logistic cycle and a transverse collaborative approach so that the project steering committee can respond immediately and propose solutions. In our knowledge centre, indicators will measure the accuracy of our hypotheses during the implementation steps, by keeping track of attendance, examination result, and job entry or re-entry rates compared to more traditional resource and distance learning centres.

Facilitated access to knowledge centres

The concept of a knowledge centre aims at responding to potential learners' needs by offering a space where it is possible to seek information, education, and entertainment. The goal is to meet the general request for job market flexibility, lifelong learning, and leisure activities. It is a place where people should keep coming during their entire lives, to prepare for a new professional activity or at least to brush up their skills.

Helping learners to overcome time constraints

The first obstacle is a general lack of available time to devote to study. This is observed with a majority of potential learners. In fact, learning patterns are changing: learners do not have long time periods available for study, unless they can get specific leaves or have not found a job. According to this approach and to make access as easy as possible, knowledge centres are to be set up in towns as well as in rural areas, to be open all day long and late at night, with kindergarten, cafeteria, administrative and technical staff who can provide guidance and social help when needed. Practical aspects of day-to-day life have to be handled or facilitated while attending sessions at these centres, so learners can concentrate on knowledge acquisition processes within specific time spans.

Mixing learners to promote convivial exchanges

It appears necessary to offer a constant opportunity to meet similar as well as different people in knowledge centres. They are to be made accessible to all sorts of potential learners. For the convenience of our study, one can classify this population into three categories that can overlap: schoolchildren and students, adults eager to acquire general knowledge, and adults in professional training. Information, education and entertainment offers vary according to targeted audiences. Different types of paths are offered according to individual needs and potentials, in a graduation of increasingly specialized hard knowledge or soft knowledge (where social practice and interpersonal exchange are more valued).

Schoolchildren and adults in a quest for general knowledge have need of knowledge acquisition and construction, linked to the school curriculum, for example; the latest developments in the technical and scientific research field; environmental issues; and new technical tools. Local schoolchildren, that is to say college students as well as school pupils, will be able to use a knowledge centre to learn rarely taught foreign languages through videoconferences, access data bases via the Internet, and so on. Another category of learners in the knowledge centre wants to follow appropriate training in order to improve job qualifications. All these persons may benefit from a desire to learn they can share while exchanging information on specific subjects of interest. This hypothesis needs of course to be verified.

Unique service window for the socially isolated

Another segment of the population, the underprivileged and socially excluded, should also be invited to come to knowledge centres. It is not appropriate to hide the fact that the socially excluded show little interest in the new communication and information technologies. They have suffered too much already in being offered gadget solutions to their problems, and they have been treated as pawns in high-tech deals by hardware merchants with local authorities. We understand their first reaction of distrust when confronted by our offer. The only way to turn around the situation is to offer all kinds of social assistance in knowledge centres concentrated at a specific administrative window, in order to solve social problems as much as possible, so that this kind of learner can concentrate on his or her practice and quest for knowledge.

Appropriate tutoring and knowledge exchange network

Traditional knowledge building for learners seems to conform to teachers' injunctions and dogmas. This process sometimes results in learners being living replicas of their teachers. Repetition and evaluation exercises are mainly used to verify knowledge acquisition processes in traditional classrooms. In this context, schooling failure occurs as soon as the master-pupil relationship is scrambled by too great a number of pupils for a single teacher, when what is taught is too far from practical cases to be solved in job situations, or when too long a period of study is required to get a degree. In knowledge centres, the learning context is more flexible: learners can study alone, in groups with or without a tutor, participate in videoconferences, or use email to be in contact with teachers. Because of teachers' scarcity, constant evolution of knowledge fields and learning needs considerable expansion. Learners' autonomy that is greater than in traditional classrooms has to be promoted.

Compensating for media-related cognitive hurdles

The role of a traditional teacher can be divided into four in the context of education and training in a knowledge centre: he/she is the designer of multimedia courses to be used by learners alone or in groups, an expert available at a distance (through telephone and videoconference) for specific classes and remedial activities, an animator for telematics exchanges (forum, email, etc.) and, finally, a tutor-mediator in a context of hybridization of face-to-face and distance teaching. An important effort of customization of multimedia design is to be made because distance learning devices can disturb the traditional way of learning[3]. In order to compensate for this handicap, specific skills have to be developed by learners. Therefore, pedagogy is less a knowledge transmission process than a way of inculcating methods to learners so that they know how to identify proper information, and to classify it and integrate it within their own knowledge representations. The expert teacher, who is available at a distance, intervenes by telephone or videoconference: his/her role is to give exact references for the knowledge content and to stimulate learners in live sessions. The animator of the telematic system uses email and forums to discuss issues with learners, to answer basic questions (those most frequently asked) and to pass on the ones he/she cannot answer to the distant teacher-expert who is the specialist in his/her field.

Knowledge exchange network boosting learner confidence

Knowledge exchange networks are to be used as a mean of intensifying exchanges between learners. The objective is double: to unlock those who have failed at school and to create a mutual desire to learn. Knowledge content exchanged in a network is usually basic training in maths, literature, etc. as taught in a secondary school. If successfully done, this exchange can constitute a solid brush-up of the basic knowledge required to go further in any specialized training ('I teach you cooking, you teach me arithmetic' and so on). The principle on which a knowledge exchange network functions is that you can be taught only if you teach something to someone else. It does not have to be the same person. The mediator's role is to identify the learning needs of each of the participants and the domains in which they know something that is in demand to be learned by others. The first step is to identify who is in need of teaching, and who can share his/her knowledge and then constitute a network of pairs in order to regulate the exchanges. An important side-effect of this process is that the person who is teaching realizes that he/she is worth something since he/she teaches something to someone else. It is more likely, although it has to be substantiated by further research, that an apprentice teacher involved in a knowledge exchange network will be inclined to search for additional information if challenged on a specific subject. Furthermore, he/she may go back to study with a more relaxed, although more organized, learning method.

Appropriate tutoring absolutely needed

The mutual desire to learn can be boosted if there is a clear linkage between the knowledge acquisition process and the social behaviour of the learner that is commonly shared in knowledge exchange networks. Therefore, the external and internal system of tutors and mediators within the knowledge centre has to convey a specific behaviourist model of knowledge access which is as informal and as friendly as possible. It is not our intention to diminish the role of the teacher who should remain, more than ever, the reference point in terms of knowledge and, most of all, must show how to retrieve the proper information, validate it and help in the process of assimilating it. Facilitated access to face-to-face tutors is also to be provided according to our analysis, in order to avoid discouraging learners confronted with a teacher at a distance who is inevitably more difficult to understand. To study in a group with the help of a tutor-mediator can therefore remedy the abruptness of synchronous distance training if proper pedagogical content and methods are used. Less than knowledge providers, tutor-mediators become models, conveying values of social exchange and communication, paying great attention to learners' needs, making themselves available as often as possible. They must be successful in unlocking learners' potential, restoring their self-confidence, and showing them an approach to knowledge made of self-respect: the ones who do not know should not be ashamed, because they know something on which they can build further knowledge and therefore they will soon compensate for their ignorance.

Customization of learning modules to learners' needs and job market requirements

Modularity is an important aspect allowing the greatest flexibility in training offers. Educational designers have to segment content in short modules, considered as value units to be capitalized. Learners can organize their study time according to their own schedules, provided administrative schooling rules are flexible enough to accommodate various study paces and validate them.

Discovery classes for schoolchildren and students

Specific classes are to be organized for schoolchildren and students, during one or two-week periods, in knowledge centres on a given topic: astronomy, hydrography, etc. Their pedagogical objective is to bring learners to the scientific process of building hypotheses that they have to verify by measuring experimentation results. This leads to a knowledge acquisition process of trial and error supported by a network of domain specialists and a team of local animators and teachers who come with the students from their regular schools. Children and students can therefore get acquainted with methods of scientific investigation and be stimulated in their own discovery of specialized domains which will result in an overall knowledge increase for each of them. For schoolchildren and other general audiences, without limitations due to a required degree of knowledge, it is possible to offer scientific game applications based on multimedia simulations and experimentations in a knowledge centre. This necessitates important equipment in multimedia hardware and software (such as microcomputers, CD-Roms, network servers, connections to the Internet, and a cable/satellite reception site).

Offering appropriate job-oriented training

Can we bypass the assumption that no matching between job and training is really possible or effective? For us, adult learners are mainly stimulated by a job offer at the end of their training cycle. If we keep that in mind, it seems to us that open and distance learning (ODL) designers should be part of steering committees composed of decision-makers and employers, assessing job trends in a given job market based on economic forecasts, and taking joint policy decisions in order to create jobs in a specific area for various economic sectors. Can this type of coordinated action in a knowledge centre help learners to get adequate training ? If the answer is yes, ODL designers should try to shorten the production cycle starting from job forecasts so that corresponding training offers are ready when jobs are offered.

Within this framework, learning plans are to be customized to learners' specific needs. The necessary steps are the candidate learner passing through the accreditation of prior learning (APL) process to get an accurate list of his/her current competencies and identification of qualifications required from the description of the specific job envisioned. The matching process involves identifying specific competencies, needed to fulfil a position, to be acquired through the learning plan. To get an accurate and customized learning plan, segmentation of curriculum content in small modules is to be carefully designed within a framework linked to job capacity requirements through national vocational qualifications (NVQs) analysis type and learner profiles.

Professional training plans

Appropriate professional training plans have to take into account these two complementary approaches:

- translation in terms of learners' competencies of their learning path (where they are and where they want to go, taking into account job market trends): elaboration of their profiles, as diversified as possible, in order to integrate them in different professional and pedagogical paths;
- formatting of training content in various pedagogical modules according to a competencies grid analyzing skills and knowledge to be mastered when each module is successfully completed (knowledge, know-how and skills references, etc.), allowing better identification of what contents can best fit the requirements of the pedagogical learning path.

The determination of the individualized training offer should include the following steps:

1. Job offers to be selected
   - selection of a group of job offers by potential learners (through a connection with employment data bases for example),
   - analysis of requested competencies to fill these positions.
   Once a job offer is identified, a study of its characteristics has to be translated into requested competencies, and defined from an official repertory such as NVQs.
2. Accreditation of prior learning (APL)
   - with an online assistance system and a professional career counsellor, analysis of the applicant learner competencies,
   - competencies analysis with an APL methodology should be used as prescribed by institutional bodies entitled to undertake this type of evaluation.
3. Training modules choice
   According to qualifications required for a job that a learner would like to apply for, a choice of appropriate training modules is to be made based on analysis of competency references attached to them: what competencies will be gained by learners when they pass the final test.
4. Individualized training plan
   According to the analysis of competencies to be acquired by learners and those which they possess already (as checked with APL), training plans have to be

built in order to acquire needed competencies that learners lack at present and that they need to apply for specific job offers.

This original approach needs to be validated in pilot projects to be started soon.

CONCLUSION

The key point is to see how citizens can really appropriate the new multimedia technologies in innovative situations such as the ones we are developing. By trying to answer their specific needs related to job and employment, access to education and culture, and in creating new services in a social-pull approach, we hope that citizens will feel driven to participate and become actors instead of being passive consumers. The interest in dealing with small towns is that we can observe community interaction and try to promote it by appropriate communication channels based on personal relationships. Self-reliance can be a key to success: a citizen should be able to get information about his/her immediate surroundings as well the outside world and decide to act accordingly, creating and improving with others the conditions of their lives. The role of steering committees with citizens' representatives is crucial in keeping a social dialogue open in order to improve services that more adequately meet social needs.

As the METASA project was interrupted at the end of 1996, the implementation steps for our knowledge centres has had to be postponed. Nevertheless, it is our intention to continue with a future European project and the same partners. In the experimental phase, indicators will keep track of attendance, examination results, and job entry or re-entry rates, compared to more traditional distance learning centres. We will check to see if accommodating learners regarding their time constraints, compensating for ODL devices training disturbances through face-to-face tutoring, and customizing training content to job requirements, can be decisive elements in making our knowledge centres a success.

Distance learning can compensate for the handicap of living in a remote area, provided a strong tutoring service is available supported by knowledge exchange networks, and with adequate tools to talk with distant experts. The development of interpersonal exchanges in knowledge centres can help individuals to return to training and to consider it part of their lives. As a consequence of their professional skills enhancement, they may find new jobs and occupations, created for or by them. Knowledge centres that provide basic access to the information highways as a public service are the condition for equal opportunity for all.

It should then become possible to build networks based on mutual interests among learners within and between knowledge centres, contributing to the creation of competency chains through extended knowledge exchange networks, and developing an harmonious computerized citizenship connected to other citizens of the world.

REFERENCES

Arnaud, M., Dubois, H., Fualds, V., Jaeckl, L., Missri, M., Perret-Clermont, A.-N., Perriault, J., Porte, L., *Humanities, workpackage 4, research and evaluation, final report*, CNED/LARIC, Poitiers, 1996.

Cesar, M., Time's role in peer interaction, *International Conference 'Mind and Time'*, Neuchâtel, Switzerland, September 8-10, 1996.

EuroStudyCentres, Development and Implementation, EADTU, Milton Keynes, 1994.

Greenfield, P.M., Cocking, R.R., (Eds) *Interacting with video*, Ablex, Norwood, 1996.

Grossen, M. Pochon, L.-O., *Learning mediated by computers: to what extent is it 'situated?*, Workshop on Learning in Humans and Machines, European Science Foundation, Aix-en-Provence, September 21-23, 1995.

d'Iribarne A., Eveno, E., Lenz, B., Lopez, A., *METASA (Multimedia European Experimental Towns with a Social-pull Approach) Research final report, workpackages 3 and 4*, LEST, Aix-en-Provence, 1996.

Perriault J., *Synchronous and asynchronous media in an hybrid learning process: effect of time compression and expansion*, Fifth Eden annual conference, July 8-10, 1996, Futuroscope Poitiers, France.

Shaw, A., *Social Constructionism and the Inner City: Designing Environment for Social Development and Urban Renewal*, MIT, Dept of Media Arts and Sciences, 1995.

---

[1] d'Iribarne A., Eveno, E., Lenz, B., Lopez, A., *METASA (Multimedia European Experimental Towns with a Social-pull Approach)*, Final Research Report, Workpackages 3 and 4, LEST, Aix-en-Provence, 1996

[2] d'Iribarne A., Eveno, E., Lenz, B., Lopez, A., *METASA*, ibid., p. 18

[3] Perriault J., *Synchronous and asynchronous media in an hybrid learning process: Effect of time compression and expansion*, Fifth Eden Annual Conference, 8-10 July 1996, Futuroscope, Poitiers, France

What does it mean to be 'virtual'?

Colin Beardon
University of Plymouth, Earl Richards Road North
Exeter EX2 6AS, UK
Tel/Fax: +44 1392 475028
Email: c.beardon@plym.ac.uk

Abstract

The role of language in thinking and reasoning about technology and society is examined with respect to the naming of new technologies.

The paper first describes the evolution of the word 'artificial' through its use in 'artificial intelligence' and argues that a common interpretation of the latter term was made possible by an ambiguity in its constituent terms. Emphasis is then placed upon the word 'virtual', arguing that its traditional use was first adapted to meet the general needs of computing, and then a more specialized meaning has emerged associated with the concept of 'virtual reality'. This new sense is roughly synonymous with 'potential'.

Empirical evidence is provided of the use of the word, based upon various dictionary definitions, quantitative research using electronic corpuses (the British National Corpus, INSPEC database of scientific and technological abstracts, and three newspapers) and a discussion of definitions given by practitioners and theoreticians in the field.

INTRODUCTION

When we think about the future of a new technology we usually do so in words - through written reports, at conferences, in articles, etc. - and whilst most of our time is spent looking at particular technologies in detail it is important, from time to time, to look at the words we use for words are also a form of tool and used incorrectly they can result in misleading conclusions. This paper will look at one particular word which has come to be used widely in debates about the future of computing, and that word is 'virtual'. It has had quite a long history, being used to describe 'virtual addressing' in the 1970s, but it has achieved spectacular notice since the term 'virtual reality' became popular around 1990.

An Ethical Global Information Society J. Berleur & D. Whitehouse (Eds.)

It will be shown that there is a process whereby the words we use to describe technology originate from ordinary usage, but then grow to produce new senses of the word which gain wider currency in debates about society in general. The ambiguity of sense that naming a technology introduces means that the names themselves are often ideologically loaded. To put it simply, these terms can be persuasive, providing obstacles to certain ways of thinking about the future, giving quasi-scientific legitimacy to some aspects of the relationship of technologies to human life, and introducing a sense of inevitability concerning certain technological developments.

It may be thought that little hangs on a name but the choice of words can be very significant. Words are an important aspect of the way we understand and negotiate the wider significance of new knowledge and they are part of the raw material for projections into the future. A technology gains meaning through the words used to express it and these are rarely chosen capriciously. Technological projects often have a number of competing names during the early stages: for example, the technique now known as 'virtual addressing' was first called 'paging'.

Naming (especially where it involves complex names containing more than one term) is a poorly understood process and until recently there has been little linguistic research into the topic. The juxtaposition of names has no fixed interpretation and there can be numerous implied relationships between the terms, possibly as many as the relationships expressible in language in general. For example, relations between the terms can involve modalities: a 'bus stop' is where a bus is *supposed* to stop, not necessarily where it *does* stop. Compound names are rarely simple devices and the brevity that is their appeal leaves them open to wide ambiguity of interpretation.

So, when it comes to giving a technology a name there is nearly always an ideological content. The word 'computer' itself emerged from a field of contenders. In 1945 it was used exclusively to refer to human beings who performed complex calculations. Its extension to describe an electromechanical device was compatible to views, expressed by Turing (and Babbage before him), that the work of the machine was comparable to the work of well-ordered human beings working at desks with pen and paper. Not everyone agreed with this and Norbert Wiener, for one, articulated a more humanistic role for the technology which he expressed through an alternative name for the device: a 'cybernetic' machine.

With terms such as 'artificial intelligence' and 'virtual reality', the constituent words are so powerful that their juxtaposition is overloaded with potential meaning. Through their technological development there is an accompanying process of lexicalization (whereby they become recognized as a single linguistic unit with a definite meaning) by means of which new refinements or interpretations of their constituent terms are produced. Benjamin Woolley refers to this when he says,

> 'Virtual' was and remains a much grander word, scandalously underused, a huge vessel of semantic vacuity waiting to have meaning poured into it. Computing has provided some of that meaning ... (Woolley, 1993, p. 58)

If computing has provided new meaning to words like 'artificial' and 'virtual', then how does this take place, and what are the implications for rational public discourses about technology?

THE 'ARTIFICIAL'

Before tackling the contemporary phenomenon surrounding the word 'virtual', it is advisable to establish a theoretical model based upon a past example. For this reason, the evolution of the word 'artificial' with respect to 'artificial intelligence' will first be briefly examined.

Words are not static referents with a meaning fixed for all time. While the word 'artificial' indicates today an opposition to nature or what is natural, this is a fairly recent development. In the seventeenth century it was used to mean something like 'clever' (i.e. 'displaying special art or skill') and by the nineteenth century it was a synonym for 'deceived', 'cunning' and 'affected' and associated with terms such as 'untrue', 'counterfeit', 'illegitimate', 'skilful', 'sly' and 'insincere' (Roget, 1852). But it is in the sense of 'unnatural' that it is commonly used today.

The Concise Oxford Dictionary (1982) lists various senses in which the 'artificial' is opposed to the 'natural':

1. made by art; not natural ... (i.e. concerned with the process of making)
2. not real (artificial flowers, limb) ... (i.e. concerned with the product)
3. affected, insincere, factitious, not arising naturally ... (i.e. concerned with the intention)

The application of the term 'artificial' to early computers (when it was referred to as 'an artificial brain', for example), raises the question of which of these senses was being used. Computers had a clear claim to be considered 'artificial (1)' in that they were without a doubt manufactured objects. The introduction of the novel compound term 'artificial intelligence', however, introduced an element of ambiguity and they soon became portrayed as 'artificial (2)' in that they were being proposed as products capable of imitating human intelligence (Turing, 1950).

Figure 1. Types of definitions of 'artificial intelligence' (Author's analysis of answers given in Negrotti, 1991)

Model or simulate human intelligence	27%
Develop a theory of human intelligence	16%
Produce behaviour which would be considered intelligent in a human	15%
Extend human intelligence or capabilities	7%
Develop human attributes in computers	6%
Extend the powers of computers	6%
Provide an intellectual challenge	4%
Other definitions	19%

By 1983 it would appear that this process was well established, at least within the scientific community. At the 8th International Joint Conference on Artificial Intelligence (IJCAI), held in Karlsruhe in that year, one hundred artificial intelligence (AI) researchers and developers were asked to provide short definitions of artificial intelligence. Their answers (summarized in Figure 1) indicate a strong view (68%) that building computers that imitate human behaviour is central to the discipline of AI.

The strong connection between 'artificial' and 'imitation' (and hence its connection to artificial (2) rather than artificial (1) in the Oxford English Dictionary (OED)) is reflected in the definitions provided for the lexicalized term 'artificial intelligence' in many present day dictionaries. In these entries there is no implied opposition of 'artificial' to 'natural' but instead frequent comparisons are drawn with human behaviour.

- *artificial intelligence*: Study of how to make computers do things that people can do, such as make decisions, see things etc. (Longmans Dictionary of Contemporary English, 1995).
- *artificial intelligence*: The study of how to produce mechanisms that have some of the qualities that the human mind has, such as the ability to understand language, recognize pictures, solve problems and learn (Cambridge International Dictionary of English, 1995).
- *artificial intelligence*: The development and use of computer programs to copy intelligent human behaviour (Oxford Advanced Learners' Dictionary, 1995).
- *artificial intelligence*: A type of computer technology which is concerned with making machines work in an intelligent way, similar to the way the human mind works (Collins COBUILD English Dictionary, 1995).
- *artificial intelligence*: The computational reproduction of intelligent action (Macmillan Dictionary of Information Technology, 1989).
- *artificial intelligence*: The property of a machine capable of reason by which it can learn functions normally associated with human intelligence (McGraw-Hill Dictionary of Computers, 1984).

There is at least a *prima facie* argument here that the development of 'artificial intelligence' in its technological and popular sense was made possible through the exploitation of an ambiguity in the meaning of the word 'artificial'. While no one could argue that computers were manufactured, and were thus properly described as being 'artificial (1)', proponents of AI, and particularly 'Strong AI' as defined by Searle (1980), went on to assume that they were also 'artificial (2)', which is to say that computers could potentially imitate aspects of human behaviour. It has been argued elsewhere that this conception of the status of computers in our societies was dominant in the 1960s and 1970s and had a number of unfortunate implications (Beardon, 1994).

THE VIRTUAL

Traditional definitions of 'virtual'

The word 'virtual' is seen today as roughly meaning 'almost', but it is not without its own history. It was derived from the same root as 'virtue' and originally meant 'morally virtuous'. By the nineteenth century it was synonymous with 'nonexistence' and 'intrinsicality', and associated with terms such as 'unreal', 'potential', 'subjective' and 'instinctive' (Roget, 1852).

Its current meaning was expressed in the Oxford English Dictionary (1933),

virtual
4. That is so in essence or effect, although not formally or actually; admitting of being called by name so far as the effect or result is concerned.

To be a 'virtual X', according to this definition, is to be 'almost an X'. Contemporary dictionaries have concentrated exclusively upon this sense of the word.

virtual almost, even if not exactly or in every way (Cambridge International Dictionary of English, 1995).

virtual almost or nearly the thing described, but not completely (Oxford Advanced Learners' Dictionary, 1995).

Longmans Dictionary of Contemporary English (1995) identifies two such senses,

virtual
1. virtual peace/darkness/destruction etc. something that is so nearly complete peace etc. that any difference is unimportant.
2. virtual leader/prisoner etc. someone who is in fact a leader, prisoner, etc. but not officially one.

There seems very little disagreement of substance between these different definitions and, with respect to general usage of the word, there seems to be unanimity that a 'virtual X' is not an X but it is almost an X.

Uses of 'virtual' within computing

The adjective 'virtual' has been used in computing at least since the 1960s and has been applied to many objects (see Figure 2). An examination of the terms in this list reveals some unusual senses of the word 'virtual'.

Figure 2. Uses of 'virtual' as a premodifier in computing terminology (derived from various computing dictionaries)

virtual access method	virtual facility	virtual private network
virtual address	virtual input/output	virtual reality
virtual button	virtual interface	virtual service
virtual call	virtual machine	virtual space
virtual cathode	virtual manager	virtual storage
virtual circuit	virtual memory	virtual support
virtual device	virtual network	virtual system
virtual disk	virtual password	virtual terminal

For example, the following definition of 'virtual address' is based upon the distinction between a syntactically valid location and something else which is referred to (unproblematically) as an 'actual location'.

virtual address: A symbol that can be used as a valid address part but does not necessarily designate an actual location (McGraw-Hill Dictionary of Computers, 1984).

It could be claimed that a virtual address has the same effect or result as an actual address for the programmer, though it is not the same kind of thing for the operating system designer, but this is an argument about relativities. It can be argued that a virtual address is still an address, and the operating system designer cannot legitimately claim to represent 'actuality' whereas the programmer does not. Rather, the point is that a virtual address is an indirect, rather than a direct, address or, to be more precise, it is more indirect than some other forms of address. The term 'virtual' in this case seems to be used to indicate a level of indirection (i.e. what is thought of as a real address to one group of people is not thought of in that way by another).

In another example, the following definition of 'virtual machine' introduces the notion of a simulation:

> *virtual machine*: In computing, a simulation of a computer and its associated devices by another computer system (Macmillan Dictionary of Information Technology, 1989).

Whilst this is a similar use to that in 'virtual address', in this case the computer system that is doing the simulating and the machine that is being simulated might exist in exactly the same sense (theoretically, they could be the same machine). An appeal cannot be made to some underlying 'actuality' in this case but, rather, it is the process of simulation (or indirection) which makes the use of the word 'virtual' appropriate.

The majority of cases in computing seem to imply a degree of simulation or indirection, whereby one group of users appears to be further away from some supposed 'reality' than another group. The Macmillan Dictionary of Information Technology provides a definition for 'virtual' as an adjective within computing that is formulated largely along these lines.

> *virtual* In computing and data communications, pertaining to a facility that is offered to a user, or system, as if it were a physical reality (Macmillan, 1989).

With the exception of one term on this list, which we shall return to later, it does appear that the use of the word 'virtual' in computing prior to the emergence of the term 'virtual reality' has introduced a new sense of the word, rejecting the traditional sense in which it is synonymous with 'almost' and developing a new sense which is roughly synonymous with 'simulated'.

USAGE

Usage of the word 'virtual'

So far it has been assumed that the phenomena described in this paper are not only real but are significant. In this section it will be shown that the word 'virtual' is being used much more than it used to be, that the term 'virtual reality' has brought about a quantum increase in its usage, and there is some evidence that the word is being used in new ways. We will do this by studying sizeable bodies of real language usage, as captured in various electronic forms.

For several years, the usage of the word 'virtual' has been increasing at an average rate of about 30% per annum and this rate has itself been increasing. These findings are drawn from INSPEC (an annual CD-ROM database of scientific and technical abstracts); and the CD-ROM full-text versions of three United Kingdom newspapers (*The Guardian, The Independent* and *The Times*). The results are summarized in Figure 3.

Figure 3. Number of occurrences of the word 'virtual'

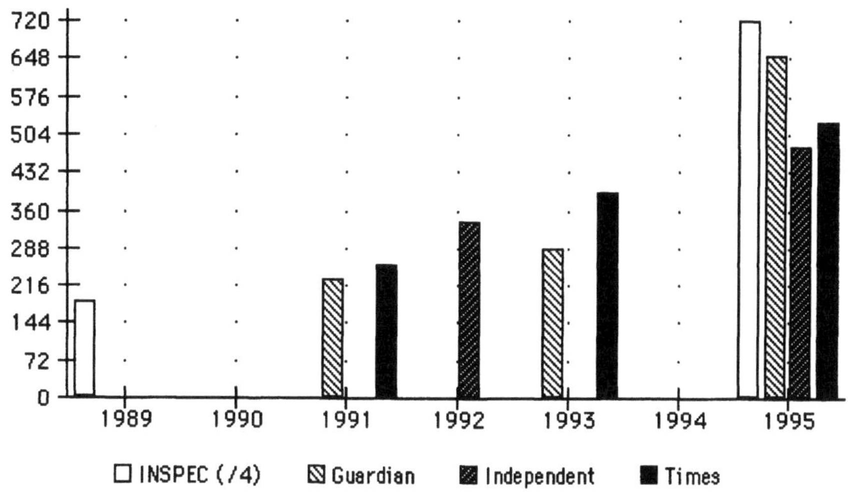

In order to determine which nouns were usually modified by the adjective 'virtual' a search was made of the British National Corpus, an electronic corpus containing approximately 200 million words of contemporary English usage. The 883 sentences retrieved yielded a total of 888 simple noun phrases, which in turn yielded 300 different head nouns. The most common of these are shown in Fig. 4.

Figure 4. Most common head nouns pre-modified by 'virtual' in BNC

virtual reality	116	virtual disappearance	13	virtual store	8
virtual monopoly	45	virtual collapse	12	virtual computing	6
virtual networks	29	virtual certainty	11	virtual demise	6
virtual memory	26	virtual eliminators	11	virtual destruction	6
virtual machines	25	virtual prisoners	11	virtual dictatorship	6
virtual particles	24	virtual standstill	11	virtual impossibility	6
virtual processors	21	virtual circuits	9	virtual library	6
virtual absence	15	virtual exclusion	9	virtual persons	6
virtual strangers	14	virtual freeze	8	virtual war	6
virtual worlds	14	virtual silence	8		

An initial attempt was made to divide the occurrences into two classes of use: 'technical' which refers to a specific technical or scientific discipline and includes pairs such as 'virtual memory' (computing), 'virtual image' (optics) and 'virtual subject' (linguistics); and 'traditional' which is unrelated to any particular technical sub-language and includes such pairs as 'virtual monopoly', 'virtual absence' and 'virtual strangers'.

It was found that, while a large number of cases could be classified in this way, certain examples did not fit either group. These could be described as cultural extensions of technical usage, e.g. 'virtual worlds', 'virtual library' and 'virtual touch'. By admitting a third, 'cultural' category it was possible to classify all instances, with the exception of 'virtual reality' which was deliberately not classified at this point. The distribution of different head nouns and number of occurrences by class is shown in Figure 5.

It was noticed that the most common examples of traditional use ('virtual monopoly', 'virtual absence', 'virtual stranger', 'virtual disappearance' and 'virtual collapse') all have negative connotations. An analysis of the entire sample found this to be a general trend (70% negative; 16% neutral; 14% positive). A tentative conclusion could therefore be drawn when the word 'virtual' is used as a synonym for 'almost' it is more likely to qualify a head noun with negative connotations. No such trend could be found with other classes of usage.

Figure 5. Use of 'virtual' by class in BNC

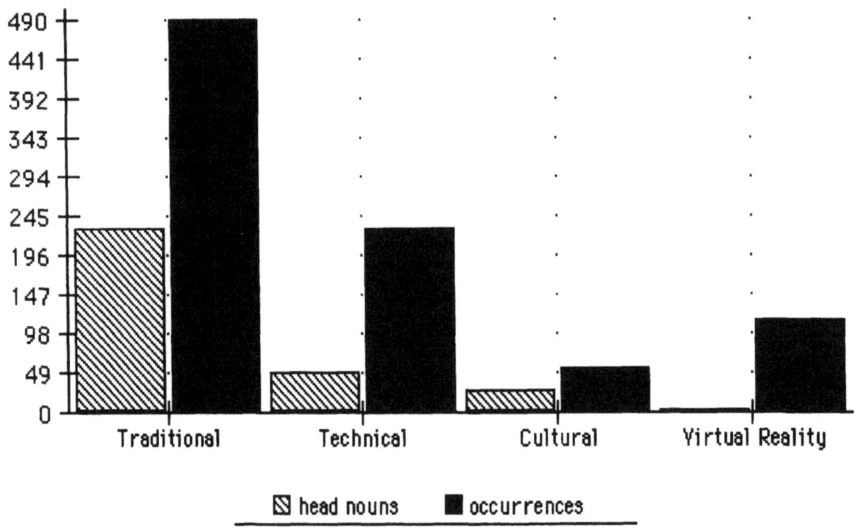

Growth of usage of the word 'virtual'

Examples from four CD-ROM series were searched in order to quantify the change of usage of the word 'virtual' over time. The INSPEC database of scientific and technical abstracts for 1989 and 1995 gave an indication of change over a 6 year period, though as it is not a full-text database it cannot be considered to be a representative sample of usage. Nevertheless, the extent of the time range was considered useful. Searches were conducted for all the head nouns appearing in Figure 1, and the results are shown in Figure 6.

Figure 6. Use of 'virtual' by class in INSPEC

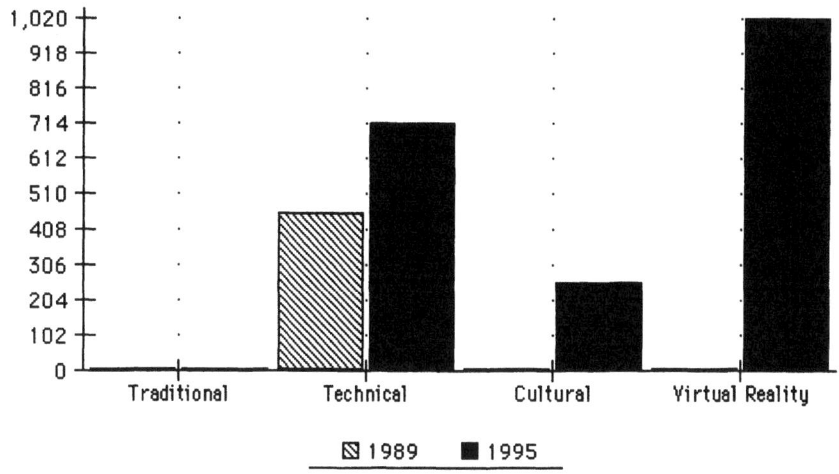

As we may expect from technical abstracts, the sample was heavily skewed towards technical usage and against traditional usage, but what is of particular interest in the growth in 'cultural' usage from practically no examples in 1989 to 9% of the total in 1995.

Figure 7. Percentage distribution of 'virtual' by class in newspapers

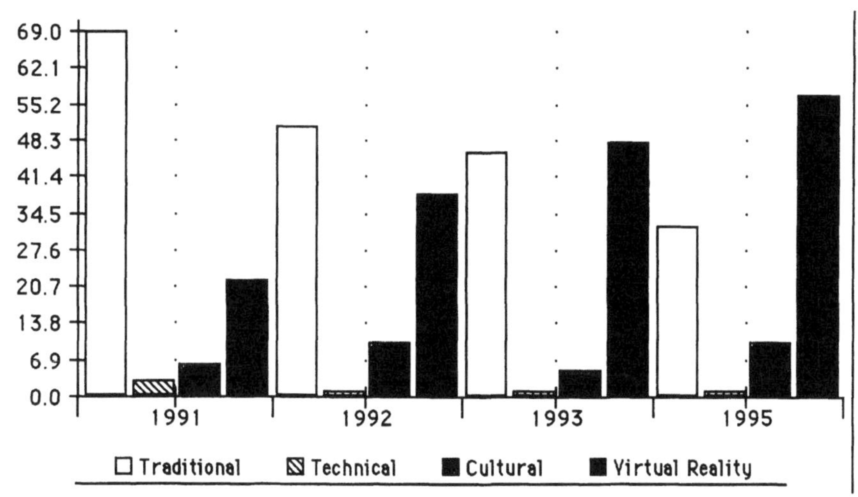

A second search was undertaken using the full-text of *The Guardian*, *The Independent* and *The Times* newspapers for various years between 1991 and 1995. The combined results are shown in Figure 7 and clearly indicate a massive growth in the use of the term 'virtual reality', a significant growth in 'cultural' usage (given the increasing size of the samples, and a decline in technical and traditional usage).

These findings show that there has been a spectacular growth in the use of the word 'virtual', spearheaded by its use in the term 'virtual reality' since about 1989, but also supported by an increase in the extensions of the word into 'cultural' domains.

The use of 'virtual' in 'virtual reality'

If the word 'virtual' has traditionally been synonymous with 'almost' (with a tendency towards negative connotations), and it has come to be applied in computing synonymously with 'simulated' (without negative connotations), then which sense is being used when we talk of 'virtual reality'?

The definitions of virtual reality given by practitioners involve several key components. These are: that virtual reality is produced by computational machinery of some kind; that it is based upon images and sounds produced by this equipment; and that it has the effect upon the person experiencing virtual reality that they are immersed within it and can interact with it or the objects within it. The following four quotations illustrate all these points.

- Virtual reality is the use of computers and human-computer interfaces to create the effect of a three-dimensional world containing interactive objects with a strong sense of three dimensional presence (Bryson, 1996, pp. 62-63).
- VR refers to interaction with computer generated spatial environments constructed to include and immerse those who enter them (Bricken, 1994, p. 163).
- Virtual reality (VR) immerses the user in a three-dimensional (3D) environment that can be actively interacted with and explored (Green and Halliday, 1996, p. 46).
- Virtual Reality (VR) systems ... are distinguished by using real-time updates of the user's head orientation and position to redraw (often in stereo) 3D images in real-time (Deering, 1996, p. 54).

However, the term 'virtual reality' has become lexicalized and in the definitions that now appear in dictionaries we find a divergence from what the technologists are saying. While the technologists stress the technology involved, all the dictionary definitions describe virtual reality from the subjective standpoint of the person experiencing it (using words like 'seems' and 'looks like'). Only one of the dictionaries taken for this study mentioned interaction.

- *virtual reality* is an environment which is produced by a computer and seems very like reality to the person experiencing it (Collins COBUILD English Dictionary, 1995).
- *virtual reality* an image produced by a computer that surrounds the person looking at it and seems almost real (Longmans Dictionary of Contemporary English, 1995).

- *virtual reality* a system in which images that look like real objects are created by computer and appear to surround a person wearing special equipment (Oxford Advanced Learners' Dictionary, 1995).
- *virtual reality* is a set of images and sounds produced by a computer which seem to represent a place or a situation in which a person experiencing it can take part (Cambridge International Dictionary of English, 1995).

This shift of emphasis, from technical description to subjective experience, is significant. Virtual reality, in technical discourse, is about levels of representation and abstraction. In general discourse, it is about appearance, belief and reality, that is to say it is presented as an ontological issue.

What is 'virtual' in 'virtual reality'?

To some people virtual reality is an ontological issue and, echoing Neil Postman's (1992) double-negative, 'We believe, because there is no reason not to believe', they argue that virtual reality can be defined as 'the suspension of disbelief'.

William Bricken appears to argue this way when he uses the concept of 'presence' to address the subjective aspects of virtual reality.

> Presence is the impression of being within the virtual environment. It is the suspension of disbelief which permits us to share the digital manifestation of fantasy (Bricken, 1994, p. 167).

For Bricken virtuality is founded upon a contrast with physical reality,

> Broadly, virtual reality is that aspect of reality which people construct from information, a reality which is potentially orthogonal to the reality of mass. ... Physical reality is built of mass while virtual reality is built of bits (Bricken, 1994, p. 163).

In a previous section it was mentioned that one example of the use of the word 'virtual' in computing pre-dated virtual reality yet did not function as a synonym for either 'almost' or 'simulated'. In the definition of a 'virtual terminal' it is clearly implied that it is used to refer to an ideal type and not necessarily a real terminal.

> *virtual terminal*: In peripherals, an ideal terminal that is defined as a standard for the purpose of uniform handling of a variety of actual terminals. A terminal processor thereafter converts the signals of the real terminal to conform to the standards of the virtual terminal (Macmillan Dictionary of Information Technology, 1989).

Woolley expresses a similar notion with respect to the notion of 'virtual machine',

> A computer is a 'virtual' machine - a virtual Turing machine, to be precise. It is an abstract entity or process that has found physical expression, that has been 'realized'. It is a simulation, only not necessarily a simulation of anything actual (Woolley, 1993, pp. 68-9).

Woolley points to a new sense of the word 'virtual' that is not opposed to 'actual' or 'physical', but is opposed to 'realized'. A similar point is made, and expanded, by Pierre Levy who makes essentially the same distinction but uses the opposite words to Woolley when he writes,

> I would like to draw an important philosophic distinction between two dialectic couples, the possible/real one and the virtual/actual one. Following

> some suggestions of Gilles Deleuze, I would say that the possible is a ghost reality: already completely defined, it only lacks existence. The realisation is not a creative process, it is just a selection among determined entities.

and later says,

> ... virtuality, indeed, does not mean imaginary. Strictly speaking, the virtual is not the opposite of the real but the opposite of the actual (Levy, 1997).

Despite their confusing use of terminology, both Woolley and Levy are saying the same thing. 'Virtual' is no longer being used in opposition to 'physically real' but is used as a rough synonym for 'potential' (a concept not unrelated to Aristotle's concept of *entelechy*). Levy makes this clear by showing how a virtualization can have a physical existence,

> Virtualization is not necessarily a disappearance. On the contrary, it is often a materialization process. This can easily be shown from the example of technology. The design of a new tool is a virtualization of many actions. When someone designs a tool, instead of focusing on the action, he makes the focus on something much more general, on a type of problem. The tool is not an answer to such or such particular situation but the materialization of a general function.

and

> ... the image is virtual on the hard disk and actual on the screen. Virtualization is digitisation and actualisation is display. The image is even more virtual when its digital description is not a stable deposit in the computer memory, but when it is calculated in real time by a program from a model and a flow of input data (Levy, 1997).

This type of 'virtuality' is roughly synonymous with 'potential' in the sense that it manifests itself as a stored general function which can be activated in order to produce a specific output depending upon the context of use. This is a long way from being a simple synonym for 'almost' and, on the way, it has turned into a term that will admit of degrees (Levy, 1997).

CONCLUSION

When we try to think about the future of a particular technology, or to think about new technologies in general, we are forced to use words as our tools. In this paper it has been demonstrated how those tools may be first borrowed but then, through their interaction with the technology itself, they become changed. Ambiguities are exploited and new senses of words are formed which can have a currency outside of the technical domain within which they were created.

This was shown in the first instance with the term 'artificial' which has always been ambiguous and which was interpreted ambiguously by some of those who speculated about the capabilities of computers to imitate human beings within what was a strictly modernist paradigm. The term 'virtual' did not contain such ambiguity but its use within the same modernist paradigm of computing produced a new sense of the word, roughly synonymous with 'simulated'. More recently, the postmodernist concept of 'virtuality', as embodied in the term 'virtual reality' has yielded yet another sense of the word, roughly synonymous with 'potential'.

It may appear that words as tools are therefore unreliable, selected to do one job they become transformed into something else; but we should remember that rigid, inflexible tools are also unreliable as they are soon broken and discarded. It is better to see language as an important arena in which culture and technology come to terms with each other and the output from which, in the form of new terms and new word senses, provides the parameters within which our thoughts about the future are frequently trapped.

REFERENCES

Beardon, C. (1994) Computers, postmodernism and the culture of the artificial. *AI & Society*, **8**, 1-16.

Bricken, W. (1994) Inclusive Symbolic Environments. In K. Duncan and K. Krueger (Eds.), Linkage and Developing Countries, *Information Processing '94*. Vol. III. IFIP/North Holland, Amsterdam, 163-170.

Bryson S. (1996) Virtual Reality in Scientific Visualization. *Communications of the ACM*, **39**, 5, 62-63.

Cambridge International Dictionary of English (1995). Cambridge University Press, Cambridge.

Concise Oxford Dictionary (1982) 7th Edn. Oxford University Press, Oxford.

Collins COBUILD English Dictionary (1995). Harper Collins, London.

Deering M F. (1996) The HoloSketch™ VR sketching system. *Communications of the ACM*, **39**, 5, 54-61.

Green M and Halliday S. (1996) A geometric modelling and animation system for virtual reality. *Communications of the ACM*, **39**, 5, 46-53.

Levy, P. (1997) Welcome to Virtuality. *Digital Creativity*. **8** (1), 3-10.

Longmans Dictionary of Contemporary English (1995) 3rd Edn, Longmans, Harlow, Essex.

McGraw-Hill Dictionary of Computers (1984) S.B. Parker (Ed.) McGraw-Hill, NY.

Macmillan Dictionary of Information Technology (1989) 3rd Edn, D. Langley and M. Shain (Eds.), Macmillan, London.

Negrotti, M. (1991) One hundred definitions of AI. In M. Negrotti (Ed.) *Understanding the artificial: On the future shape of artificial intelligence*. Springer-Verlag, Berlin. 155-57.

Oxford Advanced Learners' Dictionary (1995) 5th Edn, Oxford University Press, Oxford.

Oxford English Dictionary (1933) Oxford University Press, Oxford.

Postman, N. (1992) *Technopoly: The surrender of culture to technology*. Knopf, New York.

Prentice-Hall (1995) *Prentice-Hall Illustrated Dictionary of Computing*. 2nd Edn. Ed. by J.C. Nader. Prentice-Hall of Australia, Sydney.

Roget, P.M. (1852) *Thesaurus of English Words and Phrases*. Edition publ. 1962, Longmans, Green & Co, London.

Searle, J.R. (1980) Minds, Brains, and Programs. *The Behavioural and Brain Sciences*, **3**, 417-424.

Turing, A. (1950) Computing Machinery and Intelligence. *Mind*, **LIX**, 236.

Woolley, B. (1993) *Virtual Worlds*. Penguin Books, London.

14

Information technology for persons with a disability: A vision for the International Federation for Information Processing

Geoff Busby, MBE and Diane Whitehouse***
** British Computer Society Disability Group, c/o GEC Computer Services Limited, Great Baddow, Chelmsford Essex CM2 8HN, United Kingdom*
Tel: +44 1245 242950, Fax: +44 1245 478317
*** PhD Programme London Business School, Regent's Park, London NW1 4SA, United Kingdom*
Tel: +44 171 262 5050 X3646, Fax: +44 171 724 7875
Email: dwhitehouse@lbs.lon.ac.uk

Abstract

For the information technology industry, there is considerable potential in developing information and communication technologies that can enhance the lives of people with a disability (who number over 500 million worldwide).

Information and communication technologies can offer many different and creative solutions to the needs of persons with a disability: they can enable increased social citizenship, culture, democracy, and equality of access. But the kinds of technologies that are useful to people with a disability are also of use to society as a whole. Designing for all kinds of people, whether able-bodied or disabled, is simply good design. To create this change in perception, we need to work with positive images of disabled people and to influence the attitudes of computer scientists, systems designers and developers, and information and communications specialists.

Where does the International Federation for Information Processing fit in to such an approach? As an international federation of professional computing associations, it can take many constructive and progressive actions. Among these, it can promote the best practice of a few computer societies; it can extend its own

An Ethical Global Information Society J. Berleur & D. Whitehouse (Eds.)

position on equality of access; it can help in changing perceptions; it can act as a facilitator for consumers' needs; it can lead the world community in terms of IT values; and it can act as a watchdog, creating awareness of the social implications of information and communication technologies for the use of all people, including people with a disability. It is in this latter area particularly that potential, future directions for IFIP's Technical Committee 9 lie. It is here that the paper places its emphasis.

INTRODUCTION

The International Federation for Information Processing (IFIP) has considerable potential for influencing the kinds of information and communication technologies (ICT) available to the public at large, and disabled users specifically. Within this context, it is particularly important that IFIP's Technical Committee (TC) 9 researches the social implications and the social consequences of ICT in general and for persons with a disability especially. TC9 is potentially IFIP's interface between society and technology. TC9 could really help the information technology (IT) industry and profession in this area, showing information technologists how to be socially conscious, to know what technologies are available, and what the social reasons for this are.

The paper highlights potential, future directions for IFIP's TC9, using disability issues as an example. We have chosen this particular focus because, as individuals involved in and active in this field, this is our own personal area of concern. Hence, the paper emphasizes the interface between information and communication technologies and disability.

The paper does not specify a particular strategy for IFIP. Rather, the paper's intention is to focus on a vision for IFIP; it assumes that visions and values must enter the daily lives of organizations (Kanter, 1990). It focuses on the kind of vision that is often seen as prefacing an organization's mission, aims, and objectives (Bryson, 1988; Smith, 1995). At a later stage of preparation and planning, exact times, dates, places, and precise actions can be discussed.

Nor does the paper concentrate on any one specific disability but rather it deals with a range of disabilities. Its intention is to raise readers' general levels of awareness rather than to detail the conditions of a single impairment. (Indeed, some impairments - cerebral palsy, for example - often involve multiple incapacities.) The paper also assumes that disability is neither fixed nor absolute; it is not a condition in its own right nor the result of a personal limitation; and it has very little to do with the body. Rather, disability is a social construct (Oliver, 1989; Barton, 1996; Hales, 1996; Oliver, 1996).

The paper's aim is to put ability issues on the agenda so that individuals and groups become aware of the issues at stake, perceptions are changed so that disability is taken into account during the design process and, as a result, disabled people begin to have the IT tools available to them to facilitate their greater knowledge and to enable their greater access into the community and society. The paper's message is that universal design is do-able.

The paper first examines these concerns by giving an overview of the potential for user participation and involvement of persons with a disability. It later reviews contemporary figures relating to the numbers of people with a disability worldwide, the case for designing IT for people with a disability and using IT more, and commonly-held perceptions of disabled people including media and marketing examples. It then turns to assess what actions IFIP can take to improve attention to this field, and what TC9 specifically can do. Throughout the paper run the themes of culture and democracy in a global world.

CULTURE, DEMOCRACY, USER PARTICIPATION AND INVOLVEMENT OF PERSONS WITH A DISABILITY

Information and communication technologies can provide the potential for increased citizenship, culture, and democracy to persons with a disability. What society provides should be accessible to all. Attention needs to be paid to the full participation of disabled people in society, their complete access and involvement, and the diversity of cultures that result. IT can particularly offer to people with a disability increased access to schooling, further and higher education, employment, housing, leisure, lifestyle, welfare, culture, politics and decision-making.

Here we take culture to mean that which enables each and every one of us to master our own destiny (Berleur, 1994 citing Touraine, 1984). For us, therefore it means equality of access. People need to have an understanding and knowledge of information and communication technologies in order to increase and expand their own potential use of these technologies; this is as true for people with a disability as it is for able-bodied people. It is considered to be among the intellectual and moral responsibilities of computer scientists and information and communication technology practitioners to make information and technology comprehensible (Berleur, this volume). Indeed, a wider range of communications may need to be used when explaining information and communication technologies to people who have a disability (for example, drawings and pictures, short words and sentences, tapes, photos, symbols, sign language, or deaf-blind communication) (Change, n/d). Care and attention also needs to be paid to involving people with a disability in the design process of information and communication technologies. There needs to be real understanding and knowledge in order to control IT. It is this growing awareness which will help people with a disability to shape their own destinies. People with disabilities are part of the social tapestry; having them present, visible, and participating is tremendously important for the richness of the embroidery of social citizenship. It is through talking about their experiences, their circumstances, their understanding, and their culture that disabled people - like all other communities - can share in what is common to us all (Berleur, 1994).

More user involvement in design and needs assessment is required. Currently, many disabled people are not allowed to choose the most appropriate technologies for their requirements: whether, so to speak, they require a Mini Minor or an Alfa Romeo. Technologies are imposed on them; they are not allowed to ride their own wheels or to turn their own machines on or off. In a more democratic world, these are the kinds of tasks that disabled people ought to be able to do for themselves.

Democracy implies the capacity to participate fully in voting, in polling, and other forms of decision-making as well as running for office and taking up political positions. This participation in the community or society is as important for people with a disability as it is for able-bodied people. Some important British examples of disabled people involved in national politics include eminent politicians such as Lord Jack Ashley, David Blunkett, and Emma Nicholson. Each of these individuals who has a particular disability has developed longstanding political careers, held important political portfolios, and initiated prominent legislative developments.

In the potential opening-up of electronic democratic spaces, care needs to be taken that these spaces are open and available to persons with a disability. Communications are all-important so that persons with a disability know what the available methods and political procedures are. It is also important that research into the innovative possibilities offered for election and voting procedures by such new technologies as the Internet also consider the precise circumstances of access and involvement of individuals with a disability. Many different forms of access may need to be considered because disabilities can be many, various, and even multiple. And, of course, the numbers of disabled people worldwide are enormous.

THE GLOBAL PERSPECTIVE ON PERSONS WITH A DISABILITY AS POTENTIAL MARKETS

There are tremendous opportunities offered to information technology (IT) manufacturers and developers in terms of persons with a disability as a market for IT. In Britain alone, the number of people with a disability is estimated at 6 million by the general household survey (FEFC, 1996, p7), a figure which does not include the elderly at large. Recent figures indicate that disabled British individuals have an annual disposable income of over £33 million. There are an estimated 33 million people with a disability in Europe and around 50 million in the United States (The Economist, 1996).

Even though there are few international studies, we should not forget the massive numbers of persons with a disability in developing and newly developed countries. Disabled people live in all the countries of the world, and particularly detailed studies of their conditions have been undertaken in India, Jordan, the Occupied Territories, the Lebanon, Zanzibar, and Zimbabwe (Coleridge, 1993). In China, for example, there may be as many as 50 million disabled people (Ming, 1993).

Although the figure is disputed, one estimate of the total world population puts the number of disabled people at approximately 500 million, so that perhaps ten per cent of the world's population has either a permanent or a temporary physical, sensory, or mental impairment (Despouy, 1991). Surrounding the disabled too, there is also their cultural community, and their carers. In addition, the new wave of the elderly is as yet unquantifiable (Age Concern, 1996; Brower-Janse, Maddy D. *et al.,* 1997). In some sense, we are all only temporarily able-bodied (TAB).

At a global level, it is often those from the wealthiest backgrounds who have access to IT; too often it is the children of the wealthy, for example, who are in special schools or at special centres. In Britain, attention is paid to insufficient IT equipment in deprived areas such as southeast London, Liverpool, or Glasgow but, if these areas have problems, what about the global dearth of IT for people with disabilities, in continents like Africa, Asia or southern America?

In these figures lies a global, multicultural, challenge; indeed, a global, multicultural opportunity. Enormous numbers of disabled people could be helped by IT. Clearly, there are plenty of possibilities for marketing good, well-designed products to persons with a disability. In all contexts, the question to be asked of people in the IT industry is: are your products geared up and designed to appeal to this expanding community?

The case for IT for persons with a disability

What is good design? Good design is commonsense - it's that simple. Why is good design commonsense? Good design is commonsense because:

- it serves potential markets
- it serves the community
- it makes a better product
- it opens up new areas of technology
- it allows consumers to look at technology from a new perspective.

Design that designs for all sorts of people, able-bodied and disabled, is simply good design. Good design of information and communication technologies matters to us all because we are all only temporarily able-bodied (TAB). In reality, the differences between disabled and able-bodied people are minute, and large numbers of people become disabled as they age.

It is this kind of enhancement to the lives of people through the new information and communications technologies that can improve citizenship, culture, and democracy (Berleur, this volume). Good design would produce a better world, one that is more integrated and more multicultural.

Within this general context, two pieces of recent legislation are of particular importance: the United States' Americans with Disabilities Act (ADA) (1990) and the British Disability Discrimination Act (DDA) (1995). The implications of these laws require greater research but this is not the focus of this paper, and these issues have been more adequately covered elsewhere (for example, Gooding, 1994).

One example of good, new design of information and communication technologies is telecommunications. Its affordances offer considerable improvements to users with difficulties in hearing, speech, sight, mobility, or dexterity. For example, for people with quiet or with no voices, British technologies such as Claudius II or Ferntech 320, telephones which 'speak' recorded phrases or which allows users to make calls unaided using a single switch, are invaluable (British Telecommunications plc, 1996). Similarly, the Deaf and Disabled Telecommunications Program of the California Public Utilities Commission provides new speech-to-speech services facilities for those who have a quiet voice or who have no voice (Interactions, 1996).

The economics of taking good preventative measures are also very important: good design can have a huge impact economically. Good design can help avoid many disabling conditions, like repetitive strain injury (RSI) where it is keyboards and mice that often cause injuries. Information technology goods and equipment need to be designed so that they do not cause damage. Good design will then spread and will become available to everyone, able-bodied and disabled alike.

Well-designed information and communication technologies can help produce a better society and help designers not to be destructive in the human sense. Can the IT industry afford not to take action?

Why we need to use IT more

Technology is keeping more and more people alive, including many people with a disability. For example, the numbers of people with a severe learning disability is growing. In Britain alone, there are currently 50,000 people with a severe learning disability aged between 25-34 years old, and 30,000 between the ages of 35-44. Increasingly, such individuals are living until much older ages, often until age 60 or more (Mental Health Foundation, 1996).

Yet, at the same time, we are not using information and communications technologies enough. Many technologies are still under-used. The technologies that are available could be used much more in a quality way to help the rapidly expanding community of disabled persons. The dichotomy is that, while more disabled people may be alive, their everyday lives in the community may prove to be a difficult struggle.

Of course, there are dangers for disabled people in the new information and communication technologies, particularly in terms of possible social exclusion (Whitehouse, 1993), but then there are dangers for everyone. Rather, there are possibly even more opportunities for disabled people for access and communication than they would have had otherwise.

Technologies in general can offer so many opportunities to disabled people. Take the provision of television subtitles: simply having subtitles can make watching the television into a much more enjoyable experience for a person who is tone deaf. Or announcing railway station or bus-stop names over the loudspeaker: this can make an all-important difference to the travel journey for someone who is blind or someone who cannot read very well. Technology can also offer self-support, control, and security systems for people with a disability (Mangan, 1993, p49). It can enable users to activate or de-activate security alarms, dial up to one hundred numbers on the telephone, open and shut curtains, or turn the television on or off.

In Britain, for example, community care is now available (HMSO, 1990). However, carers are often only interviewed once and that is the extent of their training. A lot of carers have never come into contact with people with a disability or with elderly people before. Carers may know the standard answers in a given situation but apparently they do not know what to do in an emergency. Carers need to have quick and easy access to a source of expertise, just like para-medics in the middle of Africa. This could be done by making CD-Roms or online communication available to them. Imagine you are a carer and you have a portable computer or a laptop computer with you, or access to a CD-Rom, you would be able to follow a quick lesson on how to set up and use a hoist, for example, if you needed it.

Another example is that the educational ethos of the three Rs (reading, 'riting, and 'rithmetic) still dominates. Yet, in ten years' time, people may not need to read or write: people will just be able to speak and a machine will respond. Not everyone will need to be a mathematician. Education will have to change because information and communication technologies will increasingly do a lot that people currently have to do for themselves intellectually.

Information and communication technologies can offer creative solutions to the needs of people with disabilities. If we take the example of learning difficulties, we can cite the exploration of such technologies as talking screen and sentence scanning software, symbol systems, wide ranges of switches (for example, large, sensitive, flat switches), letter grids, concept keyboards, visual stimulation systems, vibration systems using music tapes and cuing music, audio-visual interaction systems, and virtual reality systems to enhance the learning abilities and lives of children, young adolescents, and mature adults with learning disabilities (Ability, 1997).

Increasingly, the relationship between the television, telecommunications, and the computer will become seamless. It will become chips with everything. Artificial intelligence, virtual reality, the information highway, multimedia, broadband communications, and CD-Rom technology: these are the kinds of technologies that can be useful to people with a disability.

But these are not just technologies that are useful to people with disabilities; they are also useful to society as a whole. Take for example, the Internet. It is no longer in the hands of IT specialists. It used to seem weird when people communicated with each other using computers; now it is becoming more and more common. People are increasingly surfing the Internet as part of their leisure activities. Like cable television, the use of the Internet will become more and more widespread (Kehoe, 1996).

To sum up, the kinds of technologies that are useful to people with disabilities are useful to society as a whole. They make using information and communication technologies easier and more accessible to all.

PERCEPTIONS OF PERSONS WITH A DISABILITY

What are your personal perceptions of persons with a disability? Disability is more of a social perception than a medical status (Oliver, 1996). A distinction needs to be made between what is medical and what is social. Look at the kinds of words used to describe someone who has a disability: for example, they are said to be 'suffering from' a particular 'handicap' or are 'wheelchair bound'.

Images of disabled children get over-used. Disabled children are presented as objects, and the associated messages are very patronising. Images of disabled children are accompanied by the message, 'Give, give, give, to help these poor children.' But they are not poor children. The message really ought to be: if a person cannot drive a car, they may simply need to be given a lift. This is the kind of insight that is very important for IT designers.

When IT people think of persons with a disability, all too often they think of those who are partially sighted or blind. Why is that so? Partly because visual difficulties are culturally easier to accept and partly because they are easier to handle in the sense of being a well-defined problem.

There are currently many advances in the fields of computer engineering, opthamology, and biology. These sciences are collaborating to bring sight to the vision-impaired through electronic prostheses; specialized image-processing cells;

ocular implants; semi-conductor technology, and computational neural networks (IEEE, 1996).

Why is Stephen Hawking shown on *Star Trek*, for example? He is used to send out a message about people with disabilities; he focuses the public's attention on the capacity of technology to improve lives (Smith, 1994).

With all Geoff Busby's qualifications, he too is caught in much the same conundrum: he is also used to send out a message. But Geoff just wants to do his job. He hates it when strangers become interested in the fact that he is married, or that he has children, or assume that, because he works with computers or has an MBE, he must be brilliant. He is not a bitter person because he is disabled and because he has cerebral palsy. He has his good times and he has his bad, but he enjoys his work and using the gifts and abilities that he has been given. For Geoff, it is a huge bonus that he can do the work he does and that he can use the gifts in his possession.

So, people at large need to think in terms of new images of the disabled. Designers need to consider people's abilities and disabilities. What can people do and what can they not do? People need to start considering each other's needs. What would information technology have meant, for example, to the Irish poet and author, Christy Brown, whose early life was portrayed in the feature film, *My Left Foot*?

What kinds of images do persons with a disability have of themselves? Ask a person who has no verbal communications what his or her aspirations are. Then give him or her a portable computer and a voice synthesizer. See what kind of effect that can have. Using a voice synthesizer, for example, can be crucial. For the thousands of people who cannot speak, this application alone can help enormously. Voice chips cost peanuts, so they should be on standard offer in IT equipment.

What communication means to you and what it means to someone else can be very different. For example, for Geoff Busby who uses a voice synthesizer, it means he can put his ideas across in a voice which, while he knows it is not his own, is at least comprehensible to the audience. Geoff enjoys customizing his 'voice' by adding his own idiosyncratic speech patterns as well as adding humorous cartoons to his presentations. Because his own, physical, voice is no longer exhausted, Geoff can also add spontaneous quips or jokes to his presentations, and the audience is able to understand these clearly. For Geoff, communication also means gaining more access to information that he needs. He hopes to do far more of this in the future through the use of CD-Roms, satellites, videos, and web technology. He is optimistic that progress in this particular technological domain will mean that he will no longer have to visit specialized broadcast studios to undertake such tasks.

Another British Computer Society Disability Group (BCS DG) colleague, Ken Stoner, founder of the IT can Help project, explains what communication means to him. Ken has had motor neurone disease for ten years and lost his voice and handwriting ability seven years ago. He says that life would be a very sad affair without his computers. Ken's wheelchair-mounted laptop synthesizer means he can join in any conversation, give long presentations or lectures, and tell jokes in the pub without forgetting the punch lines (he has input the lines in memory). Ken's desktop computer and laser printer allow him to carry on with his voluntary work for people with disabilities, for example through the IT can Help network, which would not otherwise be possible. In this way, Ken continues to make an extremely valuable contribution to his community.

For Diane Whitehouse, technology means the opportunity to communicate and correspond with colleagues at a distance, regionally, nationally, and internationally. It means being able to work more easily on collaborative projects.

To sum up, it is particularly important for IT designers and systems personnel not to limit their perceptions of individuals with a disability. They need to overcome the legacy of negativism that surrounds disabled people; they need to see people as people (Nelson, 1994). Information technology designers need to consider users' abilities and disabilities. It is important for the computer industry to be flexible in analyzing and assessing people's information and communication technology needs. The way forward is to consider designing for all, and incorporating all needs and abilities.

Media and marketing images of persons with a disability, erotica and pornography

In Britain, at least on television, there is what is called the 'nine o'clock watershed'. Certain sexual or violent images can only be shown on television after nine at night. The television viewer has the choice of keeping the television channel on or switching it off. But what if that viewer cannot turn the television on or off him or herself?

Many people gasp when the word pornography is mentioned. Yet information and communication technologies, multimedia, and virtual reality can help satisfy the social, emotional, and even sexual needs of people with disabilities. Electronic pornography is one form of access some people with disabilities have to 'love'; telecommunications may be the only means of communication, sensitivity, and chitchat that some disabled people have.

Advertising, however, is often overlooked, and much advertising has a sexual content. Marketing experts use sexual images for advertising purposes, and it seems to work: if the images did not work, and if people did not succumb to marketing messages, marketing firms would not use them. So, in a way, individuals with a puritanical attitude make some sense when they say that titillating images have an effect. Western society is, however, hypocritical because some of its members object to explicit erotica or pornography while many sales and marketing techniques are based on implicitly sexual imagery.

Information and communication technologies and interactive media, television, CD-Roms, and the Internet, are all bringing to audiences and consumers sexual imagery. While spectators watch an apparently intellectual television programme, suddenly the advertising bombards them with sexual images. Pornography comes looking for the audience rather than the audience having to look for it.

The images used in commercials and in advertising can be just as 'dangerous' as pornography: they offer misleading, unrealistic, overly perfect images of what people are, what realistic role models are, and what life is: images that can be very offensive to disabled people. These images can be found on television programmes such as *Baywatch*, on the Internet, on pop videos or in the lyrics of pop records. They project stereotypes in a world in which all women have a wonderful figure and all men have a 40" chest: of course, very few individuals live up to these perfect images.

People with disabilities now send out messages. From the early 1990s onward, there has emerged a whole new awareness, susceptibility, and perception (Nelson, 1994)[1]. More enlightened marketing companies are introducing people with disabilities in advertising in a positive manner. For example, the North American markets feature participants in the ParaOlympics who advertise sports gear. Good-looking disabled people are now sell swimming costumes. In television adverts advertising swimwear, the camera will eventually pull back at the end of a shot, to show only then that the attractive, champion male swimmer in the pool is a wheelchair user: a sort of shock tactic, but a useful and positive tactic. People with disabilities now star on stage and on screen in positive, non-patronising plays, films, and television programs. Media forums on disabilities are being set up in countries like Britain to examine best codes of practice for the portrayal of persons with disabilities in various media.

To sum up, information technologists should not impose a particular code of ethics on to people with regard to pornography; they should not set themselves up as God. There is a risk that information technologists will go too far in mandating certain behaviours, or in being overly 'ethical'. Information technologists should not take orthodox frameworks and impose them on whole communities of people. Globally, there are considerable cultural differences between regions and countries in terms of what they find acceptable or not: different cultures and societies accept different norms. An identical set of judgements cannot be used for everyone. Clearly, there are attenuating circumstances that may have to be considered, especially with people with disabilities.

WHERE DOES IFIP FIT IN?

More than any other facet of advancement of modern society, the new developments in the field of information and communication technologies, such as virtual reality, artificial intelligence, and multimedia increase the potential for social citizenship, culture, and democracy to even larger numbers of people. This is especially true for persons with a disability, and particularly for disabled people in the developing countries, where there lies even greater potential. It is our role, as members of IFIP, to make sure that these new technologies are available to everyone. Our role should be to spread the word.

In the disabilities field, there are extensive opportunities for developing the IT industry that are currently not being recognized. IFIP needs to create an awareness and a vision for the IT industry to follow, particularly with regard to the blossoming new information and communication technologies such as virtual reality, multimedia, broadband communications, and telecommunications. IFIP needs to know that people with disabilities want to make use of these technologies

---

1 Some interesting examples of positive images of persons with a disability, often using information and communications technology, can be found in magazines such as *Abilities*, *Ability Network*, *Disability Today*, and *Freedom*. (These guides for the disabled and lifestyle magazines all originate in Canada. There are, of course, similar magazines in other countries.)

in their everyday activities. Similarly, the IT industry needs to listen to its users, whoever those users are. Users are everybody; and people with disabilities want to be included in the use of information technology, not excluded.

IFIP can particularly help because it is a global, international organization with access to many different parts of the globe and many different computer societies. IFIP is an international federation of professional and technical organizations concerned with information processing, and the national groupings of these associations which has been in existence since 1960. As a federation, it is dedicated to improving worldwide communication and understanding among practitioners of every nation about the role that information processing can play in all walks of life. In a sense, IFIP is the United Nations (UN) of information and communication technologies.

IFIP could act as a facilitator of people's desires, ideas, and aspirations with regard to IT. IFIP could be the go-between or intermediary between consumers and suppliers. IFIP is in a unique position to do this; it is truly international in its reach - it is not just locked into a North American perspective.

Within IFIP, there need to be people with disabilities who can argue the case for the new disabled markets, new market awareness, new technological opportunities, and for the full realization of the potential of all people. IFIP needs to think about enhancing its leadership role: disabled people should be more visible and more involved in decision-making. (Sadly, at the moment, some people who have a disability are not able to attend certain IFIP meetings because they cannot stay in particular hotel accommodation or because the physical access to buildings is simply not there. Also, there appear to be insufficient industrial contacts within IFIP for people with disabilities to get sponsorship to attend meetings. These limitations need to be considered when organizing meetings and conferences.)

IFIP has the responsibility to explore much wider access to its members and potential members than exists currently. It can ensure that disability issues are covered as a theme in its conferences and workshops. It can ensure that all conferences, workshops, and meetings are physically accessible and have a full range of communication facilities available. It can also encourage all computer societies to have a policy or position on information and communication technologies for people with a disability and to enable the fullest possible access to all potential members. Visionaries can build accessibility into all IT products for all consumers.

Some good examples of what professional computer societies are now doing to help persons with a disability include associations in Austria, Britain, Denmark, Germany, Greece, Holland, Hungary, and soon Ireland. Computer societies considering what they might do in this area can build on the good practice illustrated, for example, by the British Computer Society Disability Group (BCS DG). Established in 1975, the BCS DG now has over five hundred members. BCS DG has a high degree of involvement at both board and volunteer levels of persons with a disability; it lobbies widely for the technology needs of persons with a disability; it liaises with other influential bodies working in this area, such as The Computability Centre; it organizes the IT Can Help project which provides free advice and assistance on technology for persons with a disability and it organizes other special projects from time to time; it is a source of information through its brochures, pamphlets, and meetings; and, last but not least, it publishes an informative, increasingly high-quality and high-profile magazine on the information and communication technologies available to persons with a disability.

IFIP needs to have an inspirational role, to be a leader in IT values and ethics. If IFIP can lead the IT industry in an awareness of this particular area, of the potential that can be offered by information and communication technologies to persons with a disability, it would be doing the IT industry a big favour. But IFIP should not just be a marketeer. While IFIP can act as a promoter of the potential offered by new information and communication technologies, it needs to do so in an ethical way.

IFIP needs to act in a responsible manner. It can also be a watchdog. It needs to be professional in its understanding of the social implications of the technologies being developed. For, what good are information and communication technologies if they are not designed for people, and if they are not useful to people?

What about TC9?

This is where Technical Committee (TC) 9 can especially help. TC9 can make people aware of the social implications of the information and communication technologies currently being developed, making sure that these technologies are well designed for the use of all people, including persons with a disability. It is important that the computer industry does not make the mistake of certain other design professions - such as the field of architecture which is prone to create disabilities through inappropriate design.

The culture of TC9 needs to be spread within IFIP. TC9's brief is concerned with the relationship between computers and society: it examines the influence and social consequences of IT applications on individuals, groups, and societies; it promotes social accountability; it facilitates research; it seeks to enhance the quality of life for all as a result of computer use, and to humanize the use of all information systems. Working with academics, practitioners, researchers, and users, TC9 should become the interface between society and the good design of information technology for all people, including people with disabilities.

So, TC9 can help in two principal ways: firstly, by listening to what society has to say and then feeding those findings into IFIP and, secondly, by feeding news about the new information and communication technologies out to society. TC9 can help to harmonize a global society. TC9's role could bring high-level thinkers in touch with society, helping to change their ideas about the effects of IT on societies.

TC9 can become the human interface between society and technology: showing people what the new tools are that are on offer and what the opportunities or the dangers are. It can also act as the interface with the more technical of the other TCs and working groups (WGs) within IFIP. Many of IFIP's other TCs and WGs have members who are working on completely abstract problems or technologies: they are not looking at cause and effect and pay no attention to the whole, global effects of those technologies. But TC9 is composed of experts in this field who can provide this kind of holistic view. TC9 can fill the current void; it can act as the go-between between information and communication technologies, society, and persons with a disability.

TC9 could investigate the various innovations and new applications that form part of the new information and communication technologies. TC9 has the expertise to say whether a particular innovation is useful or not. This kind of assessment is a social task, a social responsibility.

As members of TC9, we need to think about how to make our analyses and interpretations more internationally widespread so that they are absorbed into government policy at all levels. Society as a whole needs the kind of research that TC9 does in order to make decisions. We have to begin to analyze what are the needs of persons with a disability, what are their wants, and how information and communications technologies can enhance their lives. The facts and figures - outlined in this paper, for example - ought to be hitting people in the face. So too, a good, high-profile, media event would teach people all over the world about the social effects of information and communication technologies.

TC9 could do the research, look at the potential advantages and disadvantages of specific technologies, and investigate their potential applications and implications. But we should not say that a particular technology is good or bad, because that is about playing God. (One particular weakness is that TC9 could become too judgemental - though there may be occasions on which we may actually need to take a stand.) Ideally, TC9 should simply indicate its opinions which will be, by TC9's very nature as a multicultural group, multicultural. It should be part of TC9's role to express diversity rather than to mandate a particular worldview. TC9 should be able to express the opinions of the whole world including the views of those 500 million people with a temporary or permanent disability.

SUMMARY AND CONCLUSIONS

There is considerable potential in developing information and communication technologies to enhance the lives of people with a disability, who total over 500 million across the globe. Information and communication technologies can provide many different and creative solutions to the needs of disabled people, bringing them increased citizenship, culture, democracy, and equality of access. However, the technologies that are useful to people with a disability also make important social and economic contributions to society as a whole. It is simply good design to design for all kinds of people, whether able-bodied or disabled. To create this understanding, we need to work with positive images of disabled people and to influence the attitudes of computer scientists, systems designers, systems developers, and information and communications specialists.

What is IFIP's role in this new development? As an international federation of professional computing associations, IFIP can start many constructive, progressive initiatives. Among these, it can promote best practice among computer societies worldwide; it can examine its own position on equality of access; it can help in changing perceptions; it can act as a facilitator of consumers' needs; it can lead the world community in terms of a new culture and democracy of IT values; and it can act as a watchdog, creating awareness of the social implications of information and communication technologies for the use of all people, including people with a disability. Of all IFIP's technical communities, TC9 ought in particular to be participating in such an initiative.

ACKNOWLEDGEMENTS

The authors would like to thank Paula Goossens, Luc Goffinet, and at least two anonymous reviewers for their helpful insights into the development of this paper.

REFERENCES

Ability (1997) Tools for learning. *Ability*, 19. March 1997. Chelmsford: British Computer Society Disability Group (BCS DG). Guest editor: Diane Whitehouse.

Age Concern (1996) *Older people in the United Kingdom. Some basic facts.* August. London: Age Concern

Barton, L. (editor) (1996) *Disability and Society: Emerging Issues and Insights.* London & New York: Wesley Longman Limited

Berleur, Jacques (1994) *Des rôles et missions de l'Université.* Namur: Presses Universitaires de Namur

Berleur, Jacques (this volume) *Culture and democracy revisited in the global information society. Summary of a position paper.*

British Telecommunications plc (1996) *The BT guide for people who are disabled or elderly. The latest products and services to help you use the phone.* London: BT plc

Brower-Janse, Maddy D.; Fulton Suri, Jane; Yawitz, Mitchell; de Vries, Govert; Fozard, James L. & Roger Coleman (1997) User interfaces for young and old. *Interactions* March & April, 4 (2), 34-46

Bryson, J. (1988) *Strategic Planning for Public and Nonprofit Organisations.* London: Jossey-Bass

Change (n/d) *Change. An organisation representing people with both a learning disability and a sensory impairment.* London: Change

Coleridge, Peter (1993) *Disability, Liberation, and Development.* Oxford: Oxfam (UK and Ireland)

Despouy, L. (1991) *Human Rights and Disability.* New York: United Nations Economic and Social Council

Economist, The (1996) Disability Law. Crippling? *The Economist.* December 7, 1996, 37

FEFC (Further Education Funding Council) (1996) *Inclusive Learning. Report of the Learning Difficulties and/or Disabilities Committee.* September. Coventry: FEFC

Gooding, Caroline (1994) *Disabling Laws, Enabling Acts: Disability Rights in Britain and America.* London: Pluto Press

Hales, Gerald (editor) (1996) *Beyond Disability: Towards an Enabling Society.* London: SAGE Publications in association with the Open University

HMSO (Her Majesty's Stationery Office) (1990) *National Health Service and Community Care Act.* London: HMSO

IEEE (1996) Toward an artificial eye. *Spectrum.* May. 33 (5). New York: The Institute of Electrical and Electronics Engineers, Inc.

Interactions (1996) People with speech disabilities sought to use new telephone support service. *Interactions.* November/December. 3 (6), 10

Kanter, R.M. (1990) Editorial. Values and economics. *Harvard Business Review.* May-June. 68, 4

Kehoe, Louise (1996) California surfing could flood phone networks. *Financial Times.* Friday, October 25.

Mangan, Tom (1993) Overcoming disability - a UK perspective. In *Computers and Society*, edited by Beardon, Colin & Diane Whitehouse. Oxford: Intellect Press, 46-52

Mental Health Foundation (1996) *Building Expectations. Opportunities and Services for People with a Learning Disability.* London: Mental Health Foundation

Ming, Guo (1993) Demographic features of people with disabilities in China. *Disability, Handicap, and Society.* 8, 207-210

Nelson, Jack A. (1994) Broken images: portrayals of those with disabilities in American media. In *The Disabled, the Media, and the Information Age*, edited by Jack A. Nelson. Westport, CT: Greenwood Press, 1-17

Oliver, Mike (1989) Disability and dependency: a creation of industrial societies. In *Disability and Dependency*, edited by L. Barton. London: The Falmer Press, 6-22

Oliver, Mike (1996) *Understanding Disability: From Theory to Practice*. Basingstoke & London: MacMillan Press

Smith, Michael R. (1994) Assistive technology and software: liberating all of us. In *The Disabled, the Media, and the Information Age*, edited by Jack A. Nelson. Westport, CT: Greenwood Press, 127-144

Smith, R.J. (1995) *Strategic Management and Planning in the Public Sector*. Harlow, Essex: Longman in association with the Civil Service College

Touraine, Alain (1984) *Le retour de l'acteur. Essai de sociologie*. Paris: Fayard

Whitehouse, Diane (1993) Overcoming disability: An overview of social and technological developments. In *Facing the Challenge of Risk and Vulnerability in an Information Society*, edited by Berleur, J., Beardon, C., & R. Laufer. Elsevier Science Publishers B.V. (North-Holland), 183-196.

Gardening: A metaphor for sustainability in information technology-technical support

Ellen Christiansen, Associate Professor
Dept. of Communications, University of Aalborg,
Langagervej 8, DK-9220 Aalborg Oest, Denmark
Email: ellen@hum.auc.dk

Abstract

Based on an empirical study of how technical support people work in a nonprofit research and consulting institute, the notion of gardening, first coined by Nardi, is unfolded as a metaphor for a sustainable way of making use of information technology (IT). Sustainability is defined as development characterized by optimal interaction in and between the resource systems and the economic and social systems.

Using Bateson's classification of interaction, symmetric and complementary, and of changes in interaction, feedback and calibration, a framework for understanding technical support as gardening is unfolded. Examples from a case study are used to illustrate how the technical support people in a specific organization, working as gardeners, play three different roles simultaneously: as experts (decision-makers, gatekeepers, creative planners) when working with the technology and wrapping up after productions; as colleagues, engaging in collaborative learning when working with users; and, when it comes to the outcome of joint efforts, they are like parents, taking pride in seeing the users walk away with the results even though their own contribution is invisible and maybe not even acknowledged. Furthermore, it is discussed how an organization can establish gardening relationships around technical support of the local design and use of IT.

An Ethical Global Information Society J. Berleur & D. Whitehouse (Eds.)

INTRODUCTION

'Development that meets the needs of the present without compromising the ability of future generations to meet their own needs'
WCED: *'Our Common Future'*

This paper takes up the challenge of developing a conceptualization of what sustainable information technology (IT)-technical support may mean. Inspired by Gregory Bateson's philosophy, I assume that the distinction between environmental resources on the one side, and humans as mental systems intentionally misusing these resources on the other, is a false dichotomy. Nature is One[1], but with a two-level structure: matter governed by embodied developmental principles. Carl Jung, following the Stoics, called matter *pleroma* and the governing principles, the mind, *creatura*. Bateson, in his epistemology (1958, 1979), built on these concepts together with the idea that the processes of interaction between different forms of matter are what cause the development of both. He categorized interaction in two types: symmetric and complementary interaction. The changes in interaction he saw as caused by differences in response, of which he found two types: feedback and calibration.

In *Mind and Nature* (1979), Bateson describes this typology of process as follows:

> 'I labeled the processes with the general term *schismogenesis*' [a term Bateson borrowed from Kretschmer, meaning 'first determining character within the individuals and beyond that creating intolerable stress'], and having put a label on the processes, I went to the *classification* of them. It became clear that a fundamental dichotomy was possible. The processes of interaction that shared the general potentiality of promoting schismogenesis were, in fact, classifiable into two great genera: the symmetric and the complementary. I applied the term *symmetric* to all those forms of interaction that could be described in terms of competition, rivalry, mutual emulation and so on (i.e., those in which A's action of a given kind would stimulate B to action of the same kind, which in turn would stimulate A to further similar actions and so on. If A is engaged in boasting, this would stimulate B to further boasting, and vice versa.) In contrast, I applied the term *complementary* to interaction sequences in which the actions of A and B were different but mutually fitted each other (e.g., dominance submission, exhibition-spectatorship, dependence-nurturance). I noted that these paired relationships could likewise be schismogenic (e.g. that dependency might promote nurturance, and vice versa)' (Bateson, 1979, pp. 191-92).

By putting these principles to work, side by side, Nature ensures survival of the fittest as well as (part of) the accidental deviation. Bateson suggested that a way to become conscious about Nature's way is through conscious reflection on 'the pattern that connects' levels of process and form and accordingly re-orientation of action-patterns. This kind of reflection-in-action he labelled deutero-learning, a concept which relates to the term double loop learning or learning to learn.

I take sustainability in a Batesonian sense to be in line with the WCED-definition of sustainability quoted initially. In *Mind and Nature*, Bateson remarks:

> 'It seems that we must ask: What characterizes those adaptations that turn out to be disastrous, and how do these differ from those that seem to be benign and, like the crab's claw, remain benign through geological ages? The question is pressing and relevant to the contemporary dilemmas of our own civilization. In Darwin's day, every invention appeared benign, but that is not so today. Sophisticated eyes in the twentieth century will view every invention askance and will doubt that blind stochastic processes always work together for good. We badly need a science that will analyze this whole matter of adaptation-addiction at all levels. Ecology is perhaps the beginning of such a science, although ecologists are still far from telling us how to get out of an atomic armaments race. In principle, neither random genetic change accompanied by natural selection nor random processes of trial and error in thought accompanied by selective reinforcement will necessarily work for the good of either species or individual. And at the social level, it is still not clear that the inventions and stratagems which are rewarded in the individual necessarily have survival value for the society, nor vice versa, do the policies that representatives of society might prefer necessarily have survival value for the individuals' (Bateson, 1979, pp. 173-74).

Even though we know all too little to be sure, it might be worth trying to characterize optimal levels of interaction, the most sustainable ways of interaction, in order to apply the concept of sustainability to policy-making and planning. As suggested by Barbier (1989), the concept must be made operational and applicable to all forms of economic and social activity in a more concise, systematic and rigorous way. So, when I try to put Bateson's and others' ideas to work by analogy using the gardener-metaphor, I have to admit the intuitive character of my project, as when I suggest parallelling the symmetric and the complementary type of interaction with the different ways a gardener cultivates, nurtures, harvests, and composts her material. However, the case study (Christiansen, 1996b) from which I report here, came into being because I witnessed on a daily basis for quite some time how technical support was done in this organization, and I found that what I saw was actually an instance of a mixture of symmetric and complementary interaction that deserved the label 'good gardening' and that might serve as an example of sustainable conduct.

Using the gardener metaphor for the design and use of IT is not my idea. Bonnie Nardi, in her wonderful book on end-user programming (1993) coined it when she pointed to the gigantic potential that may be found in facilitating end-user computing by employing 'super users' as local gardeners. Nardi (1993) uses gardener as a metaphor for a super user of a certain kind: a person who

- is responsible for nurturing fellow employees and providing *strong support* so that employees can perform as effectively as possible
- is coming from the rank and file: who *knows the domain*, the users, the frustrations and problems
- has a genuine interest and *enjoyment in assisting* less knowledgeable users on the one hand and, on the other hand, has a desire to learn the way around an operating system and a programming language
- has *great communication skills*

- is *trusted* by all parties
- provides an important *bridge* between systems administrators on the one side and domain experts on the other, and can also communicate with users
- *makes managers feel confident* that the standardization and integrity of the macros, programs and data used by their staffs will be maintained
- *is discovering and bringing to the group a new productivity tool* that would not have been found by the average user just trying to get work done
- makes a special effort to *keep up with advances in the field* and to be cognizant of the changing work practices in which s/he is not directly participating[2].

I am inspired by Nardi's examples and application of the metaphor of gardening but have extended it to apply to dedicated technical support.

AN ETHNOGRAPHIC STUDY OF HOW IT-TECHNICAL SUPPORT PEOPLE WORK

Encouraged by the correspondence between what I witnessed daily and what I had learned from Nardi, I set out to do a field study on the work of two technical support people, the systems administrator and the audio-visual support person ('the video-maker') in a small, nonprofit research and consulting institute. The institute, founded in 1986, has a yearly revenue of about 4 million US dollars and employs about 55 research scientists, staff, and consultants. At the time the study was carried out, a total of 124 computers (57 on site, 11 off site, 7 servers and the rest distributed in schools and other places) were serviced by the systems administrator. When the systems administrator went on trips or vacation, her job was covered by the video-maker. Video is used in most of the research and consultancy work done at the institute: data from school or workplace settings are videotaped, analysis is done by detailed examination of the video tapes, and video is used as a medium for communicating the findings to clients and scientific communities and as a medium for instruction. The video-maker puts up cameras, shoots the videos and edits presentations and tutorial videos in collaboration with researchers. Apart from the ongoing support for data collection and analysis, in 1995 ten videos were produced ranging from 7 to 25 minutes. Since the field study began, additional support personnel have been hired for the systems administrator as well as for the video-maker.

The data for this case study consist of 24 hours of observation, 4 hours of videotaped video editing, and 5 hours of videotaped interviews and videotaped focus group discussions. The results have been thoroughly discussed with the individuals studied in order to clear up misunderstandings and get their full consent regarding the use of the data. Clearly, the people I studied were not end-users in the sense defined by Nardi but people whose jobs it is to make information technology a valuable contribution to products, in this case, teaching and training material, reports, presentations, papers. Then, what did I see?

In addition to the communicative skills regarding translating from the technical world to the world of applications and being responsive to actual needs and levels of competence emphasized by Nardi, I found that skills for physical installation and repair, in sum for coping with the physical world, were crucial. This physicality showed up as a practical ability, an inclination to nurse the technology, monitor the conditions, diagnose repair, and reuse equipment: as a caring and playful attitude towards the machinery.

Also, it seemed important that the bridging position, mentioned by Nardi, between management and employees comprised bridging across the different communities of practices within the institute. Because of the knowledge about everyone's needs and wishes gained through bridging, the support people seemed to operate from a notion of a common good with respect to the use of technology with, it seemed, the acceptance of the people in the organization to take action accordingly.

Unlike the gardeners profiled by Nardi, the technical support people I met did not come from the rank and file of those they were supporting. They were hired as technical support persons. Both had, when we first met, an academic degree as their educational background, several years of experience from other companies, plus 3-4 years of experience at the institute. Both also had a personal professional network outside the organization, the systems administrator with technical support people and people in the software industry, and the video-maker with other video-makers, mostly freelancers. Compared to what I have seen in similar organizations, these two support people got a lot of work done and maintained quite a high technical standard on a low budget. Because of this, and because people at all levels in the organization frequently expressed gratitude for what they did, I assume their work was successful from the point of view of the organization. My impression from being around the institute for a year was that of a growing technical competence among people in the organization which I, more than from their actual teaching, ascribe to the way in which they created a safe atmosphere for people's experiments and for peer learning.

To give an impression of what their way of working was like, I specify the metaphor of gardening to cover four distinct areas of technical support work:

- *cultivation* of the technical equipment, programs and infrastructure
- *nursing* users, the peer learning through which the technical support of the production is accomplished
- *harvesting*, presenting high quality products of which the technical support is an important, yet transparent, feature
- *composting*, making sure that byproducts of the production processes, and parts of all kinds are kept for potential re-use.

Cultivating ...

As far as the cultivation of equipment is concerned, immediate and cost-effective repair is important. To obtain this goal, good formal and informal relationships to a network of vendors seemed crucial. Another important parameter was the ability to make informed choices balanced by an overall vision and strategy for expansion of the IT use. The following observation from the study illustrates this.

> '... The computer at the reception desk has crashed. While the receptionist is away for a meeting, the systems administrator sits at the reception in the receptionist's chair, drinking soda, rebuilding the desktop of the computer and meanwhile taking care of the reception. She is fixing the machine with Norton Disk Doctor, operated through her little self-made portable work bench, which includes an external hard drive on which Norton is available. This hard drive

has become her most precious and handy repair tool. It is very good for fixing high level problems on the operating system. Application breakdowns are usually taken care of by the application itself. For the rest, it is in the long run cheaper to take them to the repair shop, where all replacement parts come free from the vendor. Actually, it has been on her mind to become licensed herself in order to get the parts for free, but you have to be a retailer to get them for free, so it wouldn't work. Instead she tries to bargain and get the prices down as much as possible. This machine crashed because the receptionist kept rebooting it several times, which may have caused a good deal of damage.'

'One of the researchers passes by. Seeing her makes the systems administrator remember that she has a message for her, 'Oh, I just had a request from somebody about groupware and organizational learning. I referred him to you.' They engage in a conversation that, after a while, turns to Lotus Notes. Together they develop an idea about how to make really functional integration between platforms over/via the web. The researcher leaves, and Norton has succeeded so far that the systems administrator feels inclined to do a little clean up of the desktop icons. It is a matter of aesthetics, but in the flow she gets rid of some big chunks of irrelevant software. Since the reason the machine crashed was basically overload the clean up has a functional aspect, too. It crosses her mind that partly the problem has risen because she did not do the best job when installing this machine. She does a reboot to see if the machine is OK. Now another colleague comes by. She has a problem with her name popping up on the receptionist's computer. While the system administrator tries to pay attention to this problem, somebody is on the phone asking about a video conference for the board meeting on Friday with a test-run on Wednesday, of which she is in charge. She talks and takes notes, while still nursing Norton. Then she puts the guy on the phone on hold in order to go and get an email message from the video-maker (who is out of town this week) that will explain the details. While rising, she puts Norton on a new task. Back with a printout of the video-maker's message she shifts the phone to the other ear so that she can operate the mouse simultaneously. The accountant passes by with a message, and she nods. Together with the person on the phone, she goes over a scenario as to what it should be like on Friday. After this conversation, she turns back to the computer for a moment and then unpacks some new motherboards that just arrived in the mail. She is careful preserving the boxes and other wrapping material because she knows that she'll need them next time she is going to send some stuff off safely for repair. Then she shifts mode again, now listening and feeling if the computer seems up and well. The accountant comes by again and talks about some more paperwork. While waiting for Norton, she talks with the receptionist who has returned from her meeting. The receptionist explains how the machine just went berserk, and she did a reboot, and a reboot and another reboot. The system administrator takes the opportunity to emphasize the importance of never doing more than one reboot ...'

According to this fairly accurate account, the work with the disk doctor tool, the phone, and interaction between colleagues takes place simultaneously. The systems administrator restores a disk, does some teaching that should prevent further accidents, makes an appointment about conference support, exchanges information about forthcoming software investments, unpacks some new equipment, stores the wrappings and takes care of some paperwork in less than one hour.

Nursing ...

When it comes to nursing, that is to say, peer learning, Nardi points out that the skills for this are a special gift:

> '... A person who is technically skilled but uninterested in intensive interpersonal interaction may not have much of a green thumb when it comes to helping other users. By the same token, a person without sufficient technical skill would not be an effective gardener ...' (Nardi, 1993, pp. 117-18).

But even the most responsive gardener cannot make sure all by herself that the users in the organization who need technical support get what they need to produce the best possible products. Time would not allow her to support each and every user when needed. What can be done, and what the support people I studied did, is always to be attractive role models in their behaviour, and thereby put up an umbrella of inspiration under which the users can experiment safely, and safeguard experiments by being immediately accessible as firefighters if something gets out of hand.

> 'You try to make them feel good about whatever it is they try to learn. And give them the pros of a piece of software as opposed to the negatives, so you just try to make them feel good about what they are doing, and then hopefully it works out and then they go out and they learn and they come back and they can teach us actually! It happens. They actually learn something and they can say to you, 'You can do this,' and then we go, 'Oh I didn't know that,' and so ... For instance a colleague taught herself Illustrator and you know now, when people want to learn Illustrator, we just refer them to her.'

But quite often nursing and cultivation does not come out as nice and easy as that. An example where one of the senior researchers has asked for help to learn how to receive and send faxes via modem when working from home may illustrate a far more typical condition.

> 'This guy is always busy so the technical support person is not frustrated when the meeting is re-scheduled a couple of times, and she is also prepared for interruptions during the planned one-hour session. She even tries to take advantage of getting his attention by bringing her proposal for next year's budget, since he is responsible for the budget and this might be her only chance to give him an informal introduction to her line of thought. In advance, she has made a few small stickers to put on his computer with short cuts for what he needs to do to get his faxes through. He is working on his computer when she arrives. Somehow the conversation starts out on a question about how to re-arrange address books in the email software. He has scenarios prepared, and he operates the mouse. She responds to his scenarios and explains the possibilities. During this, he gets a lot of small arrangement problems cleared up. She tries to stop him and make him reflect and learn. They get into discussion about the procedure of organizing mailing. She tries to use the screen as a prompt of what to talk about concerning mailing. Gently she turns the conversation towards today's issue of faxing via modem. She suggests

doing an actual test and begins to explain the basic principles and to fix the telephone so as to take the example all the way through. He protests, he wants to move on since he has more problems, but now she is insisting. It takes some time for the fax to get through, and meanwhile he asks, 'How do I know, the document is send,' and grabs the mouse to demonstrate his problem. Doing this reminds him that he does not know the difference between single click/double click. She explains both the clicks and also about the word-install names, then the machine crashes. This tends to happen when this specific text editor runs together with the mail system. She has to get the machine up again. She takes the opportunity to announce, that in a short time she will be releasing a field researchers' survival kit which will help telecommuters, for instance, to build up their machine when it crashes. Now he asks how to fax. So at that point the planned session starts, 45 minutes after the meeting began. He talks about the fax and she explains. Then they turn to talk about HP fax, and talk prices. His machine is still working to get up again. She returns to the issue of crashes. He asks, 'Can you teach me how to build up my desk top?' And he continues talking about a new monitor he wants, and goes from there to the budget, while she seeks to establish a definition of what it means when a computer crashes. She goes and gets the Norton utilities, in order to instruct him about that. While she is away, he reads through the draft of the computer budget. From now on the conversation follows two parallel tracks: the budget and the issue of rebuilding a desktop. It takes until his secretary comes and takes him to his next appointment.'

Harvesting ...

A third aspect of gardening is harvesting, that is to say presenting high quality products of which the technical support is an important, yet transparent, feature. How this works is illustrated in the following example, where the video-maker tells me about his work:

> 'When I cooperate with people around editing, what we basically do: we take the analog videotape and digitize it. When they bring me the tape, then I automatically sit there and I am editing it in my head while I am looking at it. OK, so what I have the researcher do or whoever I am working with, they sit down and they identify the clips they want to use, and since there is a limited amount of hard drive space on this machine, it can only store up to like an hour of video and two hours of audio, so what I do is I have them identify the clips they want to do, then I digitize them, put them on a track sheet to edit, and then at that point I have the person that I am dealing with come in and sit down and then we decide, you know, is this really the clip you wanna use, and what kind of transition you want to do, and then if we are gonna do voice overs or any sort of graphics, you know that we are going to put in between the clips, that's when we decide or that's when I have that person decide ... That is my background as a film and TV major: I kind of can get a sense of what they want and then the best way to show people what they want to show them, you know, with the videotape that we have collected. That is the best part of my job, that is what I was trained to do.'

'... What if they do not want to collaborate, and just want me to do it? Well, those rare cases, where people say, 'Just go ahead and do it!', that, of course, gives me the creative freedom. But the part I don't like about that is, when they say, 'I don't know, you just do it!' And then I do it and they don't like it, you know, and it is, 'Well, why didn't you say something then?'

'... What do I do if their ideas seems kind of odd? Well, then I try to explain to them why that won't work, you know, and I'll say: 'That's a great idea, but you know, this probably would work better, you know. Try it this way,' because they'll come up with these ideas and these ways they want to do things and sometimes it is not feasible, you know, for one thing or, if it is possible, it is going to cost a lot of money to reproduce it and that sort of thing ... But with this new video editing system I have got with the cube, I haven't had any problems with having to say no to people on their ideas.'

'... And then it is funny, because then, after we do the video tape, they'll take it and they'll look at it for a few times and they'll look at it with other people and then they'll come back and say, 'You know what: maybe we can improve on it with this,' and then I'll go, 'Yeah, that is true, we can cut that out and we can add this and do this in stead of that,' so they are learning as well.'

'... I have given them a sort of a guideline, in the sense that - actually mostly it is by repetition - if there has been one particular group that has done more than one video, then after the second time then they kind of get a sense of what I and the machine can do, what they want, and then if there is something else that they think about that they might want, then they'll say, 'Well you know, can we do it this way?' And, more often than not, we can do it that way and then we just improve on it in that way. So they are learning as well and they are learning to step outside of that boundary, that guideline sort of thing ... [Then] it becomes more fun, because they are more knowledgeable and then they, we kind of feed each other, and then they'll come up with an idea and then I go, 'Oh yeah, that will be neat, and then, plus we can do this on top of it,' and so it's a nice interaction there.'

When shadowing the support people I was somewhat puzzled by seeing them with a smile say good-bye and good luck to researchers who went off to a client with a presentation that was the result of maybe several days of intense cooperation between researcher and support person. Of course it is part of their job. But what kind of a professionalism is it that accepts and maybe even enjoys to see others receive the applause for what has been accomplished in collaboration? Maybe a label like 'back stage professionalism' would be appropriate. At least, the support staff I talked to, said that they like to work back stage, 'to be behind the camera, not in front if it.' They seemed to prefer a parental role, like when children run out into the garden, eat all the peas or plums they can, and continue their play while their parents watch them and, even with a happy smile, clean up the mess they left. If there is going to be another harvest, there must be someone who cleans up and puts things aside. But as a career trajectory? I kept being puzzled until I overheard some conversations between the technical support staff and their peers outside the organization and heard them boast of some of their accomplishments. Then I understood that they, too, had an audience, a peer group with whom they compete and from whom they get admiration.

Composting ...

Key concepts in this aspect of the work are the notion of common good and an overall strategy: acknowledging that users are individuals with individual personalities, that they deserve respect, but that the only one able to build a bridge between the users and the concern for the common good is the person who knows the needs on both sides as well as the actual options, and takes a professional pride in striving to get the best quality solutions at the cheapest price.

What in this case made most ends meet was a consistent recycling behaviour on the part of the gardeners. One of the things I learned first was that a computer would not arrive on my desk as a total solution. Computers consist of different parts, and a solution means a combination of whatever spare parts are available and are working at the moment. I could go to the support staff and express an urgent need for a better headset, a mousepad, a printer, a monitor, a hard drive, and I would find them look around the immediate workspace then, if nothing was found there, go through a range of replacements until I got my thing, typically from someone who got a more adequate replacement by having a spare part from someone else who ... and so on.

The never-ending story of preserving, storing and reusing seems more than anything to be the 'fertilizer of the soil'. Always fill up printers with paper when passing by, always tidy up in the server room, always keep boxes and paper when unpacking so that stuff can be sent safely to repair, enjoy unpacking, checking and nursing hardware as well as software, always put on a happy face when asked for the same explanation over and over again: that is part of a never-ending story of keeping a technical support garden.

NO GARDENERS WITHOUT A GARDEN

You cannot work as a gardener unless the organization where you work allows you. When it comes to the implementation of a gardening attitude, the bottom line is the organization's actual cost-benefit assessment. I have only one organizational context to report from which is justified by the truly exploratory state of the idea, but which is, of course, still a limitation. The example given may give rise to more questions than it answers. But at least in this case, neither the management nor the users would like to be without technical support staff working with a gardening attitude even though, for the management, it meant delegation of control and even though, for the users, it meant that the gardeners' concern for the common good could prevent them from having their sweetest technological dreams come true.

The organization studied is young and enthusiastic, and rich on personal relationships across communities of practice. The technical support people are located in the office space, in cubicles similar to and next to those they are supporting. Learning is a basic value of this organization, implicitly as well as explicitly. Learning as an implicit value expresses itself in the non-hierarchical structure and in the open and informal way of communicating that allows everyone to ask for help because it is acknowledged that everyone is an expert with regard to certain aspects of the work. Accomplishments of learning are recognized and cheered. At the more explicit and formal level, quarterly, biannual and annually meetings are milestones and reference points and opportunities for coordinated reflection with respect to different aspects of the organization's activity. At these meetings, everyone participates in discussions about what has been accomplished and what should be learned and in which direction to expand. Organizational memory is a research topic for some, but certainly a boundary object for everyone.

On the economic side, expenses related to IT fall into three categories: a) investments and maintenance of network, machinery and software, b) teaching and learning how to use it, and c) productions. The use of computers and video, of the Internet and intranet, is crucial to the work at all levels in the organization. And even though the budget is limited, all three categories of IT expenses are present in the budget and are subject to the gardeners' constant efforts to balance the budget and to make sure that the productions are the *raison d'être* of the investments, and that the teaching and learning effort is made timely so as to spin off in productions. This balancing takes a specific form in each category: with respect to investments, the gardeners repair and reuse as much as possible in-house, and they do as much of the cabling, cleaning, and the soldering as they possibly can themselves. The teaching primarily takes the form of peer learning supported by firefighting when necessary, aimed at creating as many teachers and learners as possible. When it comes to the production of documents and videos, the gardeners are constantly trying to help people pay attention to waste problems, avoid unnecessary printouts, and support whatever can be done to reuse pieces so that the investment in production time is balanced by the scope of the use.

Although this organization has its collectors and those who always need the hottest software, even these people seem to accept that their needs are adjusted to the overall long-term plan for expansion, and that they will get spare parts and reused products if those solutions meet the need they have expressed. And those in the organization who are most reluctant to engage in and benefit from the IT wonder world are tempted and dragged and tempted again, but never forced against their will. The email system is used extensively to communicate news, events and problems, which makes the IT situation a dear and ready-to-hand subject of conversation, just like the weather in more unstable climate zones. Affections of all kinds can be expressed by blaming it on the technology, and the technology may even sometimes be the carrier of hope, like 'once we get on to the next version of Netscape ...'

Now, it was not exactly the Garden of Eden I studied. But this organization had a remarkably successful fit between the organizational culture, the willingness and determination of management to delegate power and authority, and the responsibility to create and develop a notion of the common IT good deliberately taken up by the gardeners. By taking a position as middle-men, they did reverse the tendency that those who were already well off with equipment and service got more because they were able to express more advanced needs. By nursing and developing the most reluctant users and preventing the most anxious from eating up all the cake just for the sake of personal appetite, they supported a balanced growth.

Along a similar vein, by acknowledging and creating pride in the entire organization, these gardeners as well as other employees created mutual relationships with the community and the neighbourhood: outdated equipment was given to schools and charity organizations, and people from the outside were invited to see, to try out, and learn about IT possibilities. And they arranged that the organization hosted exhibitions of artwork from various groups in the community - a gesture of grace, one could say, but a gesture that did a lot of good for the culture inside the organization because, in a very concrete way, it symbolized that 'we are committed to the surrounding community and we care.'

But learning implies change, and change may be experienced as unpleasant or even painful. Situated learning in today's workplaces is also learning under stress since things tend to run behind schedule. For example finishing off products, in terms of layout and final editing, is always last-minute-and-should-have-been-done yesterday stuff, and the necessary extra time for learning is usually not built into such time frames. Even in this organization, those in charge of the administration, layout, and the finishing of products tend to feel that the researchers do not take these parts of the work seriously enough. But unlike most organizations, people believe that pointing to these issues may bring about change for the better. For instance, the administration staff decided on an arrangement, a one-day workshop called 'Take your researcher to work'. The agenda was 'to increase our awareness of what it takes to get a job done.' The format was that the administration staff would put the researchers to work with some of the stuff usually taken care of by themselves to give the researchers hands-on experience and thereby to develop a shared understanding.

All in all, the responsive attitude on the side of the organization did match the situatedness[3] and the responsiveness to immediate needs, shown by the gardeners.

SUMMARY AND CONCLUSIONS

My motive throughout this paper has been to give some flesh and blood to a conceptualization of sustainability within the field of IT-technical support. I have proceeded by borrowing a couple of concepts from the philosophy of Gregory Bateson, and by extending Nardi's metaphorical use of the concept of gardening to IT-technical support. Over two sections, I have presented an example of giving IT-technical support with a gardening attitude. Now let me return to my point of departure: gardening as a metaphor for a sustainable way of conducting IT-technical support. What is it about gardening that supports the principles of sustainability?

In the introductory section I suggested sustainability is synonymous with non-disastrous or benign evolution: an evolution that manages to be adaptive without turning addictive. Bateson himself was very cautious and stated that 'We lack any systematic knowledge of the dynamics of these processes' (Bateson, 1979, pp. 174) [the processes of interaction that result in either adaptation or addiction]. In line with Bardier, I suggest that sustainable development is the optimal level of interaction of three systems: the biological and resource system, the economic system, and the social system through a dynamic and adaptive process of trade offs (Barbier, 1989, pp. 184-85). An 'optimal level of interaction' is characterized by what Bateson calls adaptive evolution, a composition of symmetric and complementary forms of interaction, adjusted by calibration and feedback. In those cases when the interaction becomes subject to reflection, it may be possible to engage in what Bateson called deutero learning, a communication about what connects different patterns of interaction, which in turn may lead to interactions of a new type. For example, when I asked the gardeners in my case study about how they encouraged users to learn about new technology, they immediately reframed my question by saying: the question is rather do we ever stop people from learning? They interpreted my understanding of learning as synonymous with teaching, compared this to their own understanding of learning as ongoing practice, then came up with a pattern they thought connected these two conceptualizations of learning and therefore would be a relevant outset for answering the question. This points to an important area of further investigation, namely the connection between sustainable development and deutero learning, and between deutero learning and the, nowadays so much demanded, double loop learning.

With examples from the case study, I pointed out four distinctive aspects of gardening

- cultivation of the soil, that is to say the technical equipment, programs and infrastructure
- nursing of plants, that is to say peer learning through which the technical support of the production is accomplished
- harvesting the fruits, that is to say presenting high quality products of which the technical support is an important, yet transparent, feature
- composting the remains, that is reusing all useful ideas, byproducts, procedures and technical components.

The cultivation of the soil, I found was characterized by the strongest possible degree of recycling, internally and in exchange with the community, but conducted by the gardeners as the experts, taking upon themselves to supersede rivalry between different, more or less resourceful, people while showing concern for the common good. Nursing the users was done on the gardeners' initiative by having any interaction turn into peer learning, so that the gardeners were the more capable peers with respect to the technical and, to a certain degree, the aesthetic aspects, while the users were more capable with respect to content so that they got what the video-maker called 'a nice interaction going on there'. When harvesting the fruits, the users would be acknowledged fully for the reports, videos, and so on by their clients, while the gardeners would be bystanders like parents. But the gardeners would be acknowledged by their colleagues in the profession outside the institute, and also by the community inside. And, in the flow of wrapping up after a production, the gardeners would be experts in composting the remains, so that all reusable parts of the process would be kept safe in order to fertilize the soil further.

In all aspects of gardening, I have found examples of both symmetric and complementary interaction. The interaction between gardeners and users is, with respect to cultivation, symmetrical in the sense that they compared themselves to other colleagues in the field of technical support in seeking to be the best. Their interaction with the machinery is complementary in the sense that they listen, they are supportive, and they talk about the computers as 'puppies' or even 'babies'. When it comes to people, the nursing, the nature of the interactions becomes complementary: 'We kind of feed each other' is the video-maker's phrase. It is primarily a human-human interaction, the machinery is a medium, something that is supposed to work transparently without breaking down and, when it eventually breaks down, the interaction becomes human-machine and becomes symmetrical, like a competition, where users usually lean back and give in while the technical support people lean forward and fight. Harvesting the fruits is characterized by complementary interaction between gardeners and users, like between parents and children, and the gardeners outsource their symmetrical interaction with gardeners elsewhere. Composting the remains is, by definition, a complementary endeavour since it is basically a matter of supply. But watching the gardeners in the process revealed the impression that at the same time they were also engaged in a competition with themselves to see how creative they could be in making sure that nothing went to waste.

The hypothesis I have tried to unfold here, by now in an absolutely explorative form, suggests that technical support could be characterized as sustainable to the extent that both symmetric and complementary forms of interaction are at play in all aspects of their work: cultivating the soil, nursing the plants, harvesting the fruits, and composting the remains. The framework would, when researched more thoroughly, offer a foundation for discussion about sustainable IT-technical support.

ACKNOWLEDGEMENTS

I am grateful to Phil Draper, Ann Mathison, and their colleagues at the Institute for Research on Learning, Menlo Park, California for having introduced me to IT-support as gardening, and I owe Bonnie Nardi a lot for having brought my attention to the important qualities she addresses under the heading of gardener. Helga Wild (1996) and Libby Bishop have provided ideas and fruitful criticism while I struggled with writing the report. Unknown referees have provided me with encouraging criticism on a former draft of this paper for which I am very grateful. My husband, John Thogersen, has spent hours discussing my ideas, and drawing on and offering me his insights on sustainable consumer behaviour.

REFERENCES

Barbier, E.: *Economics, Natural-Resources, Scarcity, and Development*. Earth Scan, 1989

Bateson, G.: *Naven*. Stanford University Press, 1958

Bateson, G.: *Mind and Nature. A Necessary Unity*. E.P. Dutton, 1979

Bjerkness, G. *et al.* (eds.): *Organizational Competence in System Development*, Lund, Studentlitteratur, 1989

Bjerkness, Gro and Tone Bratteteig: The Application Perspective - An Other Way of Conceiving EDP-based Systems and Systems Development, in Sääksjärvi (ed.): *Report of the Seventh Scandinavian Research Seminar on Systemeering*, Helsinki, 1984

Bødker *et. al.*: *The AT project*. DAIMI PB-454. Aarhus University, 1993

Christiansen, E. (a): Tamed by a rose in: Nardi, B. (ed.): *Context and Consciousness*. MIT Press 1996

Christiansen, E. (b): *A Gardening Attitude*. Technical Report. The Institute of Research on Learning, Menlo Park, California, 1996

DeDijn, H.D. (ed.): *The Way to Wisdom*. Purdue University Research Foundation, 1996

Greenbaum, J. and M. Kyng: *Design at Work*. Lawrence Erlbaum 1991

Josefson, I. (ed.): *Spraak och erfarenhet (Language and Experience)*. Carlssons, Stockholm 1985

Lave, J. and E. Wenger: *Situated Learning*. Cambridge University Press, 1991

Nardi, B.: *A Small Matter of Programming*. The MIT Press, 1993

Suchman, Lucy A.: *Plans and Situated Actions*. The Problem of Human-Machine Communication. Cambridge University Press, 1987

Thoresen, Kari: Principles in Practice: Two Cases of Situated Participatory Design in D. Schuler and A. Namioka (Eds.): *Participatory Design*. Lawrence Erlbaum Ass., 1993

Wild, H.: Distributed teams, mobile workforce, distant education, remote work: Are we living on credit? Paper presented at EDRA 1996, June 1-2, 1996, Salt Lake City, Utah, USA

(WCED) World Commission on Environment and Development: *Our Common Future*. Oxford University Press, 1987

---

[1] For a further elaboration, it might be relevant to take up Spinoza's argumentation on the oneness of nature and his reflection on nature (DeDijn, 1996).

[2] Another word for these qualities could be 'caring rationality'. In Scandinavia, researchers have for decades conducted research on computing in organizations from an end-user perspective (Bjerkness, G. *et al.*, 1989; Bjerkness & Bratteteig, 1994; Bødker *et. al.*, 1993; Christiansen, 1996a; Greenbaum & Kyng, 1991; Josefson, 1985; and Thoresen, 1993). One of the key concepts that has developed through this work is the notion of a caring rationality as opposed to a technical rationality. The similarities between a gardening attitude and a caring rationality are not taken up here but they are worth further theoretical investigation.

[3] Situatedness is described by Suchman (1987) with respect to how we cope with computers, and by Lave and Wenger (1991) with respect to learning in the workplace as intrinsic to practical problem-solving.

16

Information society and civil society: Non-governmental organizations and computer-mediated communication in Latin America

Ricardo Gómez
510 Landreville, ap. B
Verdun, Quebec, H3E 1B4 Canada
Tel/fax: +1 514 768 6805
Email: gomezr@total.net

Abstract

The globalization of information and communication poses new challenges to this emerging civil society, as it provides new risks of censorship and control, but at the same time offers new opportunities for global networking and collective action. There seems to be very little research on the ways non-government organizations (NGOs) are confronting the information society and its effects. This paper explores current issues on computer-mediated communication (CMC) and virtual communities, and describes the preliminary findings of ongoing research of CMC uses in NGOs in Latin America. These findings suggest that an enhanced sense of belonging to a global civil society may be a positive effect of current uses of CMC by NGOs in the region.

THE PROMISED LAND OF THE INFORMATION SOCIETY

The information society has been acclaimed as an instrument for democracy, for postmodernity, and for control. It has been presented as the opportunity for every individual to communicate with the rest of the world and to bring about participatory democracy (Gore, 1996; Miles, Rush, Turner and Bessant, 1988; NTIA, 1993), and as the opportunity for the state or the market to control every individual (Poster, 1995; Rheingold, 1993; Sparks, 1994; Splichal, 1994) and constitute a police state in a global hypermarket (Proulx and Senecal, 1995). At

An Ethical Global Information Society J. Berleur & D. Whitehouse (Eds.)

the same time, it has been held responsible for the shattering of the grand narratives of progress and modernization, and the reconstitution of the public sphere as a fractal image of postmodern identities (Poster, 1995; Turkle, 1995; Vattimo, 1992). Nonetheless, there is increasing evidence that neither the happiest dreams nor the worst nightmares that have been proclaimed for the information society have been realized. Furthermore, I share Pierre Lévy's optimism when he claims that technological changes that upset the former balance of power and paradigms introduce the possibility of unprecedented changes and of new alliances and strategies (Lévy, 1990). Change is at the same time a risk, a challenge, and an opportunity. In the face of the globalized new world of the information society, what can be the role of civil society which is vital to the construction of genuine democracy?

Computer-mediated communication (CMC) is at the root of emergent practices in the information society. Among other things, CMC has introduced a new form of social organization between people who share an interest and not necessarily a territory or a cultural identity. Virtual communities are 'social aggregations that emerge form the Net where enough people carry on those public discussions long enough, with sufficient human feeling, to form webs of personal relationships in cyberspace' (Rheingold, 1993, p.5). Growing use of CMC has generated new forms of virtual communities (Jones, 1995a) or networlds (Harasim, 1994), established as places for social exchange, education or work. The growing process of the commercialization of the Internet has added a fourth networld, the virtual supermarket.

The possibility of creating and sustaining these virtual communities or networlds has been analyzed from different perspectives. Jones suggests that, through them, new opportunities emerge for education and learning, for the establishment of counter-cultures, for the restructuring of human-machine interaction, and for the revitalization of participatory democracy (Jones, 1995a). Are these claims any different from the euphoria accompanying the Global Information Infrastructure (GII)? Rheingold points out that 'the political significance of CMC lies in its capacity to challenge the existing political hierarchy's monopoly on powerful communication media, and perhaps thus revitalize citizen-based democracy' (Rheingold, 1993, p.14). Splichal is more cautious when he says that the nature of civil society, as well as that of the state and the economy, is 'decisively affected' by recent technological developments in computer-mediated communication; his optimism stops with the recognition that organizational changes in the economy, the state and civil society are possible and that, based on the experience of eastern and central European countries, total state control or repression is no longer possible, although it may still happen locally and temporarily (Splichal, 1994).

What is the direction of this effect? How will each sector appropriate the new tools and uses? In fact, how are these tools socialized?

THE CONSTITUTION OF VIRTUAL COMMUNITIES

Harasim insists it is not the CMC tools themselves but their use that is important in the constitution of networks into networlds. For this process to happen, a purpose, a place, and a population are required. Networlds or virtual communities are not constituted from technological tools if there is not a common *purpose*, an agenda, a timeline, which is then pursued in a *place*, one that can be a virtual café, classroom or commons, by a set of *participants* whose roles are clearly agreed (Harasim, 1994). Swerdlow insists that when people are already familiar with each other, what he calls 'the power of skin', then the opportunity is created to continue through electronic relations (Swerdlow, 1995). But Jones does not seem to be bothered by the need for familiarity or even of information exchange; he goes even further to say that virtual communities are bound not by transmission of information but by *ritual sharing* (Jones, 1995a). Ritual sharing in a virtual community can lead to all sorts of practices, such as the multiplication of identities and construction of cyberworlds in Multi-User Domains (MUDs), explored at length by Sherry Turkle. She points out that virtual reality can be seen as another reality, not necessarily in competition with real life; the boundary between virtual and real is fuzzy and, in that boundary, new cultural symbols and meanings can emerge. She points out that real life 'is just one more window', and not necessarily the best one (Turkle, 1995).

What is it then that fosters the interest in using CMC to constitute virtual communities of interest, networlds in which social, educational, commercial or democratic values can be ritually exchanged?

Virtual communities have been studied among computer-game players (Freidman, 1995; Fuller and Jenkins, 1995), MUD users (Turkle, 1995), and Usenet participants (Baym, 1995; MacKinnon, 1995; McLaughlin, Osborne and Smith, 1995). Many of these studies detail how the community is constituted through shared interests and practices, establishing roles and rules of conduct, and generating a virtual reality (VR) with varying degrees of connection with real life (RL). Sherry Turkle presents three different scenarios illustrating the effects of the move towards virtuality. She calls the first the Disneyland effect, in which denatured and artificial experiences seem real. The second is the artificial crocodile effect, when both the fake and the simulated realities seem more compelling than the real, thus devaluing the world of direct, unmediated experience. The third is the effect by which a virtual experience may be so compelling that we believe we have achieved more than we actually have. She concludes that, rather than making virtuality and real life compete, we will need to figure out ways in which we can get the best of both (Turkle, 1995).

The effects of introducing CMC, especially electronic mail, have been well documented in businesses, education and research. Rheingold suggests that CMC has the potential to change society at three levels: among individual human beings, in person-to-person interaction, and at the political level, especially if there is a strong community of users among citizens (Rheingold, 1993). Sproull and Kiesler (1991) have studied the effects of CMC in networked organizations. They differentiate two levels of effects of CMC: the first level is easier to anticipate, and includes the anticipated technical changes related to planned efficiency gains, cost displacements and added value, resulting from the introduction of CMC in organizations. Second-level changes (in which people start to change the ways they spend their time and value what is important, shifting social patterns, and the interdependence between members of the group) are generally slow and unanticipated, and are not necessarily caused by the technologies alone but rather are shaped by the interactions and uses the community gives to them. These findings seem to be confirmed by other more recent studies in organizations, cooperative research, and education, including the fact that most of the social or second-level changes are unintended and unanticipated. Management tends to focus on productivity and efficiency gains but there is a consistently reported gain in organizational commitment, solidarity, participatory and egalitarian decision-making, and better decisions being reached (Garton and Wellman, 1994; Johnson-Lenz and Johnson-Lenz, 1994; Kaye, 1992; Rice and Steinfeld, 1994; Valacich, Paranka, George, and Nunamaker, 1993). Furthermore, there seems to be agreement in that the *way* CMC is used is more important than its frequency.

TOWARDS A VIRTUAL CIVIL SOCIETY?

Nonetheless, there is extremely little literature describing or analyzing concrete uses and meanings of CMC in virtual communities as part of civil society, although there is much debate and speculation about its possibilities. We are living in a time in which new forms of relationships and interactions are possible. This presents many risks, and many opportunities. We face new technologies that allow decentralized, multimedia, hypertextual, elastic, and interactive communication in a context of familiarity, ease of use, and instant feedback at a global scale. While the state and the market, both nationally and globally, have many privileges and advantages in accessing and using these technologies for hegemony, profit and control, civil society has also a role to play in using, understanding, and shaping the new media, and appropriating them for the democratic process. We are facing an opportunity for the 'transnationalization of civil participation', as Thorup puts it (in Frederick, 1992); there are increasing indications of an ongoing globalization from below, as opposed to the dominant globalization from above that has been so heavily criticized by Hamelink (1995). For Mark Poster (1995), a new dialogue is possible that configures subjects in a differentiated cosmopolitanism, far removed from the homogeneous massification resulting from the new communication technologies that has been feared or extolled for so long.

Transnational civil participation for a differentiated cosmopolitanism in a process of globalization from below, such is the promise of CMC for development and democracy. But more research is needed in order to overcome the idealization of the new uses of this new technology. Otherwise, we can repeat the uncritical analyses of experiences using radio and video, but this time joining with Al Gore's euphoric claims of the GII as a metaphor for democracy.

The process of globalization from below is not a new idea, but it is an emergent process that has only recently begun to be shaped and formed. Networks are popular and non-governmental organizations (NGOs) are important new actors in the international scene; they have been slowly gaining recognition and space in forums and decision spaces for global affairs. Although civil society is not a homogeneous group pursuing common aims, and NGOs are not its sole members, the blooming NGO movement throughout the world constitutes a new actor on the national and international scene. NGOs are becoming increasingly important actors both in their own societies and internationally. As Harris suggests, their challenge may be to come up with communication strategies that 'recognize and address the vastly changed international politico-economic scenario in which the negative consequences of financial monopolies, environmental degradation and unsustainable development are increasingly being felt in the so-called developed countries of the North' (Harris, 1996, p.8).

It has been shown how communication technologies such as radio, video and desktop publishing have been appropriated as democratic tools (Girard, 1993; Thede and Ambrosi, 1991). These technologies have allowed a decentralization of communication resources and helped to break down hierarchies of power. 'For the first time in history, progressive forces have access to communication tools previously reserved to corporations and the military' (Frederick, 1992, p.22). In the same way, the recent emergence of computer-mediated communication has played an important role in the revitalization of the civil society. As Frederick puts it:

> 'a global civil society is best seen in the worldwide movement of NGO and citizens advocacy groups uniting to challenge problems that are substantially different in scope and character from any that have faced the world before. Problems such as the proliferation of nuclear weapons, imbalanced resource use, hunger and poverty, the destruction of the rain forests, and the developing greenhouse effect are so large in scope and have such geographically dispersed effects that they confound local—even national—solutions' (Frederick, 1992, p.219).

NGOs AND THE GLOBAL CIVIL SOCIETY

NGOs had generally been very isolated from each other, but there has been a recent trend towards their articulation around some of these global issues. They are becoming increasingly visible at United Nations (UN) and other international forums as their power and capacity to communicate and coordinate actions increases. The 1992 Earth Summit in Rio de Janeiro is frequently regarded as a landmark, a turning point in the emergence of the global civil society (Afonso, 1996; Preston, 1994). The Earth Summit provided for the first time a meeting place in which world affairs were debated with a large participation of civil society. There were 100 heads of state and 178 nations represented, and a total of 35,000 people attended, the largest meeting of this kind ever. But most significantly, over one thousand NGOs registered at the conference, with about one third of them from the third world. At the parallel NGO summit that took place simultaneously with the UN meeting, over 9,000 organizations took part; this was the largest face-to-face forum for NGO representatives from all around the world in a meeting of this kind (Preston, 1994).

Not only was the attendance by NGO representatives unprecedented, but an open electronic communication system was put in place by the Association for Progressive Communications (APC), providing email, international electronic conferences, and access to databases related with the UN Earth Summit. In this way, issues that were being discussed at the Summit and at the NGO meeting were available for consultation both on-site and internationally, via the APC electronic communication network[1]. After the Rio Summit, APC has provided similar communication services at other major international conferences: the World Human

Rights Conference in Vienna (1993), the Conferences on Population and Development in Cairo (1994) and on Women and Development in Beijing (1995), and the Social Summit in Copenhagen (1995). The impact of this participation still remains to be further evaluated but, as Afonso states, it is now clear that on the international political scene 'the APC network now plays a key role, and constitutes an indispensable media to keep track of the experiences of civil society throughout the world' (Afonso, 1996, p.152).

While it may be true that NGOs worldwide have gained access to the lanes of the information society via the APC Network services among others, much remains to be accomplished in terms of global practices towards democratic communication. We need to focus on the more concrete aspects of NGOs' use of CMC, and of electronic mail in particular since, of all the CMC tools, electronic mail remains the most readily available and used by NGOs. This is true especially in Latin America, where the APC nodes have until very recently offered exclusively line-driven, text-based connections to the network, providing access to email and electronic conferences. Until the end of 1995, it was not very easy for NGOs to get Internet access in most countries that had it, and the APC was the only alternative they had to use email (NGLS, 1995).

Nonetheless, email has been shown to be powerful enough to enact the 'ritual sharing' that constitutes virtual communities. What is yet to be seen is the actual use of these technologies, limited as they may seem, by the people in the NGOs involved. Most of the literature on the effects of CMC focuses on business, education or recreational virtual communities, and there is no guarantee that the same kind of effects hold when the users are NGOs in the construction of a virtual community for a global civil society. Moreover, there is only little evidence that the increased use of CMC by the NGO community has in fact helped to promote such a global civil society, or that it has had a positive impact on the democratization process as a whole.

EMERGING PRACTICES IN LATIN AMERICA

An ongoing study in Latin America[2] shows that there are four main kinds of perceived effects of using CMC in NGOs: speed of communication, enhanced networking, better information, and reduced cost. Furthermore, there is a growing awareness of the possibilities offered by CMC to strengthen the coordination between diverse actors in civil society in a global field of action. I will briefly discuss some of the emerging findings of this study, which may help us to understand the actual uses and perceptions of CMC among NGOs in a Latin American country.

The speed of communication is, for obvious reasons, the most frequently mentioned effect of the use of CMC, and needs not be described in detail here; it is one of the self-evident first-level effects described by Sproull and Kiesler (1991), as discussed before. But second-level effects are not far behind in the perceptions of users, most of whom report a sense of enhanced networking with CMC, which has allowed them a better coordination of activities based on shared interests with partners in the same country and around the world. Persons and institutions with common interests are perceived to be more easily brought together, independently of where they are located; the perception of a global scope of action is more easily achieved. Furthermore, initial data indicates that new contacts have been made possible for NGOs, providing more new partners with whom to exchange information. Users also report that CMC makes it possible to maintain the relations with their partners on a more regular basis, shortening geographical distances, and strengthening internal communication between branches of an organization, both nationally and internationally. Finally, some NGOs point out relationships with funding agencies have also been improved with the use of CMC.

In this way, *CMC is perceived to strengthen the bonds within the NGO community both nationally and internationally*. This is materialized in an increased sense of knowledge and understanding of what others are doing, and better chances of exchanging information with those who share common particular interests. Communication with them is perceived to be more frank, direct, and continuous, allowing faster decisions and timely solutions, and encouraging 'joint efforts and proposals among a community of interests that is more tightly bound'. As one respondent puts it, CMC 'has helped me understand the day to day activities of the diverse and sometimes disperse action of NGOs, and also how deeply involved they all are in the process of construction of a (better) society.'

This perception has also expanded the geographical boundaries of partnerships to a larger perspective of a *global NGO community* confronting similar problems in different contexts. 'We have enlarged our frame of action and learned to conceptualize the problems from a global perspective,' points out one respondent; the possibility of embracing a 'solidarity without borders' is explicit or implied in a number of statements in the survey. Nonetheless, this perception of a global perspective is only a slow, continuous process. As one respondent comments, 'electronic mail is something that NGOs will need to be able to handle because in the long run this will allow them to have a global network of NGOs and carry out joint activities.'

The idea that the service provider provides a virtual meeting place for NGOs in the country is the most commonly reported reason to choose it among other commercial service providers. The APC node is perceived to group progressive, national NGOs; its non-commercial, alternative, and progressive character is a strong element of attraction for NGOs to join it, as well as the fact that it was established and promoted by a coalition of well-known NGOs in the country. The sense of belonging to an alternative family of NGOs in an alternative network for CMC, both at national and international levels, is strongly present. As one respondent candidly explains, 'it groups all of us alternative people.' All these perceptions share the sense of belonging to a common group, a virtual NGO community that exists and that is further bound together through a sort of ritual sharing in order to become stronger as a consequence of using CMC.

It is important to note that even though solidarity, support, and a sense of community may indeed be strengthened with partners who are accessible though email, the relationships with those who are not connected can deteriorate. In fact, as some point out, many NGOs or other partners are not currently using or cannot afford this kind of communication, and are thus excluded from these networks. Increased access to CMC resources may limit this exclusion.

In sum, there is a generalized perception that CMC has at least positively affected the relations between NGOs and its partners, as it has allowed 'a slow tightening of the ties (among NGOs) with information about common interests and projects.' It is perceived to be 'an excellent way to speed communications to organize meetings and other international events, to prepare joint proposals, publications and other documents collectively or in co-authorship.' Furthermore, it has contributed to strengthening the sense of belonging to a global community, sharing many interests, concerns and activities; in order to reduce the exclusion of partners from the enhanced networking possibilities of CMC, access to its resources has to be more widespread and available, even to grassroots and community organizations.

Better information is perceived to be another major effect of using CMC among NGOs. This means having access to more abundant, more updated and more relevant information, accessible through more channels and from more sources, and with more powerful tools to search and gather new information. Furthermore, information is also better since it is easily two-way, making feedback more fluid. In the words of one of the respondents, CMC 'has allowed us to be informed about important issues, and to express our opinions on them.'

Low cost of communication is the last major recurrent issue that is reported in relation to the use of CMC. Almost half of the respondents perceive that with CMC their communication costs are lower than they would be with other media. Some note that reduced costs are not only a matter of lower phone bills, but also reduced use of paper, envelopes and other office supplies, and less time spent on the task. Nonetheless, only a few respondents claim the need to cut costs as a reason to start using CMC in the first place, although the second most common reason to choose the APC node as service provider was the affordability of its services, especially when if first began to provide them. Several respondents point out that the APC node was the first to offer affordable services for the NGO community in the country even if, for some of them, this meant expensive long distance calls to the capital city. Nonetheless, this situation has changed so that comparable or better service is offered commercially; but it is not clear to what extent lower fees would cause any particular NGOs to seek a commercial service provider.

On the other hand, the need for more training and for more upgraded equipment is the most commonly expressed means of improving the NGOs' use of CMC. Lack of funds to pay for such items is reported to be of concern among several of them. Moreover, one respondent points out that electronic communication requires access to the only computer the institution has, and it is always in use for many other tasks. In this way, cost reduction may not be immediate but may be long term, because CMC 'requires a large initial investment, not only in technology but in training and support in order to be able to make daily use of the system.' Therefore, users are aware that there are many NGOs which cannot afford to start using CMC at this point, with the consequences described above.

Negative effects are barely mentioned by those who are already using CMC. However, these include the increased work pressure brought about by more information and by the exclusion of partners outside the electronic reach of the strengthening of networks. The lack of privacy and security in communications, and the predominance of the English language in CMC at an international level, are also perceived as limitations. On the other hand, some NGOs mention the poor phone and telecommunications infrastructure as barriers that limit their use of

CMC, especially in remote regions of the country, where the phone service is unreliable or non-existent.

PREFERRED PARTNERS: TOWARDS A GLOBAL CIVIL SOCIETY?

According to the data collected in this study, the preferred partners for communication exchanges among Latin American NGOs using CMC are groups and institutions with shared interests, concerns or activities. These are mainly other NGOs, both in the country and internationally, but occasionally they can include other networks, associations, universities, press agencies, international and bilateral organizations, and even government agencies. The most salient characteristic of the communication partners is their variety within a shared community of interests; other features seem to be secondary. As one respondent notes, they communicate 'with very many organizations and institutions, of all kinds', but most respondents go on to define their preference for those who share their own field of expertise, concern or intervention, be it the environment, human rights, women, popular communication, housing, sustainable agriculture, or grassroots development, among others.

A small proportion of respondents also emphasizes the importance of establishing communication with universities and research institutes, some with particular stress on their libraries, databases, and education programmes. Even though the focus of these contacts is still the area of specialty or intervention of each particular case, hinting the same community of interest I have just described, it is noteworthy that these partners are sought to acquire valuable information for education, training, and research.

Despite the apparent heterogeneity in communication partners and counterparts reported, a common thread is implied in all of them. They represent organizations and institutions of civil society, brought together into communities of interest, exchanging information and strengthening linkages and networks in a global scope of action. As one respondent points out, 'there should be more communication and exchange of information with those who are in other countries and with different networks ... in order to strengthen the organization of civil society.'

There are only a few explicit mentions of the notion of civil society in the respondents' comments, but the implied message is palpable in at least half of them. NGOs appear to be using CMC slowly to enlarge the scope and strengthen the bonds between different sectors of civil society. These could be the first steps towards the transnationalization of civil participation, the differentiated cosmopolitanism that is made possible with the use of CMC among NGOs worldwide.

Further research on these issues is still needed if we are to understand the scope of the contribution of CMC to the strengthening of a global civil society.

REFERENCES

Alfonso, C. (1996). Electronic Networks and Political Action at the Service of Civil Society. In A. His (Ed.), *Communication and multimedia for people* Paris: Transversales Science/Culture, (pp. 148-152).

Baym, N. (1995). The Emergence of Community in Computer-Mediated Communication. In S. G. Jones (Ed.), *CyberSociety: Computer-mediated communication and community*, Thousand Oaks, CA: Sage (pp. 138-163).

Frederick, H. (1992). Computer-Communications in Cross-Border Coalition-Building: North American NGO Networking against NAFTA. *Gazette* (50), 217-241.

Friedman, T. (1995). Making sense of software: Computer games and interactive textuality. In S. G. Jones (Ed.), *CyberSociety*, op. cit. (pp. 73-89).

Fuller, M., & Jenkins, H. (1995). Nintendo and New World Travel Writing. In S. G. Jones (Ed.), *CyberSociety*, op. cit., (pp. 57-72).

Garton, L., & Wellman, B. (1994). Social Impacts of Electronic Mail in Organizations. *Communication Yearbook*, 18, 434-453.

Girard, B. (Ed.). (1993). *La Passion Radio*. Paris, Montreal: FPH, AMARC.

Gore, A. (1996). Global Information Infrastructure - GII Delivery at the International Telecommunications Union Conference in Buenos Aires, March 21, 1994. In A. His (Ed.), *Communication and multimedia for people*, op.cit., (pp. 69-77).

Hamelink, C. (1995). The democratic ideal and its enemies. In P. Lee (Ed.), *The Democratization of Communication* Cardiff, UK: WACC, University of Wales Press, (pp. 15-37).

Harasim, L. (1994). Networlds: Networks as social space. In L. Harasim (Ed.), *Global Networks: Computers and International Communication*, Cambridge, MA: MIT Press, (pp. 15-34).

Harris, P. (1996). Globalisation, civil society and communication. *Media Development*, 43(3), 8-9.

Johnson-Lenz, P., & Johnson-Lenz, T. (1994). Groupware for a small planet. In P. Lloyd (Ed.), *Groupware for the 21st. century: Computer supported cooperative working toward the millennium*, London: Adamantine, (pp. 269-285).

Jones, S. G. (1995). Understanding Community in the Information Age. In S. G. Jones (Ed.), *CyberSociety: Computer-mediated communication and community*, Thousand Oaks, CA: Sage (pp. 10-35).

Kaye, A. (1992). Computer conferencing and mass distance education. In M. Waggoner (Ed.), *Empowering Networks: Using computer conferencing in education*. Englewood Cliffs, NJ: Educational Technology.

Lévy, P. (1990). *Les technologies de l'intelligence*. Paris: La Decouverte.

MacKinnon, R. (1995). Searching for the Leviathan in Usenet. In S. G. Jones (Ed.), *CyberSociety*, op. cit., (pp. 112-137).

McLaughlin, M., Osborne, K., & Smith, C. (1995). Standards of Conduct on Usenet. In S. G. Jones (Ed.), *CyberSociety*, op. cit., (pp. 90-111).

Miles, I., Rush, H., Turner, K., & Bessant, J. (1988). *Information Horizons: The long-term implications of new information technologies*. Brookfield, VT: Gower Pub.

NGLS. (1995). @t ease with e-mail: A handbook on using electronic mail for NGOs in developing countries. New York: United Nations Non-Governmental Liaison Service NGLS, Friedrich Ebert Foundation.

NTIA. (1993). The National Information Infrastructure -NII: Agenda for Action. In A. His (Ed.), *Communication and multimedia for people*, op.cit., (pp. 50-68).

Poster, M. (1995). *The Second Media Age*. Cambridge: Polity Press.

Preston, S. (1994). Electronic Global Networking and the NGO movement: the 1992 Rio Summit and Beyond. Swords & Ploughshares: A Chronicle of International Affairs, 3(2), online at gopher.american.edu.

Proulx, S., & Senecal, M. (1995). Is Technical Interactivity a mere pretense of Social Interaction and Democracy? *Technologies de l'information et société*, 7(2), 131-145.

Rheingold, H. (1993). *The Virtual Community: Homesteading on the electronic frontier*. New York: Harper-Collins.

Rice, R., & Steinfield, C. (1994). New forms of organisational communication via electronic mail and voice messaging. In J. Adrianson & R. Roe (Eds.), *Telematics and Work*, Hillsdale, NJ: Lawrence Erlbaum, (pp. 109-137).

Ruth, S., & Ronkin, R. (1992,). Aiming for the elusive payoff of user networks: an NGO perspective. Paper presented at the annual meeting of the International Society for the Systems Sciences, July 1992, Denver, CO.

Sparks, C. (1994). Civil Society and Information Society as Guarantors of Progress. In S. Splichal, A. Calabrese, & C. Sparks (Eds.), *Information Society and Civil Society*, West Lafayette, IN: Purdue University Press, (pp. 21-49)..

Splichal, S. (1994). From Civil Society to Information Society? In S. Splichal, A. Calabrese, & C. Sparks (Eds.), *Information Society and Civil Society*, op.cit., (pp. 50-77).

Sproull, L., & Kiesler, S. (1991). *Connections: New ways of working in the networked organization*. Cambridge, MA: MIT Press.

Swerdlow, J. (1995). Information Revolution. *National Geographic Magazine*, 188(4), 5-37.

Thede, N., & Ambrosi, A. (Eds.). (1991). *Video the Changing World*. Montreal: Black Rose Books.

Turkle, S. (1995). *Life on the Screen: Identity in the age of the Internet*. New York: Simon & Schuster.

Valacich, J., Paranka, D., George, J., & Nunamaker, J. (1993). Communication concurrency and the new media. *Communication Research*, 20, 249-276.

Vattimo, G. (1992). *The Transparent Society*. Baltimore: Johns Hopkins University Press.

---

[1] The APC is probably the most often cited case of CMC use for democratization of communication, but it is by no means the only one. The work of the Electronic Frontier Foundation and of Computers for Social Responsibility are frequently mentioned, and the proliferation of local public-access freenets in many cities in North America have made major contributions to democratizing cyberspace. Their reach is, nonetheless, far more localized and has had less impact on the global arena than the APC.

[2] This study is part of the author's dissertation research. The findings reported here are based on a survey administered to all NGOs affiliated with an APC service provider in a Latin American country, and on follow-up in-depth interviews with some of the respondents.

Culture and communication - The interplay in the new public commons: Usenet and community networks

Michael Hauben
PO Box 250101, New York, NY 10025-1531, USA
Phone: +1 212 787 9361, Fax: +1 212 662 6442
Email: hauben@columbia.edu

'Any document that attempts to cover an emerging culture is doomed to be incomplete. Even more so if the culture has no overt identity (at least none outside virtual space). But the other side of that coin presents us with the opportunity to document the ebb and flow, the moments of growth and defeat, the development of this young culture.'
(John Frost, *Cyberpoet's Guide to Virtual Culture*, 1993)

Abstract

As we approach the new millennium, social relationships are changing radically. In 1969, the anthropologist Margaret Mead spoke of an 'approaching world-wide culture'. While Mead wrote of a global culture made possible by the electronic and transportation advances of her day, her words actually foresaw fundamental changes that have been substantially enhanced by the computer communication networks that were just beginning in 1969. A new culture is being formed out of a universal desire for communication. This culture is being formed and formulated both by new technology and by social desires. People are dissatisfied with their conditions, whether traditional or modern. Much of the new communication technology facilitates new global connections. This paper will explore the effect of new communication forms on human culture and of human culture on these new communication forms.

An Ethical Global Information Society J. Berleur & D. Whitehouse (Eds.)

THE EMERGING GLOBALIZATION OF THE EVERYDAY

The extensive development of transportation and communication technologies in the twentieth century has linked the world together in ways which make it relatively simple to travel or to communicate with peoples and cultures around the world. The daily exposure of the world's peoples to various cultures makes it impossible for almost any individual to envision the world consisting of only his or her own culture (Mead, 1978). We really are moving into a new global age which affects most aspects of human life. For example, world trade has become extensive, many words are similar across languages, and sports and entertainment are viewed simultaneously by global audiences. The exposure to media and forms of communication helps spread many of these cultural elements. While television and radio connect people with the rest of the world in a rather impersonal and often passive fashion, computer networks are increasingly bringing people of various cultures together in a much more intimate and grassroots manner.

Culture is a difficult concept to define. For example, Tim North has gathered seven different definitions (North, 1994, chapter 4.2.1). One common category in some of these definitions is the passing of previously learned behaviour from one generation to the next. Another common category in the definition of culture is the importance of experience and patterns of behaviour shared among a group of people. Historically, culture has changed slowly and has been passed on from generation to generation. In the last half of the twentieth century, however, for most peoples the rate of cultural evolution has been accelerating. Mead (1978) writes that while, in the past, culture was transmitted from the older generation to the younger with slow change from generation to generation, today the younger generation learns from both its elders and from its peers. The learning from peers is then shared with the elders. Human culture is set by how people live their lives (Graham, 1995). Culture is created and reinforced through how a person lives in the context of society and of social movements. The individual is taught the culture of his or her society while growing up, but those perceptions change as he or she matures, develops, and lives an adult life. Culture is not statically defined. Rather, a person grows up into a culture and then changes it as that life progresses through time (Mead, 1956).

As people increasingly live a more global lifestyle, whether mediated through media, travel or actual experience, culture is changing. This global experience is facilitated by the ability of the individual to interact with people from other cultures and countries on a personal level. Images and thoughts available via mass media show these cultures exist but, when people get a chance to talk and interact, differences become less of an oddity and more of an opportunity (Uncapher, 1992).

There are those who claim this global culture or mass culture is snuffing out individual differences to make a pre-packaged culture. These critics call for the isolation of communities from each other so that their uniqueness can be preserved. This criticism misses the point that human culture is a dynamic element of society, and freezing it would produce a museum of human society. Uncapher (1992) correctly points out that what these critics do not recognize is that, more and more, the people of various cultures are understanding the power of the new communication technologies. More and more people are reacting against the mass media and corporate dominance and calling for a chance to express their views and contribute their culture to the global culture. Margaret Mead tells a story (1978, pp. 5-6) of returning to a village in New Guinea which originally requested medicine and trade goods. On this later visit, rather than asking for more contributions of western civilization, the villagers requested their songs be recorded via tape recorder in order to contribute their own culture to the outside world. The presence of radios made the villagers aware of the music of others, and they wanted a part of their culture broadcast around the world.

GLOBAL CONTACT OVER COMPUTER NETWORKS

The new media of Usenet news, electronic mail and the Internet facilitate the growth of global interactive communities. These forums are made available through community networks, universities, the workplace, Internet access providers, and other public access locations (Hauben and Hauben, 1997). Human culture is ever evolving and developing, and the new public commons are of a global nature. A growing number of people are coming together online and living more of their daily lives with people from around the world. Through the sharing of these moments by people, their cultures are coming to encompass more of the world not before immediately available.

Usenet newsgroups are a relatively young medium of human discourse and communication [1]. In a recent study of the global online culture, Tim North (1994, chapter 5.2) asks the question, 'Is there an on-line culture and society on Usenet?' His conclusion is that there is a definite Usenet culture. He lists four of the important defining aspects of this culture:

1. The conventions of the culture are freely discussed;
2. The culture is not closed to outsiders and welcomes new members;
3. There is a strong sense of community within the net culture;
4. It is what you say, not who you are, that matters.

North proposes, however, that Usenet cannot be considered as a separate society. Rather Usenet is 'a superstructural society that spans many mainstream societies and is dependent upon them for its continued existence' (North, chapter 4.2.2, p. 4).

North argues that the net does not need to provide the physical needs made possible by a society. He writes: 'In this superstructural view, the Net is freed of the responsibilities of providing certain of the features provided by other societies (e.g. reproduction, food and shelter) by virtue of the fact that its members are also members of traditional mainstream societies that do supply them' (North, chapter 4.2.2, p. 4).

Rather, those who use the net live in their offline society and come to the net for other than physical purposes. Others are studying the online culture and the connection to the growing global culture (Avis, 1995; Graham, 1995; Jones, 1991).

Usenet technology was developed by graduate students in the late 1970s as a way to promote the sharing of information and to spread communication between university campuses. This design highlights the importance of the contribution by individuals to the community. Thus the content of Usenet is produced by elements of the community for the whole of the community. In the forming of this public space or commons, people are encouraged to share their views, thoughts, and questions with others (Hauben and Hauben, 1997). Usenet provides the chance to contribute to discussions and to interact with other people; it has become a truly global community of people hooking their computers together to communicate. People desire to talk and to communicate with other people (Graham, 1995; Woodbury, 1994).

Both the technological design of opening a computer up to accept the contributions of others and the desire to communicate led to the creation of an egalitarian culture (Jones, 1991; North, 1994; Woodbury, 1994). People have both a chance to introduce and to share their own culture and a chance to broaden themselves through exposures to various cultures. As such, the Usenet culture is an example of a global culture which is not a reflection of purely one culture. Instead, Usenet incorporates cultural elements from many nations and builds a new online culture (North, 1994).

COMMUNITY NETWORKS MAKING ONLINE ACCESS AVAILABLE

Community networks provide a way for citizens of a locality to hook into these global communities for little or no cost (Graham, 1995). Community networks also provide a way for communities to represent themselves to others connected online (Graham, 1995; Weston, 1994). Without access made available through community networks, through publicly available computer terminals or local dial-in phone numbers, only those who could afford the monthly charges or who have access through work or school would represent themselves (Avis, 1995). Particular portraits of various cultures would thus be only partially represented. Also, when access is available and open to all, a greater wealth of contributions can be made.

There is a strong push in Canada and Canadian communities to get online. A lot of grassroots community network building is taking place. A Canadian national organization, Telecommunities Canada, stresses the importance of contributing Canada's various cultures to the online community and, in this way, of making a contribution to the whole community (Graham, 1995; Weston, 1994). In a similar way, Izumi Aizu (1995, p. 6) says that Japan has 'an opportunity to bring its own cultural value to the open world' and, he continues, '(i)t also opens the possibility of changing Japan into a less rigid, more decentralized society, following the network paradigm exercised by the distributed nature of the Internet itself.'

There is something to be said about the attraction of representing one's self to the greater community. The many-to-many form of communication where an individual can broadcast to the community and get responses back from other individuals is an empowering experience. No longer do you have to be rich and powerful to communicate broadly to others and to represent yourself and your own views. This power is making it possible for individuals to communicate with others with similar interests (and different interests) around the world. Grassroots organization is boosted and even the formation of local community groups is accelerated. Development of the commons to the exclusion of the big media representations makes this a grassroots medium or a new enlarged public commons (Felsenstein, 1993).

The online culture is primarily a written one, although much of the text is generally written in an informal, almost off-the-cuff fashion. While people will post papers and well thought-out ideas, much of the conversation is generated in an immediate response to others' messages. This text can feel like a conversation or a written version of oral culture. Stories akin to the great stories of pre-history come about. Legends and urban myths circulate and are disseminated (Jones, 1991). Pictures and other non-text items can be sent in Usenet messages but these non-text items are primarily transferred and not modified, thought about, or communally worked on as are the textual ideas. The common, shared, online language is English (Aizu, 1995). However, other languages exist in country hierarchies, in newsgroups, and in mailing lists, along with Internet Relay Chat (IRC) channels, gopher sites, and world wide web (WWW) pages.

Text also means that body language and other non-verbal clues need to be spelled out. Extra-sensory emoticons [2] have been invented (for example, <grin>, <laugh>, and so on) along with smileys. Smileys are textual drawings of a person's face with a smile or grin rotated 90 degrees counter-clockwise so as to be typeable and printable on computer text screens and printouts [3].

CONCLUSION

North writes how there is a distinct Usenet culture, and that this culture is open and welcoming to newcomers (1994). He also notes there can be unfriendliness to 'newbies' but he focuses on how the online culture is documented and available for people to learn from documents available online [4]. This description of culture and netiquette (the online word for net etiquette) is available to learn from and open to discussion. Bruce Jones (1991) sums up the net culture:

> '...the usenet network of computers and users constitutes a community and a culture, bounded by its own set of norms and conventions, marked by its own linguistic jargon and sense of humor and accumulating its own folklore' (p. 2).

Both North (1994) and Jones (1991) elaborate on what they see as an egalitarian tendency or tendency to contribute to the community's benefit. Jones writes:

> '...the people of the net owe something to each other. While not bound by formal, written agreements, people nevertheless are required by convention to observe certain amenities because they serve the greater common interest of the net. These aspects of voluntary association are the elements of culture and community that bind the people of usenet together' (p. 4).

The global culture is formed in several ways, none of which is a generic, corporate, rubber stamp. People are taking charge. They are bringing their own cultures into the global culture and spreading this new culture around the world. This is taking on a general form and an online form. The online form provides a strong means by which people can spread their ideas and culture which in turn affects the broader global culture. This broader global culture also affects newsgroups or online media. The ability to express oneself to the rest of the world is addictive and the rapid increase of new people joining the online global community makes that manifest. 'The voice-less and the oppressed in every part of the world have begun to demand more power ... The secure belief that those who knew had authority over those who did not has been shaken' (Mead, 1978, p.5).

NOTES

[1] Usenet was initiated in 1979.
[2] Emoticons are icons which are used to include emotion and other meta-messages otherwise not transmittable in written online communication forms.
[3] Examples include :-) traditional smile ;-) wink, etc. See Sanderson, 1993, for more examples.
[4] The online culture is described and written about in FAQ (frequently asked question) files in various newsgroups, the various news.newuser newsgroups, and in other readily available files (North, 1994).

REFERENCES

Aizu, Izumi. (1995). Cultural Impact on Network Evolution in Japan Emergence of Netizens [On-Line]. Institute for HyperNetwork Society. GLOCOM (Centre for Global Communications), International University of Japan.
Available WWW: http://www.glocom.ac.jp/Publications/Aizu/nete&c.html

Avis, Andrew. (1995) Public Spaces on the Information Highway: The Role of Community Networks. Unpublished master's thesis, University of Calgary, Calgary, Alberta, Canada.
Available WWW: http://www.ucalgary.ca/~aavis/thesis/thesis.html

Felsenstein, Lee. (1993, May). The Commons of Information. *Dr. Dobbs' Journal* 18-22.

Frost, John. (1993). Cyberpoet's Guide to Virtual Culture.
Available WWW: http://homepage.seas.upenn.edu/~mengwong/cyber/cgvc1.html

Graham, Garth. (March 29, 1995). A Domain Where Thought is Free to Roam: The Social Purpose of Community Networks. Prepared for Telecommunities Canada for CRTC public hearings on information highway.
Available WWW: http://www.freenet.mb.ca/tc/crtc.brief.html

Hauben, Michael and Ronda Hauben. (1997) *Netizens: On The History and Impact of Usenet and the Internet.* Los Alamitos, CA: IEEE Computer Society Press.
Also available WWW: http://www.columbia.edu/~hauben/netbook/

Jones, Bruce. (1991) An Ethnography of the Usenet Computer Network: Proposal for a PhD Dissertation in Communications. University of California, San Diego. Dept. of Communication.
Available FTP: weber.ucsd.edu Directory: /Usenet.Hist/ File: diss.proposal

Mead, Margaret. (1956). *New Lives for Old: Cultural Transformations - Manus, 1928-1953.* NY, NY: William Morrow & Company.

Mead, Margaret. (1978). *Culture and Commitment: The New Relationships Between the Generations in the 1970s.* Garden City, NY: Anchor Books/Doubleday.

North, Tim. (1994) The Internet and Usenet Global Computer Networks: An investigation of their culture and its effects on new users. Unpublished master's thesis, Curtin University of Technology, Perth, Australia.
Available WWW: http://www.vianet.net.au/~timn/thesis/

Sanderson, David W. (Ed.). (1993). *Smileys.* Sebastopol, CA: O'Reilly & Associates.

Uncapher, Willard. (1992). Between Local and Global Placing the Media-scape in the Transnational Cultural Flow . Available WWW:
http://www.eff.org/pub/Net_culture/Global_village/between_global_and_local.paper

Weston, Jay. (Nov. 26, 1994). Old Freedoms and New Technologies: The Evolution of Community Networking. [On-Line]. Paper presented at the Free Speech and Privacy In The Information Age Symposium: University of Waterloo, Canada
Available WWW: http://www.nptn.org/cyber.serv/tdp/jweston

Woodbury, Gregory G. (1994, Fall). Net Cultural Assumptions. Net Culture Assumptions II - Historical Perspective *Amateur Computerist Newsletter*, 6
Available FTP: wuarchive.wustl.edu Directory:/doc/misc/acn/ File: acn6-2.txt.

18

On cultures and information technology applications in organizations

Pertti Järvinen
University of Tampere
P.O. Box 607, FIN-33101 Tampere, Finland
Phone +358 31 2156777; Fax +358 31 2156070
Email: pj@cs.uta.fi

Abstract

Some empirical studies concerning usage of new information systems and of general office systems (such as word processing systems) show that all the potential features of those systems have not been used at all. The reason for this is suspected to lie in organizational cultures. There are, however, very few studies on how information technology (IT) applications fit in with an organizational culture. In this paper, firstly, a typology of organizational cultures is presented and, secondly, an analysis is made of how harmonious the fit is between IT applications and a certain cultural type. It is shown that IT applications and organizational cultures mutually affect each other. Advances in IT, together with policy level decisions being made in organizations, may lead to increasingly complex situations. The fit between IT and varieties of organizational culture represents a new challenge for IT design and the IT community.

INTRODUCTION

The recent development of the Internet has brought the global village a bit closer. The so-called global world is most probably not the whole world, but the metaphor has its importance in terms of culture (Berleur, this volume). Global business on the superhighway and its potential implications for the office of the future has been sketched and evaluated (Glasson, 1996) with differing views on whether technical aspects or social ones will dominate.

Organizations today face unprecedented change in their environment. Information technology (IT) continues to be integral to creating products and delivering services, as well as a critical enabler of business strategy execution

An Ethical Global Information Society J. Berleur & D. Whitehouse (Eds.)

(Henderson and Venkatraman, 1993). It is clear that, even though IT has evolved from its traditional orientation of administrative support toward a more strategic role within an organization, there is still a glaring lack of fundamental frameworks within which to understand the potential of IT for tomorrow's organizations.

The modern resource-based theory of the firm (Conner and Prahalad, 1996) considers the firm as a collection of heterogeneous resources: physical and human resources, knowledge, organizational routines and culture. The latter, the organizational culture spread over the whole organization can form a sustainable competitive advantage.

Quinn *et al.* (1990) have in the field of management collected models and cultures of management. Some models emphasize either control or flexibility, some models stress the importance of either a firm's internal arrangements or its external relationships. In this paper, *the analysis is directed at how a potential or a real IT application fits in with a particular organizational culture.* This study will in some sense be more complete and wider than others because Knoll and Jarvenpaa (1994) in their covering review of literature showed that the earlier organizational-IT fit research has mainly considered internal aspects within a stable environment.

Kling and Jewett (1995) in their social analysis of computing systems speak of two dimensions of these systems, which they term: I. Closed/open systems, and II. Rational/natural systems, taken from Scott (1992). Kling and Jewett's dimension of closed/open systems corresponds to the dimension referred to in this paper as 'internal/external', and their 'rational/natural systems' dimension quite closely corresponds to what is called here the dimension of 'control/ flexibility'. Kling and Jewett mainly emphasize the consequences of computing or networking for the work organization and workers, whereas here the emphasis is on the analysis of cultures.

The rest of this paper is structured in the following way: in the section that follows a typology of organizational cultures is selected and presented. Thereafter, a detailed analysis is given of how to make a potential or real IT application fit in with a particular organizational culture. Before the final summarizing discussion, some organizational policy issues are considered.

TYPOLOGY OF ORGANIZATIONAL CULTURES

In this section, some basic concepts like organizational climate and culture are first defined. Thereafter follows an analysis of some potential frameworks for structuring an evaluation of the IT-organizational cultural fit. The typology chosen identifies four main categories of organizational culture.

The FOCUS-group (1996) reports considerable discussion about the meaning of the words 'climate' and 'culture'. The group prefers the following definition: 'Organizational climate is the collective perception of the relatively stable value orientations in the organization in its entirety, which influence the behaviour of the members regarding the efficient functioning of the organization and which is presented in a descriptive way by the members of the organization'. The construct of organizational culture appeared more recently than organizational climate. In the domain of organizational culture there are two approaches, namely an organization is a culture and an organization has a culture. In the first approach, the organization has a culture with symbols, stories, myths which is meaningful to the employees. That is, the way of working together and organizing has a special meaning for the people who work in the organization. This view of the organization excludes cultural typologies, because each culture is considered to be unique.

In the second approach, an organization has a culture besides other organizational variables like structure, leadership, reward systems, etc. Organizational culture is the glue which holds the organization together (Deal and Kennedy, 1982). This approach promotes the study of organizational culture as a system of shared meanings, assumptions, and underlying values (Schein, 1985).

Quinn (1988) has identified an evolution of management models starting from the beginning of this century. He finds four classes of model: the rational goal, the internal process, the human relations, and the open systems models. Each model belongs to one quadrant formed by two dimensions. Does the model emphasize the internal affairs of the organization or its relations to the external environment? Is the organization oriented towards flexibility or towards controlling/maintaining the current situation? Quinn *et al.* (1990) characterize these models by using the terms market, hierarchy, clan, and adhocracy. They divide each quadrant into two parts, create eight roles, and call the result the competing values framework. These eight roles of managers do not fit in well with the purpose of the present analysis where the emphasis is on cultural types. Therefore, the formulation of organizational cultures made by Smart and St. John (1996) has been selected, and this is summarized in Figure 1.

These four organizational cultures will be considered as ideal types in the Weberian sense and are briefly characterised below.

The *clan* culture (upper left quadrant in Figure 1) is characterized as having high flexibility, individuality, and spontaneity, as well as internal emphasis, a short-term time frame, and a focus on smoothing activities. In clan cultures the primary leadership style is that of a mentor or facilitator, bonding mechanisms emphasize loyalty and tradition, and the strategic approach focuses on human resources and cohesion.

The *hierarchy* or bureaucracy culture (bottom left quadrant in Figure 1), like a clan culture, has an internal emphasis, a short-term time frame, and a focus on smoothing activities but differs in its emphasis on stability, control, and predictability. The dominant leadership style is that of the coordinator or organizer, rules and policies are the primary bonding mechanisms, and the strategic emphasis is on permanence and stability.

The *adhocracy* culture (upper right quadrant in Figure 1), like the clan culture, emphasizes flexibility, individuality, and spontaneity but differs in its emphasis on external positioning, a long-term time frame and achievement-oriented activities. The entrepreneur and innovator leadership styles are prevalent in adhocracy cultures, the bonding mechanisms emphasize innovation and development, and growth and acquisition of new resources constitute the primary strategic emphases.

The *market* culture (bottom right quadrant in Figure 1) shares an emphasis on external positioning, a long-term time frame, and achievement-oriented activities with the adhocracy culture but differs in its valuing of stability, control, and predictability. The leadership style most compatible with the market culture is that of the producer or hard-driver, while goal attainment provides a bonding mechanism, and the strategic emphasis is on competitive actions and achievements.

Figure 1. Typology of organizational cultures

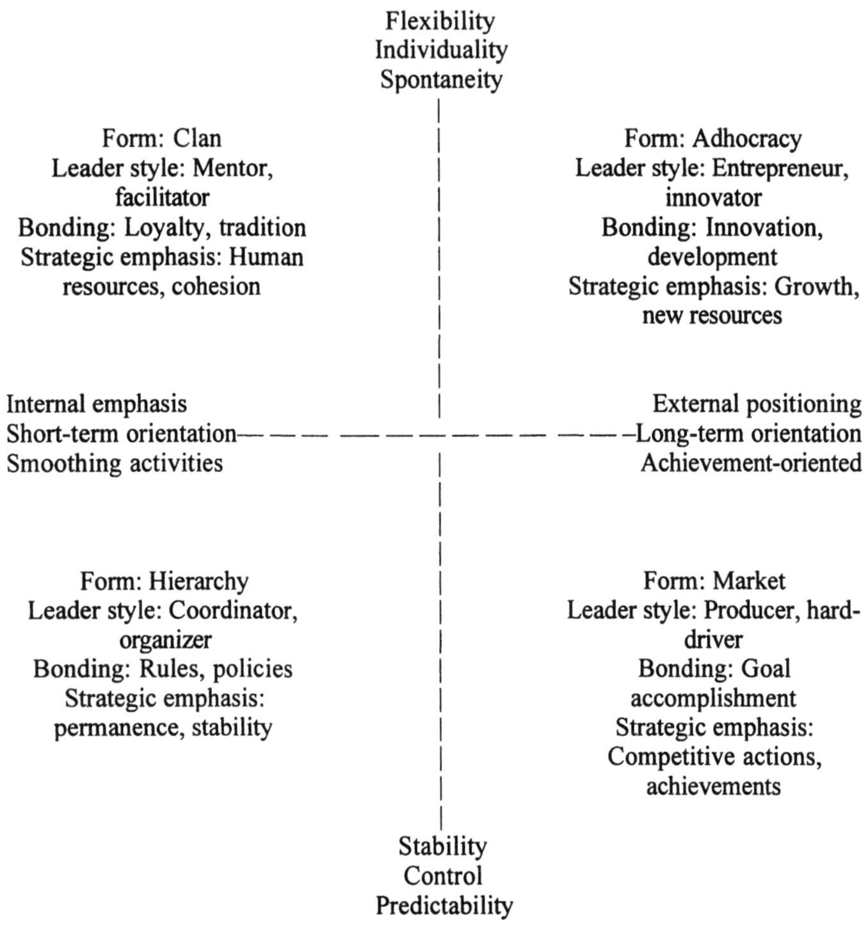

Before using the typology, mention needs to be made concerning democracy, another key concept in this discussion, at the organizational level. In the organizations emphasizing flexibility, their participants share a common interest in the survival of the organization and engage in collective activities to secure this end. It is important to note that organizational *democracy* will be realized in those organizations emphasizing flexibility.

In the next four sections, our analysis of potential and real relationships between cultural types and IT applications will contain both empirical studies and conceptual speculations, i.e., so-called thought experiments. In each section, a cultural type is first characterized together with some features of IT applications supporting this type, and then some cases are described from the literature. General comments and organizational policy issues are considered in a separate section after the detailed analysis.

IT AND HIERARCHY

An organization oriented towards the individual and towards the control of individual behaviour has a rules-oriented culture. A bureaucratic organization is a prototype. Order, discipline, and systematic work are important. The IT applications developed to support a hierarchical organizational culture contain rules and procedures. A questioning/answering system is a good example where a program controls a dialogue with a user. Our first example below describes how the information systems (IS) development was controlled, and the second example how the new IS can support empowerment.

Orlikowski (1991) has described how a large international consulting firm used a Computer-Aided Systems Engineering (CASE) tool to control the work of systems analysts. The firm hired college graduates and MBAs without any computing experience and trained them with their own methods. The firm reviewed the newer consultants every two years. The new CASE tool was designed to enforce a specific sequence of design activities. The older consultants found that systems development activities with the new CASE tool required less skill than earlier. Somebody else could immediately continue the work performed earlier by another colleague. Orlikowski found that the firm exercised the systemic form of control by a socialization process which comprised a 'significant area of cultural control - control of conduct'. The firm could in real time evaluate and control the current project on the basis of records made by the CASE tool. Hence Kling and Jewett (1995) said that 'this firm's use of the customized CASE tool has some important parallels with Perrolle's (1986) characterization of intellectual assembly line'.

Kling and Jewett (1995) paid attention to Zuboff's (1988) 'informating' concept and its positive application. Zuboff defined her key concepts 'automate' and 'informate' as follows:

> 'To "automate" is to replace human activity with a machine (computer) which is faster, more reliable, more subject to control etc. The goals of automation have typically been those of cost reduction, efficiency, and productivity. Automation means applying technology in ways that increase the self acting and self regulating capacities of machine systems, thus minimising human intervention. Intelligent technology can be used to automate, but even as this occurs, the technology has the capacity to translate those automated activities into data and to display those data. Information technology symbolically renders processes, objects, behaviours and events such that they become visible, knowable and sharable in a new way. The word Zuboff coined to describe this second function is "informate".'

Zuboff (1988) reported an intriguing case of informating in her study of an expense tracking system in a paper plant. Operators in the plant learned about the costs of making paper from a computerized subsystem that had been added to their equipment controlling the paper-making process. By experimenting with their equipment they were able to reduce the costs of producing paper significantly, because the new system informed them about the costs of chemicals and other ingredients.

Kling and Jewett (1995) saw some features of the human relations school or the clan culture in Zuboff's findings, because the operators felt that they owned the system and it empowered them. This might be a special case. In general, the informating concept may be applicable in cases where the object of work is material or human (not data) and the new computing system makes the object more visible. An application of IT may then, as in Zuboff's case, cause some emergent organizational changes.

IT AND CLAN

An organization oriented towards people and with internally oriented flexibility has a supportive, clan culture. In this cultural type the human being takes a central position. People trust each other, help each other and feel at home in the organization. In an organization following the clan culture, the IT is applied by building an infrastructure to support cooperation and sharing knowledge. Our example concerns groupware in an IT firm. One department was established to help customers to solve their problems with the IT products delivered by the firm.

Orlikowski (1995) examined the use of a groupware technology (Lotus Notes) in the context of customer support to understand how the technology was used to enable organizational changes over time. Building on its successful implementation of the groupware technology two years earlier, the customer support department brought about many organizational changes that altered the nature and distribution of work, forms of collaboration, utilization and dissemination of knowledge. Some of the organizational changes were planned and some were emergent; use of the new electronic mechanism for collaboration led to an interesting emergent change in the department: it shifted the form of collaboration from being primarily reactive to being primarily proactive. Because all specialists had access to the database of customer calls being worked on in the department, they browsed through each others' calls to see which ones they could help with. Rather than waiting to be asked if they had solutions to particular problems (reactive collaboration), they actively sought problems that they had solutions for (proactive collaboration).

Silver *et al.* (1995) judged that (1) 'in an organization that values individuality over teamwork, groupware systems - especially those that operate with anonymity - may fail to achieve their desired consequences of promoting productive collaborative work. On the other hand, when coupled with other measures, such a groupware system might be used as part of a conscious effort to make the corporate culture more team oriented'. Thus it is very important to note that the relationship between organizational culture and IT systems might work in two opposite directions.

IT AND MARKET

An organization oriented towards the goals of the organization and towards the control of the means to reach these goals has a market culture. Everyone works in the same customer-oriented direction. Productivity is emphasized. People who contribute to the realization of goals are rewarded. The IT applications can be built to help managers to control the optimal use of resources. Our example concerns the introduction of the IT package to the consulting company whose market culture was in conflict with the idea behind the package.

Orlikowski (1992) explored the introduction of groupware into an organization to understand the changes in the work practices and social interaction facilitated by the technology. The chief information officer of a large international consulting firm carefully chose a new groupware package (Lotus Notes) to help the firm to manage its expertise and transform its practice. Results suggested that people's mental models and the organization's structure and culture significantly influenced how the groupware was implemented and used. Specifically, in the absence of mental models that stressed its collaborative nature, groupware was interpreted in terms of familiar, personal, stand-alone technologies such as spreadsheets. Further, the culture and structure of the firm provided few incentives or norms for cooperating or sharing expertise, for example, the consultants' incentive structure was based on having 'billable time' from clients for each of their activities. The firm's managers failed to modify this incentive structure. The consultants had no way to bill the significant amount of time (15-30 hours) taken to learn to use the new software or the time spent writing case reports that might help another consultant.

IT AND ADHOCRACY

The adhocracy culture emphasizes organizational flexibility, and relationships between the firm and its environment. The specialists in such a firm are oriented towards searching for all kinds of new things. The following elements are typical of an adhocracy culture: growth, taking risks, creativity, competition, individual responsibility, being open to scientific findings, and following courses to improve knowledge and skills. The example considered below is a hypothetical case, a sketch of an adhocracy type firm and how its arrangements can be supported by IT.

Boland and Tenkasi (1995) claimed that knowledge-intensive firms are composed of multiple communities with specialized expertise, and are often characterized by lateral rather than hierarchical organizational forms. Producing knowledge to create innovative products and processes in such firms requires the ability to have strong perspectives within community, as well as the ability to take the perspective of another into account.

Boland and Tenkasi presented models of language, communication, and cognition that can assist in the design of electronic communication systems for perspective making and perspective taking. By appreciating how communication is both like a language game played in a local community and also like a transmission of messages through a channel, and by appreciating how cognition includes a capacity to narrativize our experience as well as a capacity to process information, Boland and Tenkasi identified some guidelines for designing electronic communication systems to support knowledge work. The communication systems they proposed emphasize that narratives can help construct strong perspectives within a community of knowing, and that reflecting on and representing that perspective can create boundary objects which allow for perspective taking between communities.

Boland and Tenkasi also presented a 'plausible, but admittedly utopian form of a knowledge intensive firm'. They structured their representation by considering it from the technological, organizational and cultural aspects. Technologically, they expected that computing, imaging, and communication devices have become ubiquitous. The information environment in this hypothetical firm is a seamless integration of multimedia devices for collection, storage, processing, and display. The organization is replete with systems based on the channel model and language games model. Once certain kinds of knowledge are established and the perspective of a community of knowing becomes mature, the decision routines are embedded in project management and other kinds of software, although such decision premises are always subject to question and revision. Graphics, texts, models, audio, and video applications are all radically tailorable to a user's needs. Hyperlinks from an element in any one application to elements in any other application are fully supported, making contextually rich, complexly layered, representations the norm. Groupware is highly developed, with multimedia meetings, and discussion groups in a wide variety of issue forums. A sophisticated vocabulary of electronic forums for initiating, replying or commenting on decision models and discussion topics has emerged through an open process of structuration (Giddens, 1979).

According to Boland and Tenkasi, organizationally, the firm is characterized by a critical density of interdependent knowledge communities. The organization uses lateral teams extensively in which the vertical authority structure plays a muted role while the principle of value-adding activities of knowledge creation and knowledge application are carried out in a changing 'mosaic' of lateral project teams.

Culturally, the idea that doing work in a knowledge-intensive firm means perspective making and perspective taking in communities of knowing has taken hold and has shaped both individual and group identities. Individuals have a reflexive awareness of their ways of processing information as well as their narrative modes of cognition. Members of the firm enter into and make readings of communication episodes with an open awareness of the hermeneutic circle in which they tack back and forth from an interpretation of the larger context of a perspective to an interpretation of the detailed elements of the message at hand. They realize that debate is a win-lose polarizing strategy that rarely results in true synthesis or creative insights. Dialogue, in contrast, is mutually reinforcing, working together through language. It is a realization that we can assume a perspective taking orientation and benefit from opening ourselves to the horizon of another.

Within the organizational, cultural, and technological environment sketched by Boland and Tenkasi, communities of knowing are using advanced groupware facilities to conduct meetings, construct multi-author documents, and coordinate their promises and deadlines, all with the capability of accessing data and knowledge through a worldwide network of knowledge repositories.

Since groups form and reform in a knowledge-intensive firm employing a lateral organization, Boland and Tenkasi proposed five classes of electronic communication forums for enhancing perspective making and perspective taking: 1. Task narrative forums, 2. Knowledge representation forums, 3. Interpretative reading forums, 4. Theory building forums, and 5. Intelligent agent forums.

GENERAL COMMENTS AND SOME ORGANIZATIONAL POLICY ISSUES

First, some comment is given on the analyses in the previous four sections, and then organizational policy issues are considered such as electronic mail, end user computing, and outsourcing. The few examples above show that cultural type can have an influence on the usage of a certain IT applications. If the latter does not fit in with the organizational culture of a firm, some problems will appear. The examples also show that the IT applications which do fit in very well with the cultural type can trigger positive processes not planned at all.

Electronic mail and a computer network in an organization gives employees the chance to communicate freely with each other and to form news and discussion groups. The employer exercizing hierarchical control may not like to see that some clan subcultures will emerge in the network that are difficult to control. Silver *et al.* (1995) estimated that, given the information sharing and communication capabilities of IT, traditional organizational hierarchies are giving way to adhocracies and networked organizations.

Kumar and van Dissel (1996) recently studied how to manage conflicts and cooperation in interorganizational systems. The highest form of interdependence between interorganizational units is the reciprocal dependency where units feed their work back and forth among themselves, that is, each receives input from and provides output to others, often interactively. The authors claim that group technologies may diminish risks of socio-political conflicts but, at the same moment, they pay attention to another aspect. They evaluate that group technologies, at their current level of evolution, at best provide a value-neutral platform for enabling such interorganizational systems. At worst, which is usually the case, they incorporate the value judgements of the culture in which they were conceived and developed.

End user computing, in contrast to corporate computing, may contain the independent use of spreadsheets, graphics, word processing, queries and report generation, and desktop publishing (McLean *et al.*, 1993). Capable employees can build their own IT applications which may cause some overlapping and conflicting effects with corporate computing. These surely are not desired in the organizations emphasizing control in their culture.

McFarlan and Nolan (1995) recommended that the outsourcing contract of an organization with an IT firm should last at least 10 years. In a turbulent world such a contract cannot then be restrictive. For the IT firm it is profitable to install similar IT applications into many organizations. We can now imagine what would happen if the IT firm were to develop its applications which previously supported a particular cultural type, such as a hierarchy, in such a direction that they would support another cultural type say, for example, a clan. Some control concerning the selected cultural type in the organization will be moved to another firm.

We can conclude that some technical advances in IT like groupware and local area networks, and some organizational policy issues like end user computing and outsourcing, can in some cases create problems with sustaining a selected cultural type.

DISCUSSION

The analysis of the four cultural types and consideration of wider issues shows that the question of how a potential or real IT application fits in with an organizational culture can be solved rather easily at the IT application level. There are IS supporting each cultural type. The advances in IT technology and some political issues clearly increase the complexity of this problem area. Managers must be also aware of cultural aspects when they are making decisions on the development of a new information system, on purchasing new IT technology for the organization, and on making contracts with an IT firm.

The above analysis was widely based on examples in order that the reader could make his or her own judgements when following the argument. The purpose was in this way to support intersubjectivity.

The reengineering of organizations has recently been connected with the new opportunities offered by IT. At the same time a more horizontal division of labour is emphasized, but as Barley (1996) wrote 'hierarchical practices and ideologies have a way of reemerging even when managers are sincere about adopting more collaborative practices'. The most critical inference to be drawn from Barley's ethnographic study of technicians' work was: 'The most serious barriers to adapting successfully to a changing world of work are likely to be cultural, ... if technicians are at all typical of what a significant proportion of work will be like in a post-industrial economy, the difficulties of reengineering firms will pale before the cultural and institutional changes that we may need to contemplate'.

In the longitudinal development program (Harkness *et al.*, 1996), the Bose leaders very early recognized that process improvement techniques (such as Business Process Reengineering and Total Quality Management) and the existing organizational culture needed to be synthesized into a pattern of work that leveraged the strengths of both.

One aspect still needs to be taken into consideration, namely the possible combinations of cultural types. There are some ideas to support such a view (Quinn *et al.*, 1990) that, on the one hand, the hierarchy and the adhocracy and, on the other hand, the clan and the market are complementary rather than mutually exclusive. In the discussion of adhocracy above, reference was made to Boland and Tenkasi (1995) who stressed that 'individuals have a reflexive awareness of their ways to process information as well as their narrative modes of cognition', that is, the researchers recommend the use of two complementary models. Nonaka (1994) also recommended a similar arrangement called a 'hypertext organization' for creating knowledge in an organization. The core feature of the hypertext organization is the ability to switch between the various contexts to accommodate changing requirements from situations both inside and outside the organization.

Those contexts can be situations such as the acquisition, generation, exploitation, and accumulation of knowledge. Each context has, according to Nonaka, a distinctive way of organizing its knowledge creation activities. Heterarchical self-organizing activities are indispensable for generating new knowledge as well as for acquiring 'deep' knowledge through intensive, focused search. On the other hand, a hierarchical division of labour is more efficient and effective for implementation, exploitation, and accumulation of new knowledge as well as acquisition of diverse information through extensive, unfocused search.

The complementary use of the hierarchy and the adhocracy, on the one hand, and the clan and the market, on the other hand, means a new challenge for the IT community. Thus, for the same firm, where there is an emphasis on efficiency, information systems need to be built that support those processes and, where creativity is emphasized, other information systems need to be designed that support these processes.

REFERENCES

Barley S.R. (1996), Technicians in the workplace: Ethnographic evidence for bringing work into organization studies. *Administrative Science Quarterly* **41**, (3), 404-441.

Berleur J. (this volume), Culture and democracy revisited in the global information society. Summary of a position paper.

Boland R.J. and R.V. Tenkasi (1995), Perspective making and perspective taking in communities of knowing. *Organization Science* **6**, (4), 350-372.

Bunge M. (1967), *Scientific Research I. The Search for System*. Springer-Verlag, Berlin.

Conner K.R. and C.K. Prahalad (1996), A resource-based theory of the firm: Knowledge versus opportunism,. *Organization Science* 7, (5), 477-501.

Deal T.E. and A.A. Kennedy (1982), *Corporate cultures: The rights and rituals of corporate life*, Addison-Wesley, Reading.

FOCUS-group (1996), First organizational cultural unified search, Vlaams Instituut voor Zelfstandig Ondernemen, Limburg, manuscript.

Giddens A. (1979), *Central problems in social theory*. MacMillan, London.

Glasson B. (1996), Global business on the superhighway: Implications for the office of future, In Terashima and Altman (Eds.), *Advanced IT tools*. Chapman & Hall, London, 117-128.

Harkness W.L., W.J. Kettinger and A.H. Segars (1996), Sustaining process improvement and innovation in the information services function: Lessons learned at the Bose corporation. *MIS Quarterly* **20**, (3), 349-368.

Henderson J.C. and N. Venktraman (1993), Strategic alignment: Leveraging information technology for transforming organizations. *IBM Systems Journal* **32**, (1), 4-16.

Kling R. and T. Jewett (1995), The social design of worklife with computers and networks: An open natural systems perspective. In Yovits (Ed.), *Advances in Computers* No 39, Academic Press, Orlando, 239-293.

Knoll K. and S.L. Jarvenpaa (1994), Information technology alignment or 'fit' in highly turbulent environments: The concept of flexibility. *Proceedings of the 1994 ACM SIGCPR Conference*, March 1994, pp. 1-14.

Kumar K. and H.G. van Dissel (1996), Sustainable collaboration: Managing conflict and cooperation in interorganizational systems. *MIS Quarterly* **20**, (3), 279-300.

McFarlan F.W. and R.L. Nolan (1995), How to manage an IT outsourcing alliance. *Sloan Management Review* **36**, (2), 9-23.

McLean E.R., L.A. Kappelman and J.P. Thompson (1993), Converging end-user and corporate computing, *Communications ACM* **36**, (12), 79-92.

Nonaka, I. (1994), A Dynamic Theory of Organizational Knowledge Creation. *Organization Science* **5** (2), 14-37.

Orlikowski W.J. (1991), Integrated information environment or matrix of control? The contradictory implications of information technology. *Accounting, Management & Information Technology* 1 (1), 9-42.

Orlikowski W.J. (1992), Learning from Notes: Organizational issues in groupware implementation, In *Proceedings of CSCW'92*, ACM, New York, 362-369.

Orlikowski W.J. (1995), Evolving with Notes: Organizational change around groupware technology, URL: http://ccs.mit.edu/CCSWP186.html (June 1995).

Perrolle J. (1986), Intellectual assembly lines: The rationalization of managerial, professional, and technical work. *Computers and the Social Sciences* **2**, (3), 111-122 (also in Dunlop and Kling, 1991, *Computerization and controversy: Value conflicts and social choices*. Academic Press, San Diego, 221-235).

Quinn R.E. (1988), *Beyond rational management*. Jossey-Bass, San Francisco.

Quinn R.E., S.R. Faerman, M.P. Thompson and M.R. McGrath (1990), *Becoming master manager - A competency framework*. Wiley, New York.

Schein E.H. (1985), *Organizational culture and leadership*. Jossey-Bass, San Francisco.

Scott W.R. (1992), *Organizations: Rational, natural and open systems*. Prentice-Hall, Englewood Cliffs.

Silver M.S., M.L. Markus and C.M. Beath (1995), The information technology interaction model: A foundation for the MBA core course. *MIS Quarterly* **19**, (3), 361-390.

Smart J.C. and E.P. St. John (1996), Organizational culture and effectiveness in higher education: A test of the 'Culture Type' and 'Strong Culture' hypotheses. *Educational Evaluation and Policy Analysis* **18**, (3), 219-241.

Zuboff S. (1988), *In the age of the smart machine: The future of work and power*. Basic Books, New York.

The role of Ukrainian universities in the development of the global information society

Helen Kaikova, Vagan Terziyan*, Seppo Puuronen***
** Software Department, Kharkov State Technical University of Radioelectronics, 14 Lenina av., Kharkov, Ukraine*
Phone: +380 572 409 446;Fax: +380 572 409 113
Email: vagan@milab.kharkov.ua
*** Department of Computer Science and Information Systems, University of Jyvaskyla, Finland*
Phone: +358 14 603 028; Fax: +358 14 603 011
Email: sepi@jytko.jyu.fi

Abstract

This paper presents an observation of the positive experience obtained by Kharkov State Technical University in the area of education specialists for the development of an information society programme. Economic problems postponed the beginning of the information society programme in Ukraine. Nevertheless, Ukraine now has good possibilities to apply the best experience of western universities and speed up the process of transferring existing education to the European level. The paper also presents an analysis of the main trends that are taking place in that education. The paper uses the example of one of the leading Ukrainian technical universities to show the possible ways of positive changes in education in the framework of developing the national infrastructure of Ukraine. The examples show how the universities' sciences can be involved in large-scale transEuropean projects connected with problems of the global information society.

An Ethical Global Information Society J. Berleur & D. Whitehouse (Eds.)

INTRODUCTION

Ukraine is a republic located in eastern Europe and it is a founding member of the Commonwealth of Independent States which, in December 1991, succeeded the USSR. With a total area of 603,700 square kilometres and a population of 51 million, Ukraine is now the second largest country in Europe (after Russia). Traditionally, Ukraine has had a high level of science and education. It has hundreds of universities and research institutes, and it has had quite a high level of universal and obligatory secondary education. Economic problems connected with disintegration of the states of the former USSR, and the Chernobyl catastrophe, postponed the initiation of the information society programme in Ukraine. The ongoing process of infrastructure development presupposes the solution of several problems connected with Ukraine's cultural and ethical peculiarities.

The information society programme has started in Ukraine. Its first official document, *National Information Society Programme of Ukraine: Urgent Steps for the Period 1996-2,000*, was signed in Kiev on October 30, 1995 by the head of the Agency for Information Society Problems who is attached to the president of the Ukraine. The document notes that Ukraine's current level of information society development is unsatisfactory (2-2.5% when compared to western countries). It also includes the analysis of factors that are slowing down the process of successful development of the information society programme. The budget funds are planned to support:

- development of the national infrastructure;
- development of the national telecommunication system;
- information support development of the strategic directions of state interests, security and defence, and the social sphere.

The urgent steps are to develop the basis for standards and laws for the information society programme of Ukraine to be coordinated with international standards.

THE ROLE OF EDUCATION IN THE INFORMATION SOCIETY OF UKRAINE

We suppose that Ukrainian universities are able to make an essential input to the success of the information society programme through:

- education of a new type of specialist;
- cooperation with foreign universities to apply their best experiences in education;
- research on the strategic directions of the global information society;
- spreading the culture of the information society;
- developing exchange programmes for teachers and students;
- applying to European foundations to support joint projects.

To become the driving force in information society development, universities have to develop a lot in their own organization. We suppose that universities have to:

- develop curriculums for computer science specialisms towards the best standards of European education and, at the same time, to keep up the best national traditions (for example, high levels of mathematical studies);
- pay more attention to language studies, cooperation, and negotiation skills to prepare for the possibility of wide exchange programmes;
- reconsider economic education in the universities by taking into account essential changes in national economics;
- develop the administrative structure of universities by applying evaluation techniques which are based on well-defined formal criteria;
- develop a system of funds distribution between and inside universities based on formal criteria (such as international conferences, papers, exchange programmes, doctoral theses, etc.);
- begin to use and to teach the use of legal software;
- find possibilities to install Internet and world wide web (WWW) facilities in the universities.

We consider that such changes in universities would help very much in developing the national infrastructure because of the following trends:

- cooperation between western and Ukrainian universities is growing. Western partners very often help with computers and with the organization of Internet connections. New modern courses introduced in Ukrainian universities will need facilities quite soon for teleeducation and teleconferences using the experience of the best lecturers from abroad. The requirements to apply to most European Community foundations mean it is necessary for universities to find new partners, and to establish new contacts. In such a situation, the infrastructure of Ukrainian higher education institutions will be developed quite fast;
- Ukrainian companies also need partners in western countries as well as new information technologies and good specialists. This means that contacts (including information exchange and electronic connection) will grow between those universities which are first involved in the European infrastructure and Ukrainian companies. Thus, Ukrainian companies are also expected to join the information society quite soon;
- scientific schools and research laboratories in Ukrainian universities already have results and experiences at their disposal in traditionally strong areas of national research that allow them to start some large-scale transEuropean projects together with western partners. This would affect very much the role of Ukraine in the European infrastructure and make it possible to earn essential funds for developing the information society programme of Ukraine.

Kharkov State Technical University of Radioelectronics (KHTURE) is one of the main universities educating specialists for the information society programme of Ukraine. KHTURE is the main institution to develop the information society programme in the most industrially and scientifically developed region, the northeast of Ukraine. The way that has been selected to improve the level of research and teaching activities in KHTURE is international cooperation and use of the experience of western universities. KHTURE's Faculty of Computer Sciences, with four specialities and twelve scientific schools in the area of computer science, is the leading faculty among Ukrainian universities. It develops curriculums, methods, and teaching aids that are applied to education in similar faculties of other technical universities. The research and educational laboratory, Metaintelligence, as part of KHTURE, has the main goal of participating in the development of the information society programme of Ukraine through international research and cooperation. Research topics of the laboratory include: knowledge and metaknowledge engineering; expert systems and multiple experts' problems in medicine; metamodels and metatools for information processing; mathematical methods and tools for biosignal analysis; metamathematics; computer-supported cooperative work; intelligent navigation in information systems; and human-computer interfaces.

In this paper, we show some experiences of KHTURE and the Metaintelligence Laboratory in developing education and research projects within the framework of the information society programme of Ukraine.

DEVELOPING CURRICULUMS FOR COMPUTER SCIENCE SPECIALITIES

The new curriculum, which has been developed at KHTURE in cooperation with the University of Jyvaskyla (Finland), includes the following main changes in comparison with traditional education in Ukraine (Kaikova *et al.*, 1997):

- economic education has been extended twice, and its contents takes into account changes in Ukrainian economics towards a market orientation;
- mathematical education still has an essential role in the curriculum but it is also improved by developing the contents of some courses, for example, statistics, symbolic mathematics, and optimization methods;
- the curriculum includes a choice of one main speciality from two: artificial intelligence (AI) and information systems. The traditionally high quality AI education will be strengthened by additional up-to-date courses. The block of information systems courses has been totally renovated. It includes the following courses: information management; tools of personal and group work; object-oriented development of information systems; designing information systems; an advanced course on developing information systems; theoretical foundations of information systems; strategies for information technologies and business development; computer-supported cooperative work; and management strategies for information technology and its assessment;
- educational and industrial training, which was previously distributed throughout the whole 5-year education using summers, has now been reorganized into the system development project according to the best experiences of the Department of Computer Science and Information Systems of the University of Jyvaskyla;
- language education is extended almost twice and language studies are planned to be improved essentially by modern methods and by student exchange.

In the new curriculum, software systems are expected to be developed and used during many courses, for example: in general studies, small information and expert systems will be included; in economic studies, accounting and other economic systems will be used; in mathematical studies, training systems will be used; in artificial intelligence studies, some research prototypes will be produced, and most masters' theses will also include development of software that implements or verifies the ideas presented. Students will also be supposed to produce and present software in workshops, conferences, and exhibitions as previously.

Recent plans in the education area are to develop the university infrastructure and to organize distance education (lectures and summer schools) using the lecturers and telelearning facilities of the University of Jyvaskyla, which is the main foreign partner of KHTURE.

The authors are optimistically considering the perspectives of Ukrainian computer science education and its effect on the fast development of the information society in the Ukraine. They are also sure that cooperation between European partners (companies and universities) and Ukrainian universities seems to be beneficial to both sides.

MULTIPLE EXPERTISE AND TELECONSULTING: TELEMEDICINE SYSTEMS DEVELOPMENT

This project has been initiated by the Metaintelligence Laboratory together with students from KHTURE. It concerns the area of artificial intelligence applications in telemedicine. The project brings together the experience of Ukrainian researchers with computer-based intelligent medical systems, and the experience of Finnish researchers in the area of telecommunications, with their common experience in the area of multiple experts and, in addition, the expertise of German researchers in developing adaptive procedures of time series analysis and their application to problem settings in the biosignal analysis. The main goal of the project is to manage multiple expertise obtained from experts-physicians in different countries in order to develop a decision support medical system for broad earmarking based on telecommunication tools.

Project objectives

The project brings together the experience of Ukrainian researchers in computer-based intelligent medical systems (Dzundzjuk, 1989; Grebenyuk *et al.*, 1994, 1995) and signal processing (Bondarecko *et al.*, 1994; Terziyan and Tkachuk, 1995), with the experience of Finnish researchers in the area of telecommunications (a completely new, innovative telematic studio; local and remote multimedia groupware; computer-aided negotiation suites; telelearning environments; simulation; virtual reality, SUN and Silicon Graphics; Internet, and WWW services) and computer-supported cooperative work (Auromaki and Kovalainen, 1994a, 1994b), with their common experience in the area of multiple experts (Gerasin *et al.*, 1994; Puuronen and Terziyan, 1996, 1997a, 1997b; Terziyan and Puuronen, 1997), and also with expertise of German researchers in the development of adaptive procedures of time series analysis and their application to problem settings in biosignal analysis (Griessbach and Schack, 1993; Griessbach and Witte, 1996; Schack *et al.*, 1995).

The long and successful history of research cooperation between Ukrainian and Finnish Universities and some reasons to develop it further are presented in Kaikova and Terziyan (1997). The very important results obtained in the Institute of Biomedical Engineering and Medical Informatics (at the Technical University of

Ilmenau) and the mutual interest in cooperation was the reason for including the German partner in the project.

Research methods

Multiple experts voting-type technique

The voting-type technique to manage knowledge obtained from multiple sources was proposed by Professor S. Puuronen (of the University of Jyvaskyla) and Professor V. Terziyan (from Kharkov State Technical University of Radioelectronics) (Gerasin *et al.*, 1990; Puuronen and Terziyan, 1996, 1997a)

The technique is based on the derivation of the most supported opinion of the group of experts and its further refinement using a multilevel structure of knowledge sources or concepts.

The final statement (diagnosis) obtained as a result of the refinement process takes into account the opinions of all the experts according to their area of competence and the level of their expertise.

Metaclassification technique with multiple statistical methods

The first version of an intelligent system for statistical data processing MetaHuman-96 (MH96) was developed by researchers from the Metaintelligence Laboratory (at the Kharkov State Technical University of Radioelectronics) for the decision of medical diagnostics problems (Dzundzjuk *et al.*, 1989; Grebenyuk *et al.*, 1994, 1995). The problem of medical diagnostics was solved with the help of modern methods of discriminant and regressional analysis using information from training sets. MH96 contains the metamethod to support a user's decision-making about choice of method for a specific problem in medical diagnostics. The metamethod advises a user on the selection of one of the methods available in the system or offers a combination of them. The system allows the management of various medical databases (the user is allowed to configure structures of databases) and, using these data, the making of an analysis of a new object of diagnostics.

Adaptive procedures for biosignal analysis

The researchers from the Institute of Biomedical Engineering and Medical Informatics (at the Technical University of Ilmenau) led by Professor G. Griessbach are focused on the development of adaptive procedures of time series analysis and their application to problem settings in biosignal analysis. In the computer-aided analysis of biosignals, adaptive time series analysis methods are gaining more and more in importance (Griessbach and Schack, 1993). Due to their recursive proceeding, they permit an online evaluation of the time series and, due to their adaptive properties, a quick adaptation to changes occurring in the time series. In addition, they are robust against the great variety of signal structures, thus representing an algorithmic initial approximation equally for deterministic signals with trend and transient signals. The recursive consistent estimate functions for parameters of stochastic processes are the mathematical background to the adaptive procedures.

Dynamic methods in the spectral domain are necessary to analyze biological signals because of the frequently nonstationary character of the signals. At present, not only the development of other adaptive parameters (e.g., adaptive recursive test statistics) is being investigated but also their mathematical-algorithmic properties. In addition, they are implemented by means of object-oriented technologies (Griessbach and Witte, 1996). An adaptive procedure was proposed for fitting time-dependent models to nonstationary signals which is suitable for online calculations (Schack *et al.*, 1995).

The essential role in developing telemedicine projects belongs to students of KHTURE who are already well educated in developing large software systems. Installation of such teleconsulting centres in Ukraine, first of all, helps persons who have suffered the hard consequences of the Chernobyl catastrophe, and also gives them the possibility of using the experience of foreign experts.

INTERNATIONAL TELECONSULTING CENTRE ON MATHEMATICAL EXPERTISE

Another important positive tradition in research in countries of the former Soviet Union is the high level of results in the area of mathematics. Now, it is very important and useful to make all those results that have been obtained during the long history of the main mathematical schools in Russia and other eastern countries available to European and to world society. One example of a possible way to establish access to this mathematical expertise is discussed in this section. The example supposes that the profit gained from realizing such a possibility can be used by Russian and Ukrainian universities to develop their own infrastructures.

Modern technological processes consist of complicated movements of media in different phases and dynamic phase transitions on free surfaces: melting, solidification, evaporation, condensation, etc. Most of the current mathematical models of phase changes include only a part of the physical phenomena (for example, separate Stefan equations or separate Navier-Stokes equations). For many physical situations, it is very important to take into account interactions between different types of processes and media. The physical experiments in this area are very expensive and it is difficult to get the full information about any processes of interest. One can make inaccurate conclusions about the behaviour of the physical system. For this reason, the correct construction of the complete model, coupled with a system of equations for different processes and media with phase transitions, has a big and practical interest. Using the expert system, investigators can choose different mathematical models according to their needs:

- mathematical models of stationary flow and heat mass transfer with fixed or unknown boundaries between the phases;
- mathematical models of deformation and thermodynamic state of solid bodies with a boundary between solid and liquid phases;
- quasi-stationary mathematical models of phase change problems (the stationary Navier-Stokes and the constitutive equations for free solid part and nonstationary thermodynamic equations);
- nonstationary mathematical models of phase change problems (melting processes, the nonstationary Navier-Stokes and constitutive equations for free solid part and the nonstationary thermodynamic equations).

Theoretical analyses of these mathematical models include the proofs of smoothness, uniqueness, and stability. Finite element method is used for the numerical analysis of phase change problems. Using this method one can get:

- numerical simulation of the stationary boundary problems for the Navier-Stokes equations, using the domain decomposition method, parallel algorithms, multi-resolution method, and grid refinement;
- numerical simulation of the initial boundary problems for the nonstationary Navier-Stokes equations for arbitrary domain shapes using the projection method, domain decomposition methods, and up winding schemes;
- numerical simulation of boundary value problems of a solid and a mixed medium in an arbitrary domain;
- numerical simulation for the coupled phase change problem.

In this project, the expert system will suggest to the investigators the models for the different phase change problems and their numerical simulation. The models will include thermodynamic and constitutive equations for each phase and physical natural conditions on the unknown boundary between the phases. The expected results are: using the expert system, the investigators can choose some of the mathematical models, test whether they are correct or not, and get a numerical simulation of the problem.

The International Teleconsulting Centre on Mathematical Expertise (TELEMATH) is planned for installation at the Laboratory of Scientific Computing of the University of Jyvaskyla. The TELEMATH Centre will sell services to a wide network of users all around the world. The structure of the TELEMATH Centre is presented in Figure 1.

The expert system of TELEMATH is intended to solve complex multiphase and multiinterface problems using knowledge of mathematical models and methods acquired from multiple experts-mathematicians.

The area of expertise covers the mechanics of the continuous media investigated by the variations of the finite element method, and also different mathematical models: reaction-diffusion; the heat conduction; the laminar and turbulence flows of viscous compressible and incompressible liquid and gas; deformation of the solid body with different reological laws; coupled with problems from the phase changes, free boundaries, and others.

TELEMATH learns by acquiring expertise from different experts through an intelligent expert interface using a special methodology of mathematical knowledge acquisition and representation or unique expert language for mathematical knowledge description. The expert system receives a problem from a user through the intelligent user interface, controls its correctness, selects a mathematical model, determines the region's geometry, initial conditions and boundary conditions, selects a method (the type of the finite element, the order of approximation, domain discretization, the way of solving the final system of equations), derives the solution and introduces it to a user. The system is able to organize a teledialogue with experts in cases when it cannot itself make a decision. It is also possible to expand the knowledge bases by new models and methods permanently obtained from the experts. The organization of the expert system, methodology of knowledge acquisition, language, classification technique, and interfaces are supposed to be easily reoriented to new groups of models and methods.

Figure 1. Structure of teleconsulting centre on mathematical expertise

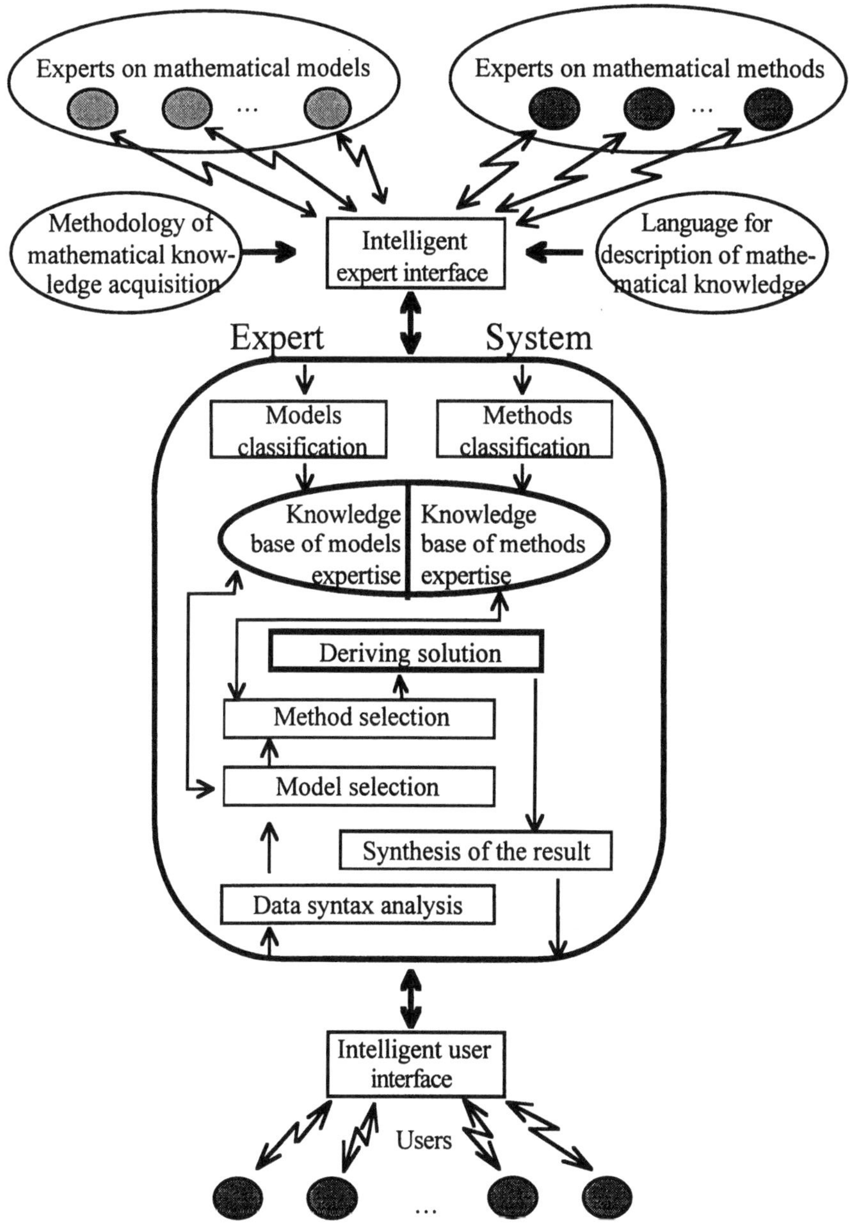

The project uses methods described elsewhere in this paper. The *voting-type technique* is used to manage knowledge obtained from different experts about the same mathematical object. It allows consensus among the experts concerning the description of a method or a model. The *metaclassification technique* is used to describe metamethods of selecting mathematical methods for a problem solution.

The project brings together the experience of Ukrainian researchers (from KHTURE) in the development of large computer-based intelligent systems, classification techniques, and multiple expertise, with the experience of Russian mathematicians (from St. Petersburg State Technical University and North-West Polytechnic Institute) in the area of mathematical models for the mechanics of continuous media and variations of the finite element method (Erunova and Rivkind, 1990, 1991), with the experience of Finnish researchers (from the University of Jyvaskyla) in the area of telecommunications and information technologies. The project is also supposed to use students widely to develop and to classify mathematical methods and to develop software.

CONCLUSION

This paper presents an observation of the positive experience gained by Kharkov State Technical University in the area of education specialists for the development of an information society programme. Economic problems have postponed the beginning of an information society programme in Ukraine. Nevertheless, Ukraine now has good possibilities to apply the best experience of western universities and speed up the process of transferring existing education to the European level. The paper also includes an analysis of the main trends that are taking place in that education. It presents an optimistic view of a future Ukrainian education and its essential role in the process of developing the information society in Ukraine. It uses the example of one of the leading Ukrainian technical universities to show possible ways of developing the organizational structure, education, and research activities in Ukrainian higher education institutions in order to participate in the development of the global information society.

ACKNOWLEDGEMENTS

We are grateful to the Centre for International Mobility and Ministry of Education of Finland whose support made it possible for Helen Kaikova and Vagan Terziyan to develop this research in Finland.

REFERENCES

1. Auramaki E., Kovalainen M., Computer Support for Sharing Expertise in Process Disturbances. In: *Proceedings of XIII European Annual Conference on Human Decision Making and Manual Control*, Espoo, Finland, 1994a.
2. Auramaki E., Kovalainen M., Computer Support for Sharing and Extending Expertise in Paper Process. In: *CSCW94 International Workshop*, North-Carolina, USA, 1994b.

3. Bondarenko M., Terziyan V., Tkachuk A., Multilevel Models for Representation of Quasi-Periodical Temporal Patterns, In: *Signal/Image Processing and Pattern Recognition*, Second All-Ukrainian International Conference, Kiev, Ukraine, 1994, pp. 76-80.
4. Dzundzjuk B., Terziyan V., Severina L., Development of Expert Health-Protection Systems Based on Discrete Mathematics, *Bionics Problems Journal*, 1989, **42**, 104-109.
5. Erunova I.B., Rivkind V.J., Study of the Problem of Liquid Evaporation, *Vestnic Leningrad University*, 1991, **2** (8).
6. Erunova I.B., Rivkind V.J., On Estimates of the Rate of Convergence of Approximate Methods of Calculating the Flow of a Viscous Incompressible Fluid with a Free Surface in Domains with Corner Points, *Soviet Mathematics Doklady*, 1990, **313** (6).
7. Gerasin S., Kaikova H., Terziyan V., An Interval-Based Approach to Multiple Experts Opinions Processing: Successive Severance Method, *Bionics Problems Journal*, State University Publications, 1990, **44**, 41-46.
8. Grebenyuk V., Kaikova H., Terziyan V., Fundamentals of Multilevel Pattern Recognition, In: *Signal/Image Processing and Pattern Recognition*, Second All-Ukrainian International Conference, Kiev, Ukraine, 1994, pp. 25-29.
9. Grebenyuk V., Kaikova H., Terziyan V., Multilevel Automatic Diagnostics Based on Models of Speech Behavior, In: *Radioelectronics in Medicine Diagnostics*, International Conference, Moscow, November 1995, pp. 131-139.
10. Griessbach, G., Schack, B., Adaptive Quantile Estimation and its Application in the Analysis of Biological Signals. *Biometrical Journal*, 1993, **35** (1).
11. Griessbach, G., Witte, H., Complex adaptive procedures for EEG monitoring, Kongreband zum 'Hans-Berger-Kongress 1996'.
12. Kaikova H., Terziyan V., Puuronen S., Software Engineering Education in the Ukraine: Towards Cooperation with Finnish Universities, In: *Intern. Symposium on Software Engineering in Universities*, Rovaniemi, Finland, March 1997, pp. 109-116.
13. Puuronen S., Terziyan V., Modelling Consensus Knowledge from Multiple Sources Based on Semantics of Concepts, In: *Challenges of Design, ER96 International Conference on Conceptual Modelling*, Cottbus, Germany, October 1996, pp. 133-146.
14. Puuronen S., Terziyan V., Voting-Type Technique of the Multiple Expert Knowledge Refinement, In: Sprague R. H., (Ed.), *Proceedings of the Thirtieth Hawaii International Conference on System Sciences*, Vol V, IEEE Computer Society Press, 1997a, pp. 287-296.
15. Puuronen S., Terziyan V., Colleague-Oriented Interpretation of Knowledge Acquired from Multiple Experts, In: *PACES/SPICIS97 The Joint Pacific Asian Conf. on Expert Systems/Singapore Intern. Conf. on Intelligent Systems*, Singapore, February 1997b.
16. Schack, B., Bareshova, E., Griessbach, G., Witte, H., Methods of Dynamic Spectral Analysis by Self-Exciting ARMA Models and their Application to Analysing Biosignals. *Med. & Biol. Eng. & Computing*, 1995, **33**, 492-498.
17. Terziyan V., Puuronen S., Multilevel Context Representation Using Semantic Metanetwork, In: *CONTEXT-97-Intern. and Interdisciplinary Conference on Modeling and Using Context*, Rio de Janeiro, Brazil, February 1997, pp. 21-32.
18. Terziyan V., Tkachuk A., Multilevel Models for Speech-Based Diagnostics, In: *Radio-Electronics in Medicine Diagnostics*, International Conference, Moscow, November 1995, pp.140-143.

PART FOUR

Democratic Challenges

Ethical and social issues of 'teleservices' for disabled and elderly people

Julio G. Abascal
Informatika Fakultatea, Euskal Herriko Unibertsitatea, Basque Country, 649 postakutxa, E-20080 Donostia, Spain
Tel.: + 34 4 3 218000. Fax: + 34 43 219306
Email: julio@si.ehu.es

Abstract

In recent years the implantation of '*teleservices*' as an alternative for the social integration of people with disabilities and elderly people has been observed. Telematic services such as *teleteaching, telework, teleshopping, telecare, telesurveillance, teleleisure* appear to be the panacea for the complete social and labour integration in developed countries. In this paper some aspects related to ethical and social issues of teleservice proposals are studied. Other matters in question, such as technical feasibility (which is not always evident) or economic profitability (for a very high anticipated cost), are not discussed here. As a conclusion, a list of conditions for every project of implementation of teleservices for disabled and/or elderly people is proposed.

INTRODUCTION

The development of telecommunications, from the telegraph to broadband networks, has promoted crucial changes in human relationships, maybe without precedent in human history. Similarly, the diffusion of computers has caused a big impact in the life of the citizens of developed countries. But the combination of both information technology and communication has resulted in another technology, telematics, with a social action that goes much further than its direct components. It is foreseen that the diffusion of telecommunications will allow in the short term the apparition of new services offered from remote computers connected to telematic networks. Some of these services are already active, while

An Ethical Global Information Society J. Berleur & D. Whitehouse (Eds.)

others are only proposals of intentions sometimes without a complete specification. Even if nowadays telematic services are aimed at every kind of user, it is said that some of these services were originally proposed to alleviate the problems, such as social and labour integration, of disabled and elderly people. In the next section certain teleservices are explained briefly.

TELEMATIC SERVICES FOR DISABLED AND ELDERLY PEOPLE[1]

From the time of the industrial revolution, family relationships have notably changed in industrialized countries. The extended family, including grandparents, aunts and uncles, parents and children living in the same house, has evolved to a nuclear family including only parents and children until the latter become independent. In many cases, modern houses and flats are not conceived for big families and the lack of adequate space for the elderly restricts their integration. Thus, grandparents and single or widowed relatives who used to find a place in the extended family must now live on their own. Other alternatives, such as residential institutions, are nowadays being abandoned. This possibility is only considered adequate for people with special needs due to mental or physical diseases. The emergent alternative is the development of technologies that allow elderly people to live on their own with the highest comfort and the minimum risk.

A similar analysis can be made of the social situation of people with disabilities. The conclusion can also be the convenience of telematic services to help them to experience a more autonomous life.

Even if some of these teleservices lack an accurate specification, I will try to describe some of them superficially in order to analyze their impact.

- *Telealarm.* The user is equipped with a device that automatically or manually generates a call to a remote surveillance centre when he or she suffers an emergency due to an accident, disease, security problem, etc.[2]. Different ways to operate this service (with and without family participation) and diverse technical support are being tested (telephone[3], text telephone, video-telephone, interactive television).
- *Telecare* is proposed as a distant medical attendance service. In some cases care is limited to health advice by means of speech or/and written communication[4]. More complex systems may include teleexploration, and diagnostic and therapeutic advice. Remote patient monitoring and transmission of physiological signs may be required in this case.
- *Teleinformation* services offer elderly people valuable information about diverse aspects of ordinary life: public transport, emergency telephone numbers, relatives' addresses, etc. In some cases they may include advice about everyday tasks, developing and agenda planning (schedule for medical treatment, doctor's appointments, and special days like birthdays, holidays).
- Different kinds of *interpersonal telecommunication services* (that can include speech, image and text transmission like video-telephone[5], telefax, or electronic mail) have been tested to decrease the isolation of disabled people. When elderly people lack these services, they tend to use alarm systems to simply 'speak with somebody'.

- There exist proposals for diverse services that can be included in the *teleleisure* section. They may include information about sports, hobbies, and culture.
- Services like *teleshopping* have been extensively promoted and do not need any more explanation.

  In addition, there exist some telematic services specially intended for people with severe motor restrictions that may impede their access to places where various activities are usually developed. It is said that telework and teleteaching were first conceived for disabled people, but people with other kind of restrictions (for example, people living in very isolated villages) can also profit from these services.
- *Telework* offers the possibility of carrying out remunerated work from home using a personal computer and telematic communication, usually via a telephone network[6].
- *Teleteaching* offers different levels of distance education using computer-aided instruction via telematic networks in addition to the usual remote teaching methods.

It is important to mention that these telematic services for disabled and elderly people are highly conditioned to the availability of human-computer interfaces well adapted to the physical and cognitive characteristics of users. Even though there are several interesting projects in progress in this area[7], the problem is not yet adequately solved in many cases.

WEAK POINTS OF TELESERVICES

Competence, technology acceptability and user needs

In advanced societies it is frequently assumed that the introduction of telematic services will by themselves result in the integration and the happiness of disabled and elderly people[8]. But, even if technological advances enhance the quality of life of this population, there are two important factors that can miscarry this objective: the lack of ability of the hypothetical users to handle complex devices, and also the acceptability of the services[9].

There exists an open discussion about the low level of technology acceptance by elderly people. Rejection is frequently due to the low quality of the interface: automatic cashiers (or automatic teller machines) are a paradigmatic example. Moreover, some studies show that adequately trained elderly people are in general able to use technology[10]. In addition, it is expected that the acceptance of technology by elderly people will increase with the ageing of people accustomed to technology.

Another possible cause of the rejection of telematic help systems can originate in a deficient evaluation of user needs. Frequently, the emergence of new technological advances moves engineers to imagine hypothetical benefits for disabled and/or elderly people if these technologies were to be applied to solve assumed user needs[11]. These assumptions, when they are not based on in-depth studies about users' interests, needs, wishes, and likes lead to misconceptions that produce systems unsuited to the target user group and hence they are rejected. Only serious studies about user needs[12] can result in systems that truly satisfy these needs and therefore have the possibility of being accepted by users.

Technology for human contact

The introduction of technology to allow elderly and disabled people to be more autonomous and socially productive may lead to the substitution of human relationships for technology; frequently it is easier for families to pay for devices than to dedicate time to personal relationships. This same scheme can be reproduced at the social level: institutions may prefer to create telematic services than to maintain traditional social and care services.

To avoid this possibility, it is convenient to verify that proposals for the provision of telematic services do not lead to the restriction of personal contact or the elimination of other non-technology based services.

Privacy and freedom

Advances in global positioning systems (GPS) technology, satellite communications, sensor technology and so on, allow the existence of teleservices which include systems registering data about the geographic position of the patient or his/her vital signs and sending them to a remote surveillance centre. This centre is immediately informed about any danger or change in the user's situation. Thus, telesurveillance allows chronically ill patients, who would usually be hospitalized, to live at home.

The idea seems to be very attractive but one cannot forget that these systems can interfere with the capacity of patients to make their own decisions (like deciding not to obey medical prescriptions if they wish). Even if some patients would prefer to be under telematic surveillance at home rather than to remain in hospital for long periods of time, this alternative can be inadequate in other cases. So, people living alone or without a serious pathology can be compelled to accept these services under family or social pressure. In addition, the proliferation of these kinds of devices can lead to a socially accepted 'watched freedom'. While some countries are regulating the use such devices, the majority lack laws to protect patients' rights from the excesses produced by technology[13].

Labour integration

Telework is one of the more promoted teleservices. This telematic service offers the worker the possibility of developing his/her work from a remote site (usually from home), thereby avoiding unnecessary commuting. From the point of view of the company, telework also offers advantages: among them, the possibility of using contractors for short periods of time or to carry out particular tasks. In addition, there is no need for space for workers (in some cases arriving at the 'virtual company' concept).

In fact, telework is an interesting alternative not only for people with disabilities. Currently, telework is open to able-bodied people to carry out diverse activities that do not require a worker's physical presence in the company. This profusion of telework jobs poses several social problems that are not going to be treated here, including the unsteadiness of contracts, excessively long working timetables, and labour rights[14].

Users with severe movement restrictions, who make up a large percentage of the disabled population, are very interested in telework because of their difficulty in accessing companies' premises. But they also find difficulties in using computers. The majority of people with disabilities wanting access to telework have mobility restrictions that make the use of standard interfaces (screen-keyboard-mouse based) difficult. So, these people require special interfaces that usually produce slower communication rates. Even though promising work is in progress trying to enhance communication speeds (by means of special keyboards, word prediction systems, and so on), nowadays the communication rate attained by people with severe movement restrictions remains too slow to be competitive in a production environment.

Nevertheless, the major problem for people with disabilities considering telework is the possibility of enlarging their isolation. One cannot forget that the desire of people with disabilities to access the labour market is related to their need to integrate into productive society as a 'full member' (obtaining resources to become autonomous and self-confident), but it is also motivated by the need to get in touch with people other than their families and therapists. From this point of view, telework can become a solution to the problem of obtaining a job. But the possibility of accessing only the productive part of the labour activity exists, while remaining outside the socialization that accompanies the working environment.

It has been said that telework is a good way of integrating disabled people because it does not differentiate between disabled and able-bodied people. However, what kind of 'integration' is possible when there is an interposed telematic network that hides the fact that, on the other side, there is a person who is 'different'? In addition, if telework becomes an extensively used service, competition among the disabled and non-disabled may become imbalanced because of the productivity question. As a result, people with disabilities may again be relegated from the labour market.

HIDDEN MOTIVATIONS FOR THE IMPLANTATION OF TELESERVICES

Sometimes the planning, development and implementation of teleservices are based on different motives than those mentioned. To understand that there can be other reasons for implementing teleservices, one cannot forget that the disabled and elderly populations have in general low economic power that results in a not very attractive market for business[15].

Let us analyze three of these possible 'occult' motivations, that are easily detectable in some teleservices projects.

a. The availability of the technology

Experience frequently reveals that the only justification for backing projects related to telematics for disabled and elderly people is the availability of the necessary technology. These 'advances' are justified by themselves without any study of needs, feasibility, cost/benefit, social impact, and so on[16].

b. The use of the disability flag to obtain funding for general purpose projects
Some companies have found, in the provision of telematic services to disabled and elderly people, a way to open up a broader market. In this way, funding obtained to develop services for disabled and elderly people is sometimes used to carry on projects destined for a wider population where disabled people are only a small proportion. This explains the lack of adequate evaluation of user needs: teleservices are not actually devoted to disabled and elderly users.

c. The use of the disabled and elderly population to test services intended for a broader population
In connection with the previous point, these projects can be used not only to obtain funding for services that are really for the general public, but also to test their market perspectives, feasibility, acceptability, and so on.

ANOTHER APPROACH TO TELESERVICES

'*Disintegration*' and compensatory measures

If teleservices became a massively applied solution for disabled and elderly people in the future, they could produce loneliness and social *disintegration*. The possibility of carrying out the majority of everyday tasks (work, study, leisure, and communication) from home may inhibit socialization and human contact. Let us look at an example. If a student with a severe physical handicap wants to attend a university course, it is necessary to carry out work to eliminate the architectural barriers present in the majority of old buildings. But, increasingly, people wanting to sign up for degree courses are directed to universities that give their courses remotely (distant universities) through teleteaching services. In this way, the existence of this telematic service may become an excuse not to face the expenditure of making every university building accessible. The distant university is a legitimate alternative for every student (disabled or not) if he or she wants it. But if it is the only way for disabled people to access higher studies this imposition results in being discriminatory with respect to the other citizens.

A similar situation may be caused by the introduction of telework as a solution for disabled people, because it may instigate the disappearance or the reduction of existing integration measures (like laws existing in some countries that force companies over a certain number of workers to employ disabled people).

Thus, it is evident that compensatory measures are needed to avoid the *disintegration* effect that can result from the introduction of some teleservices.

Telematic services and evaluation of the technology

The cliché, 'every scientific advancement and hence its technological application is good' frequently impedes a deeper evaluation of the technology. For this reason, it is very difficult to find rigorous studies about the social impact of teleservices in the target population and its environment[17].

The request for an evaluation of telematic services for disabled and elderly people is frequently opposed using the following arguments[18].

1. 'If you are against current technology you want to go back to the Stone Age'[19].
2. 'If there is a need for corrective measures, they must be provided by the administration'.

In relation to the first point, the dilemma cannot be posed as 'technology or nothing'. The aim is 'technology *with* the necessary complementary measures'. In the case that concerns us, elderly or disabled people must receive guarantees that the implementation of telematic services will not have a negative influence on their social integration.

The model of contaminant industry

With respect to the second argument, it is accepted that some corrective measures are necessary but they are left to the administration. Following this model, while the agent that uses the technology obtains the benefits, the administration, on behalf of all the population (with its money) must bear the expense of compensating for the damage. This has been the procedure frequently used by contaminating industries. Continuing with this example, the emergent proposal for this problem is to ask the contaminating agent to establish systems in a way that avoids contamination (or to pay for it). In the case of telematic services the designer of the teleservice (that is, the potential social *disintegrator*) should create the necessary compensatory measures to avoid *disintegration*. It is also fundamental that these measures are included in the implementation plans of the teleservice.

Conditions for teleservices

From the analysis of the potential impact of teleservices in the target population and its environment, the need for some corrective measures and guarantees has been stated in this paper. In summary: in order to prevent the above mentioned problems and dangers from arising, telematic services for disabled and elderly people must fulfil the following conditions:

- be based on rigorous studies of user needs
- avoid the 'substitution of human contact for teleservices'
- respect the freedom and the privacy of the user, taking into account the ethical aspects
- avoid the experimentation of new services with elderly and disabled people
- include the necessary socializing measures to compensate the tendency to loneliness.

To become effective, these conditions should be supported by social awareness of the potential dangers of teleservices if they are applied massively without control. While the legal regulation of some aspects of teleservices is active in a small number of countries[20], greater efforts in developing laws that protect the disabled and elderly as potential users of teleservices are necessary.

CONCLUSIONS

As has been previously outlined, industrialized society tends to isolate disabled and elderly people. To overcome this problem, some telematic services have been proposed as a way to promote the social and labour integration and to enhance the autonomy, quality of life and security of both disabled and elderly people.

In this paper the real motivation behind some of these proposals has been discussed. The need to avoid damaging effects on the user population has been emphasized. From this point of view, this paper suggests a list of conditions that should be required for all implantation projects of new telematic services for disabled and elderly people, to ensure that their implementation is carried out with enough guarantees for the users. Obviously these conditions require a larger development, and legal and social support to guarantee their application and effectiveness.

REFERENCES

(Augustsson-91) L. Augustsson. *Access to the USA - Recent Disability Legislation.* The Swedish Handicap Institute, 1991.

(CE-88) Council of Europe. *Legislation on the Rehabilitation of Disabled People.* Strasbourg, 1988.

(Edwards-95) Alistair D.N. Edwards (Ed.). *Extra-Ordinary Human-Computer Interaction. Interfaces for Users with Disabilities.* Cambridge University Press, Cambridge, 1995.

(Hyppönen-96) H. Hyppönen (Ed.). *Future Actions in the Field of Telematics and Disabilities.* COST 219. CEC-DGXIII (EUCO-TELE 219/CTD/96). Finland, 1996.

(IHAC-95) Information Highway Advisory Council. *Connection Community Content. The Challenge of the Information Highway. Final Report of the IHAC.* Minister of Supply and Services. Canada, 1995.

(Pereira-94) L. M. Pereira and J. I. Lindström (Eds.). *Videotelephony for Disabled and Elderly People.* COST 219. CEC-DGXIII (EUCO-TELE 219/CTD/94). Lisbon, 1994.

(Roe-95) P. R. W. Roe (Ed.). *Telecommunications for all.* COST 219. CEC-DGXIII. Luxembourg, 1995.

(Sanmartín-90) J. Sanmartín. *Tecnología y futuro humano.* Anthropos, 1990.

(Taipale-95) V. Taipale and L. M. Pereira. The Social Aspects of Telematics, Disabled and Elderly People and The Future Challenges. In (Roe-95)

(Tapiovaara-95) P. Tapiovaara (Ed.). *Services for Independent Living.* COST 219. CEC-DGXIII (EUCO-TELE 219/CTD/95). Finland, 1995.

(Tetzchner-91) S. von Tetzchner (Ed.). *Issues in Telecommunication and Disability.* COST 219. CEC-DGXIII (EUR 13845 EN). Brussels, 1991.

(Thakkar-90) U. Thakkar. 'Ethics in the Design of Human-Computer Interfaces for the Disabled'. *ACM SIGCAPH Newsletter,* No. 42 June 1990.

ACKNOWLEDGEMENTS

Many thanks to the colleagues, including the referees, who have made comments, suggestions, and corrections to the multiple previous versions of this paper.

---

[1] The association of disabled people and elderly people (sometimes under the denomination of people with special needs) is frequently rejected because both communities often present different characteristics and needs. This association, which is very common in institutional, social, and research and development programmes, is due to the intention to apply the same technical solutions to both populations.

[2] See Emergency Services and Alarm Systems by J. I. Lindström and M. Martin (Roe-95).

[3] See, for instance, M. Martin, Emergency Telephones (Tetzchner-91).

[4] See, for instance, M. Gauci, The Provision of Care [in Malta] Through the Telecare Service (Hyppönen-96).

[5] See (Pereira-94).

[6] See Telework as an Employment Option for People with Disabilities by B. Murray and S. Kenny (Tetzchner-91).

[7] See, for instance (Edwards-95).

[8] This idea is very similar to the 'technologic determinism' concept (Sanmartín-90).

[9] See C. Rott, Elderly people and new technology: Psychological issues of competence and assistance (Tapiovaara-95).

[10] Attitudes and Acceptance by S. Bjfrneby *et al.* (Tetzchner-91) refutes the myth of the technological incompetence and disinterest of elderly and disabled people in using technology through experiments carried out in England, Portugal, and Norway.

[11] Designers of input devices for interfaces should integrate disabled user needs as an integral part in their designs (Thakkar-90).

[12] Such as the study mentioned by S. Collins *et al.* in Telecommunications Needs as Expressed by Elderly People and People with Disabilities (Tetzchner-91).

[13] With respect, the innocence showed by engineers in relation to ethical problems resulting from technological applications turns out to be very curious, to say the least. The cliché used by scientists is 'technologies are neutral by themselves' (Sanmartín-90).

[14] Some of the ethical and social questions posed by telework are considered in the interesting Appendix IV of the report entitled *Connection Community Content. The Challenge of the Information Highway. Final Report of the Information Highway Advisory Council* (IHAC-95), where the representative of the Canadian Labour Congress in the Advisory Council explains his opinion about the impact of telework on employment and in the workplace.

[15] But they can become an interesting potential market in the opinion of M. Martin, People with Special Needs as a Market (Tetzchner-91).

[16] This behaviour is based on two very common assumptions in the area of science/technology: 'the application of the technology always supposes an advancement' and 'the availability of the technology is the only requirement for its application'. J Sanmartín calls *technologic imperative* the tendency to accept, in the name of human progress, that 'all the things that are technically feasible must be done'. He identifies this idea as one of the commonplaces of industrialised society. Following this philosophy, 'the innovation will be beneficial if we ensure that the conditions for its application are the correct ones' (Sanmartín-90).

[17] Evaluation of the technology before its application is hardly accepted by scientists and engineers. Even if, nowadays, it is generally recognised that, for instance, the use of nuclear technology should have been evaluated before its extensive implantation, people are reluctant to evaluate other emerging technologies, such as genetic engineering, that pose ethical questions. This social resistance to the evaluation of technology may come from the false idea that criticism can destroy one of the pillars of the technologically developed and supported society.

[18] These arguments are in fact very similar to the ones used when doubts and criticisms are shown in relation to the implantation of some other technologies that are arising.

[19] (Sanmartín-90).

[20] Information about existing legislation in Europe can be found in these volumes (CE-88; Augustsson-91).

21

The global information society and the implications of self-organization

Frans A.J. Birrer
Computer Science & Society
P.O. Box 9512, 2300 RA Leiden, Netherlands
Fax: +31 71 5276985
Email: birrer@rulwinw.leidenuniv.nl

Abstract

The emergence of the information society shows many of the characteristics of a self-organizing process. This is certainly true of its currently most publicized branch, the electronic highway. Self-organization, however, implies that it is not possible to steer the process in any direction one might choose; attempts to steer should carefully take into account the social system's own dynamics. A brief analysis of the main imperatives and trends around the electronic highway suggests that we should not be focusing our attention too exclusively on the development of the electronic highway as such. Right now, trends like globalization, decentralization and deregulation are having a much stronger impact. Though information technology (IT) is sometimes called one of the reasons for these trends, they are commonly pursued for quite different reasons. In turn, the trends will shape the future use of IT as well as a lot of other things. If we want the information society to develop in a democratic way, we must face those more general trends.

DIAGNOSTICS FOR THE INFORMATION SOCIETY: THE INSTRUMENT OF SOCIOCYBERNETICS

The information society is developing fast. Structures emerge from numerous initiatives taken in a largely unorchestrated, often even uncoordinated manner. It is hard to get a global picture of what is going on, and what we are heading for. Yet such a general view is exactly what we need, if we want to find out where we stand, and what initiatives are needed. Without it, we run the risk of being caught by the issue of the moment, while missing out on the heart of the matter.

An Ethical Global Information Society J. Berleur & D. Whitehouse (Eds.)

In such a situation one particularly needs some kind of overall framework to structure the analysis of what is happening. In this paper, I will use a sociocybernetics approach.[1] Sociocybernetics is a special branch of the systems paradigm. If one wants to analyze certain complex, interacting phenomena, one can hardly avoid the notions of systems theory. Sociocybernetics is confined to the study of social systems, and takes a specific interest in the phenomena of steering. Steering, here, refers to internal processes that drive the system in a certain direction ('self-steering') as well as attempt to steer the system from the outside. The notion of steering makes it possible to ask more specific questions about the direction of developments, and about the possibilities for intervention.

THE INFORMATION SOCIETY AS A SELF-ORGANIZING SYSTEM

If there is one currently 'hot' notion from the broad range of systems perspectives that seems particularly applicable to the current developments in the information society, it must be the notion of 'self-organizing system'. The information society does not develop from a preconceived plan, it emerges from the complicated dynamics that result from the initiatives and interplay of many actors exploring new technological possibilities.

There exists no unique definition of the notion of self-organizing system. The term is often used in a rather loose way; as a general term, it functions as a metaphor rather than as a specific model. In the present analysis, the following characteristics of self-organization will be in focus: (i) the structure of the system emerges from a complex interplay of its parts (ii) the dynamics of the system cannot be steered in arbitrary directions (since it depends on the drives and interplay of the parts). I take this to imply the following with respect to what we can and cannot know or predict about such a system:

(1) How existing patterns are kept up by the interplay of various actors is in principle open to analysis. For such an analysis, we must to a certain extent standardize an actor's behaviour, as subjected to more or less predictable 'impulses' (with this term, I am of course not referring to universal drives of behaviour but rather to behaviour as canalized by culture and institutions existing at that particular time and place).

(2) As a first approximation, we can also try to estimate how this existing field of impulses would work out if a new resource, such as a new technology, were introduced. We can analyze what new kinds of opportunities become available to the actors, and the incentives they present.

(3) We cannot - or only to a very limited extent - predict the emergence of entirely new patterns (that is, patterns that do not follow from the two preceding lines of analysis).

(4) We can, to some extent, foresee possible dissonances, that is, consequences of the processes predicted along the lines of (1) and (2) that may not be really wanted by some or all of the actors. We must realize here that we are making a normative anticipation in the name of the actors, which may prove to be wrong.[2]

(5) We cannot predict how actors will actually react to these dissonances. Dissonances may be relieved either by countervailing channels existing in the

present system, or by changing the procedures along which the system operates.[3] But discrepancies between outcome and desirable outcome may also lead to (i) new blind impulses (what is called 'technological fix', that is, fighting the unwanted consequences of a certain technology with another one, which again leads to new unwanted consequences, and so on), or (ii) attempts to put the discrepancy out of one's mind (repression, ostrich behaviour). This implies that dissonances can be manifest, but also latent (that is, not formally recognized by the actors).

(6) Finally, the canalization of impulses by culture and institutions as mentioned under (1) is not static. There are shifts in institutional and cultural rules that we must take into account. I use the word 'trends' to denote these shifts (for the topic to be treated here, decentralization, deregulation, and globalization are examples of relevant trends). We can, with some caution, extrapolate such trends for the near future.

ANALYSIS PART I: THE 'BLIND IMPULSES'

In a self-organizing social system, technology is not a neutral tool, the use of which can be headed in any conceivable direction. As a first approximation, we can see the new technology as a disturbance, inducing the existing blind imperatives to carve new pathways. First order changes can be identified by examining how the technology lowers (or raises) thresholds to perform certain actions. Since the most dramatic changes are currently expected from electronic communication (the Internet, electronic highway, etc.), this will be the main focus. It will be useful to differentiate between specific functions of electronic communication. We can use the following categorization:

Informing

Impersonal: providing certain information on the net. The information may be accessible by anyone, or only by a selected group of people (for instance, persons who pay for access).

Personal: sending unsolicited information to one or more specific persons.

Requesting information

Impersonal: such as by posting a request for information or advice on a list, accessible by others, in the hope that someone is willing to reply.

Personal: consulting a specific person.

Exchanging opinions

This involves all mutual exchanges with a major evaluative component, which are beyond the informative.

The categories are not completely exclusive (there may not always be a clear-cut division between information and opinion), but for the present purpose they are good enough. Since major changes with the Internet lie in new ways of getting together, exchanges that take place in an already existing communicative relation have been left out.

What kind of structural changes can be expected in each of these areas? In light of what was said earlier about self-organizing systems, this question decomposes into three parts:

(i) In what direction will the natural impulses and imperatives of the social system lead, given the new technological possibilities? This question can be answered by examining what thresholds are lowered compared to the old situation.

(ii) To which types of manifest and latent dissonances might this natural flow of events give rise? Here we must anticipate what consequences might be manifestly or latently disturbing to the actors, as explained before.

(iii) Are there any existing mechanisms through which counterforces could push back disturbing effects?

Let us now briefly pass through the various categories.

Impersonal informing

Thresholds lowered. Information can be made accessible to a very large public with relatively little effort. Whether the information will actually reach those persons for whom it might be useful is far less obvious. Despite the existence of search engines, the selection problem on the Internet is far from solved.

Potential dissonances. The most obvious nuisance is information overload. Ackoff already suggested that the problem of a manager is not a lack of information, but an excess of it, and the lack of a selection mechanism.[4] This is equally true of the average Internet user.[5] If more and more information is provided, the selection problem will become increasingly urgent.

Countermechanisms. Browsers can solve only part of the information overload problem. It is also the way in which information is offered that would have to be guided somehow. Though this may not be impossible in principle, it seems to run counter to the current feel of individual freedom on the Internet. But even if selection were easier, the sheer amount of available information would in many cases still be overwhelming.

Personal informing

Thresholds lowered. Automated sending of messages can now be done at very low cost. If one has an email address list, pushing one button is enough to send a message to each individual on the list.

Potential dissonances. A main threat here is junkmail.[6] Since it is so easy to send electronic messages by means of address lists, we might all become flooded with messages; the selection of the relevant ones would become very time consuming, and in extreme cases even the receiving computer system may be overloaded.

Countermechanisms. As far as the source of junkmail can be identified, this problem could be addressed more directly than that of information overload. Insofar as it is possible to send messages where the source cannot be traced, email terrorism might become a real problem.

Impersonal requests for information

Thresholds lowered. The net provides instant access to expert communities on an already endless list of topics. Whether one gets a useful response or not depends, of course, on the willingness and capacities of others to answer.
Potential dissonances. I see no imminent dissonances here.

Personal requests for information

Thresholds lowered. For personal requests for information, the change could be less significant than in the previous cases. Though the current culture on the net seems to lower psychological distances, and seems to make it easier to put a question to someone with whom one has never had contact before, it is also clear that if this were to happen on a large scale, well-known people would probably get a larger number of requests than they could possibly answer.
Potential dissonances. Like in the previous category, there seem to be no major impending dangers here. Getting many requests may be tiresome, but if one simply does not reply any more, the number of requests will probably drop.

Opinion exchange

Thresholds lowered. There are already discussion lists on almost any topic one could think of. Easy accessibility as well as brief response time have created possibilities that have not been available in any other form before.
Potential dissonances. Some have questioned the usefulness of many Internet exchanges (informative or otherwise).[7] Some fear a tendency towards superficiality[8], pseudocommunities[9] or fragmentation, scattering and alienation[10]. Scanning the interchanges taking place on the Internet may occasionally give rise to feelings of support for such concerns. On the other hand, being patronizing can be dangerous, and it is far from obvious that those interchanges have actually driven out less trivial pursuits.
Countermechanisms. Although the dangers of cultural degradation should not be exaggerated, we must at the same time realize that these effects work behind our backs. We usually are not conscious of them. Because they are so intangible, it is hard to think of effective countermechanisms.

There are a few issues that relate more or less to all of the above categories. Among those are issues that have to do with the (mis)use of information derived from the net. The issue of privacy is one example. Privacy problems, however, are not specific to the net, and they are already addressed by specialized platforms. Registering the entrances at a certain site, for example, for the purposes of profiling or for direct marketing) is another example. The use of IT for direct democracy has similar dangers. Already in 1977, Laudon pointed out that direct democracy by means of the electronic highway could lead to profile research identifying best selling strategies for what has already been decided, rather than result in different decisions or in politicians being more responsive to the wants and needs of citizens.[11]

Finally, dissonances can also arise because some groups or individuals will *not* be actively involved in the use of electronic communication, and thereby become disadvantaged. Here, schooling is of course the keyword. But in order for schooling to be effective, we must be able to present tasks that are motivating and really useful to the ordinary citizen. The inventory above suggests that such tasks may not be immediately available.

On the whole, the main short-term effect seems to be that communication in already existing communicative relations can become more efficient. There may be some threshold lowering for new communicative relations for very specific purposes, but structural short-term change in the information used by citizens is blocked by the phenomenon of information overload.

ANALYSIS PART II: THE 'TRENDS'

The canalization of impulses that was used to get a first approximation of the direction of developments is of course not invariant. It is itself subject to change. Because changing the rules of the game usually requires discussion, the forces behind such changes are of a cultural nature; they are prone to fashion, and they may even be outright ideological. Shifts in (thinking about) the rules of the game will be called trends. Even if strongly ideological, a trend often contains an idea that makes some sense as long as it is balanced against others; the ideological character lies in the fact that this one aspect is blown up as if there were no other considerations and no trade-offs.

The development of electronic communication is canalized by trends; at the same time, developments in electronic communication may reinforce (or work against) existing general trends.[12] Some trends that are particularly relevant here are the following:

Decentralization
Deregulation and liberalization
Economic globalization
Cultural globalization
Postmodernism

Each of these trends will now be discussed briefly. In line with the preceding sections, the focus will be on potentially harmful effects of certain trends and, of course, on their interplay with electronic communication.

Decentralization

There has become an increasing awareness that not all decisions should be made at a central level. Not only would the centre be overburdened, many decisions mainly concern local interests anyway. Since decision- and communication-assisting IT has also developed in a direction of decentralization, the two trends seem to reinforce each other.[13] It is sometimes suggested that this leads to more democratic control. That, however, very much depends on the way in which the decentralization is carried through. If decentralized processes are strongly standardized, local autonomy may decrease instead of increase.[14] All this applies to the public sphere as well as private organizations.

Deregulation and liberalization

We already saw that in a self-organizing system predictability is limited, and so are the possibilities for steering. The state as implementor of some kind of blueprint master plan for society is not a feasible option. In many western countries there is a trend to reduce the role of the state, and to leave more to deliberation procedures between parties or to market regulation.[15] Again, however, this withdrawal of the state may reduce the possibilities for a citizen's counterforce. Although the relation between electronic communication and deregulation/ liberalization is more indirect, there is significant coupling through the previously discussed trend of decentralization.

Economic globalization

The economy is becoming more and more a world economy. Economic decisions in one country are tied to decisions in other countries. Companies can choose where they will conduct their activities, and play off different communities against each other in order to get the most profitable conditions. Modern communication technology is among those factors that make companies more independent of a specific location (some already speak of the virtual organization [16]). The result is community autonomy being handed over to firms or to the economic imperatives on which they act. Once more, the result is a serious weakening of potential counteracting forces.

Cultural globalization

Modern communication technologies have enormously increased people's exposure to cultures other than their own. There is no doubt that this exposure has led to a rather asymmetric adaptation, dominated by western, Anglo-Saxon culture. It is hard to say to what degree this is a bad thing. One may regret that old traditions disappear. Cultural diversity is valued by many as a good in itself. But given our present lifestyle, there are objective reasons for having intensive worldwide communication. Economic globalization makes us interdependent, and there are many other important problems that need to be solved worldwide as well with respect to the environment. To establish adequate deliberations on a world scale, we need a thorough understanding of each other's cultures. If this understanding leads to assimilation, this is not necessarily a bad thing, as long as it is not an involuntary handing over of autonomy. On the other hand, we must realize that the value of a cultural practice is hard to evaluate, and that one might throw something away of which one did not realize the value.

Postmodernism

Postmodernism is in a sense a philosophical summary of the previous trends. According postmodernism, the time of the big stories (such as political ideologies) is over. There is no unifying framework any more; life and experience are local and fragmented. It is often assumed that this is a good thing for democracy but, again, that is an overhasty conclusion.[17] Not only are counterforces often most effectively mobilized when the scale is large, they also very much depend on comparisons to other practices as an important argumentative weapon; overemphasizing fragmentation deploys counterforces of an important part of their argumentative force. This shows how trends like globalization and decentralization, that apparently go in quite opposite directions, can in fact be seen as two sides of the same coin: it is the counterforces that are fragmented, leaving the field open to the dominant (economic) forces and powers, which then can induce their own uniformities.

Trends like 'deregulation', 'decentralization' and 'globalization' are very powerful at the moment. I put these indications between quotes because, as already indicated, they operate as ideologies; what actually happens under their banner may be very different from what the words suggest. Probably, the trends have self-organizing qualities too. But even though there may be an underlying dynamic that drives the process in a particular direction, it is easier to use canalizing impulses to explain certain structures than to explain changes in the canalization itself, because the drives are much less tangible. For this reason, I have so far treated the trends merely as an exogenous input.

One can, however, suspect at least some of the drives behind the trends. In general, persistent dissonances mostly have to do with load-off effects of some kind. An actor benefits by performing a certain action while others pay the costs. Particularly persistent are situations that present a prisoners' dilemma or a tragedy of the commons (which is in fact a load-off problem and a prisoners' dilemma at the same time). Take information overload. It is due to each individual's wish for personal expression even if, at a collective level, this leads to ineffectiveness. Junkmail is the pursuit of personal interests at the expense of others.

For the potential dissonances arising out of the trends discussed, very similar observations can be made. Deregulation and economic globalization may selectively favour the position of certain parties against that of others. As we saw, certain trends, if pushed too far, will seriously weaken democratic counterforces. Trends like decentralization, deregulation and globalization are attractive to a decision-maker who wants to avoid personal risk: they make it relatively easy to push aside the need for active policy in favour of a construction in which policy-makers only acts as facilitators of other people's negotiations and do not have opinions or initiatives of their own. Attractive as this may seem to the decision-maker, it is severely damaging to the overall problem-solving potential. After all, decision-makers are often installed for the very reason that parties have great difficulty in finding an appropriate solution themselves, because they are involved in a prisoners' dilemma or because the less powerful might be overrun.

Avoidance of personal risk can also be observed in policy initiatives with respect to the information society.[18] Here too, there is a tendency towards vague rhetoric; there is often insufficient study of what is happening or could realistically happen in the near future and, as a consequence, the resulting programmes do not have sufficiently reflected and concrete goals.

Right now, the impact of the trends seems much stronger than the impact of the electronic highway. Even though these trends are often pictured as unavoidable consequences of the developments of IT, they are not; the drives behind them are of a quite different nature. It is therefore imperative that we do not restrict our view to the electronic highway. The really powerful determinants currently are the ideologies of decentralization, deregulation and globalization. The main direct impact of the projection of electronic utopias will act as an argument to support trends that actually are pursued for very different reasons. These ideological policies, in turn, will shape the long-term development of the electronic highway; already, many decision-makers seem interested only in a vigorous commercialization of the net. As a result, publicly important options could be cut off before they even materialize. This will not be stopped unless we find ways to countervail the decision-makers' desire for personal risk avoidance. Like blind impulses, trends also form a self-organizing system. They cannot be changed by direct planning. Our basic task is to eliminate the procedural and rhetorical hiding places that shield biased decisions from external criticism, and to find democratic mechanisms through which countervailing power can be mobilized and effectuated. Maybe we also need a new type of citizen, a citizen who is much more aware of decisions made in various parts of society, and who is willing to influence those decisions more actively. Information technology could support such a project. But then the goals would have to be set very differently from the way they are being set now.

CONCLUSIONS

It is not the electronic highway, but the trends of 'decentralization', 'deregulation' and 'globalization' that are the most powerful determinants of present developments. We should not be fooled about the true nature and impact of these trends by the rhetoric that accompanies them.

Attempts to influence the development of the electronic highway in the long run will not be successful unless they address these trends, particularly if one is interested in strengthening democracy. Democracy is not an automatic consequence of current IT developments, as is sometimes suggested; on the contrary, if IT is to be used for strengthening democracy, we need a significant change in the present societal structures, providing citizens with real opportunities to influence decisions. We must make sure that decisions of public importance are accounted for in terms of explicit and verifiable arguments. Improvement of the quality of (and participation in) discussions on such decisions is of key importance, and should be stimulated by education of the public as well as of decision-makers.

With respect to the electronic highway this implies at least the following: (i) citizens must have access to the net at a price that is affordable for everyone, (ii) all information that has public relevance should be freely available on the net, in a form that is as understandable and as transparent as possible to the general public, and (iii) citizens should be enabled with real possibilities to influence decisions.

We must beware of technocracy and utopian schemes. Assuming that everything operates ideally is unrealistic and dangerous. Social systems cannot be steered in any way we choose. We must be prepared to formulate concrete diagnoses, and to make specific, well-considered interventions.

ACKNOWLEDGEMENTS

I would like to thank the members of the Dutch study group for sociocybernetics and the participants at the conference for their comments.

REFERENCES

Ackoff Russell L., Management Misinformation Systems, *Management Science*, 14, no. 4, B-147-156 (December 1967)

Beniger James, *The control revolution*, 1986, Harvard University Press, Cambridge (MA)

Berghel Hal, Cyberspace 2000: dealing with information overload, *Communications of the ACM*, 40, no. 2 (February 1997) 19-24

Besser Howard, From Internet to Information Superhighway, in: James Brook, Iain A. Boal (eds.), *Resisting the virtual life. The culture and politics of information*, 1995, City Lights, San Francisco

Birrer Frans A.J., Expertise, context and problem orientation. A constructive realism perspective on science and expertise, 1994, Technical Report 94-45, Dept. of Computer Science, Leiden University

Birrer Frans A.J., Client-oriented anticipation in expert-advised problem solving, 1996, Technical Report 96-40, Dept. of Computer Science, Leiden University

Bryant Tony, The myth of the information society, in: Jacques Berleur, John Drumm (eds.), *Information technology assessment* (Proceedings 4th Human Choice and Computers Conference), 1991, North-Holland, Amsterdam

Danziger James N., William H. Dutton, Rob Kling, Kenneth L. Kraemer, *Computers and politics. High technology in American local government*, 1982, Columbia University Press, New York

Dutton William, The political implications of information technology: Challenge to power?, in: Jacques Berleur, Andrew Clement, Richard Sizer, Diane Whitehouse (eds.), *The information society. Evolving landscapes*, 1990, Springer, New York

European Commission, Green paper. Living and working in the information society: People first, 1996

Frissen P.H.A., *De virtuele staat. Politiek bestuur, technologie: een postmodern verhaal*, 1996, Academic Service, Schoonhoven

Geyer Felix, & van der Zouwen J., Cybernetics and social science. Theories and research in sociocybernetics, *Kybernetes*, 20, no. 6, December 1991

Information Society Forum, Networks for people and their communities. Making the most of the information society in the European Union (Report to the European Commission), 1996

Laudon Kenneth C., *Communications technology and democratic participation*, 1977, Praeger, New York

Miller Steven E., *Civilizing cyberspace. Policy, power, and the information superhighway*, 1996, ACM Press, New York

Abbe Mowshowitz, Virtual feudalism: a vision of political organization in the information age, in: P.H.J. Frissen, A.W. Koers, I. Snellen (eds.), *Orwell of Athene? Democratie en informatiesamenleving*, 1992, SDU, The Hague

Qvortrup Lars, The information age. Ideal and reality, in: Jennifer Daryl Slack, Fred Fejes (eds.), *The ideology of the information age*, 1987, Ablex, Norwood (NJ)

Robins Kevin, Webster Frank, Information as capital. A critique of Daniel Bell, in: Jennifer Daryl Slack, Fred Fejes (eds.), *The ideology of the information age*, 1987, Ablex, Norwood (NJ)

Schiller Herbert I., Communication of knowledge in an information society, in: Jacques Berleur, Andrew Clement, Richard Sizer, Diane Whitehouse (eds.), *The information society. Evolving landscapes*, 1990, Springer, New York

Stoll Clifford, *Silicon snake oil. Second thoughts on the information highway*, 1995, Doubleday, New York

Talbott Stephen L., *The future does not compute. Transcending the machines in our midst*, 1995, O'Reilly, Sebastopol (CA)

Zuboff Shoshana, *In the age of the smart machine. The future of work and power*, 1988, Basic, New York.

---

1 For an overview of sociocybernetics, see [Geyer & Van der Zouwen, 1991].

2 I have argued elsewhere [Birrer, 1994; 1996] that such normative anticipation on behalf of actors is quite a common phenomenon in science and scientific expertise, even though it is not often acknowledged.

3 This again follows from the limited possibilities for active steering in a self-organizing system. The behaviour of the system cannot be adjusted in arbitrary ways or directions; any attempt to

steer should take into account the imperatives that are at work in the system. In order to get different overall outcomes one has to change the procedures of the system itself, so that the blind imperatives are canalized in a different way.

4 [Ackoff, 1967].

5 See, for example, [Berghel, 1997].

6 See, for example, [Miller, 1996, p. 272-274].

7 [Stoll, 1995].

8 [Besser, 1995].

9 *Cf.* [Beniger, 1986].

10 [Talbott, 1995].

11 [Laudon, 1977].

12 That has often been the role of IT, see, for example, [Beniger, 1986], [Bryant, 1991], [Danziger, *et al.*, 1982], [Dutton, 1990], [Qvotrup, 1987], [Robins & Webster, 1987], and [Schiller, 1990].

13 [Frissen, 1996].

14 *Cf.* [Beniger, 1986], [Zuboff, 1988].

15 *Cf.* Miller's description of an economic tragedy of the commons [Miller, 1996, p.387-80].

16 [Mowshowitz, 1992].

17 *Cf.* [Talbott, 1995].

18 For example, [European Commission, 1996], [Information Society Forum, 1996].

Information highways: A threat to democracy?

Marie d'Udekem-Gevers[1]
Cellule Interfacultaire de Technology Assessment (CITA)
Institut d'Informatique, Facultés Universitaires Notre-Dame de la Paix, Rue Grandgagnage, 21,
B-5000 Namur, Belgium
Phone: + 32 81 72 4973, Fax: + 32 81 72 4967
Email: mgevers@info.fundp.ac.be

Abstract

This paper focuses on the potential impacts of the information highways on democracy. It begins by showing with concrete examples that this new technology, like other communication networks, is a tool which allows integration and cohesion to be increased. But the paper stresses that to improve communications does not mean making society more equal and more democratic. The second part of this paper considers how to build up the information highways according to official documents of the European Union. It underlines that the liberalization of the telecommunications sector required by the official texts and the basic importance given to market forces and to competition can be considered a threat to democratic values. There is a serious risk of increasing inequalities. There are also problems linked to services and to content such as issues in financing nonprofit services, threats to the freedom to communicate and to operate on the network, risks of information being limited, and so on.

INTRODUCTION

Information highways (IH) are defined here as the international broadband networks projected by governments in most economically developed countries. Such networks (or more probably networks of networks) will be able to transmit numerical and multimedia information and will allow interactivity. They are examples of new information and communication technologies (ICT).

An Ethical Global Information Society J. Berleur & D. Whitehouse (Eds.)

They are considered, particularly in the European Union (EU)[2],as leading to the emergence of the information society (IS). While the last expression is more frequently used in EU documents than in those on the IH, both are considered here as referring to the same framework of reflection.

In this paper, the main question is that of evaluating the risks of the IH for democracy[3], particularly, for democratic *values* i.e., consensus values on which any democracy is based. The democratic process itself (for example, the mechanism of representative and direct democracies) will not be discussed here.

A CHANCE FOR DEMOCRACY?

Opportunities offered by the information highways

Like any communication network, information highways (IH) are *tools* which allow social integration and cohesion to be increased via communications. Moreover, thanks to the access to information and databases, the IH can also contribute to levelling society. Thus, they could help the democratic basis for society to be enforced.

Indeed, analysis of existing communication and information networks (such as the Internet and Freenets) shows that they produce the emergence of new[4] community concepts. Practically, new communities based on ICT can be classified into two types on the basis of their extension in space: local communities and scattered communities. According to Beamish's vocabulary (1995), the first type is most often named either community network or civic networking and the second type, virtual community or online community.

'A "community network" is a network of computers and modems that are interconnected via telephone lines to a central computer. The system provides local information and a means for community residents to communicate electronically. (...) Community networks are located and support a specific physical place' (Beamish 1995, Abstract). A community network characteristic is 'the belief that the system, and its communication and information, can strengthen and vitalize existing communities... It is believed that community networks can be used by the local community to find and build solutions to their problems' (Beamish 1995, p. 2). 'Increased communication and information will increase the sense of community, increase involvement in the community, and serve as a tool to solve some of the problems facing the community at a grass-roots level... Community networks will *improve democratic governance and empower citizens to become more active and informed*[5] (Media Access Project 1994)' (Beamish 1995, p. 3; emphasis added). The first community network was created in Berkeley during the mid-1970s. Since this period, these networks have grown in number in the United States (US). And, ever since 1993, they can receive public funding. In Europe, Application Ten of the Bangemann Report, named City Information Highways and suggested by Hervé (1996a, p. II), corresponds to some extent to the concept of community networks. In this framework, trials are currently being undertaken in six selected cities (Naestved, London, Eindhoven, Venice, Trieste, and Bologna) (see Kooi, 1996). Among other examples, let us also mention the European projects of digital cities called METASA and MIND (Hervé, 1996a p. V, VIII, IX) involving Parthenay (France), Arnedo (Spain), Weinstadt (Baden-Wurttemberg Land) and Torgau (in the former East Germany). The case of Parthenay is particularly worth a mention: in this little city, the concept of active citizenship as defined by Hervé[6] (1996b, p. 18) is being put forward and reinforced via telecommunication networks. Another famous European example is De Digitale Stad Amsterdam[7].

An online community is 'a social group of any size that shares common interests, whether those be social, professional, occupational, or religious ... They gather together electronically in newsgroups or mailing lists to discuss specific topics which range from academic research to hobbies. There are no geographic boundaries to on-line communities and participants can be located anywhere in the world' (Beamish, 1995, p. 6). Examples of online communities are very numerous and different. Jerusalem One, for instance, is a network which allows the Jewish diaspora to keep in touch. Via the Association for Progressive Communications (APC) network, a virtual community of more than 20,000 non-governmental organizations (NGOs) from poor countries can now hold discussions and be heard by people in rich countries (see Afonso, 1994, and Bissio, 1994). Let us remark that participating in an electronic forum can be really democratic: all the opinions can have the same weight, from the point of view of visual presentation (Bissio, 1994).

Outside these new types of communities, social cohesion can be improved via the IH *if* the possibility of communicating (particularly the possibility of expressing oneself and of producing information) and/or of accessing information (particularly in the domains of education, health, and/or administration and public information) is *given to people previously excluded or disenfranchised*; groups at risk (such as women, disabled people, the elderly, the unemployed, the homeless[8]); minorities, isolated or poor regions, or less favoured countries. Let us take the case of women, for example. 'The new media actually provide many new vehicles for women to redress imbalances. In cyberspace, no one needs to know what gender you are. Furthermore, research has shown that the new media provide opportunities to overcome gender differences. Computer conferencing ... and Net discussion groups have been found to change criteria for leadership - moving the most succinct (often women), rather than the forceful and verbose, to the fore ... And as for women who choose to be homemakers, the I-way can reduce rather than increase isolation and stratification' (Tapscott 1996, p. 295). As summarized by Tapscott (1996, p. 294), technology can be a great leveller.

'Overall, then the capacity that information and communication technologies *offer* to put individuals and groups in contact with one another to request a service, to exchange knowledge, to transmit information and so on, promotes participation in community life and a renewal of sociability which are necessary to effective democracy' (High Level Expert Group on the IS, 1996, p. 78; emphasis added).

Status of the information highways

But the fact is that, while the IH do offer these possibilities, they do *not automatically result* in improving social cohesion! And the idea of brotherhood and equality brought by a communication network is nothing other than a utopia.

Nevertheless it is frequent and old. '... The creation of a network of networks ... will bring ... strong democracies ...' Gore states (1994), for example. As pointed out by Mattelart (1995a and 1995b), this kind of utopia has appeared since 1793, with the installation of the optic telegraph between Paris and Lille. It re-emerges whenever communications (either transport or signal transmission) show a major technological leap (Mattelart, 1995b). For example, in 1832, Michel Chevalier, a disciple of Saint-Simon, after observing the installation of the first railway in England, wrote that communication decreases distances between different points but also between social classes. And he concluded that to improve communications means thus to make society more equal and more democratic. According to Mattelart's analysis, the same idea is used by Wiener in 1948 (with the information society) and by McLuhan in 1960 (with the global village).

But communication, by itself, is not social progress (Ramonet, 1996). And the IH, like other ICT, are only instruments: they can be used either positively or negatively! Not only NGOs but also racist or paedophile associations can profit from their possibilities. Moreover, the IH offer an opportunity to reduce social disparities *if and only if everybody has access.* This *sine qua non* condition implies, in turn, that there is a political will for equity and that the *laissez-faire* conditions suggested by the global market economy are seriously counterbalanced. As we are going to see now, it is far from being established.

HOW TO BUILD THE INFORMATION SOCIETY ACCORDING TO EUROPEAN UNION OFFICIAL DOCUMENTS

Let us thus have a look at the history of the information society in Europe and in European Union official documents.

After the publication in 1993 of the Commission of the European Communities (CEC) White Paper, *Growth, Competitiveness, Employment - The challenges and ways forward into the 21st century*, the Council requested that a group of prominent persons from the private sector (members of the executive staff of such firms as Bull, Canal Plus, Olivetti, La Société Générale de Belgique) prepare a report on the IS. This report, issued in May 1994 and entitled *Europe and the global information society - Recommendations to the European Council* is generally referred to as the Bangemann Report. It includes the following sentences: 'The *market* will drive ... the prime task of government is to safeguard *competitive* forces ...' (p. 9; emphasis added). 'The Group recommends member States to accelerate the ongoing process of *liberalization* of the telecom sector by opening up to *competition* infrastructures and services still in the monopoly area ...' (p. 12) 'The group believes the creation of the IS in Europe should be *entrusted* to the *private sector* and to *market forces* ...' 'There will be *no need for public subsidies,* because sufficient confidence will have been established to attract the required investment from private sources' (Bangemann, *et al*, 1994, p. 30).

All these statements can be considered as reflecting the main principles of neoliberalism.

In its action plan (Com (94) 347 final) which was published in July 1994 and is the basic official document about the IS, the CEC supports the conclusions of the Bangemann Report and concludes (p. 4): 'The Community will assume its responsibilities for setting the appropriate regulatory environment. In parallel, the private sector is invited to play its entrepreneurial role and launch without delay concrete initiatives for the prompt deployment of the IS'. Moreover, an important characteristic of this action plan is the little concern paid to the social dimension of the IS. Emphasis is essentially on economic issues and goals. Let us note that, from this point of view, the action plan contrasts with its US equivalent: the *National Information Infrastructure: Agenda for Action* (IITF, 1993). In the latter, the economic and social aims of the IH have the same priority.

The insufficient concern about the social issues and goals of the IS in the EU is so clear that it has been denounced and underlined by both reflection groups created in 1995 in the framework of the action plan itself (ISPO, 1995). Indeed the High Level Expert Group on the IS[9] (1996, p. 1) remarks: 'So far, the IS policy debate has been dominated by technological issues and more recently the appropriate regulatory economic environment, neglecting by and large, some of the broader issues implicit in the society notion'. As for the IS Forum[10] (1996b, p. 10), it declares that more needs to be done to assert the moral and social dimension of the IS and also states that questions of public and individual interest, of setting social and professional standards, and of defining objectives which sustain democratic and individual liberties should be regarded by the European Commission as of equal importance as the need to foster the conditions for economic exploitation.

But it seems that things could improve now. While the CEC does not recognize its past lack of social concern[11], it has recently written (on July 24, 1996) a Green Paper entitled *Living and Working in the IS: People First* in order to promote wide discussion and awareness of the social and societal issues involved (see Com (96) 389 final, p. 4). But this paper is far less precise than those of both reflection groups, and looks like a catalogue of pious wishes. And there is another, perhaps more promising, sign: the Commission (see Com (96) 395, final and Com (96) 607) has defined four new priorities to be taken into account, among which, people first. Moreover, it has explicitly declared (see Com (96) 395 final, p. 1a) that all these priorities have the same importance. After these promises, let us wait now for the facts.

A THREAT TO DEMOCRACY?

Let us now tackle the main question asked in this paper: are the information highways a threat to democratic values? The answer is that, when implemented within the framework of deregulated global markets and with weak concern for social issues, this new technology could become threatening to democracy.

Conflicting principles

Indeed, the rules of the market do not overlap with those of democracy (see Table 1). To be clearer, let us give concrete expression to the main principles of democratic ethics: let us choose here to consider, for example, *freedom of all human beings*, *equality* and *fraternity*. To these three basic values, let us add a less romantic one: *efficiency*. This last principle is of course also at the basis of neoliberalism (as of any other economy theory). But the three others characterize democracy. Corresponding values from some liberal leanings (such as those of the Chicago School) are fully justified by efficiency in the framework of the global market. They could be defined respectively as follows: *freedom of enterprises to trade*, *inequalities based on income differentials* and, last but not least, *competitiveness*. They are opposed to democratic values.

Table 1: Comparison of principles of the democratic ethics and rules proposed by some global market economy advocates

Principles of *democratic* ethics	Rules proposed by some global *market* economy advocates
Freedom of all human beings	Freedom of enterprises to trade
Equality of all human beings	Inequalities based on income differentials
Fraternity of all human beings	Competitiveness
Efficiency	Efficiency

Factual risks

If access to the IH is based only on market laws, and information is considered as a marketable good, two major classes of issues for democratic principles arise, linked to *access* and linked to *content*.

Let us note that all these issues are increasing because, in the framework of the globalization and of the convergence of telecommunication/computer science/audio visual sectors, huge enterprises and conglomerates which vertically integrate the production and distribution of content are now being set up.

Issues linked to access

The Declaration of Human Rights[12] states that everyone has the right of *equal* access to public service in his or her country. A new version of public service called universal service is proposed in the EU as an essential element of the IS (see title of Com (96) 73 final). Universal service means *a defined minimum set of services of specified quality which is available to all users independent of their geographical location and, in the light of specific national conditions, at an affordable price* (Com (96) 419, p.9). As underlined by Hercberg (1996) and Barrère (1996), this definition is imprecise and very restrictive. Moreover, it must be noticed that the crucial question of affordability is left to member states. 'With the adoption by the European Parliament and the Council of the Voice Telephony Directive in December 1995[13], the Community has now for the first time identified the *common scope of universal service obligations* in the EC ... The obligations ... comprise the provision of voice telephony service via fixed connection which will also allow a fax and a modem to operate as well as the provision of operator assistance emergency and directory enquiry services ... and the provision of public payphones. Users should also have access to published information about the cost and prices of services, about their quality and whether targets for quality are being met. By including network access within the scope of universal service, users are given the possibility of accessing not only the defined voice telephony service but *all* services that can be provided over today's telecommunications networks (i.e., every citizen will be able to access interactive and on-line information services including the Internet, provided they have a computer and a subscription with an Internet service provider)' (Com (96) 73 final, pp. 4-5). This definition of scope shows clearly that access is unfortunately limited to technical means, thus to the pipeline[14], and does *not* extend to the content, that is, to specific information (except about costs and prices) and specific services (such as, for example, community services). The IS Forum does not agree with this definition and recommends universal public access to basic online services such as public information, education, and health (IS Forum 1996a, p. 5).

Moreover, in a liberalized environment, financing universal service is not easy and offering an affordable price to all users looks somewhat problematic, mainly in the short term. Issues appear at the level of the current basic telephone service and at the level of the new services of the IH. Indeed, on the one hand, telephone bills could rise for residential consumers (who make few long-distance and international calls) because of the process of tariff rebalancing resulting from political decisions in favour of the liberalization of the sector (Com (96) 73 final, p. 9). This trend is already evident on the scale of the whole EU for the period 1990-1995: the available data 'shows that important changes in tariff structures are underway, and, in particular, the general trend of increases in fixed elements in the tariffs ... (connection and rental), as well as *higher charges for local calls* at peak hours and in most Members States, corresponding reductions in regional, long distance and international calls' (Com (96) 73 final p. 41; emphasis added). Let us remark also that deregulation in the US produced a shortening of two points in the rate of telephone connection (see Torres, 1996). On the other hand, 'the new services will mostly be financed by subscriptions and could be an expensive item for consumers'; thus, access at affordable prices is by no means guaranteed (IS Forum 1996a, p.15).

As a result, there is a risk of increasing inequalities: society could now be divided between *information haves* and *have nots* (or perhaps also between information wants and want nots). This risk is frequently denounced and generally considered as the greatest one in the IS (see, for example, IS Forum 1996b, p. 9). As pointed out by Mansell (1995, p. 50), as liberalization and competition take hold, the supercarriers will continue to pursue their goals in international markets and they will become increasingly reluctant to bear public service responsibilities. However, in the interest of both equity and efficiency in the market, there is a need to ensure that a common public network continues to evolve. The risk of increasing disparities[15] does exist at several levels: inside society in industrial countries, between regions (for example, of the EU) and, obviously, between North and South.

Inside society in the industrial countries, several groups are threatened as excluded from information. These groups[16] have been listed by the High Level Expert Group on the IS (1996, p. 34) as follows: people with reduced mobility or impaired physical ability to communicate, the elderly, early and active retired persons, low income families, the unemployed, women, persons with learning disabilities, and illiterate people. Let us note this remark of Tapscott (1996, p. 296): 'As for differences between old and young, there is little doubt that the generation of 10- to 25-year olds, are effortlessly embracing the new media. Rather than a generation gap, there is a danger of *generation lap* where cyberspace is part of life of one generation and an uncomfortable place for preceding ones'.

Existing inequalities between regions of the EU are well known. For example, the whole of European scientific innovation is considered to be concentrated in ten islands (see Hilpert, 1991): the south-east of England, Paris/Ile-de-France, Frankfurt, Munich, Turin, Rotterdam/Amsterdam, Rhine-Ruhr, Stuttgart, Lyon/Grenoble, and Milan. The Commission itself recognizes (Com (96) 389 final, p. 21) that 'disparities between regions within the same Member State have tended to widen over time'. There is some evidence that disparities are currently still growing. Indeed, as pointed out by the High Level Expert Group (1996, p. 42), the pace of liberalization of the telecommunications market in the less-favoured regions of the EU seems to be now less rapid than in the core regions. In the future, the risk of increasing inequalities between regions is perhaps higher yet. Indeed, '... given the deregulation and privatization of telecommunications, information and communication technologies services will be provided on a commercial basis thus raising, on the one hand, the question about the commercial viability of privatized telecom services in less-favoured regions and, on the other hand, the risk that only the more affluent and/or core regions will benefit from the more competitive pricing and new services following liberalization' (High Level Expert Group on the IS, 1996, p.41). In other words, 'a major concern is that commercial or market forces may lead to a concentration of investment in geographical areas which appear to be the most profitable ...' (IS Forum 1996b, p.17). Let us remark that the CEC is perfectly aware of the issues of access to the IH. After its *Communication on universal service for telecommunication* (see Com (96) 73), it declares (see Com (96) 389, p. 22): 'there remain important questions concerning the level and quality of access of less favoured and less populated regions, groups with special needs, and public institutions ... to the full range of IS service'.

The problem of increasing inequalities between the world's North and South is still more worrying. Recent indicators (UNDP, 1996) show that the gap between rich and poor countries is widening. United Nations Development Programme administrator, J. G. Speth, concludes: 'If present trends continue, economic disparities between industrial and developing nations will move from inequitable to inhuman' (The Straits Times, July 17, 1996). As clearly underlined by Renaud (1996, p. 94), there are three serious obstacles to the IH in the less developed countries: the lack of solvency, insufficient infrastructures, and the widespread illiteracy. Thus, the development gap is probably going to become still wider. The southern countries were unfortunately not invited to the G7 summit of February 1995 on the information society in Brussels. To try to compensate for this absence, another G7 meeting devoted to information society and development was organized with the participation of thirty developing countries in May 1996 in South Africa. But, at this summit, most of the poorest countries (which are generally also less connected to worldwide telecommunications networks - see Elie, 1996) were not represented. According to the conference theme paper: 'Even in the developing countries, the private sector should be primarily responsible for financing the development of the IS' (ISAD Conference - press information, 1996). Moreover, the South was encouraged to open its countries to the global market.

But, once open to competition, the poor countries (particularly in Africa) could be threatened by delocalized telecommunications infrastructures (see Renaud, 1996, p. 95): indeed low earth orbit satellites (for example, the Iridium satellites now built at Motorola, Arizona) could be used. And this, in turn, could be a new risk for development, as Renaud (1996, p. 95) remarks. Indeed, on the one hand, the financing of local infrastructures could be more difficult and, on the other hand, more qualified jobs could also be delocalized.

Issues linked to content

As to the issues for democracy linked to the services and the content of the IH in the framework of pure neoliberalism, they are numerous.

First of all, the question of how to finance nonprofit services (such as education, help to people, health) can be asked. The public's need for online services is unlikely to be fully satisfied by market forces (IS Forum 1996a, p.17). Thus the democratic principle of *fraternity* (or solidarity) is likely to be neglected.

Other issues are threats to *freedom of any human being*. Indeed, the freedom to communicate[17] and to operate (i.e., use services, etc.) on networks is generally endangered. Privacy and freedom from intrusion are threatened. As pointed out by the IS Forum (1996a, p. 11), there is a strong commercial interest in monitoring online activities and the transactions of citizens, building detailed consumer profiles which can then be used for a wide range of purposes (such as marketing or credit decisions) for which the data were never intended. New techniques developed by Webtrack, NetCount or Internet Profiles, called I/PRO, already allow the manager of an Internet site to know by whom the site has been visited (see Stagliano, 1996, p. 92). There is also a risk of being flooded with stupefying entertainment programmes, needless gadgets and useless services. This is already illustrated by what happens in trial projects on the IH made by consortiums of firms in various cities (for example, Orlando, Omaha (Nebraska), Castro Valley (California), Alexandria (Virginia)) around the US. As reported by Johnson (1996, p. 15-16), executives from Time-Warner, Inc. are proudly showing a video about the Full Service Network currently being tested in Orlando, Florida. The video shows happy suburban families using their set-top boxes to play games, watch movies, browse electronic magazines, and order pizzas and bedroom sets. There is also a danger of being overrun with advertisements. Moreover, the quality and the diversity of the information is also likely to be threatened: this is underlined by both the IS Forum (1996b, p. 13) and by the High Level Expert Group on the IS (1996, pp. 70-71). 'With the deregulation and internationalization of [ICT] industries, the abilities of individual governments to impose standards of practice on communications providers in the IS is significantly weaker, whilst the risk of information terrorism and political manipulation paid for by influential groups or companies grows' (High Level Expert Group on the IS, 1996, p. 78). There is a risk that information circulating on the highways is limited (for example, to the sensational and spectacular), distorted, and no longer pluralistic. And, as pointed out by Dolhem (1996), this threat exists here and now. Dolhem (1996) gives as proof the current struggle of Microsoft, the software champion, to offer content: after launching the cyberspace news magazine called Slate, Bill Gates' firm has recently joined with the National Broadcasting Company (NBC), the most important US television channel. Both firms have invested nearly one billion US dollars to create a new network mixing television and computer, and have begun to broadcast continuous news since July 15, 1996. Moreover Bill Gates has announced a new online newspaper on the web, Cityscape, which will give pieces of information on the big US cities. To sum up, if political power is left to business groups, these groups could push for an information superhighway that delivers much less public benefit but maximizes their own projected benefit (Johnson 1996, p. 17). Thus, there is a risk of being treated as consumers to be targeted rather than citizens to be connected (Johnson, 1996, p. 16). There is a danger of a large-scale enslaving of minds (Schiller, 1994).

CONCLUSION

The analysis of official documents related to the information society shows that current European Union policy focuses mainly on competitiveness and pays far less concern to social issues than to economic challenges. In this framework, implementation of the information highways could become a threat to principles of consensus such as freedom, equality, and the fraternity of all human beings.

'While markets must drive most developments, public interest must be safeguarded' (The IS Forum, 1996a, p. 12). Thus, while encouraging the market, governments and public authorities at all levels must also act as active guarantors of democratic values. As suggested by the IS Forum, they must show a greater readiness to assume their responsibilities in this matter.

Only when this condition is met, will it be possible to target the European model defined by the European Commission (Com (96) 389 final, p. 30) as built both on competition between enterprises and *solidarity* between citizens and member states.

ACKNOWLEDGEMENT

The author wants to thank Renaud Delhaye and Domenico Rossetti di Valdalbero for their corrections and suggestions, and Claire Lobet-Maris for her comments.

REFERENCES

Afonso C.-A. 1994, Réseaux électroniques et action politique au service de la société civile, *Le Monde Diplomatique*, juillet 1994.

Bangemann M. *et al.* 1994, *Europe and the global information society - Recommendations to the European Council*, CD-84-94-290-EN-C, Brussels, 26 May 1994, 36 p.

Barre Ch. 1996, Citoyens, ou... nécessiteux? *Le Monde Diplomatique*, janvier 1996.

Beamish A. 1995, *Communities On-Line: Community-Based Computer Networks*, submitted to the Department of Urban Studies and Planning in partial fulfillment of the requirements of the degree of Master in City Planning at the Massachusetts Institute of Technology, February 1995.

Bissio R. 1994, Cyberespace et démocratie, *Le Monde Diplomatique*, juillet 1994.

Commission of the European Communities 1993, *White Paper - Growth, Competitiveness, Employment - The challenges and ways forward into the 21st century*.

Commission of the European Communities 1994, *Europe's Way to the Information Society. An Action Plan* - Communication from the Commission to the Council and the European Parliament and to the Economic and Social Committee and the Committee of Regions, Com (94) 347 final, Brussels, 19.07.1994.

Commission of the European Communities 1996, *Universal Service for Telecommunications in the Perspective of a Fully Liberalized Environment - An Essential Element of the Information Society*, Com(96) 73 final, Brussels, 23.03.1996.

Commission of the European Communities 1996, *Green Paper - Living and Working in the Information Society: People first*, Com (96) 389 final, Brussels, 24.07.1996. Available at http://www.ispo.cec.be/infosoc/legreg/cdocs/people1st.htlm

Commission of the European Communities 1996, *Information Society: from Corfu to Dublin - The New Emerging Priorities* Com (96) 395 final, Brussels, 24.07.1996.

Commission of the European Communities 1996, *Europe at the Forefront of the Global Information Society: Rolling Action Plan* - Communication from the Commission to the Council and the European Parliament and to the Economic and Social Committee and the Committee of Regions, Com(96) 607 final, Brussels, 27.11.1996.

Com (96) 419 1996, ONP VT Directive XIII/96/53 rev3, *Proposal for a European Parliament and Council Directive on the application of ONP to voice telephony and on universal service for telecommunications in a competitive environment*, 11 September 1996.

Dolhem N. 1996, Télécybervision, *Le Monde Diplomatique*, août 1996, p. 19.

Elie M. 1996, Internet et développement - Un accès à l'information plus équitable? *Futuribles*, Novembre 1996, pp. 43-64.

European Parliament and Council 1995, *Directive 95/62/EC on the application of Open Network Provision (ONP) to Voice Telephony* (the Voice Telephony Directive), OJ L321.

FCC (Federal Communications Commission) 96J-3 1996, *In a Matter of Federal-State Joint Board on Universal Service - Recommended Decision*, Adopted: November 7, 1996, Released: November 8, 1996, CC Docket No. 96-45.

Gore Al 1994, Plugged into the world's knowledge, *Financial Times*, September 19, 1994.

Groupe de Lisbonne 1995, *Limites à la compétitivité - Pour un nouveau contrat mondial*, Editions La Découverte, Paris, février 1995, 227 p.

Hercberg S. 1996, Des services publics garantis de l'intérêt général, *Le Monde Diplomatique*, juin 1996, pp. 8-9.

Hervé M. 1996a, *Autoroutes de l'information urbaines - Le défi du partenariat public/privé*, City Information Highways Workshop, Evolution, Eindhoven, 22 mai 1996.

Hervé M. 1996b, Changer la ville!, *Transversales Science Culture*, **41**, pp. 14-19.

Hilpert 1991, *Archipelago Europe*, mentioned in Hingel A.J. 1993, *Note sur un nouveau modèle de développement européen*, La Prospective - FAST, CCE, FOP 361, pp. 21-23.

High Level Expert Group on the Information Society 1996, *Building the European Information Society for us all - Interim Report*, January 1996, available at http://www.ispo.cec.be/hleg/hleg.htlm

IITF (Information Infrastructure Task Force) 1993, *The National Information Infrastructure: Agenda for Action*, September 15 1993.

Information Society Forum 1996a, *Networks for People and their Communities - Making the Most of the Information Society in the European Union - Fisrt Annual Report to the European Commission from the Information Society Forum*, June 1996.

Information Society Forum 1996b, *Networks for People and their Communities - Making the Most of the Information Society in the European Union - Fisrt Annual Report to the European Commission from the Information Society Forum - Supplement Containing Groups Reports*, June 1996, available at http://www.ispo.cec.be/

ISAD (Information Society and Development) Conference - South Africa, 13-15 May 1996 Press information.

ISPO (Information Society Project Office) 1995, *Europe's Way to the Information Society, Updated Version of the Action Plan, Status of the 15th December 1995.*

Johnson J. 1996, The Information Superhighway: a Worst-Case Scenario, *Communications of the ACM*, February 1996, **39** (2), pp. 15-17.

Kooi A. 1996, *City Information Highways: an assessment of on-going projects*, City Information Highways Workshop, Evolution, Eindhoven, 22 mai 1996.

Mansell R. 1995, From telephony to telematics: equity, efficiency and regulatory innovation, in *Information Superhighways - Multimedia users and futures*, Emmot S.J. Ed., Academic Press 1995, pp. 35-60.

Mattelart A. 1995a, Les nouveaux scénarios de la communication, *Le Monde Diplomatique*, août 1995, pp. 24-25.

Mattelart A. 1995b, Une éternelle promesse: les paradis de la communication, *Le Monde Diplomatique*, novembre 1995, pp. 4-5.
Media Access Project and People for the American 1994, *A Proposal to Improve Democratic Governance via the National Information Infrastructure. Draft.*
Miller P. 1996a, The Building Blocks of Electronic Democracy, *The CPSR Newsletter*, **14** (2), pp. 1-2 and 18-19.
Miller P. 1996b, CTCNet and the Movement for Democracy, *The CPSR Newsletter*, **14** (2), pp. 5 and 21.
Ramonet I. 1996, Changer d'ère, *Manière de Voir*, Hors-série (*Le Monde Diplomatique)*, octobre 1996, pp. 6-7.
Renaud P. 1996, L'avenir informatique du Sud, *Manière de voir*, Hors-série (*Le Monde Diplomatique)*, octobre 1996, pp. 94-95.
Schiller H.I. 1994, Reléguer le bien public sur les bas-côtés, *Le Monde Diplomatique*, mars 1994.
Schuller D. 1996, Democracy and Democracyware, *The CPSR Newsletter*, 14 (2), pp. 10-15.
Sérusclat F. 1995, *Les nouvelles techniques d'information et de communication: l'homme cybernétique?*, Office Parlementaire d'Evaluation des Choix Technologiques, Tomes 1 and 2.
Stagliano R. 1996, Publicité du troisième type, *Manière de Voir*, Hors-série (*Le Monde Diplomatique)*, octobre 1996, pp. 91-92.
Torres A. 1996, Une nouvelle proie, les télécommunications, *Le Monde Diplomatique*, janvier 1996.
Tapscott D. 1996, *The Digital Economy - Promise and Peril in the Age of Networked Intelligence*, McGraw-Hill, New York.
The Straits Times 1996, *Gap widening between rich and poor nations: UN report*, July 17 1996.
UNDP (United Nations Development Programme) 1996, *The Human Development Report 1996.*

---

1 With the financial support of the Belgian Federal Office for Scientific, Technical, and Cultural Affairs (Interuniversity poles of attraction, Phase IV).

2 For example, according to the Bangemann Report technocratic vision (1994, p. 21, § 2): 'Communications systems combined with advanced technologies as keys to the information society.'

3 The term democracy is of course polysemic. Thus, it will not be defined here.

4 When defining its vision towards the IS, the High Level Group of Experts (1996, p. 83) acknowledges the possibility of a new concept of community.

5 On this subject, see also Tapscott (1996, p. 304), Sérusclat (1995, t. 1, pp. 69-89), Miller (1996a, p. 19) and Schuller (1996, pp. 14-15).

6 'An active citizen is responsible, autonomous, cooperating, and inventive.'

7 Amsterdam is one of the thirteen cities which participate in the European project called Telecities.

8 See, for example, Miller (1996b).

9 This group is composed of fourteen members.

10 This forum gathers 128 members from five main fields of activity: users, social groups, content and service providers, network operators, and institutions (see Com (96) 607, p. 14).

11 See Com (96) 389 final, p. 4: The Commission's Action Plan ... placed an important emphasis on social and societal questions.

12 *Cf.* Article 21 (2) of the Declaration of Human Rights (such as that adopted by the United Nations General Assembly in 1948).

13 Directive 95/62/EC. See also Com (96) 419.

14 Let us remark that such a definition of universal service limited to the pipeline has also been recently adopted in the US (see FCC 96J-3).

15 See the Groupe de Lisbonne (1995), for example p. 174.

16 See also Beamish (1996), pp. 8-9.

17 *Cf.* Article 19 of the Declaration of Human Rights: Everyone has the right to freedom of opinion and expression; this right includes freedom to hold opinions without interference and to seek, receive and impart information and ideas through any media and regardless of frontiers. See also Article 29: In the exercise of his rights and freedom, everyone shall be subject only to such limitations which are determined by law solely for purposes of securing due recognition and respect for the rights and freedom of others and of meeting the just requirements of morality, public order and the general welfare of a democratic society.

23

Privacy at risk in the global information society

Simone Fischer-Hübner
Faculty for Informatics, University of Hamburg
Vogt-Koelln-Str. 30, D-22527 Hamburg-Stellingen
Tel: +49 40 5494 2225; Fax: +49 40 5494 2226
Email: fischer@rz.informatik.uni-hamburg.d400.de

Abstract

Privacy is a fundamental civil right which has to be protected in a democratic society. In the global information society, individual privacy is seriously endangered. An increasing amount of personal data is being transferred around the world and communication data of users could be easily traced and used to create individual communication profiles. International privacy regulations, besides the European Union Directive on Data Protection, will be needed because the communication using the new information infrastructure will be global.

This paper discusses privacy risks in the global information society. It also compares the Bangemann report and action plan with other national information infrastructure programmes (of the United States, Singapore, Japan, Canada, and Denmark) and critically analyzes their different approaches to privacy protection. The difficulties for a common harmonized approach to privacy protection, due to cultural differences, are shown. Moreover, privacy enhancing technologies are discussed. Finally, minimal requirements for a socially and privacy acceptable design and use of the information infrastructure are suggested.

INTRODUCTION

In the United States (US), the Clinton government started the National Information Infrastructure (NII) Programme (Clinton, 1993) for the further development of information highways to strengthen US communication and information technology. European politicians and industrialists did not want to miss out on opportunities for participation in the new information technology (IT) market and did not want to be put at a competitive disadvantage. A group of representatives,

An Ethical Global Information Society J. Berleur & D. Whitehouse (Eds.)

mainly from industry, under the chair of the vice-president of the European Union (EU) commission, Martin Bangemann, therefore elaborated a report and an action plan for the EU (Bangemann, 1994) to carry Europe forward into the global information society. In addition, many other nations (such as Canada, the Scandinavian countries, the Netherlands, Singapore, and Japan) meanwhile developed their own strategies. The Bangemann report and most other information infrastructure programmes promote initiatives such as teleworking, distance teaching, research networks, telematic services for enterprises, road and air traffic management systems, health care networks, public administration networks, and network access for all households through applications such as telebanking and video on demand. The programmes are mainly motivated by economic interests. They generate new jobs and economic growth, and provide better chances for people constrained by geography or disability. Furthermore, they help to overcome structural problems such as in traffic or in health care. On the other hand, the new information infrastructure will change our lives completely, and it bears different risks for society (CPSR, 1993; Fischer-Hübner and Schier., 1996). Individual privacy will be especially endangered, as more and more sensitive personal data can be quickly transferred around the world. Moreover, an increasing amount of transactional data for network services will be available and can be collected at different sites around the world. These data can be used to generate consumer and communication profiles. Privacy as a fundamental civil right (in Germany, a constitutional right) has to be protected in a democratic society. An international harmonization of privacy legislation, besides the EU Directive on data protection, is needed because in the global information society privacy is becoming more and more of an international problem.

This paper discusses privacy risks in the global information society. It shows that, due to cultural differences, there are significant deviations in the EU approach to privacy protection from the privacy regulations of other countries which have developed information infrastructure programmes. These different approaches to privacy protection are critically analyzed. Furthermore, privacy enhancing technologies are discussed, because they can be used technically to enforce legal privacy requirements. Finally, minimal requirements for a socially and privacy acceptable design and use of information highways are suggested.

PRIVACY

An often used definition of privacy is the one by Alan Westin: 'Privacy is the claim of individuals, groups and institutions to determine for themselves, when, how and to what extent information about them is communicated to others' (Westin, 1967).

In general, the concept of privacy has three aspects (Rosenberg, 1992; Holvast, 1993):

- *territorial privacy* (by protecting the close physical area surrounding a person);
- *privacy of the person* (by protecting a person against undue interferences, such as physical searches or information violating his/her moral sense); and
- *informational privacy* (by controlling whether and how personal data can be gathered, stored or selectively disseminated).

Data protection is the protection of personal data in order to guarantee privacy and is only a part of the concept of privacy.

The emphasis of this paper is on the discussion of informational privacy of individuals. Individual informational privacy has also been defined by the German Constitutional Court in its Census Decision of 1983 as the term *right of informational self-determination*, meaning the right of an individual to determine the disclosure and use of his/her personal data on principle at her/his discretion.

In order to protect this right, privacy laws of many western states as well as the EU Directive on data protection (EU Directive, 1995) require basic privacy principles to be guaranteed when personal data are collected or processed. These include:

- purpose binding (personal data obtained for one purpose should not be used for another purpose without informed consent);
- necessity of data collection and processing (the collection and processing of personal data shall only be allowed, if it is necessary for the tasks falling within the responsibility of the data processing agency);
- the data subject's right to information and the right to correction, erasure or blocking of incorrect or illegally stored data;
- control by an independent data protection authority (also called supervisory authority, data protection commissioner, or ombudsman); and
- requirement of adequate technical and organizational security mechanisms to guarantee the confidentiality, integrity, and availability of personal data.

THREATS TO PRIVACY IN THE GLOBAL NETWORKED SOCIETY

In the global information society, privacy is seriously endangered. A key problem is that the traffic on a global network (for example on the Internet) crosses international boundaries and is not centrally managed. On the Internet, there is no overall responsibility assigned to a certain entity, and there is no international oversight mechanism to enforce legal obligations (especially data protection legislation), as far as they exist (Budapest Draft, 1996).

There are severe privacy risks, because personal data about the users or other data subjects are available and can be intercepted or traced at different sites around the world. Major risks are:

Transmission of great quantities of personal data

Meanwhile, the global information society is evolving rapidly and many new information highways for the health sector, public administration, research and private life are being developed. There is a growing amount of personal data, such as sensitive medical data, business data and private data that are accessible and are communicated through networks across state borders. Sensitive personal data can easily be communicated to or routed via countries without an appropriate privacy level. Messages transmitted in plain text could be intercepted or modified. Especially, the secret services are interested in controlling message content.

Communication and consumer profiles

A side-effect of global communication is that connection data are available at different sites around the world revealing details about communication partners, time of communication, services used, connections, and so on. These transactional data may reveal who communicated with whom, when, for how long, and who bought what for what price. Users leave an electronic trace which can be used to create consumer or communication profiles.

Every electronic message contains a header with information about the sender and recipient, as well as the routing and subject of the message. This information could be intercepted at each site passed. There is normally no anonymity of communication, because the recipient of an electronic mail (even if the email is encrypted) can determine the sender's identity through the sender's email address which normally contains information about the user's name, background (for example, university or company), and location.

Communication profiles could be created by the service provider to whom the user is connected (like Internet or mailbox providers). Service providers are recording personal user data (such as user name, login name, address, bank connection, and status) as well as accounting data for billing purposes. Users are normally identified and authenticated by the service providers, and their communication behaviour (for example, access to news or world wide web (WWW) sites could be easily traced and supervised by the providers.

Also, personal user data could be recorded at remote servers. A WWW server can only record the Internet Protocol (IP) addresses of requesting users, which normally do not reveal the user's identity. But techniques, such as Netscape's so-called cookies, could be used by the remote WWW servers to monitor the user's accesses to web pages. Cookies are variables that a server provider can store and later retrieve from the local WWW browser of the user. If a user is identified by the server as having ordered goods or registered for software, the cookies of this user revealing his/her interests in particular web pages can be related to his/her name or email address by the server.

There are several possibilities for the (mis)use of such communication profiles. For example, marketing agencies have a special interest in communication profiles, which can be used to send advertisements to consumers addressing their specific needs or interests. Also, the secret services are interested in information about users' access to newsgroups or WWW pages so as to have the ability to monitor the communication behaviour of individuals under suspicion.

Network insecurity

Another problem of the global information society is whether the requirements of appropriate technical and organizational security mechanisms to protect the personal data on the information highways and to provide network reliability can be guaranteed sufficiently. The Internet, an important contemporary information highway that consists of several thousand computer networks with several million users, is known for a lot of critical security holes. Accidents, such as the Internet worm, chain letter attacks, hacking attacks (such as the KGB hacking incident), sniffer-password attacks, IP address spoofing, and malicious agents have demonstrated the insecurity of Internet technology.

Major reasons for Internet security problems are the lack of standardized cryptographic authentication, buggy host software, and the difficulties in system administration. There is no overall responsibility for security on the Internet; each site is responsible for its own security. The specification of the new improved IP version 6 is offering support for end-to-end encryption and authentication mechanisms in its protocol definition. However, encryption and authentication mechanisms can only be used in a secure manner with an infrastructure for key distribution which is not part of the specification.

Since security was not a main issue when the Internet was initially designed, it is now virtually impossible to fix many security holes.

In conclusion, in the global information society, privacy is at risk and is becoming more and more an international problem. Consequently, internationally harmonized privacy regulations are needed for an adequate level of privacy protection. Furthermore, data protection commissioners demand that privacy protection should be technically enforced and should already be integrated in the system design.

PROBLEMS OF AN INTERNATIONAL HARMONIZATION OF PRIVACY LEGISLATION

In the Bangemann report it is written:

> '...Without the legal security of a Union-wide approach, lack of consumer confidence will certainly undermine the rapid development of the information society. Given the importance and sensitivity of the privacy issue, a fast decision from Member States is required on the Commission's proposed Directive setting out general principles of data protection.'

In the EU, privacy protection will be enforced by *the EU Directive on the protection of individuals with regard to the processing of personal data and on the free movement of such data* (EU Directive, 1995). The EU Directive was formally adopted in 1995 by the European Council. It has to be used by member states to amend their respective national laws (where necessary) to comply with the requirements of the directive by 1998. Besides the privacy protection of individuals, another objective of the EU Directive is to require a uniform minimum standard of privacy protection to prevent restrictions on free flow of personal data between EU member states for reasons of privacy protection.

Even if the EU Directive can help to enforce a relatively high standard of data protection in Europe, it will not be able to protect privacy sufficiently in the global information society. As discussed above, personal data can easily be transferred or routed across state boundaries to countries without any data protection legislation, where its information content or communication data can be intercepted. Privacy is therefore an international problem, and an international harmonization of privacy regulations is needed.

The critical question remains whether a common harmonized approach to privacy will be possible due to cultural, historical, and political differences. Anthropologists have stated that, on a low level, privacy (especially privacy of the person and of the close surroundings) is a human physiological need. But, on higher organizational levels, privacy is basically a cultural construct and there are considerable cultural variations in privacy needs and interests (Lundheim and Sindre, 1994). In addition, experiences from World War II, especially the practice of the Nazi government in amassing and misusing great amounts of personal details about the population, have caused a greater sensitivity to privacy in western European states (Madsen, 1992). Another problem can be seen in non-democratic societies, where individual privacy is normally not protected by legislation. On the contrary, in these countries privacy is often invaded by the state.

In the following sections, the privacy approaches of technologically developed states that have set up information infrastructure programmes are compared with the EU approach. Thereby, considerable distinctions in the different national approaches to privacy protection are shown. Furthermore, all the approaches are critically analyzed to determine the insufficiencies of privacy legislations.

European Union

According to the Bangemann report, the EU Directive will provide protection of privacy through the member states in the global information society.

The EU Directive makes no differentiation between rules applied in the public and in the private sector. The EU Directive is focused on personal data protection. It sets out general rules on the lawfulness of data processing which should also enforce the basic privacy principles mentioned in the earlier part of this article on privacy. It could be used to enforce a relatively good level of data protection in Europe. However, it has also been criticized that some rules (especially the criteria for making data processing legitimate - Article 7) are very general and allow a variety of specific implementations in national laws. These differences in interpretation could hinder the goal of reducing divergences between national laws.

The EU Directive also contains provisions for the transfer of personal data to third countries outside the EU. According to Article 25, the export of personal data to third countries, which do not provide an adequate level of protection, is prohibited. However, in open and free networks, such as the Internet, with no central agency of control, it is technically difficult to enforce this requirement (Koch, 1995).

It has also been criticized that many rules of the EU Directive include exceptions that are mandatory and may hinder states in providing a stricter standard of privacy protection (Greenleaf, 1995).

Singapore

The information infrastructure plan *IT2000 - A Vision Of An Intelligent Island* was formulated by the Singapore government in August 1991 (Singapore, 1991). By 2000, Singapore, the Intelligent Island, should be among the first countries with an advanced information infrastructure that will link government, business, and people. Singapore, like most other Asian states, does not have any privacy protection laws so far. On the contrary, privacy does not seem to be a topic at all. Intensive surveillance by security services is justified by Singapore's Internal Security Act. While promoting the use of the SINGNET (Singapore's Internet sub-network), the government is trying to control the content of the information transmitted over the net at the same time (Madsen, 1995).

Japan

In June 1993, the Information Industry Committee of the Industrial Council in Japan issued a report stating the need for the government to promote information technology. In May 1994, the Ministry of International Trade and Industry (MITI) published a *Programme for Advanced Information Infrastructure.* In this programme under the topic *Improvement of Environment for Realizing Advanced Information Society*, only security measures, and not privacy issues, are discussed (Japan, 1994).

Japan, on the other hand, is one of the very few Asian countries to have implemented a data protection act. The awareness of privacy in Japan has resulted more from economic self-interest than from any longstanding tradition of ensuring individual privacy (Madsen, 1992). The Japanese *Act for Protection of Computer Processed Personal Data* was made official in December 1988. In addition, cities, towns, and villages have also enacted local privacy regulations. However, the Japanese data protection act only applies to national government organizations. Moreover, it does not install an independent data protection authority to control data processing. In 1989, MITI issued formal guidelines entitled *Protection of Personal Data Processed by Computers in the Private Sector*. However, these guidelines for privacy in the private sector are not mandatory and can only be adopted internally by private companies.

United States of America

In 1993, the Clinton/Gore government presented the *National Information Infrastructure (NII) Programme - Agenda for Action* (Clinton, 1993). So far, the US has been criticized for being the first in technology but the last in data protection (Madsen, 1992). The US Privacy Act of 1974 only covers the public sector. Besides the Privacy Act, there is only a non-uniform patchwork of various privacy and computer security legislation. The US does not have a data protection authority to oversee privacy protection and to act if there are complaints from data subjects about unfair or illegal use of their personal data. Consequently, the only way for data subjects to fight against data misuse is through the courts.

It has been realized that the NII does not only promise many benefits, but is also increasing risks to privacy. Therefore, the Information Infrastructure Task Forces (IITF) Working Group on Privacy has developed privacy principles with the goal of providing guidance to all participants in the National Information Infrastructure (IITF, 1995). They are intended to be applied to governmental and private sectors, and are based on the idea that all participants (information providers, collectors, users, and data subjects) of the NII have a shared responsibility for the proper use of personal information..

General Principles for All Participants require that all NII participants should ensure and respect information privacy, information integrity, and information quality.

Privacy approaches in selected information infrastructure programmes

Information Infrastructure Programmes	Privacy regulations	Criticisms to privacy approaches
Singapore *IT2000 - Vision of an Intelligent Island, 1991*	--	- Internal Security Act allows intensive surveillance - attempts to control information content transmitted over the net
Japan *Programme for Advanced Information Infrastructure*	Japan Data Protection Act (1988)	- applicability to public sector only - no data protection authority
Report by *Information Industry Committee of Industrial Structure Council*, 1993	MITI Guideline *Protection of Personal Data Processed by Computers in the Private Sector* (1989)	- not mandatory
USA *National Information Infrastructure (NII) Programme*, 1993	US Privacy Act (1974) + Privacy Acts of states	- applicability to public sector only - no data protection authority
	IITF-WG on Privacy - Privacy Principles (1995)	- not mandatory - shared responsibility of data protection agency/usees will not work - no control of independent data protection authority
Canada *The Canadian Information Highway*, discussion paper: 1994 Final report by *Information Highway Advisory Council*, 1995	Canada Privacy Act (1982) + Privacy Acts of Quebec and Ontario CSA *Model Code for Protection of Personal Information* (1996)	- applicability to public sector only (except Quebec) - no legislation so far
EU *Europe and the Global Information Society*, (Bangemann Report), 1994	EU Data Protection Directive (1995)	- too general, too many exceptions - art. 25 can hardly be enforced on the Internet
Denmark *Info-Society 2000*, 1994	The Danish Private and the Danish Public Authorities Register Acts (1978)	- applicability to registers only
	Utilisation of Data and Protection of Personal Data	- multifunctional use of data, not purpose binding

Principles for Users of Personal Information require information users to assess the impact on privacy of current or planned activities and to use personal information only for these activities or for compatible uses. Data subjects will be informed by the data collector about the reason and purpose of data collection and about their rights. Information users should use appropriate security mechanisms to protect the confidentiality and integrity of personal data. Information users should not use information in ways that are incompatible with an individual's understanding. Furthermore, they should educate themselves about how privacy can be maintained.

According to the *Principles for Individuals Who Provide Personal Information*, individuals should obtain information about what data is being collected and for what reason, and how it will be protected. Individuals will have a responsibility to understand the consequences of providing personal data to others and will make intelligent choices on whether to provide or not to provide their personal data. Individuals will be able to safeguard their own privacy by having the means to obtain their data, to correct them, to use appropriate technical safeguards (for example, encryption), and to remain anonymous when appropriate. Furthermore, data subjects will have means of redress, if harmed by an improper disclosure or use of personal data.

The IITF privacy principles could raise the level of data protection in the US, especially if applied in the private sector. Unfortunately, the principles only offer guidelines for those who are drafting laws and regulations but they do not have the force of law. Although the IITF privacy principles are intended to be consistent with international guidelines such as the Organization for Economic Cooperation and Development guidelines, they do not in some respect offer the same level of privacy protection as the EU directive. In practice, the idea of shared responsibility of equal partners will not always work, because data subjects (such as employees) often depend on services provided by the data processing agencies (for example, employers), so that they hardly have the chance to enforce their rights themselves. Consequently, besides the right of redress, the control of an independent data protection authority is necessary to protect data subjects efficiently.

Canada

In September 1995, the Canadian Information Highway Advisory Council presented the final report *Connection Community Content: The Challenge of the Information Highway* (Canada, 1995). In contrast to most other information infrastructure programmes, which were mainly influenced by input from representatives of the IT industry, the advisory council also included members from artistic, creative, and educational communities, and from consumer and labour organizations. It was chaired by David Johnston, professor of law at McGill University's Centre for Medicine, Ethics and Law.

The Canadian Privacy Act of 1982 which, in contrast to the US legislation, established the Office of Privacy Commissioner, only applies to federal government bodies and agencies. Only the province of Quebec has enacted specific legislation for the private sector. In order to overcome these deficiencies in the private sector, the Canadian Standard Association (CSA) is developing a model of a voluntary privacy code for use by the private sector.

Privacy protection and network security were one of five principles that were set up by the Information Highway Advisory Council. The council recommends that the government should continue to collaborate with the CSA, business, and consumer organizations, and other levels of government in order to implement the CSA draft code and develop effective independent oversight and enforcement mechanisms.

Denmark

The Danish approach is discussed to show that, even in the European Union, there is not a complete consensus on the approach of the EU Directive on data protection. The Danish Private Register Act as well as the Danish Public Authorities Registers Act of 1978 protect personal data in registers and cannot be applied to other form of personal data (for example, personal data included in electronic mail). For this and for other reasons, it is regarded as outdated and its amendment is planned.

The Danish proposal *Info-Society 2000* (DMR, 1994) was worked out by a two-member committee appointed by the government and was published in 1994 by the Danish Ministry of Research. Statements to the parliament on *Info-Society 2000* and action plans for the initiatives for the coming years were presented by the government in 1995 and in 1996.

In the *Info-Society 2000* proposal, the EU directive was criticized for being too bureaucratic. Modern legislation that makes it possible to register, combine, and use data for all legal and administrative purposes without bureaucratic procedures, was demanded. According to the report, it should be possible to collect and register non-sensitive information and to use it more or less freely, as well as to transfer it, provided that due respect is paid to the principle of transparency. The principle of transparency should, on the other hand, not be administered rigidly or inflexibly. However, the Danish public also commented critically that the free use of personal data for different purposes can endanger personal privacy. The more or less free use of personal data is actually an infringement of the internationally accepted privacy principle of purpose binding. It is not considered that there are no non-sensitive data. Also, personal data such as addresses that seem to be non-sensitive *per se*, can become highly sensitive if used for a specific purpose in a certain context. The Danish proposal gives an example of how changes to privacy legislation are discussed, not because individuals will be protected from increasing privacy risks but rather because free communication on the information highways will be legalized.

PRIVACY ENHANCING TECHNOLOGIES

In a fully networked society, privacy is seriously endangered and cannot be sufficiently protected by privacy legislation alone. Data protection commissioners are therefore demanding that privacy requirements should also be technically enforced and that privacy should be a design criterion for information systems. The Dutch Data Protection Authority (the Registratiekamer) and the Information and

Privacy Commissioner (IPC) for the Province of Ontario, Canada, have collaborated in the production of a report (Registratiekamer/IPC, 1995) exploring privacy enhancing technologies that safeguard personal privacy by minimizing or eliminating the collection of identifiable data.

The report on privacy enhancing technologies by the Registratiekamer and IPC, and a prior study of the Registratiekamer on how to design and model privacy technologies, (Registratiekamer, 1995) mainly focus on privacy technologies that permit transactions to be conducted anonymously. Extended security criteria for systems with high privacy requirements should cover a diversity of privacy enhancing security aspects such as:

- *Anonymity, Pseudonymity, Unlinkability, Unobservability of users:* The privacy principle of necessity of data collecting means that personal data should not be collected or used for identification purposes when not really necessary. Consequently, information systems should guarantee that, if possible, users can act anonymously.
- *Anonymity and Pseudonymity of data subjects:* If storage is needed, personal data of data subjects should be anonymized or pseudonymized as soon as possible.
- *Purpose binding and necessity of data processing of personal data of users and data subjects:* If personal data have to be processed, the privacy principles of purpose binding and necessity of data processing can be technically supported through an appropriate security policy and access control mechanisms (for example, see Fischer-Hübner, 1994, for a formal privacy enforcing access control model).

In the global information society, privacy technologies that provide anonymity or pseudonymity for the users will be needed to prevent the creation of communication and consumer profiles. So far, there are only a few privacy technologies available for protecting user identities. Examples are:

- *Prepaid cards* (e.g., telephone cards) for charging services;
- David Chaum's *DigiCash* which is based on blind signatures. It can be used as an electronic form of anonymous payment that can be transmitted over the networks (see Chaum, 1985; Chaum, 1990). DigiCash's Ecash has been tested for several years and was used in 1995 to issue the first ecash dollars in the US. Also, an Australian bank will soon use DigiCash to issue ecash, and a big German bank and Digicash's Ecash are to launch a joint pilot project to test the use of electronic cash on the Internet.
- *Anonymous remailers* provide a free service that allows email to be sent without the recipient knowing who sent the message. The message is sent through an intermediary computer which secretly passes the message to the recipient. Anonymous remailers cannot completely guarantee email privacy. A mapping of anonymous identities to real addresses must be maintained by the remailer which, for that reason, can be a sensitive point of attack. There was an earlier incident in which the Finnish police, in cooperation of the Federal Bureau of Investigation (FBI) raided the residence of a Finnish provider of an anonymous remailer. The FBI is opposed to anonymous remailer services but formally acted on a complaint from the Church of Scientology about stolen scientology files posted on the remailer. Such incidents could probably easily happen again. Besides, unscrupulous providers could monitor the traffic that

goes through the remailers. In any case, the user has to place a high degree of trust in the anonymous remailer. For sensitive communication, encrypted messages should be sent through several remailers.

The report of the Registratiekamer and IPC (Registratiekamer/IPC, 1995) concludes that, if privacy technologies are to play a more significant role, it will be necessary to create more public awareness as well as consumer demand for them. If there is a demand, providers will probably try to respond to market forces.

Security mechanisms, such as access control or encryption, are necessary to protect the confidentiality and integrity of personal data, if personal data have to be processed/transmitted. Such security mechanisms can be better classified as data protection technologies (in contrast to privacy enhancing technologies).

The Bangemann report emphasizes the importance of encryption to protect personal data but also claims that governments may need powers to override encryption for the purposes of fighting against crime and protecting national security. In France, the free use of encryption is already restricted by law. Legal forms of the regulation of encryption are also being discussed in other European states and by the European Commission. However, as the cryptographic policy debate demonstrated, such regulations of encryption will primarily endanger the possibilities of individuals to communicate freely and to protect their own personal data. Criminals or terrorists will still find ways to hide secret messages (for example, through steganography) without being detected.

MINIMAL REQUIREMENTS FOR A SOCIALLY AND PRIVACY ACCEPTABLE DESIGN AND USE OF THE INFORMATION INFRASTRUCTURE

Only leading representatives from industry were initially invited to contribute to the Bangemann report. Consequently, economic opportunities were emphasized while social impacts were neglected. Most other information infrastructure programmes were also mainly motivated by economic interests.

For a socially acceptable design of the global information society and for a democratic proceeding, the public should be fully involved in policy-making. Representatives from public interest communities (usee organizations) and social and legal scientists, who can assess and consider the social and legal impacts adequately, especially should participate in the design of the information society. Some minimal requirements for a socially and privacy acceptable design and use of the information infrastructure are as follows (see also CPSR 1993; Fischer-Hübner and Schier, 1996):

- Democratic participation of the public in the design and development of the information infrastructure should be encouraged.
- Social and legal impacts of different initiatives should be assessed in advance in cooperation with representatives from usees' organizations and from public interest communities as well as in cooperation with social and legal scientists. Initiatives should be carefully tested in pilot projects for aspects of social acceptability. Initiatives with non-acceptable risks to privacy and/or society should not be implemented.

- Social impacts have to be considered and initiatives should be periodically reviewed to ensure that they continue to serve public interests.
- Internationally obligatory privacy regulations besides the EU directive are needed. These regulations should guarantee basic privacy principles for an adequate protection of privacy in the global information society.
- Security and privacy issues have to be considered from the beginning and should be integrated into the system design. Privacy enhancing technologies have to be implemented if possible.
- High security standards and network reliability should be required.
- Users should be permitted to use strong cryptography to protect communication.

These minimal requirements must be considered, and enforced, from the beginning and throughout the design of the information society.

REFERENCES

(Bangemann, 1994) Europe and the global information society, Recommendations to the European Council, Brussels, 26 May 1994 (Bangemann report), http://www.earn.net/EC/bangemann.html

(Budapest Draft, 1996) International Working Group on Data Protection in Telecommunications, Data Protection on the Internet, Report and Guidance (Budapest Draft), May 1996.

(Canada, 1995) Connection Community Content: The Challenge of the Information Highway, Final Report of the Information Highway Advisory Council, September 1995.

(Chaum, 1985) D. Chaum, Security without Identification: Transaction Systems to Make Big Brother Obsolete, *Communications of the ACM*, **28** (10). 1985, pp.1030-1044.

(Chaum, 1990) D.Chaum, Achieving Electronic Privacy, *Scientific American*, August 1992, pp.76-81.

(Clinton, 1993) Clinton/Gore, The National Information Infrastructure: Agenda for Action, 1993.

(CPSR, 1993) Computer Professionals for Social Responsibilities: Serving the Community: A Public-Interest Vision of the Nation Information Infrastructure, *The CPSR Newsletter,* Winter 1994.

(DMR, 1994) Ministry of Research and Information Technology, Denmark, INFO-Society 2000, November 1994.

(EU Directive, 1995) Directive 95/46/EC of the European Parliament and of the Council of 24 October 1995 on the protection of individuals with regard to the processing of personal data and on the free movement of such data.

(Fischer-Hübner, 1994) S. Fischer-Hübner, Towards a Privacy-Friendly Design and Use of IT-Security Mechanisms, *Proceedings of the 17th National Computer Security Conference*, Baltimore, October 1994.

(Fischer-Hübner, and Schier, 1996) S. Fischer-Hübner and K.Schier, Der Weg in die Informationsgesellschaft - Eine Gefahr fur den Datenschutz, in: Britta Schinzel (Ed.): *Schnittstellen*, Vieweg-Verlag, 1996 (in German).

(Greenleaf, 1995) G. Greenleaf, The 1995 EU Directive on Data Protection - An Overview, *The International Privacy Bulletin*, published by Privacy International, **3** (2), April-June 1995.

(Holvast, 1993) J. Holvast, Vulnerability and Privacy: Are We on the Way to a Risk-Free Society?, in: J.Berleur *et al.* (Ed.): *Facing the Challenge of Risk and Vulnerability in an Information Society*, Proceedings of the IFIP-WG9.2 Conference, Namur May 20-22, 1993, Elsevier Science Publishers B.V. (North-Holland), 1993.

(IITF, 1995) Information Infrastructure Task Force - Privacy Working Group: Privacy and the National Information Infrastructure: Principles for Providing and Using Personal Information, Final Version, June 1995.

(Japan, 1994) Ministry of International Trade and Industry (MITI), Programme for Advanced Information Infrastructure, May 1994.

(Koch, 1995) F. Koch, European Data Protection - Against the Internet?, *Privacy International Conference on Advanced Surveillance Technologies*, Copenhagen, September 1995.

(Lundheim and Sindre, 1993) R. Lundheim and G. Sindre, Privacy and Computing: a Cultural Perspective, in: R. Sizer *et al.* (ed.): *Security and control of Information Technology in Society*, IFIP WG 9.6 Working Conference, St.Petersburg, 1993, Elsevier Science Publishers.

(Madsen, 1992) W. Madsen, *Handbook of Personal Data Protection*, Stockton Press, 1992.

(Madsen, 1995) W. Madsen, Securing Access and Privacy on the Internet, in: *Proceedings of the COMPSEC-Conference*, London, October 1995, Elsevier Science Publishers.

(Registratiekamer, 1995) Registratiekamer, Privacy-Enhancing Technologies: The Path to Anonymity, Volume II, Achtergrondstudies en Verkenningen 5B, Rijswijk, August 1995.

(Registratiekamer/IP, 1995) Registratiekamer, the Netherlands and Information and Privacy Commissioner/ Ontario, Canada, Privacy-Enhancing Technologies: The Path to Anonymity, Volume I, Achtergrondstudies en Verkenningen 5A, August 1995.

(Rosenberg, 1992) R. Rosenberg, *The Social Impact of Computers*, Academic Press, 1992.

(Singapore, 1991) National Computer Board (NCB)/ Singapore, IT2000 - A Vision of an Intelligent Island, August 1991.

(Westin, 1967] A. Westin, *Privacy and Freedom*, New York, 1967.

The politics of privacy on the global information highway

Richard S. Rosenberg
Department of Computer Science, University of British Columbia, Vancouver, B.C. Canada, V6T 1Z4
Phone: +1 604 822 4142; Fax: +1 604 822 5485
Email: rosen@cs.ubc.ca

Abstract

In this paper, we will explore a number of political issues associated with the debate over privacy concerns on the information highway. Among the approaches that have been proposed for protecting personal privacy, especially in North America, the four main ones are government legislation, self-regulation, security, and education. In this paper, a position in support of government legislation for privacy protection is adopted and defended over voluntarism and self-regulation. Most of the sources used are reports, proposals, and statements, produced or commissioned by government agencies in Canada, the United States (US), and the European Community. Given that governments have political agendas that are shaped by a combination of forces, it is a necessary and important exercise to identify the items on these agendas and to evaluate their relative strengths in order to anticipate the likelihood that personal privacy will be adequately protected in the future. Current privacy policies in Canada and the US are similar and differ substantially from those of many European countries.

INTRODUCTION

> 'If you're worried about privacy in the emerging electronic age, you're not alone. I'm worried too ... The need for explicit policies and appropriate laws arises from the efficiency of information technology. As long as it was impractical for large amount *[sic]* of personal information to be collected and distributed, only modest regulation of privacy was needed. But once gathering and sharing information became easy, the need for explicit guidelines will be evident' (Gates, 1995).

An Ethical Global Information Society J. Berleur & D. Whitehouse (Eds.)

It will be assumed that the term privacy is reasonably well understood, although considerable debate exists about an acceptable working definition. The following definitions are useful for the present purposes:

> Privacy is the claim of individuals, groups or institutions to determine for themselves when, how and to what extent information about them is communicated to others (Westin 1967, p. 7).
>
> Privacy refers to the social balance between an individual's right to keep information confidential and the societal benefit derived from sharing information, and how this balance is codified to give individuals the means to control personal information (*Information Security and Privacy in Network Environments*, 1994, Footnote 11, Chapter 1).

Note that both of these definitions refer to the ability and indeed the right (claim?) of individuals to control personal information. The growth of commercial activity on the Internet is creating vast amounts of such information.

The technological assault on personal privacy continues to accelerate on many fronts. Whether it is the video camera monitoring virtually every banking activity as well as other financial transactions or indeed ubiquitous closed circuit systems in public squares or the increasing use of smart cards that capture enormous amounts of transactional information, virtually every action in the marketplace adds to the growing databases of personal information. On the horizon are smart cards with microchips that can store such information and much more in a distributed fashion. For network *aficionados* there are web browsers that download information to most web sites visited. Microsoft's Windows 95 has the facility to scan a user's system to determine the kinds of application programs present and then to transmit this information when the Microsoft network is accessed, unless the user actively declines to participate. Commercial networks such as America Online and Prodigy monitor the activities of their clients to make sure that certain questionable words are not being used in chat rooms, where individuals can discuss arbitrary topics in a closed environment. This list could easily be extended.

In what follows, the policies of the governments in the US and Canada will be compared with the policies adopted in the European Community. Current privacy policies in both of these countries are generally similar, with certain important differences. However, they both differ substantially from those of many European countries. These differences and similarities will be explored later as well as the social and political implications. As a preview of the choices that could be made with respect to privacy concerns, consider the following list provided in a discussion paper (*Privacy and the Canadian Information Highway*, 1994) released early in October 1994 by the Information Highway Advisory Council (IHAC) in Canada, a government appointed body: legislation and regulation, voluntary codes and standards, technological solutions, and consumer education. (See Appendix A for more detail.) In one way or another, these four approaches, individually or in concert, underlie the range of discourse in North America. Of course, the European Community has decided that the first approach is the appropriate way to proceed and has done so by virtue of the Privacy Directive adopted in June 1995, to become effective in 1998.

Some threats to privacy

One fairly insidious example, on the Internet, is the use of cookies or 'client-side persistent information' by Netscape's browser as well as Microsoft's Internet Explorer. These browsers gather information about your shopping habits and make it available for subsequent perusal by downloading it without your knowledge onto your hard drive. Of course the official Netscape line is that, 'cookies are beneficial to the Web ... shopping done via the Web could be gradually gathered in the cookies file, and then paid for (as if at a supermarket checkout) when the user enters the appropriate page. The concept can also be used to create a permanently customized view of a site - if you regularly have specific needs from a search engine, for example' (*Netscape's Cookies Crumble*, 1996). There is more, 'a Cookie program can be built to track the user's every move while connected to a particular server. This information can then be fed into a database to keep statistics on site usage so Webmasters can tailor a site to a particular user's interests ... Combine Cookie with JavaScript and a site's administrator could launch a very effective direct mail campaign without ever having asked the user for permission ... In more malevolent hands, these new tools can do far worse. For example, a Webmaster could pretend to be a particular site in order to retrieve a user's Cookie data without authorization. "If you use a server that does not encrypt its information, there is a real problem."' (Yang, 1996).

InfoSeek, a web search engine, plans to track information stored in users' cookies files to figure out where on the web they have been and anticipate what information they want. The feature will also help the company sell advertisements at a premium by letting it identify users to advertisers. 'If you type in "chicken stock", it knows you're not talking about gumbo because you've been searching through financial sites' (Fogarty, 1996). The service will also target surfers with advertising tailored to their interests (Note 1).

In October 1996, three US senators were so concerned by the gathering of personal information in a typical commercial transaction that they wrote to the Federal Trade Commission, requesting it to, 'conduct a study of possible violations of consumer privacy rights by companies that operate computer data bases. We have received calls and letters from constituents who are greatly disturbed about the compilation, sale, and usage of these data-bases. They, as well as consumers in general, are concerned about the potential intrusion upon, and violation of, individual privacy rights. There also is concern about the potential abusive and unlawful usage of the data' (Letter from Senators Bryan, Pressler, and Hollings, 1996). More specifically, they asked for the probe to include the following questions and issues:

1. Is the non-consensual compilation, sale, and usage of databases a violation of private citizens' civil rights?
2. Are the databases subject to unlawful usage? Do they create an undue potential for fraud on consumers?
3. Are the compilation, sale and usage of consumers' personal data consistent with the Fair Credit Reporting Act and federal telemarketing regulations?
4. Are there ways consumers can prevent database service companies from including their personal background information in commercial databases absent from their content?

There is reason to be concerned, and the question to be addressed next is how have various nations responded to the ongoing attacks on personal privacy.

PRIVACY LEGISLATION OR LACK THEREOF

United States

The constitutional protection of privacy in the US has been much debated with legal opinion divided as to the degree to which privacy represents a fundamental right. Surely nothing exists as explicitly as the constitutional guarantee of freedom of expression (The First Amendment of the Bill of Rights), itself a topic of endless and ongoing concern. In the case, Griswold v. Connecticut (381 U.S. 479, 484 1965), Supreme Court Justice William O. Douglas described 'zones of privacy' that are protected by the Bill of Rights (as quoted in Blackman 1993, p. 439):

> 'The right of association contained in the penumbra of the First Amendment is [a zone of privacy]. The Third Amendment in its prohibition against the quartering of soldiers "in any house" in time of peace without the consent of the owner is another facet of that privacy. The Fourth Amendment explicitly affirms the right of the people to be secure in their persons, houses, papers, and effects, against unreasonable searches and seizures. The Fifth Amendment in its Self-Incrimination Clause enables the citizen to create a zone of privacy which the government may not force him to surrender to his detriment. The Ninth Amendment provides: The enumeration in the Constitution of certain rights shall not be construed to deny or disparage others retained by the people.'

Thus, if it can be established that threats to privacy do exist, it is incumbent on the government to take appropriate steps to deal with such threats and included in these steps may be legislation, as was the case with the Fair Credit Reporting Act of 1970, the Privacy Act of 1974, and the Electronic Communications Privacy Act of 1986, among others. Indeed as Blackman (1993, p. 446) argues, 'Congress has recognized the need for and demonstrated a desire to protect personal privacy and commercial access to information, but has thus far failed to enact legislation that accomplishes both purposes in a comprehensive, effective manner. Satisfaction of Congress' intentions requires *a law that establishes a privacy standard for all industries to follow, and a mechanism to ensure its enforcement*' [emphasis added]. However, neither Congress nor the President has shown any interest in enacting legislation to protect personal privacy.

Canada

Canada is similar to the US in that there is no federal government legislation that applies comprehensively to the private sector. The Canadian Privacy Act applies only to the activities of the federal government, although in distinction to the US Privacy Act there is a federal Privacy Commissioner (as well as a Freedom of Information Commissioner). However, this position has limited powers and serves primarily as a mediator, a facilitator, and an early warning monitor. At the provincial level, there exists a wide diversity of approaches, with some provinces having limited privacy legislation while others, especially Quebec, have much more power. Indeed, Quebec is the only jurisdiction in North America whose privacy law applies to both the public and private sectors and, in this regard, is comparable to many of the laws that exist in western Europe. Note that, in the Canadian political system, federal responsibility is limited in many areas, and serious jurisdictional barriers would prevent general acceptance of federal sovereignty in the privacy area. Nevertheless, the Quebec Privacy Law (Quebec Act respecting the protection of personal information, 1993) could provide a model for appropriate legislation. (See Appendix B for more detail.)

In recognition of the importance of the Internet and the anticipated information highway, the Canadian government appointed the Information Highway Advisory Council (IHAC) in 1994 to explore a wide variety of social, political, commercial, and legal issues in order to provide necessary advice for future policies. IHAC's membership reflected many diverse interests and it produced a number of studies in such areas as intellectual property rights, access, content, education, and of course privacy, as mentioned above, prior to a final report issued in September 1995 (*Connection, Community, Content*, 1995) that contained a number of recommendations with respect to the protection of privacy on the information highway. Although the information highway is still in the future the current technological approximation, the Internet provides some of the features that are expected to make it so exciting.

Recall the four approaches presented at the outset of this paper to serve as a concise set of possibilities for dealing with privacy problems on the information highway. In brief, they are legislation and regulation, voluntary codes and standards, technological solutions, and consumer education. Let me argue that these approaches are not alternatives and their presentation tends to suggest, for example, that consumer education, as well as 'a fundamental need to educate business about the need for more enlightened approaches to the handling of personal data', will help alleviate major impending challenges to personal privacy. This statement is either naive or disingenuous. To support this position as well as the voluntary codes and standards approach would require evidence that historical examples exist in which companies have voluntarily curtailed certain activities, thereby foregoing profits in order to take the ethical high ground. The general tone of the argument in favour of voluntarism is that privacy issues are complex, government jurisdiction is a problem, the private sector is responsible, consumers need to be educated, and all in all the Canadian government is very concerned.

However, in its final report (*Connection, Community, Content*, 1995), after referring to the usefulness of voluntary codes and standards, the IHAC came down very strongly on the side of legislation, or in its own words, 'The Council believes strongly that there should be national legislation (Rec. 10.2) to establish fair information practices on the Information Highway' (p. 50). It further urges the government to continue to cooperate with the Canadian Standards Association and other organizations to 'implement the code (*Model Code for the Protection of Personal Information,* 1995) and develop effective independent oversight and enforcement mechanisms' (Rec. 10.1 and 10.2). In the end, IHAC has come to the conclusion that government legislation is necessary and will work, given an extensive consultation process with the private sector and consumer groups. So, the operating procedure that has emerged and that might also be effective in the US context is a preliminary period of industry consultation to develop an acceptable privacy code that is comprehensive and effective, followed by national legislation with regulatory, oversight, and enforcement teeth, based on this code.

Europe

Given that the US is a major world trader and enmeshed in international trading agreements, the issue of data protection of transborder data flows (TBDF) is of prime importance. The Basic Principles of National Application of the Organization for Economic Cooperation and Development (OECD) have influenced the privacy guidelines of many countries (Clarke 1989). However, with the prospect of a global information infrastructure (GII) on the horizon, it will be necessary to establish privacy principles that have worldwide application. Members of the G7, the world's leading industrial countries, met in Brussels between February 24 and 26, 1995, to discuss a host of issues related to the GII. Much of the meeting was devoted to technical issues, but social issues including privacy and data protection were also on the agenda.

Prior to the meeting, the US government produced a position paper that included the following with respect to privacy concerns (*The Global Information Infrastructure: Agenda For Cooperation,* 1995):

> The United States and other countries around the world are re-examining existing privacy policies to ensure that they apply comprehensively to the transfer of personal data over global networks. A balanced privacy policy - preserving the individual's right to privacy while maintaining the free flow of information across national borders - is important to the development of global networks and services. Working together, nations should ensure that the transport of personal data adequately takes into account the following agreed-upon international privacy principles:
>
> - Personal data should be collected only for specified, legitimate purposes;
> - The dissemination, sharing, and reuse of information should be compatible with the purposes for which it was originally collected;
> - Personal data should be accurate, relevant, and up-to-date;
> - Individuals should be informed how personal data will be used and should be allowed to examine and correct this information; and
> - Transmission of personal data should not be unduly restricted or subject to burdensome authorization procedures.

The first four points are clearly taken from the US Code for Fair Information Practices, currently being updated after some twenty years, to reflect the needs of a much more advanced information society. (See Appendix C.) The last point is directed towards perceived attempts by Europe, in the form of OECD directives subsequently amended by the European Parliament, to strengthen the privacy requirements for TBDF.

The 1992 Privacy Directive, as amended, was adopted by the European Community in June 1995. The significant part of this Directive (Directive 95/EC, 1995) for the present purposes is Chapter IV, Transfer of Personal Data to Third Countries, Article 25, Principles, which reads in part:

> 1. Member States shall provide that the transfer to a third country of personal data which are undergoing processing or are intended for processing after transfer may take place only if, without prejudice to compliance with the

national provisions adopted pursuant to the other provisions of this Directive, the third country in question ensures an adequate level of protection.

2. The adequacy of the level of protection afforded by a third country shall be assessed in the light of all the circumstances surrounding a data transfer operation or set of data transfer operations; particular consideration shall be given to the nature of the data, the purpose and duration of the proposed processing operation or operations, the country of origin and country of final destination, the rules of law, both general and sectoral, in force in the third country in question and the professional rules and security measures which are complied with in those countries.

The simple version of the first point is that no personal data can be transferred, from any member state of the Economic Community, to a third country unless that country's level of protection is adequate, where adequate means equivalent to that offered in the Economic Community. Since there are no national privacy laws for the private sector in existence in North America, it would seem to be the case that a confrontation is looming, but the Directive allows the possibility that adequate 'professional rules and security measures' may be sufficient or that satisfactorily agreed upon procedures, that could be generalized, may do as well. Thus, it is possible that the Privacy Directive may serve to spur the development of federal privacy laws or, what is more likely, special arrangements will be made between US companies and the Economic Community for the protection of personal information. In the present US political climate, there appears to be little inclination to enact comprehensive privacy legislation.

Possible North American responses to the privacy directive

The question now looms as to what impact it will have on traditional modes of privacy protection in the US and Canada and how it will influence the role of government. For probably no other reason would data protection legislation be enacted in the US today, and such a demand by the Economic Community may yet fail to have this effect, given a universal reluctance for US legislators to be seen as bowing to foreign demands. Although the US could possibly take a go-it-alone stance, such an option is probably not available to Canada. It is also possible that the acceptance by US industries of a voluntary code that meets the requirements of the European Privacy Directive may satisfy the European Community. Where this leaves the individual is up for debate, given that individual companies or industries will be the final arbiters in privacy disputes. If nothing else, however, the Privacy Directive will serve to isolate the US and focus on the inadequacies of legitimate protection of personal privacy in the private sector.

In Canada, the federal government has announced that it will move towards privacy legislation based on the Model Code for the Protection of Personal Information of the Canadian Standards Association (*Model Code for the Protection of Personal Information*, 1995). Although this code was expected to be voluntarily adopted by Canadian businesses, it requires legislative teeth to meet the standards of the European Directive. In its response to the privacy recommendations contained in the Final Report of the Information Highway Advisory Council, the Canadian government noted that, 'As a means of encouraging business and consumer confidence in the Information Highway, the ministers of Industry and Justice, after consultation with the provinces and stakeholders, will bring forward proposals for a legislative framework governing the protection of personal data in the private sector' (*Building the Information Society*, 1996, p. 25). Canadian Justice Minister, Alan Rock, has promised that such legislation will be in place by the year 2,000.

VOLUNTARISM AS A SOLUTION

United States

The Information Infrastructure Task Force (IITF) Working Group on Privacy notes that the National Information Infrastructure (NII), the Clinton Administration's term for the information highway will, by its very nature, raise the privacy stakes beyond anything that has so far existed and therefore require more comprehensive privacy principles. Consider the following comments (*Privacy and the National Information Infrastructure,* 1995):

6. While guidance to government agencies can be found in existing laws and regulations, and guidance to private organizations exists in principles and practices, these need to be adapted to accommodate the evolving information environment. This changing environment presents new concerns:

(a) No longer do governments alone obtain and use large amounts of personal information; the private sector now rivals the government in obtaining and using personal information. New principles would thus be incomplete unless they applied to both the governmental and private sectors.

(b) The NII promises true interactivity. Individuals will become active participants who, by using the NII, will create volumes of data containing the content of communications as well as transactional data.

(c) The transport vehicles for personal information - the networks - are vulnerable to abuse; thus, the security of the network itself is critical to the NII's future success.

Thus, although a set of updated privacy principles for the Information Highway is the goal of this report, the working group argues that they should not be implemented as legislation. In the report, it is stated that the purpose of these principles is to provide a 'guide' for any groups, institutions, or governments that need to design privacy regulations or laws but that these principles do not have 'the force of law'. This position is certainly consistent with the long-standing attitude of the US in opposition to broad and comprehensive privacy legislation and in favour of a piecemeal or sectoral approach, often resulting in legislation enacted under crisis situations or in response to a wellspring of public indignation. Thus, the federal Privacy Act of 1974 seems to have been enacted as a result of the Watergate events with the basic intent to reassure the public that government would respect personal privacy only if specific legislation were in place. The Fair Credit Reporting Act (1970) can be seen as a response to public opinion concerned with the accuracy and misuse of credit records by credit bureaus, banks, insurance companies, and other institutions that depend on personal credit reports.

Such narrowly-based legislation is clearly at odds with the history of privacy legislation in western Europe. Countries such as Germany (then West Germany), Sweden, and the United Kingdom have established Data Protection boards to oversee and monitor any public or private institution that collects and uses personal information. Space does not permit additional discussions of the European approach but Flaherty (1989) and Bennett (1992) are excellent references. The following two paragraphs are quite revealing (*Privacy and the National Information Infrastructure*, 1995):

> 9. Moreover, the Principles are intended to be in accord with current international guidelines regarding the use of personal information and thus should support the ongoing development of the Global Information Infrastructure.
>
> 10. Finally, adherence to the Principles will cultivate the trust between individuals and information users so crucial to the successful evolution of the NII.

Paragraph 9 states that the Principles are 'intended to be in accord with current international guidelines ...' but given that they do not have the force of law it is not clear that a mix of voluntary guidelines will satisfy the countries of Europe that have adequate legislation in place. Paragraph 10 offers the plaintive hope that 'adherence to the Principles will cultivate the trust between individuals and information users ...' What evidence is there that voluntary codes work? How will individuals know which voluntary code is in effect and how its provisions differ or are similar to other voluntary codes? What recourse will they have if they feel that their privacy has been compromised? Must they depend upon the goodwill of the 'information user'?

In October 1995, the National Telecommunications and Information Administration (NTIA) issued a White Paper (*Privacy and the NII: Safeguarding Telecommunications-Related Personal Information,* 1995), by which it hoped:

> to contribute to the broader privacy debate by addressing the privacy issues related to a specific sector - the telecommunications sector. Specifically, this paper focuses on the privacy concerns associated with an individual's subscription to or use of a telecommunications or information service. The overall purpose of the paper is to provide an analysis of the state of privacy in the United States as it relates to existing and future communications services and to recommend a framework for safeguarding telecommunications-related personal information (TRPI).

Note that this paper is a product in part of the comments received as a result of the circulation of the February (and April) 1994 NTIA 'Inquiry' paper. Forty-six formal comments were received from 'industry, the press, academics, privacy advocates, and individuals ... supplemented by consultations with stakeholders in the privacy debate, feedback from experts, and independent research'.

It is noted that the 'United States currently has no omnibus privacy law that covers the private sector's acquisition, disclosure, and use of TRPI (telecommunications-related personal information)'. But, not surprisingly, its bottom line is not to recommend such legislation, at least not yet. Instead, the White Paper hopes for the following:

> As stated above, NTIA's proposed framework draws upon the IITF's Principles and has two fundamental elements - provider notice and customer

> consent. Under NTIA's proposed framework, each provider of telecommunications and information services would inform its customers about what TRPI it intends to collect and how that data will be used. A service provider would be free to use the information collected for the stated purposes once it has obtained consent from the relevant customer. Affirmative consent would be required with respect to sensitive personal information. Tacit customer consent would be sufficient to authorize the use of all other information.
>
> This approach, if embraced by industry, would allow service providers and their customers to establish the specific level of privacy protection offered in a marketplace transaction, *free from excessive government regulation*, so long as the minimum requirements of notice and consent are satisfied ... For these reasons, NTIA believes that it is in the private sector's interest to adopt the privacy framework outlined in this paper, *without waiting for formal government action* [emphasis added].

Formal government involvement in the marketplace regulation of privacy via appropriate legislation is not on the cards, even though western Europe, Canada, and other countries have chosen this strategy. The NTIA paper recommends a modified contractual approach to dealing with privacy concerns. Under such an approach, 'companies would inform their customers about what sorts of personal information the firms intend to collect and the uses to which that information would be put. Consumers could then either accept a company's 'offer', or reject it and shop around for a better deal'. The modified contractual approach, favoured by NTIA, 'allows businesses and consumers to reach agreements concerning the collection, use, and dissemination of TRPI, subject to two fundamental requirements, provider notice and customer consent. Our recommended approach should adequately protect individuals' legitimate privacy interests without excessive government intervention in the marketplace'. Finally to reinforce its view, NTIA offers both the carrot and the stick. It recommends that the modified contractual framework be grounded in the 'principles of fair information practices released by the IITF's Privacy Working Group in June 1995'. NTIA expects the private sector to implement this framework voluntarily but '(i)f such private sector action is not forthcoming, however, that framework can and should form the basis for government-mandated privacy regulations or standards'.

Not surprisingly, the private sector has responded with the formation of something called eTRUST (eTRUST Press Release, 1996):

> The Electronic Frontier Foundation (EFF) and CommerceNet are partnering to implement eTRUST, a global initiative for establishing consumer trust and confidence in electronic transactions. Tapping the combined strength of industry and public interests, eTRUST is designed to address the issues of consumer trust in the Internet marketplace.
>
> eTRUST will build an integrated logo system which consumers will associate with trust and confidence in electronic transactions. Though eTRUST will address privacy and security concerns initially, the eTRUST brand will grow to encompass a variety of other consumer interests. A major component of eTRUST will be an awareness and education program for consumers and businesses.

The current membership is not large, but with such powerful members as Coopers & Lybrand, KPMG Peat Marwick, Firefly, and CommerceNet, it may grow. How this approach will play out in the context of the European Privacy Directive remains to be seen. Will a sophisticated public relations campaign convince the average uninformed consumer that all is well? If large companies launch such campaigns to convince the public that a particular logo guarantees privacy protection, how will the average person be expected to maintain a realistic level of scepticism and concern?

SUMMARY AND CONCLUSIONS

Early in this paper, four possible approaches were suggested: legislation and regulation, voluntary codes and standards, technological solutions, and consumer education. Most of the present effort have been to explore the legislative option and indeed to advocate its adoption as a necessary step in protecting individual privacy. By default, therefore, voluntary codes are seen at best as a temporary precursor to legislation. This perspective is supported in Canada and can be seen as a possible strategy in the US if the private sector is not aggressive in developing, employing, and enforcing adequate privacy codes. The NTIA October 1995 White Paper, although very reluctant to recommend government intervention does threaten it if industry is recalcitrant in vigorously pursuing a comprehensive and effective privacy policy. North America has taken a much more relaxed view than Europe in the development of comprehensive legislation to ensure that, in the OECD terminology, data subjects have adequate safeguards in place with respect to the collection, storage, processing, transmission, and use of personal data by government and companies alike.

To preserve anonymity and protect the privacy of users, the responsibility cannot just be left to the users themselves or to the companies that serve them. In the former case, it is too difficult and, in the latter, too much of a conflict of interest. North American governments can follow the lead of European countries and both the spirit and letter of the current OECD directive, and pass appropriate legislation to protect the privacy of their citizens in a meaningful manner. It is not necessary to threaten public well-being with government intrusiveness as in the Clipper Chip chronicles. The creation, under effective legislation, of arm's length data protection boards or commissions to monitor the establishment and operation of all government agencies and companies that collect, process, and use personal information, is the necessary action to be taken to safeguard the increasing amounts of personal data being gathered.

Enormous profits are on the horizon if the realization of the information highway matches the projections of its supporters. Surely the stakes are high enough and the rewards sufficiently great to take the initiative in drawing up appropriate comprehensive privacy legislation. Surely, we have learned that, unless adequate protections are built in from the start, they are difficult to achieve after the fact. It remains for an informed public to demand that its privacy is preserved given the relentlessness of contemporary attacks. It is the responsibility of consumer and civil liberties groups to focus a spotlight on the privacy practices of government as well as the private sector and to articulate the options currently available to the US as well as those in place elsewhere. Historically, the public has been uninformed, an untenable situation in the age of the information highway.

NOTES

1. The Netscape Navigator 3.0 permits a setting under the Options menu and the Network Preferences submenu Protocols that shows an alert when a request is made to accept a cookie or send a cookie. If this option is not set, cookies are automatically created and stored. This option is not advertised and thus most users have accepted many cookies without any advance knowledge. What is also of interest is that if acceptance is refused, it is frequently asked for repeatedly until the web site is escaped. Thus many sites will not permit entrance if the cookie is not eventually accepted.

ACKNOWLEDGEMENT

The very helpful comments of the referees are gratefully acknowledged as is the financial support of the Natural Sciences and Engineering Research Council of Canada.

REFERENCES

Bennett, Colin. 1992. *Regulating Privacy: Data Protection and Public Policy in Europe and the United States. Ithaca*, NY: Cornell University Press.

Blackman, Joshua D. November, 1993. A Proposal for Federal Legislation Protecting Informational Privacy Across the Private Sector. *Santa Clara Computer and High Technology Law Journal*, (9:2), pp. 431 - 468.

Building the Information Society: Moving Canada into the 21st Century. 1996, May. Industry Canada. Accessible from the Web site with URL: <http://strategis.ic.gc.ca/cgi-bin/dec/wwwfetch?/sgml/ih01015e_pr702.sgml>.

Connection, Community, Content: The Challenge of the Information Highway. Final Report of the Information Highway Advisory Council. 1995, September. Industry Canada. Accessible from the Web site with URL: <http://strategis.ic.gc.ca/cgi-bin/dec/wwwfetch?/sgml/ih01015e_pr702.sgml>.

Clarke, Roger. 1989. The OECD Data Protection Guidelines: A Template for Evaluating Information Privacy Law and Proposals for Information Privacy Law. Australian National University Unpublished Working Paper of 1989. © Australian National University, 1987, 1988, 1989.

Directive 95/EC. June 1995. Directive of the European Parliament and of the Council on the Protection of Individuals With Regard to the Processing of Personal Data And on the Free Movement of Such Data. Accessed from the Web page with URL: <http://www2.echo.lu/legal/en/dataprot/directiv/directiv.ht ml> on May 15, 1996.

eTRUST Press Release: CommerceNet and Electronic Frontier Foundation Partner to Implement eTRUST. October 16, 1996. Accessed from the Web page with URL: <http://www.etrust.org/07press.html> on November 16, 1996.

Flaherty, David. 1989. *Protecting Privacy in Surveillance Societies: The Federal Republic of Germany, Sweden, France, Canada, and the United States*. Chapel Hill, North Carolina: The University of North Carolina Press.

Fogarty, Kevin. Infoseek to track cookies information, *Computerworld*, October 4, 1996. Accessed at the Web page with URL: <http://www.computerworld.com/news/infoseek.html> on October 21, 1996.

Gates, Bill. Billionaire Bytes, *The Vancouver Sun*, September 14, 1995, D 4.

The Global Information Infrastructure: Agenda For Cooperation. 1995, February. Information Infrastructure Task Force. Available on the NII Virtual Library, WWW site with URL: <http://iitf.doc.gov>.

Information Security and Privacy in Network Environments. 1994, September 15. U.S. Congress, Office of Technology Assessment, Washington, DC: U.S. Government Printing Office. Also available on Web page with URL: <http://www.ota.nap.edu/pdf/data/1994/9416.PDF>.

Letter from Senators Bryan, Pressler, and Hollings. October 8, 1996. Accessed from the Web page with URL: <http://www.epic.org/privacy/databases/ftc_databases. html> on October 21, 1996.

Model Code for the Protection of Personal Information. August, 1995. Final Draft. CSA Technical Committee on Privacy, Canadian Standards Association, CAN/CSA-Q830-1995. Available at the Web site with URL: <http://www.csa.ca/>.

Netscape's Cookies Crumble. 1996, April. Australian Personal Computer Online - News. Accessed from the Web page with URL: <http://www.com.au/apc/9604/thenet/onnews.html> on May 13, 1996.

Privacy and the Canadian Information Highway. 1994, October. Communications Development and Planning Branch, Spectrum, Information Technologies and Telecommunications Sector, Industry Canada. Also available at the WWW site with URL: <http://info.ic.gc.ca/info-highway/ih.html>.

Privacy and the NII: Safeguarding Telecommunications-Related Personal Information. October, 1995. NTIA, Office of Policy Analysis and Development, Washington, DC. Also available at Web page with URL: <gopher://www.ntia.doc.gov:70/HO/policy/privwhitepaper.html>

Privacy and the National Information Infrastructure: Principles for Providing and Using Personal Information. January 19, 1995. Information Infrastructure Task Force Working Group on Privacy. Available on IITF Web site with URL: <(http:// iitf.doc.gov>.

Quebec Act respecting the protection of personal information in the private sector. 1993, Bill 68 (1993, chapter 17), National Assembly of Quebec, Second Session, Thirty Fourth Legislature.

Westin, Alan. 1967. *Privacy and Information.* Atheneum: New York.

Yang, John, a research assistant in the geology department at Florida International University as quoted in James Staten, Netscape Tricks Raise Security Concerns, *MacWeek,* March 13, 1996. Accessed from the Web page with URL: <http://www.zdnet.com/macweek/mw_1011/gw_net_tricks.html> on May 13, 1996.

Appendix A

Four Approaches to Privacy Protection in Canada on the Information Highway:

Legislation and Regulation
Protection of the enormous information holdings of governments, including medical, welfare, tax, immigration and police records, exists at the federal level and in the provinces of Quebec, Ontario, Saskatchewan, Alberta and British Columbia. The quality of coverage varies from jurisdiction to jurisdiction and, when information travels, it is not always clear which law applies.

Voluntary Codes and Standards
Voluntary codes have been the preferred approach of Canadian business and industry associations. This approach allows for flexibility in application, so that different industries can tailor their data protection schemes to the needs of their customers, the regulatory environment in which they operate and the demands of the marketplace.

Technological Solutions
Another approach to privacy protection is to use technology to safeguard personal data. Traditionally, technology has been exploited to increase the amount of information gathered, and hence has been feared rather than welcomed by privacy activists. But technology itself is neutral, and can be used to enhance privacy as well as threaten it. Technologies can be designed so that the 'default setting' is on zero information collection.

Consumer Education

There is a fundamental need to educate businesses about the need for more enlightened approaches to the handling of personal data, and to raise the awareness of consumers about how to protect themselves. Consumers need information and education about their rights, about the value of their personal information, about the risks to their privacy that new technologies can bring, and about what they can do to retain privacy.

Appendix B

In the explanatory notes that precede the Quebec Act respecting the protection of personal information, the following relevant information appears:

> The object of this bill is to establish special rules regarding the personal information on others that is collected, held, used or communicated to third persons in the course of operating an enterprise in the private sector and the rights and obligations resulting from the provisions of the Civil Code of Quebec that deal with the protection of personal information.
>
> Under the bill, a person collecting personal information for the purpose of establishing a file on another person or entering information in such a file can collect only information that is necessary to attain the object of the file ...
>
> Persons operating an enterprise are required by the bill to ensure that any personal information on others that they hold or use remains confidential ...
>
> ...
>
> The 'Commission d'accès à l'information', on its own initiative or following a complaint from an interested person, will have the power to inquire into, or entrust another person with inquiring into, any matter relating to the protection of personal information and the methods used by a person operating an enterprise and collects, hold or uses personal information or communicates it to third persons ...
>
> ...
>
> Lastly, the bill prescribes penal sanctions and ensures concordance of its provisions with the legislation currently in force.

Appendix C

Fundamental Principles of Fair Information Practice*:

- There must be no personal-data record-keeping systems whose very existence is secret.
- There must be a way for an individual to find out what information about him is in a record and how it is used.
- There must be a way for an individual to prevent information about him obtained for one purpose from being used or made available for other purposes without his consent.
- There must be a way for an individual to correct or amend a record of identifiable information about him.
- Any organization creating, maintaining, using, or disseminating records of identifiable personal data must ensure the reliability of the data for their intended use and must take reasonable precautions to prevent misuse of the data.

**Records, Computers, and the Rights of Citizens.* Report of the Secretary's Advisory Committee on Automated Personal Data Systems, US Department of Health, Education and Welfare. Cambridge, MA: The Massachusetts Institute of Technology, 1973, p. 41.

25

Growing old in an information society

Marc van Lieshout, Thea Weijers** and René van Rijsselt****
** Rathenau Instituut, P.O. 85525, NL-2508 CE The Hague*
Phone: +31 70 3421501; Fax: +31 70 3633488
Email: m.vanlieshout@Rathenau.KNAW.nl
or: marcvl@cs.kun.nl
*** TNO-STB, P.O. 541, NL-7300 AM Apeldoorn*
Phone: +31 55 5493497; Fax: +31 55 5421458
Email: T.Weijers@stb.tno.nl
**** Department of Sociology and Social Gerontology, Free University, De Boelelaan 1081C, NL-1081 HV Amsterdam*
Phone: +31 20 4446784; Fax: +31 20 4446810
Email: RJT.v_Rijsselt@scw.vu.nl

Abstract

The societal implications of electronic highways receive more attention than some years ago. Still, it is not sure whether the debate that has started contains more than cheap rhetoric. The Dutch Rathenau Institute has initiated a project to research the images and perspectives that important stakeholders have about a very specific group on the electronic highways: elderly people. The project was aimed at providing insights into the position of elderly people in the information society: are they included or excluded? In this paper, attention is focused on the role and position of elderly people as citizens: negotiating with public authorities, having rights and fulfilling obligations by means of information and communication technologies. It is argued that elderly people might need specific attention when it comes to the question whether they are 'in' or 'out'. The variety in elderly people prohibits too many broad statements, though some remarks can be made concerning their shared history, educational style, and age.

An Ethical Global Information Society J. Berleur & D. Whitehouse (Eds.)

INTRODUCTION

In the Netherlands, the Rathenau Institute (the successor of the former Dutch Organization for Technology Assessment – NOTA) initiated in 1996 a project dedicated to the question whether the pronounced concerns about the division between the 'Information Rich' and the 'Information Poor' entail more than the rhetoric they seem to be based on. A number of questions were phrased. What precisely are the arguments underlying the concerns? To what kind of visions, perspectives or expectations do they refer? Is there reason to believe that the visions are shared among relevant actors? Are the actors who are formulating the visions in which exclusion processes are present, able to articulate where these processes stem from? The project was meant to offer a reflection on the problem of exclusion that – according to some – might follow the widespread introduction of electronic highways. In that sense, the project was an assessment. It was, however, not a traditional Technology Assessment (TA). In line with the mission statement of the Rathenau Institute the traditional TA-approach has been exchanged for a broader approach that takes socio-cultural changes as a starting point, assuming that technological developments are embedded in socio-cultural practices.

In this paper, we will discuss the results of this project. We will particularly tackle the question of how the position of elderly people as citizens within the information society may change due to the informatization of society. We will start with a brief sketch of the motivation for the project and the choice of the category of elderly people. Then, a brief description of the theoretical model we used will be presented. The core of the article will be the presentation of our findings with respect to the elderly citizen in the information society. We will conclude with a discussion of the main results.

SPOTLIGHT ON ...

In tackling the question of whether processes of social exclusion are part of the contemporary diffusion of electronic highways, the focus must be oriented towards a specific demographic category. Posing the question too broadly leads to superfluous answers on non-existing problems. The change processes that are experienced in modern – western – societies lead to different problems and to different problem definitions for different social categories. Socio-economic stratifications might be a starting point to delineate groups of interest. With respect to the electronic highways it is commonplace to propose that only White Higher educated Young Male People (WHYMP) profit from the digital revolution. Women, lower educated people, the elderly, and foreigners or immigrants experience difficulties in mastering the technology and its applications. This, however, is an approach that takes the Internet and its early adopters as representative of the electronic highways and their riders. Though the Internet today undoubtedly determines many of the popular images about what the information society will look like, it would be a mistake to take that perspective too seriously. We take the electronic highways (the Internet included) as a metaphor for the process of informatization of society. This informatization is, for the time being, the sum total of processes of socio-cultural change in which political, economical, juridical, social, and technological problems seem somehow to correlate to the gathering, processing, and distribution of information.

Taking this process of informatization as a starting point, the problems that specific categories of people may experience may be more encompassing than just the problem of knowing how to connect a personal computer to the Internet.

After a small survey, the Rathenau Institute decided to take elderly people as the focal group within the project. A number of arguments led to this choice.

The ageing of society is a well studied phenomenon. In the Netherlands, some 3.4 million people are aged 55 or older (from a total population of roughly 15 million). Of this group, two million are aged 65 or older. Dutch society is confronted with a double greying process: the absolute as well as the relative proportion of elderly people (aged 55 years or older) will increase dramatically in the decades to come, while there will also be an increase in people aged 80 years or more (most of the last category will be widowed women).

Elderly people together own many of the financial resources in society. In 1989, 7% of people aged 65 or older had personal financial resources of at least 100,000 ECUs (compared with an overall percentage of 4.7% of the population). This wealth, however, is unevenly distributed. Especially those elderly people above 80 years or more – most of them widowed women who together do not form a very big group – do not have much money to spend. Many households with only one person (usually a woman) have incomes that do not exceed social minimum standards (Timmermans, 1993, pp. 14-24; Timmermans, 1997, pp. 72). Terms such as the silver generation are used to denote the average wealth of today's older people. But, it should be noted that this silver generation will not exceed 25% of the total aged community, while another 50-60% will have very limited financial resources (Timmermans, 1997, pp. 76-77).

Another argument for taking elderly people as the main group to be studied is the fact that, while elderly people seem to have longer and better lives than a few decades ago, their societal role is still very restricted. The composition of elderly cohorts will drastically change in the years to come, hinting at a built-in conflict between the societal role they are assigned to and their needs and desires in this respect (the so-called 'structural lag'). As past participants in the democratization processes of the 1960s and 1970s, it is highly unlikely that the future elderly will accept a societal position at the margin. The beginnings of this transition are visible now. Elderly people organize political parties, they empower their representatives. In the last elections, two parties that presented themselves explicitly as political parties of elderly people were elected to parliament. The political pressure of elderly parties might increase in the years to come. The societal tension between the images and roles attributed to the elderly and the positions they want to have themselves, could be studied as an effect of ongoing changes due to the informatization of society.

A last argument is the fact that elderly people are faced with many, negative, stereotypes. It is said that they should be unable to pick up the latest technological developments and, even if they can, they are unwilling to do so. They experience physical problems that forbid them to remain active, they are unable to cope with the speed of contemporary life, etc. Many of these stereotypes lack any solid foundation. Still, they are widespread and are often used in documents and in policy-making.

RESEARCHING PERSPECTIVES - HOW TO APPROACH THE ELDERLY CITIZEN?

A research panel was formed that was willing to take responsibility for the project. The authors were – in different roles – part of the panel. A theoretical framework was developed that guided the empirical part of the project. The second step was the organization and collection of empirical findings. This was done in two subsequent phases: the first was the *diversification* phase, in which as many different perspectives as possible were collected; the second phase was aimed at realizing *convergence* among the formulated perspectives. Finally, a report was written that combines the theoretical model and the empirical findings.

In this section, we describe the theoretical model we used, the societal domains we studied, and the research method.

The theoretical model

The starting point of the model was its ability to identify forms and mechanisms of exclusion processes. Within the Department of Social Gerontology of the Free University of Amsterdam, sociological research dealing with the process of ageing is part of the usual activities of the research group. The model that forms the core of the department's activities looked to be very useful for our purposes (Onderzoekprogramma, 1995). Basic to the model is the level of *independency* an individual has in his or her living surroundings. This independency has three distinct features: the level of *self-determination*, the level of *self-care*, and the level of *societal participation*. The first relates to the ability to decide for oneself what to do and how to behave. The second relates to the ability to take care of oneself in daily situations (cooking, cleaning, washing, dressing, and the like). The third relates to the ability to participate in clubs, groups, political parties, public debates, and so on.

Processes of exclusions are defined as occurring as a result of the mismatch between pressure exerted on individuals through channels that link individuals with their surroundings and their individual *competencies*. The competencies are analytically split up into abilities, restrictions, and potentialities. Exclusion may be found or determined by a diminished self-determination, self-care, societal participation, or a combination of the three. It may be typified by the following four mechanisms: *don't have to*; *don't want to*; *are not able to*; *are not allowed to*.

Having presented the socio-gerontological basis of the study, we can now tackle the question of how informatization should be included in the model. The notions from socio-gerontology were mixed with notions from technology researchers such as those from the Organization for Applied Scientific Research, Centre for the Study of Technology Policy (TNO-STB). Processes of informatization will be found on two levels: first, as part of the outer spheres, as processes exerting influence on individuals in a variety of ways (organizational, economic, technological, etc.); second, as part of the individual's competencies, that is, the potentialities, restrictions, and aspirations of the individual. Informatization is a fluid concept. It relates to the introduction of networks in working situations, but also to the reorganization of activities due to the opportunities information and communication technologies (ICT) offer. Like all technologies, ICT has a hard and a soft component. The hard part refers to the artifacts, like computers and network infrastructures, but also to computer software and network protocols, i.e., the organization of the environment. The soft part refers to the knowledge and the skills that are needed to use the artifacts, i.e., the competencies of the individual. Informatization is a process in which ICT are used to rearrange and to redefine existing social structures and patterns by referring to the gathering, processing, and distribution of information.

Figure 1. Theoretical framework 'Exclusion of elderly people'

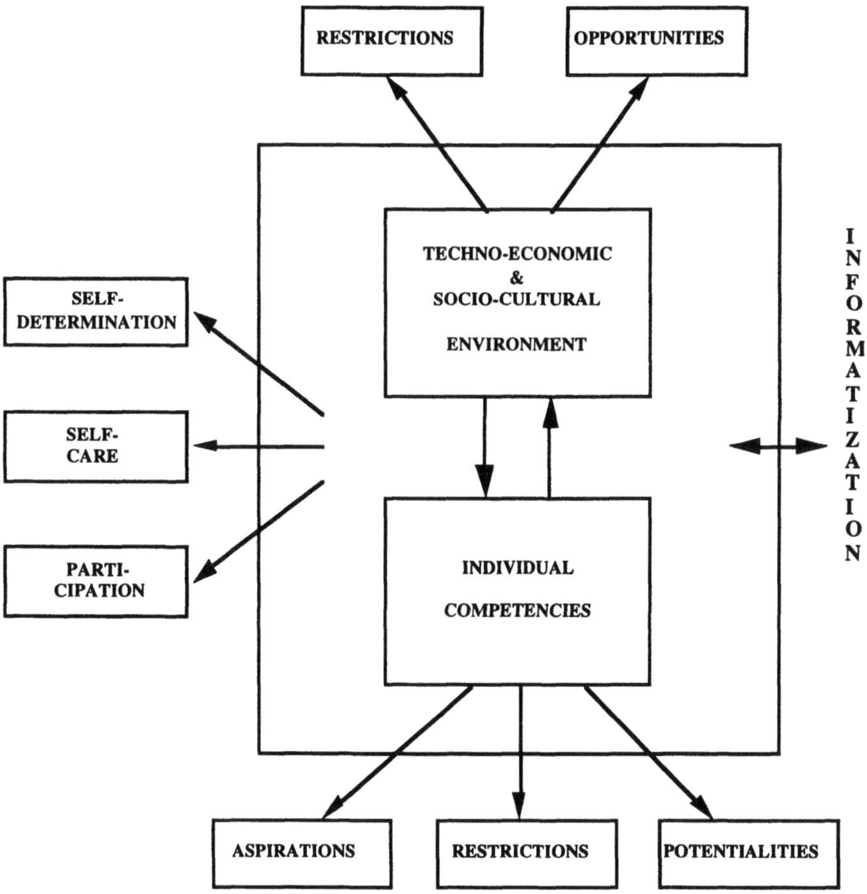

Views and perspectives on informatization will differ in their focal point: will they relate to processes in technological developments, to processes in economic structures, or to processes of socio-cultural dimensions? In our model we analytically discriminated between the techno-economic domain and the socio-cultural domain. Visions about the future information society usually include aspects of both domains. Bringing these components together in one framework leads to the model presented in Figure 1.

Societal domains of interest

Having formulated the theoretical approach, we had to decide which societal roles of the elderly should be part of the research. The heterogeneity of the conglomerate of the elderly suggests that different people may experience different kinds of pressures, while having different sets of competencies. Because the project was aimed at identifying societal mechanisms and forms of exclusion processes we decided to identify different societal domains that might be important in terms of our research objectives.

One of the most important aspects of societal participation is being part of the labour force, being employed, having a job. The Dutch situation on the labour market is rather peculiar with a very high rate of exclusion of elderly people. In the past two decades, roughly 50% of employees aged 55 or older retired. It should be mentioned that originally attractive financial arrangements were offered to encourage elderly people to retire. Today, these arrangements are questioned: they are costly and the expulsion of the elderly from the labour market is seen as apt to discriminate on the basis of age. The effect of ICT on the organization of work, in a quantitative as well as a qualitative sense, is a highly debated issue. The fact that there have been profound changes is not disputed. The role that informatization plays in these processes of change, especially when analyzed from the perspective of a specific category of workers, is not clear. The changing composition of the working force, the changes in work processes, and the changing requirements with respect to work satisfaction, together inspired us to look for processes of exclusion in this domain.

ICT, the Internet, the electronic highways, virtual reality, and all the other buzzwords, somehow seem to relate more to younger people than to the elderly. Today's culture is a youngster culture. Being old is out. Products and services are developed and presented with reference to qualities of youth: they have sex-appeal, they fit in a fast and speedy culture, they look good, etc. Products or services specifically developed for the elderly are dull, boring, clumsy, slow, big, grey, and so on. Companies avoid being associated with elderly customers. Their reluctance is based on stereotypical images of elderly people. But, even elderly people themselves seem to take these stereotypes for granted. These attitudes made the domain of the elderly consumer an interesting domain to research.

The third and final perspective related to societal participation is in the sense of being a citizen, being able to exert your civilian rights, fulfilling your civilian obligations, and being able to deal with administrative and bureaucratic procedures.

In each of these three domains, different processes in which informatization plays a role can be identified. The socio-technical dynamics within each domain follow different routes, have different value-systems and pose different kinds of questions about the impact of informatization on elderly people.

The research method

Two phases were formulated in the project: a divergence phase in which as many perspectives as possible were collected, and a convergence phase in which the similarities and differences between the perspectives were identified. The first phase was organized in three separate sessions, following the three societal domains. The method used in the first phase was the method of a – non-public – hearing. During three days, some 24 different actors were interviewed.

The results of the hearings were analyzed in view of the theoretical framework, and were presented in an evaluation report (Van Rijsselt and Weijers, 1997).

In a working conference, we checked out our findings. Apart from the 24 interviewees, another 15 experts were invited to participate. The results of the working conference were combined with our earlier findings. At the time of writing this paper, the researchers on the panel are in the process of writing the final report (Van Rijsselt and Weijers, 1997b).

THE ELDERLY CITIZEN IN THE INFORMATION SOCIETY

All three domains showed intriguing features with respect to the role and position of the elderly. We will use this paper to concentrate on the third domain: the domain of the elderly citizen. Of all the three fields, this field is most affiliated with an on-going concern of the Rathenau Institute: the debate over the restructuring of the public domain.

ICT applications fulfil a number of functions. An important one is the supply of electronic channels to get informed. Concepts such as the information society underscore the importance of information in contemporary society. The economic importance of information and information-related processes (like logistics) has led to the announcement of the successor of the industrial society: more than 60% of gross domestic product stems from information-related activities, and more than 60% of workers are information workers (Dordick and Wang, 1993). The second function is communication. Both information and communication are reflected in the acronym, ICT. Next to these two core functions of ICT, the opportunities for offering transaction facilities (like electronic banking or reservation of tickets) and entertainment (video-on-demand and games) are usually seen as important driving forces for the diffusion of ICT. In the following paragraphs, we will concentrate on the two main aspects of ICT, as reflected by its name: information and communication. To indicate the effect of the latter, we add the term 'participation' to the term 'communication', promoting our opinion that communication is the tool to enable participation.

Information over, for, and by elderly people

In a politico-administrative research project developments in administrative re-organization processes and information and communication technologies (ICT) were analyzed (Zuurmond, 1994). Two ideal types of informatization were sketched (ideal type in the Weberian sense of 'a unified conceptual approach to an analysis of both subjective meaning and structural forms' (Zuurmond, 1994, p. 14): the global and universal informatization and the local and contextual informatization. Global and universal informatization refers to bureaucratic elements like standardization, formalization, centralization, hierarchization, and specialization. The control of the specific uses of ICT in an organization remains with the uppermost, highest level. Global and universal informatization fits in a hierarchical context, with a top-down structure, and a command and control regime. Local and contextual informatization refers to the non-bureaucratic uses of ICT on the workfloor where personal preferences, flexibility, creativity, individual responsibility, and output-oriented tasks are supported by organizational and networked intelligence provided by computers and networks. This kind of informatization fits more in an egalitarian approach with a bottom-up structure and a networked structure where command and control is not exerted from a fixed centre but is distributed within the network. The empirical research of Zuurmond showed that it is not the latter use of ICT that is at hand. The Weberian bureaucracy is strengthened by new ICT. The specific uses of ICT reflect the norms and values of higher management, and reflect such organizational requirements as efficiency, speed, reduced throughput times, and reduced stocks. The norms of the local and contextual informatization, on the other hand, refer to issues like customer-oriented approaches, personalized services, quality of services, and an integral work approach instead of division in routinized and non-routinized tasks. It was shown that, at present, it is still the norms of higher management that are implemented in the use of new ICT.

Whether this result should be seen as the final outcome of the process of informatization from the last two decades, or as part of a transition period that finally will give the benefit to the more egalitarian approach, is an open issue. Activities that have been initiated by public authorities in recent years contain both approaches, and seem to be based on a mix of both normative schemes. We will discuss a few of them in the following.

Public authorities have initiated a number of activities around so-called civic service centres: one-stop shopping centres where citizens do not have to wonder which sequence of counters has to be followed in order to get information, to deposit a complaint or to renew a driving license. In a one-stop-shopping approach, the citizen's comfort seems to be increased because any administrative burden is shifted to the back-office and is supplanted by intelligent computers. In the Netherlands, an initiative has been launched by the Department of Internal Affairs, in which municipalities are invited to develop projects for developing and implementing one-stop shopping counters. One interest group is the combined group of elderly and disabled people. In several municipalities, initiatives are formulated around the development of information services to the elderly and/or disabled citizens.

Several problems surround these initiatives. First, the mixture of elderly and the disabled is a rather peculiar mix of demographic variables that leads to negative labelling processes on both sides. In general, the elderly are not disabled, just as disabled people are not elderly.

Second, not much is known about specific information requests from elderly people. In general this is because elderly people were never asked what kind of services they needed (but services were simply offered on the basis of previous experiences with uses of services by elderly people).

Third, though the number of proposals for starting a one-stop shopping centre was unexpectedly high, and showed, among other issues, a shared interest in these kinds of socio-technical innovations, many of the initiatives were part of a business redesign process that was aimed at an overall quality improvement (in line with increased efficiency, increased throughput times, increased speed of production, etc): the global and universal form of informatization.

So, while these initiatives could contribute to a strengthening of participatory functions, such as the use of facilities and being informed about need-to-know issues, in practice these functions do not seem to be at the core of the initiatives so far. The use of ICT seems to be more oriented to fulfilling internal organizational objectives, to preventing misuse of facilities (instead of stimulating the use of proper facilities), to supporting organizational changes, or to showing that public authorities are at the leading edge of developments, use the latest technologies, and belong to the category of early adopters at the cost of opportunities for the late adopters. Tentatively, we would argue that the more egalitarian approach that is visible within the initiatives legitimizes the more hierarchical one; both are based on a legitimate attempt to improve the communication between public authorities and citizens but, where the more egalitarian approach is aimed at improving the position of the citizen with respect to the local authorities, the second is aimed at improving the distribution of financial and social resources among those who are entitled to them.

A number of examples illustrate this argument. At the working conference, it was noticed that the commercial sector is more sensitive to unarticulated needs from the market. A big information-collecting organization in the Netherlands, the Air-miles organization, every three months informs roughly three million individuals about the data collected about them during these months. Use of ICT to inform citizens actively about registered information by public authorities is so far unknown. Another example of what may be called a flawed use of ICT in serving citizens is in the attribution of certain subsidies. When citizens want to apply for individual rent subsidies, they have to take the appropriate action by themselves. Meanwhile, all the information about attributing rent subsidies automatically is available to the local authorities. Similar cases were mentioned with respect to collecting any information about the changed personal situation of elderly people, where the needed information was available but not used.

A last example is the Dutch interdepartmental programme *Elderly people and the electronic highway* (Willems and Van den Wildenberg, 1996). This is a programme that has only recently been initiated. Its primary objective is to promote the independence of elderly people in line with the general policy for the aged. As an important way of promoting the participation of elderly people, it formulates the existence and feasibility of educational and promotional activities. This activity was viewed by the organization of the elderly as of great importance for the empowering of the elderly, in order to get them in touch with new technological developments and enable them to judge these developments on their significance. But then, the report argues that education and promotion activities fall outside the scope of the programme objectives. The programme focuses on combining information services on the supply side by creating a shopping site. It concentrates on stimulating the development of specific services for elderly people. In short, it promotes the market, and not the user.

All these factors relate to information, provided for or over elderly people. The line of information by elderly citizens is hardly developed, not to say almost absent. There are scarcely any initiatives initiated by public authorities where citizen panels are used to support public authorities. The website SeniorWeb – initiated by the Dutch Platform for Aged and Europe (NPOE) - is an example of an activity initiated by an organization of elderly people. SeniorWeb is a Dutch clone of the American SeniorNet. The NPOE tries to connect as many elderly people as possible to on-going developments in a globalizing world and as such plays a leading role in the world of the elderly ICT user. The initiative might increase awareness by political decision-makers and public authorities for the needs and interests of elderly people on the electronic highways.

Communication and participation

In general terms, societal participation decreases with age. First, elderly people stop working. Having a job relates to being in a cordial environment with people who share the same interests, belonging to a group with shared objectives, and to feelings of self-esteem. But it also relates to getting in touch with new, technological developments, like personal computers, word processors, and the like. The Netherlands has had a policy of 'Young for Old'. Faced with an enormous increase in young people entering the labour market at the beginning of the 1980s, it became common practice to replace older employees with younger people. In line with the aforementioned images of exclusion, it started with *the elderly don't have to work*, which after a while became *they don't want to*. The dynamics behind this shift in attitude are interesting to discuss, but fall outside the scope of this paper. The Dutch approach has led to a situation in which more than 90% of Dutch workers retire before they are 65. Higher educated people work longer than lower educated. Higher educated people thus keep in touch longer with new developments. This is not to say that work is the only place to get in touch with new technologies, but it is a place where new technologies may be introduced as part of normal practice.

The second reason for the decrease of participation is that older people are expelled from positions of political power. Reaching the age of 70 used to imply that political or administrative positions had to be renounced. Recently, the Dutch Department of Social Affairs is engaged in preparing a law that prohibits discrimination on the basis of age in the case of getting a job. Whether this will lead to a substantial increase in elderly politicians remains to be seen. For the time being, the participation of elderly people is restricted to participating in clubs and organizations and in volunteer work. The level of organization of the elderly is pretty high in the Netherlands: organizations for elderly people have as many as 650,000 elderly members, from a total of two million people aged 65+. Active participation remains until the age of 70-75. So, while the formal and political participatory channels are blocked, the informal and private ones are very vividly used until a reasonable age (Timmermans, 1997).

What remains to be shown is whether informatization contributes in a positive or in a negative way to the societal participation of elderly people. This is not an easy task. Empirically, this relationship is not well studied. Not much is known, for instance, about the use and appreciation of ICT tools and processes.

An American survey among elderly people shows that 29% of Americans aged 55+ claim to own a personal computer. The survey was held at the end of 1995. A survey in July 1994 gave a total of 21% owners, indicating an increase of 41% over a year and a half. But items such as a video cassette recorder (VCR) (81%) and cordless telephones (58%) are also found regularly in elderly households (Adler, 1996). A Dutch study in Rotterdam showed that 63% of elderly people (55+) had heard about the Internet (compared with 85% of the total population). But knowledge about Stadstext-interactive (City-text, a local interactive news bulletin board on television) was almost absent (0.5%), compared to an average acquaintance of 40% of the total population. Though many of the elderly had heard of the Internet, they did not use it. With respect to personal computers, 19% of aged Rotterdammers possess a personal computer (PC), and 4% own a PC with modem. Overall results for the Rotterdam population were 43% and 16% respectively (Kanters and Hartkamp, 1995). In the feasibility study mentioned before (*Elderly people and the electronic highway*), written on the order of the interdepartmental working group *The elderly and technology*, a figure of 18% is mentioned for PC-owners in the age range of 55 to 70, of whom roughly 20% owns a modem. Not more than 10,000 elderly PC-owners (aged 55-70 years) should be seen as users of the Internet (Willems and Van den Wildenberg 1996, p. 5).

These figures are difficult to relate to potentialities, restrictions, and aspirations of the elderly with respect to electronic communication. Possessing a PC is not necessarily an indication of familiarity with the use of the communicative functions of the PC. The interviews we held gave some perspectives on these items. First, with age, physical and cognitive *restrictions* grow. Up till the age of 75-80, however, elderly people have many mechanisms to compensate for cognitive and physiological decline. Electronic communication tools (like email) could contribute to overcoming physical as well as cognitive restrictions. Letters may be written in several steps, shopping lists may be easily filled in.

Due to our research method, we have not been able to track down the *aspirations* of elderly people with respect to the use of ICT. We will stick to a few general remarks.

To start with, elderly people do not reject new technology because it is new technology. They should be seen as critical users. They are eager to accept new tools when these tools can be shown to have a functional added value. Tools like security cameras and lifelines illustrate the potentialities of new technologies. But, while these tools are shown in the context of the care-needing elderly person, the biggest part of the elderly population is interested in the same kind of things as other people, like information about travelling and trips, communication about hobbies, daily news, etc. The growth of the number of elderly people with a PC might be a point in this respect. It is, however, necessary to raise awareness for the functions of the new ICT media. A very considerate and dedicated approach will be needed, since many of the relative advantages that the new media seem to offer to the young do not fit into the schemata of the old (like saving time, or avoiding places that may lead to unwanted social contacts).

With respect to *potentialities*, there are hardly any signs that elderly people are not able to cope with the new ICT tools, compared to other age-related groups. Information processing capacities reduce, while interpreting capacities (context-related acting) improve. Several interviewees noticed the problem elderly people have when they need to programme an apparatus; programming a VCR, using an automated ticket machine at the railway station, or programming the more advanced functions of a telephone pose problems.

An interesting explanation for these missing capacities is the notion of 'technology generations', hinting at the fact that everyone grows up with a very specific view of technology. Mental models are created in childhood with respect to how technology works. New technologies are viewed from these old perspectives. The flexibility of today's ICT is difficult for the elderly to understand. They were raised with machinery that was operated by means of handles and sticks; instructions had fixed sequences; changing instruction A with instruction B might have had very damaging consequences. Many elderly people lack the educational training to engage themselves in a situation of learning by doing. Today's ICT is much more fault-tolerant: the PC does not break down when improperly used. These malleable and flexible ICT tools work, however, in a far more complicated world than the world of a few decades ago. For elderly people, the difference between the speed of today's societal processes (from traffic to bureaucratic procedures) and the multi-faceted character of many processes based on modern technology may cause blockages that are hardly seen at all by younger people.

Whether the concept of technology generation is a proper concept to explore differences between the attitude of different generations towards socio-technical innovations is still an open but interesting question.

Next to the individual competencies, *environmental characteristics* play a role in promoting or preventing participation. First, ICT is – in a very specific sense – an individual technology. Tools like PCs, and the interfaces between computers and machines, are individually based; they presuppose one person a time. Getting money from an automated teller machine (ATM), or searching information in an electronic database, is an individual man-machine process. Within this individuality, it is the user that must trigger the process. Getting a ticket from a railway station or asking for information at an automated help desk in a public place presupposes an active role and attitude from the (older) user. Today's elderly people (aged 75+) have missed this transition to an active and participative role. Their self-image reflects a passive nature: being taken care of, and being dependent on helping institutions. This places them in a backward position and shows the need for more attention to their specific situation. The elderly people aged 55-75 will, in general, have passed by higher educational levels that might support them in bridging the transition.

Second, from a more global point of view, processes of liberalization, deregulation and individualization run parallel with informatization processes. The collective arrangements of the welfare state are supplanted by individual arrangements without a general social-serving system underneath. Individuals negotiate their specific situation with employers, public authorities, insurance companies, etc. Issues like the expected disappearance of cohesion and solidarity within society, the fragmentation of traditional norms and values and the multi-cultural composition of contemporary society, are easily related to the global dimensions of the informatization processes. These global processes are part of the modern world: the world that is formed by the stakeholders of today. These stakeholders are everyone except the elderly whose role is limited to a wait-and-see attitude. It is not an easy task to engage the older community in these processes. Of course, we might question the need for empowering, engaging, and teaching the elderly. When no specific requests are heard from this group, why bother? Taking our starting point seriously – i.e. promoting independency – offers one argument for taking initiatives. Another argument is of a more opportunistic nature. Today's men and women aged 50-60 will be tomorrow's elderly of 60-70 years. Their relative and absolute size makes them an interesting target group for marketeers. Their growing political awareness makes them a group to be aware of. Within less than a decade they might become a serious political, commercial, and societal factor within society.

CONCLUSION

The project was aimed at identifying the dynamics of exclusion of elderly people in various societal fields. The exclusion process itself was split up in several dimensions, in order to develop a more sophisticated approach (Van Rijsselt and Weijers, 1997). Each dimension can be characterized by one of the following questions. On which societal domain does exclusion occur? What kind of exclusion occurs (is it the effect of a collective societal norm or is it a free and individual choice)? Is the exclusion permanent or temporary? Is it integral or partial? Is it an active form of exclusion (active denial of rights) or passive? And finally, though exclusion has a negative tone, it need not be the result of a negative process but it may be self-chosen and self-wanted.

Confronting these dimensions with the theme of this paper, we conclude that within the societal domain we focused on, the exclusion process is not integral but covers certain areas (work, politics), that exclusion is the result of a collective societal norm (we impose and endorse a view in which elderly people are allowed to withdraw from societal activities), and that it is the result of an active process (having reached the age of 65 means a formal end to a working career). Whether the exclusion is permanent or not is difficult to answer. In a sense it is (formal work, political power positions). But many initiatives – from the elderly themselves, and also from commercial players and public authorities – are launched and developed that are directed at engaging elderly people in a variety of societal processes. Elderly people themselves take up other activities that confront them with on-going changes in society and that bring them into contact with new uses of ICT. The young elderly especially show a rather active pattern of various societal activities that enables them to keep track of new developments. The last dimension – self-chosen versus imposed exclusion – is an interesting one. We have found no signs that opposition to informatization processes grows among older people. An increasing awareness of the absence of societally significant roles for elderly people in combination with a continued hierarchical form of informatization might however lead to growing opposition, and might lead to the rise of elderly Want Nots.

We have presented arguments for the thesis that elderly people should not be treated as one single homogeneous group. The concept of technology generation has been introduced - though in a rather primitive fashion – to indicate the effect of the specific technologies with which people are raised. Then, we indicated the effect of the educational level and the awareness for a learning by doing attitude. Both arguments are only indicative, but nevertheless supportive, of the diversification among the elderly people.

We would like to make a final remark. Most of the processes mentioned before are not exclusively typical of elderly people. Of course, socio-cultural change processes are more global in scope, but also on the level of individual competencies we have tried to show that the aspirations, restrictions, and potentialities of elderly people do not necessarily differ from those of other demographic groups. It is the specific combination of perspectives, societal attitudes, and individual competencies that may give rise to processes of exclusion. A number of interviewees were rather optimistic about the trickling down of use of ICT tools. They hinted at the traditional diffusion approach in which diffusion of technological artifacts is seen as a process that starts with 'innovators', continues with the 'early adopters', goes on to the 'late adopters', and ends with the 'laggards'. This approach presupposes that the problem of diffusion is merely a problem of reaching a critical mass. Once a significant proportion of users is reached, the majority will follow. The informatization of society is, however, a process that is more complicated than a simple diffusion of artifacts. First, it is a combination of technological and social (organizational) innovations. Everything changes at the same time, and all changes influence each other. Second, it is not the mere use of an artifact but especially the significance of an artifact in a specific constellation that counts. The constellation may change rather rapidly (for instance, at the end of a career) or turn out to be useless for specific categories of users. Finally, the technological base is innovating with enormous speed, which confuses the traditional diffusion process. Before an artifact reaches a mature state it may have been overruled by the next artifact or a competing one. Laggards will remain laggards and will only experience a growing distance from the majority of users. We should not expect the information society to be the simple sum of technological innovations in which processes of change can be explained by following technological trajectories. It will be the total of socio-technical innovations, indicating the intrinsic interdependence between the social and the technological changes that occur today.

Taking the combination of elderly people, exclusion processes, and informatization processes, it seems that specific societal constraints (collective societal norms) are disadvantageous for elderly people. The most important constraint is the statement that elderly people do *not have* to participate. From this, it follows that - where participation is linked to modern technological developments - they are *not able* to participate because they lack knowledge and interest in new technologies. In the end, this leads to the conclusion that they do *not want* to participate.

The way out is not simple. It is mostly beliefs and self-fulfilling prophecies that underlie the feelings of exclusion. Many of these beliefs do not stand a proper second look, for instance, the fact that elderly people are not able to use a computer. Or the fact that they do not want to use email or other forms of electronic communication. When the added value is visible (for instance, the opportunity to receive pictures of relatives via electronic networks), elderly people will be among the first to use the new tools. With respect to societal participation, we conclude that it is not the elderly but the public authorities that are at stake.

Most of the informatization processes are directed at bringing order in their own backyard, while initiatives are launched that try to improve the information relationship with the citizen. Whether these initiatives cover civilian rights as much as civilian obligations must be doubted. The internal requirements – guided by the hierarchical approach of informatization – are, for the time being, more important than the external relationship (the empowering of citizens). Elderly people are generally seen as care-dependent, and only interested in issues related to safe housing and health care. We think we know what is best for them. And that is a peculiar thing, because, as one interviewee noted: 'We all know what it is to be young, because we all have been young. But who of us has been old?'

REFERENCES

Adler, R. 1996. *Older adults and computers: report of a national survey.* www.seniornet.com

Dordick, H. S. and Wang, G. 1993. *The Information Society - a retrospective view.* Sage Publications, London.

Kanters, E. and Hartkamp, F. 1995. *The Elderly and Information Technology in Rotterdam.*

Onderzoekprogramma vakgroep Sociologie en Sociale Gerontologie, Vrije Universiteit Amsterdam, 1995 (Research programme Department of Sociology and Social Gerontology, Free University of Amsterdam, The Netherlands).

Timmermans, J. 1993. *Rapportage Ouderen*, SCP, Den Haag (Report on Elderly People).

Timmermans, J. (ed.) 1997. *Rapportage Ouderen*, SCP, Den Haag (Report on Elderly People).

Van Rijsselt, R. and Weijers, T. 1997a. *Uitsluiting van ouderen - de dreiging verkend; evaluatierapport,* Rathenau Instituut, Den Haag (Exclusion of elderly people - the threat analyzed; evaluation report).

Van Rijsselt, R. and Weijers, T. 1997b. *Ouderen en de informatiesamenleving: een verkenning van opvattingen over aan - en uitsluiting* (The Elderly and the Information Society: a survey of attitudes on in - and exclusion). Otto Cramwinkel Uitgeverij, Amsterdam.

Willems and Van den Wildenberg 1996. *Haalbaarheidsstudie 'Ouderen en de elektronische snelweg'*, Den Haag (A feasibility study 'The Elderly and the Electronic Highway').

Zuurmond, A. 1994. *De infocratie - een theoretisch en empirische heroriëntatie op Webers idealtype in het informatietijdperk,* Phaedrus, Den Haag (The infocracy – a theoretical and empirical re-orientation on Weber's idealtype in the Information Age).

PART FIVE

The Concept of the Agora

The Internet: A new agora?

Niklas Damiris and Helga Wild***
**Apple Research Labs/Stanford University*
942 College Avenue, Palo Alto CA 94306, USA
Phone: +1 415 493 7570
Email: niklas@leland.stanford.edu
*** Institute for Research on Learning*
66 Willow Place, Menlo Park, CA 94025, USA
Phone +1 415 614 7933, Fax: +1 415 614 7957
Email: helga_wild@irl.org

Abstract

Democracy in ancient Greece relied on the active participation of the people in political life. This participation took the form of *speech* and *action*, and was supported by a certain configuration of *space*, the agora, and a certain configuration of *community*, the polis. Subsequent developments, specifically the gradual rise of the economic and the parallel dismantling of the public sphere deeply affected the balance that these factors had achieved in the Greek city-state. Most importantly, they obscured the grounding of the political discourse in space and community. As a result, democracy today has come to be associated with abstract institutions and governance mechanisms.

The Internet appears to offer new hope for a participatory kind of democracy. This is due to a rich potential for communication and an almost unlimited access to information. However, to fulfil this hope it needs to reestablish the balance between the two axes, the discursive-performative – speech and action, and the embodied – space and community.

ROOTS OF DEMOCRACY IN ANCIENT GREECE

Ancient Greece is, if not the cradle of western civilization, certainly the cradle of western democracy. Democracy took root with the foundation of the Greek city-state and its specific form of political organization, the *polis*.

An Ethical Global Information Society J. Berleur & D. Whitehouse (Eds.)

According to Hannah Arendt in *The Human Condition* (Arendt, 1958), this was accomplished by a differentiation of the social sphere into two separate realms: the realm of the house (*oikia*) made up of family, kin and slaves, which could be called the realm of the private since it was under the authority and control of the master of the house, and the realm of the political embodied in the *agora* whose institution and architecture supported people engaged in public debate.

If historians are right, the public realm of the Greek city-state was built at the expense of private social organization. It replaced in importance earlier forms of organization dependent on family and kinship. Indeed, for the citizen-members of the polis, the household existed in order to support their political life. The agora constituted the sacred space of public life. The hearth with its gods and goats, in turn, functioned as the sacred space of the household. Agora and oikia supported and complemented one another.

The material production of subsistence centred around the household. The familial existence included slaves, who contributed to the everyday life of housekeeping and were thereby also bound by the laws of the house: literally, the meaning of economy. The process of material production offered the opportunity to accumulate money through hard work and was open even to slaves. Yet, even though making money was considered legitimate, it was not in itself pertinent to the duties and powers associated with being a participating member of the agora.

If only the master of the household had the right to participate in public affairs this was because he was entitled to a viewpoint, that is, he had the right to offer his opinion in the agora as one among equals, and he had a standpoint, that is, an existentially grounded place through his position in the household[1].

Being well off was therefore a necessary, but not a sufficient, condition for being a citizen of the Greek polis. 'To live the good life,' as Aristotle called the public life of the citizen (McKeon, 1941) meant that one had to strive not merely to free oneself from the hardship of making a living without indemnity. Once that had been accomplished one was condemned to the freedom of participation in the public life which was itself equivalent to a full-time job. No one who had to labour could participate in the time-consuming activities of the polis.

One could imagine that those who could afford not to work might have wanted to enjoy a quiet life at home instead of doing politics. But, no matter how comfortable private life in the household could become for Athenians, it could never be more than a supplement even where it offered room for activities which a large number of people today would rank higher than political engagement. The reason for this was that the political life of the agora did not merely impart a better or nobler character to ordinary life. Rather, the agora *constituted* human life as a novel and autonomous form. The member of the polis had the potential to be good because, as Hannah Arendt states, 'by having mastered the necessities of sheer life, by being freed from labor and work, and by overcoming the innate urge of living creatures for their own survival, [he] was no longer bound to biological life processes' (Arendt, 1958, p. 37).

AGORA: PLACE OF ETHICAL CONDUCT

The agora was the physical place that embodied the unique character of Greek democracy. It afforded the community of free and equal men (the polis) the opportunity to engage in dialogue with one another without consideration of power, wealth, and heritage. This is where they would engage in daily intense interaction and debate and decide about the common good of the city-state. In the agora, all men were free and equal and no-one was either ruling or being ruled. In this respect, the space of the agora established its own set of rules for ethical conduct. Decisions were made by consensus, without force. Hierarchy and violence had no place in the agora; they were bound up with the realm of necessity and belonged therefore to the household.

The concern of the polis was to make the world *appear* as fully as possible by enabling every free man to take a stance. That meant that the agora saw both conflict and consensus expressed and developed. It was the duty of every participant to speak as best he could to the course and consequence of possible actions and to move his fellow men to follow him in the proposed direction. The only way in which individuals could stand out in their fellow citizens' esteem, was through important and heroic political action. This space of social appearance was established both through action in the political disputes of the agora and through action in war.

Engaging in political life was the highest form of life since it made man become properly human. Aristotle, in his definition of man as the *zoon politicon* (the political animal) and in the corollary definition of man as *zoon logon ekhon* (a living being capable of speech), makes clear how the Greeks distinguished man from animal precisely through the former's participation in political life.

Consequently, of all the activities habitually engaged in by the ancient Greeks, the two valued most highly were the ones considered constitutive of political life: *action* and *speech*. This included the possibility of *action through speech*, namely when one managed to utter the right words at the right moment (Arendt, 1958, p. 25). One can find here the origin of the place of rhetoric as the cornerstone of the educational curriculum of the Middle Ages.

To sum up the lessons from the Greek city-state for current purposes, neither individual autonomy nor being social alone was enough to guarantee democracy. The individual self embedded in the household and the family, and thereby in some form already socialized, could only develop a one-sided view of the world. The world was fully disclosed only in the political realm in which people confronted the embodied stance of others and no-one's identity was subjugated. Being social was, therefore, not equivalent to being political. While it allowed the citizen to cope with the problems associated with work and with labour, first, through cooperation in the household and, later, through competition in the market, it did not generate a political life. This required taking an ethical stance with respect to the needs of the community and taking action for the common good. Performance in the agora expressed itself through speech and action. These were grounded in the physical space and enabled by the community; space and community, in turn, were transformed by political performance into a place of ethical conduct and a polis of heroic individuals.

TRANSFORMATION OF THE PUBLIC AND PRIVATE SPHERE

Since the Greek polis, Europe has seen a great deal of change in the function and meaning of private and public realm. Ancient Rome, with its form of civic society, elevated its members to the status of citizen-soldier whose duty was to contribute to the expansion and ruling of the Roman empire. The household continued to be the place of labour, production, and economic considerations. Its value-adding function became recognized in the legal conception of private ownership.

In the feudal order of the Middle Ages, monetary and trade concerns became legitimated as motivating factors behind political ambition. With this development, the household's preoccupation with exchange and possession of the products of work started to invade the public realm. One result of this invasion was literally the transformation of the public place of political life into the marketplace where commodities were traded and exchanged for money, a development which marks the beginning of the era of capital accumulation.

By the time of the great monarchies in Europe, the economic way of thinking had embedded itself deeply into the public sphere. With the rise of state power and stately institutions, 'private' acquired the meaning of operating in a non-official function or of being excluded from public office. Later, with the rise of capitalism, this meaning of privacy took on a positive and economic flavour and privacy became associated not only with the house and family circle but also with the domain of persons acting in their private economic interests, thereby establishing a market functioning outside the rules of state institutions.

The privacy and autonomy of the household were secured through the competition of private individuals in the free market. The financial success of this new structural arrangement produced a value shift: as the private realm gained in importance it became the defining criterion of what it meant to be human. The new private self with its beliefs and opinions demanded its own public expression. This resulted in the creation of a second public sphere alongside the sphere of state institutions, that of public opinion. *Salons* in France, *coffee houses* in England, and *Tischgesellschaften* in Germany, provided the place for the formation of this public opinion while the educated bourgeois family provided the community (Habermas, 1991).

> 'The public sphere as a functional element in the political realm was given the normative status of self-articulation of civil society with the state authority corresponding to its needs. The social precondition for this "developed" bourgeois public sphere was a market that, tending to be liberalized, made affairs in the sphere of social reproduction as much as possible a matter of private people left to themselves and so finally completed the privatization of civil society' (Habermas, 1991, p. 74).

The state eventually accepted civil society as a carrier of truth and saw itself as providing the mechanisms for implementing it. For a while, state institutions and public opinion functioned cooperatively. But, as the bourgeois family became more and more a site of consumption, the public spaces, salons, coffeehouses, etc., that enabled the debates formative of public opinion, lost their grounding in the community. They either transformed themselves into capitalist enterprises (newspapers and other publishing businesses) which operated under the law of the market or turned into islands of aesthetic and intellectual life with little impact on the world beyond.

In the twentieth century, the interaction between public and private sphere has become the uneasy coexistence of welfare state and individual and human rights. It is clear that this is the result of a development long in the making. The commons which used to be dominated by cultural matters was gradually overtaken by the economic preoccupation of possessive individualism. This has led to the assimilation of the concern for the public good by the economic rationale now reinterpreted as the problem of *free riding* or, alternatively, to what has come to be known as 'the tragedy of the commons' (Hardin, 1982).

Democracy has ceased to be concerned with the creation and support of a public sphere in which people articulate their differences and develop common goals and courses for action. Democracy has become synonymous with the legal institutions and financial governance mechanisms that protect states and individuals from each other in the race for economic growth.

DEMOCRACY AND THE INTERNET

With the triumph of the 'economics-first' ideology, all technology invented since the advent of capitalism has been justified as a means to added growth. Technological innovations, like the steam engine or the car, made this glaringly obvious. They dramatically changed people's standard of living, economically understood, and literally transformed the face of the earth. Enter now a new technology – networked computers – and something different seems to be in the offing! Or is it?

In the United States today, policy experts hail the Internet as the hope for democracy. They claim that it provides a cure against the decreased participation in the political process, the disproportionate influence of a few powerful interest groups, the biased reporting in the media, and the general disaffection of the voter. The Internet can overcome, or at least improve, this situation, they argue, because it gives easy and unlimited access to information, empowers the ordinary citizen through giving ownership of the textual means of production, and makes communication among equal-minded spirits and participation in the political process so much easier, so much cheaper (Corrado and Firestone, 1996).

On the downside, they note the danger of splitting the population into those with access to the Internet and those without; not an unreasonable fear in the light of the growing impoverishment of the middle class in the United States. And there exists always a dark side to the advantages mentioned above: information is useless when one either cannot find it or one finds too much. If interest groups can influence government and media, what is to prevent their censoring influence on the Internet? Already the technologies behind the Internet are controlled by fewer and fewer companies. And economic interests invade the Internet much as they have invaded all other domains of life.

Yet the dream of a place where people could freely express their individuality and still be part of a community, much in the spirit of the agora, is very much alive on the Internet (though, as Frank Zappa said about jazz, it smells a bit funny (Zappa, 1978)). When hearing the founders of the WELL (the Whole Earth

'Lectronic Link) recount their vision of computer-mediated communication, one notices immediately their eagerness to associate it with a domain free of commercial interests and free of government intervention too, for that matter. Like the ex-hippies many of them are, they try to imagine a world where people would be freely sharing information, ideas, and software without concern for property rights, profits, and the like.

In the year 1997, most of that sounds like an impossible wish list, since business interests are powerfully setting the agenda for a utilization of the Internet different from the one originally envisioned. Interesting enough, many of the hippie founders do not seem averse to electronically conducted commerce even though they use libertarian rhetoric to rail against governments' attempts to regulate the Internet[2]. So, here we find under different guise a repetition of the old tension between self-interest, on one side, and impersonal institutions and regulations, on the other. Trying to understand the potential of the Internet for envisioning democracy has become a challenging task indeed!

The conception of democracy fostered by economic liberalism seems far removed from the agora understood as a public place with established rules of conduct where people freed from economic worries debate their differences, develop their identities, and realize common goals. And yet, there is no denying that the Internet, which is still in its fledgling stages, offers some support for the vision of a sphere where the participants could communicate widely, organize, and coordinate their activities. The question becomes then, how one could go about realizing this hope so that it can eventually transform the housekeeping mentality instead of succumbing to it?

Possibly we can get a first glimpse of an answer from the Internet itself, from the way people have envisioned and used it. Interestingly enough, the Internet has been described from its inception alternately as a community or as a space of sorts. One is tempted to see this as a poetic reimagining of one of the main axes of Greek democracy: space and community. We will discuss each one of these metaphorical takes briefly in turn.

INTERNET AS VIRTUAL COMMUNITY

The journalist Howard Rheingold, summarizing many peoples' notions of the Internet, calls it – following McLuhan – a 'virtual village' where folks would use words on screens to exchange pleasantries, engage in intellectual discourse, conduct commerce, and create art and a lot of talk. According to Rheingold, computer-mediated communication was an outpost of social habitation best characterized as an ongoing conversation conducted among people who started as complete strangers but who became over time more and more involved in each others' concerns. Computer-mediated social groups, he claims, were virtual communities: their creation and sustenance required an act of imagination. However, he also adds: 'The WELL felt like authentic community to me from the start because it was grounded in my everyday physical world. Wellites who don't live within driving distance of San Francisco Bay [which is where Rheingold resides] are constrained in their ability to participate in the local networks of face to face acquaintances' (Rheingold, 1993).

We can summarize the Internet-as-community metaphor thus: networked information technologies enables people to produce speech genres (Bakhtin, 1984) or phrase regimes (Lyotard, 1988). This means self-regulated, rule-governed enclosures in a generalized system of communication created by like-minded people, in this specific case, through electronic means. According to this vision, to *be* is to *communicate*: people 'talk-write' with the expectation of an interlocutor in mind who is preparing a response, offering agreement, sympathy or objection. The narratives of different lives become thereby intermeshed and engender new social relations and contact with people one could not otherwise encounter.

This brings communication close to being equivalent to community. Or rather, the meaning of the term 'community' receives a reinterpretation because of the way it gets used on the Internet. People speak about communities of transaction, communities of interest, communities of relationships and communities of fantasy, depending on whether one buys or sells via the Internet, discusses specific topics, works through dramatic personal events, or engages in make-believe games. Insofar as we focus on the communicative exchange aspect of community, it is to some extent justified to see the Internet as a new kind of soil which nourishes new types of community. But, as always, economic interests are also at work here. Already, these so-called communities are being advertised as fertile ground for new and emerging markets (Armstrong and Hagel, 1996), which makes one wonder whether the Internet is not employing the term 'community' in a rather euphemistic fashion.

Be that as it may, the practices on the Internet make clear that the communities fostered there are always the *product* of the discursive exchanges of the participants, not – as is the case outside the Internet – their *ground*.

INTERNET AS VIRTUAL SPACE

The community metaphor brings to mind communication and social relations; the conception of the Internet as space capitalizes on the spatial metaphors that abound in language which can be traced back to a person's ability to act on and move in its environment. The issue raised is this: as an information environment becomes increasingly persistent and perceptible does this not imply that there is 'a there there', to borrow Gertrude Stein's expression (Stein, 1933)? Or, that one can produce a *there* by the manipulations the Internet affords?

If we consider the production of space through human agents we have to introduce the tripartite distinction of space made by Henri Lefebvre. He suggests that there are three kinds of spaces for humans: a linguistic mental space (the conceived), a physical space (the perceived) and the space of social practice (the lived) (Lefebvre, 1991, p. 40). In contemplating the appropriateness of the spatial metaphor for the Internet we need to remain aware of the complexity of our normal experience of space. What is it that makes us experience space: our perception of three-dimensionality of objects, our reliance on permanent features of the environment, or our physical movements in it? How does this relate to the sense of place which is much more grounded in pragmatics of action and the temporality of the body?

To be sure, on the face of it, the Internet is pretty anti-spatial: the fundamental principle of data independence holds that a user should be able to obtain something without knowing where or how it is stored. This is the whole idea with the Internet. The fact that some items may refer to physical locations does not mean that the Internet is one of those. No distance, no continuity, no ordering! Yet, places can exist without space, as low bandwidth virtual reality environments like multi-user dungeons (MUDs) have shown.

Researchers in the area of computer-supported work have by now realized the difference between space and place. They claim that it is place that makes possible the framing of appropriate behaviour, and find that framing of behaviour on the Internet, though often organized around spatial features, nevertheless operates quite independent of them. In this fashion they reveal – after lengthy discussion – the derivative nature of the Internet's spatiality by putting the emphasis on place without space (Harrison and Dourish, 1996).

Thus, analogous to Internet communities, space too turns out to be the *effect* of actions taken, not their *starting point*. Appropriately framed behaviour creates an enclosure within the Internet which gives the participants a sense of place and this place, in turn, can be demarcated by visual clues and equipped with spatial features.

SPEECH AND ACTION

After this excursion into metaphors for the Internet, we can fully appreciate the meaning of virtuality as it is applied to both community and space. Community and space are called *virtual* on the Internet because they are effects, namely the effects of the discursive activities and the communicative interactions which the Internet affords. They are not grounding, but grounded, and thereby acquire a flavour of self-presentation.

Surprisingly, Arendt, in speaking about democracy, anticipates such a development with these remarks which sound like early advertisement for the Internet:

> 'Action and speech create a space which can find its proper location almost anytime anywhere. It is the space of appearance in the widest sense of the word, namely the space where I appear to others as others appear to me, where men can exist not merely like other living or inanimate things but make their appearance explicitly' (Arendt, 1958, pp. 198-199).

Arendt suggests that the joining of speech and action can create a space in which people can appear to one another. If we identify speech in ancient Greece with communication on the Internet – which is defensible if we take into account the transformation that a novel medium will impose – we are still falling short of the action: what would it take to make the Internet into a space for social action?

Here is a pertinent quotation from Habermas in which he justifies the need for a level of action higher than the instrumental goal-oriented one that underwrites normal activities. This higher level of action, which he calls 'communicative action' (Bernstein, 1995, p. 42), is what enables people not only to enter the space of appearance mentioned by Arendt but also to develop consensus among themselves – a necessary component of democratic practice. Communicative action depends on a language system which is appropriate to the needs of a community and is revisable if those should change.

> 'The consensus-producing power of argument rests on the supposition that the language system in which the recommendations requiring justification, the norms, and the generally accepted needs cited for support are interpreted, is appropriate ... We call appropriate that language of morals which permits determinate persons and groups, in given circumstances, a truthful interpretation both of their own particular needs, and more importantly of their common needs capable of consensus. The chosen language system must permit those and only those interpretations of needs in which the participants in the discourse can make their inner natures transparent and know what they really want ... By virtue of its formal properties discourse must guarantee that the participants can at any time alter the level of discourse and become more aware of the inappropriateness of traditional need interpretations; they must be in a position to develop that language system which permits them to say what they want under given conditions with a view to the possibility of changing conditions, and to say – on the basis of a universal consensus – what they ought to want' (Habermas, quoted in McCarthy, 1978, p. 316).

If, in other words, communicative action is to take place, the language system into which all participants enter has to be appropriate for the expression of their true wants and needs. While the Internet can be seen as providing the conditions for communication and, consequently, for action – not through speech but through communication - the appropriateness of the language system and the ensuing behaviour cannot be judged from within the Internet. It takes its validity from a 'needs interpretation' derived from the real world. From there, comes also the demand for a change in the language system and its norms for appropriate behaviour if a group of persons is not allowed proper self-presentation under the current one.

The connection to space and community outside the language system is made via the embodiment of the communicative actor and the materiality of the medium itself. The connection appeared, though obliquely, already in Rheingold's discussion of the WELL. He writes, 'People in virtual communities do just about everything people do in real life, but we leave our bodies behind.' But then he also observes, 'Wellites who do not live within driving distance of San Francisco Bay are constrained in their ability to participate ...' Although we do not equate face-to-face relations with political behaviour, they certainly are the ground for ethical conduct and are thereby intimately connected to the language of morals and to what counts as appropriate behaviour on the Internet (Levinas, 1981).

The only way the Internet can help further democratic ideals is then by tying itself closer to the world outside. This world is never really outside, but all too often cut off deliberately by a dualistically inspired desire to leave the body and all other aspects of the material world behind. Such bracketing of the real world leads ultimately to an impoverishment of the exchanges on the Internet itself.

CONCLUDING REMARKS

To sum up our thoughts on the possible use of the Internet for reestablishing political life: two main axes are necessary in establishing the basis for a participatory democracy; one stands out in explicit behaviour; the other forms the background from which the first emerges. The first axis is that of speech-and-action which appears to be one of the strengths of the Internet. The other axis is that of space-and-community which the Internet has forgotten or suppressed, and has attempted to substitute with virtual counterparts. Needless to say, we feel the substitute works at best as a reminder of the real thing, at worst as the wishful thinking of a dualistic mind. The grounding of democratic political life in space and community does not lose its relevance by being paraded in effigy on the Internet.

Lest we want to treat the creation of the Internet as culmination and institutionalization of the Cartesian schism, we must instead strengthen the relation of the Internet to the larger world and its impact on it. The challenge is to develop an understanding that does justice, first, to the self evident (and, hence, unknown) character of embodied existence and its connection to community and space. And second, this alternative world view must try to imagine not virtual communities and spaces made of words, but develop the affordances of a medium whose materiality is continuous with human embodiment. The way to this goal would also lead to a better understanding and novel use of information technology.

Following Spinoza, understanding bodies means attending to their ethics. This is very important and also relevant for grasping the sense in which the accomplishment of Athenian democracy was not only the creation of superior rationality and rhetorical skill but, most of all, the result of ethical conduct. The capacity for rationality and ethical conduct are related, but they are not interchangeable. Currently, the state of technology and the social imaginary of the culture support mainly discursive rationality. The aspect concerning the ethical remains underdeveloped. Or, to put it differently, by separating speech and rhetoric from their relation to embodied existence, technology has robbed itself of the opportunity to affirm the immanence of life. The current design of the Internet does not support embodiment and the ethics it entails. The aim of this paper is to inspire people to work on one that does ...

REFERENCES

Arendt, Hannah. *The Human Condition.* Chicago Press, 1958.

Armstrong, Arthur; Hagel, John. The Real Value of ON-LINE Communities. *Harvard Business Review.* May-June 1996.

Bakhtin, Mikhail. *Speech Genres and Other Essays.* University of Texas Press, 1984.

Bernstein, Jay M. *Recovering Ethical Life. Jürgen Habermas and the Future of Critical Theory.* Routledge 1995.

Corrado, Anthony; Firestone, Charles M., Editors. *Elections in Cyberspace: Toward a New Era in American Politics.* The Aspen Institute, 1996.

Damiris, Niklas. *Light and The Physics of Intentionality.* Under review.

Electronic Dark Ages, *San Francisco Guardian.* October, 1996.

Habermas, Jürgen. *The Structural Transformation of the Public Sphere. An Inquiry into a Category of Bourgeois Society.* Translated by Thomas Burger, MIT Press, 1991.

Hardin, Russell. *One for All. The Logic of Group Conflict.* Beacon Press, 1982.
Harrison, Steve; Dourish, Paul. *Re-Place-ing Space: The Roles of Place and Space in Collaborative Systems*, Proceedings of the ACM Conference on Computer-Supported Cooperative Work CSCW '96, Boston, Nov. 1996.
Lefebvre, Henri. *The Production of Space.* Blackwell, 1991.
Levinas, Emmanuel. *Otherwise than Being or Beyond Essence.* Martinus Nijhoff, 1981.
Lyotard, Francois; *The Differend.* Minnesota Press, 1988.
McLuhan, Marshall. *Understanding Media: The Extensions of Man.* McGraw-Hill, 1964.
McCarthy, Thomas; *The Critical Theory of Jürgen Habermas.* MIT Press, 1978.
McKeon, Robert, Ed., *Basic Works of Aristotle.* Random House. 1941.
Rheingold, Howard. *The Virtual Community.* Vintage, 1993.
Spinoza, Baruch. *Ethics.* Dover Edition. 1670.
Stein, Gertrude. *The Autobiography of Alice B. Toklas.* Harcourt, Brace and Co., 1933.
Zappa, Frank. *Roxy & Elsewhere.* LP. 1978.

---

[1] For the differentiation between viewpoint and standpoint, see Damiris (forthcoming).

[2] See a pungent critique of this attitude in *Electronic Dark Ages*, San Francisco Guardian, October 1996.

27

DEMOS: Democratic evaluation of multiple options in society

Vassilios Laopodis
European Commission, DG III.B.2 SC15 1/142
200, Rue de la Loi, B-1049 Brussels
Phone: +32 2 299 0034, Fax +32 2 296 8998
Email: vassilios.laopodis@dg3.cec.be

Abstract

The deepening of democracy and enlargement of citizens' participation in the decision-making process theoretically is, and always has been, on the agenda of all individual countries and associations of nations such as the European Union and the United Nations organizations. The emergence of the information society and its very rapid globalization potentially affects all forms of human activity. The debate on the possible threat posed by the global information society to human rights, and the potential advent of hyperpowerful governments, is counterbalanced by proposals for genuine use of the technology to bring decision-makers and citizens closer, and to allow the latter to influence decisions.

This paper discusses concepts of direct *versus* indirect democracy, without entering into a formal comparison, and some potential advantages of more direct democracy at a local level. It proposes the exploitation of commonly available tools of the global information society to introduce new forms of democratic consultation with a view to facilitating the evaluation, by citizens themselves, of the options presented and allowing them to influence decision-making.

The DEMOS model proposed, is based on exploitation of information highways, particularly the Internet, for obtaining direct participation in debates of citizens and their representative groups.

It is inspired by the momentum of the European Scenario Workshops Initiative (EC DG XIII-Innovation programme) and proposes a two-way channel using the information highways and covering all the stages of decision-making: from concepts, to action plans and reform proposals' approvals by the citizens, up to formal voting. Emphasis is given to the implementation at local/community level as an emanation of the ancient Greek *demos* (the assembly of the citizens).

An Ethical Global Information Society J. Berleur & D. Whitehouse (Eds.)

The proposed environment is presently under experimentation, in synergy with other pilot implementations for digital cities, at a European level.

INTRODUCTION

Democracy, from the Greek *demos* (people) and *kratos* (power) is considered to be an archetype for governing people in a state of justice. Nowadays, worldwide, there is a growing wave of dissatisfaction and indifference among laypeople, expressed mostly as abstinence from political actions and from voting, in practically all western countries. In ancient Greece, democracy was direct with citizens empowered (a notable limitation) participating in the decision-making process in the *agora* (market).

The present *indirect* or *representative* democratic system, however, was considered to be the best way to approach this ideal a century ago. Representative democracy was founded and developed mainly because of the existence of political and natural as well as information barriers in communicating and expressing views on a given subject at a certain time. In such systems, democracy is more susceptible to the danger of strong lobbies, persuasion, and even blackmail because many people do not have enough influence in the political decision-making process regardless of whether the system is open to all. Decisions are made by very few people (politicians and their advisers) who do not very often consult and communicate with their electoral bases except during electoral campaigns.

The democratic character of political discourse is a matter for discussion. It is believed, not without foundation, that in many cases it is controlled by elite institutions, most conspicuously political campaigns and the political media that select what messages to disseminate via limited resources of editorial space and time. This massive level of control is not a foregone conclusion.

To ensure that political discourse is democratic, a change in the political media is needed. This change refers to the agenda-setting function of the political media, whereby those who control the distribution of information set the course of the debate. In setting the course of debate, the political media perpetuates a top-down model of political discourse, in which those at the top of the information business hold control over the information provided to the public for discussion (Dutton, 1990).

The only way to promote a system where society is governed by the *people as a whole* is to abolish or to limit the powerful position of many groups in society and allow smaller groups, as well as isolated and disabled citizens, to be informed, to participate in, and to influence the decision-making process concerning all major developments in their neighbourhood, community, city, region or country. To this end, citizens should have the possibility of becoming an integral part of a system for the democratic evaluation of multiple options in society.

The issue of deeper citizens' participation in democratic decision-making has attracted a lot of attention worldwide, particularly in Europe, with the publication of several expert reports at the initiative of the European Union (European Commission, 1996a, 1996b, 1996c) and a reflection has started on improving the decision-making process through the use of information highways to abolish traditional barriers and so as to avoid, at the same time, the creation of new barriers due to computer illiteracy.

DEMOCRACY REVISITED IN A GLOBAL INFORMATION SOCIETY

The idea of a direct democratic system is envisaged by the electronic democracy concept allowing the creation of a new, virtual agora, with open, free, and extensive discussions, and with a view to making optimal decisions regarding local society.

The aim of this revisiting of concepts is not to compare direct *versus* indirect democracy as systems in order to substitute for existing systems of government, but to propose alternative ways to improve the present situation using a step-by-step approach. However, in experimenting with issues such as these, one has to take into account two major concerns and propose measures for solving them, that is, how to benefit from the strengths of direct forms of democracy while limiting their weaknesses and, if more direct democracy is to be the solution in local society, how to distinguish between the simple participation of citizens in the debate and seeking their input and feedback as opposed to responsibility for the implementation of these decisions and their follow-up.

The key element in this debate is easy and free access to public information, free expression of views, extensive discussion for better understanding and, finally, approval of measures to be taken regardless of whether their implementation will be delegated to the executive power directly or whether there will be a formal vote before decisions are taken. At an early stage towards a more direct form of decision-making, it cannot be expected that electronic assemblies of citizens make fast decisions as a continuous process, but it seems more advisable to expect an adequate environment for effective and democratic decision-making. In this respect, the role of elected representatives, even if it seems *de facto* to be limited is, in reality, enlarged by taking a different dimension. Instead of being the only decision-makers, they become guarantors of the democratic process and, in a way, process arbitrators, facilitators, and managers. This might constitute an evolution of parliaments and governments.

Modern information and communications technologies (ICT) play an important role in the vision of direct democracy because they remove constraints in space and time allowing, through computer networks and user-friendly interface tools on the Internet, the opportunity of access to free debates and exchange of thoughts and ideas, and free and direct access to public information and government sources.

Technology does not only provide answers but also imposes new political questions to be answered like, for example, what kind of legal territorial principles will be created by the new electronic highway. These new political questions will also radically influence the future organization of the state. However, in order to establish a system of direct democracy, the whole present political system needs to be changed into new structures supported by infrastructures like the Internet.

A DECISION-MAKING MODEL

A possible scenario envisages the rise of a new electronic information and decision-making layer. This layer would consist of extensive exchanges of information and public electronic discussions, leading to strategic decision-making by means of public consultation and referendums. One of the major difficulties encountered, and a potential problem of direct democracy, is the necessity for theoretically all citizens to devote their permanent attention to public electronic discussions and to be aware of what is happening all the time by consulting public or personal email-based systems and databases.

In this paper a model for the Democratic Evaluation of Multiple Options in Society (DEMOS) is proposed. Its main objective is to contribute to democratic decision-making by establishing a framework for involving and educating ordinary citizens about the information society, and by demonstrating how a platform initiative for electronic democracy may be implemented starting with smaller communities, cities, and regions. The introduction of systems like DEMOS will facilitate the following:

- establishing a favourable environment for public participation;
- providing a platform, stimulating interest in electronic democracy;
- initiating and controlling the electronic democracy process by civic and social organizations themselves;
- providing better information through the development of issue-based discussions, e.g., on sustainable development, the information society;
- providing a level playing field for all candidates;
- giving citizens an opportunity to put their views on questions asked by participants in public debates and to influence decisions, mainly at local and regional levels;
- providing an open discussion forum for citizens, available 24-hours a day;
- increasing participation, and reaching young voters and citizens with specific needs (e.g., the elderly and disabled persons).

THE ACTORS

Electronic democracy represents a major step towards the implementation of the information society involving a large number of actors, such as administrations, citizens associations, social partners, and academics.

Such an initiative will have to start with an assessment of how people can make best use of the potential of new technologies, in order not only to improve communication among themselves, with their administrations and at the global level, but also to enlarge participation in decision-making processes. However, the model is based on the assumption that citizens and administrations are fully aware of the capabilities of electronic highways, and trained to use such facilities. Therefore at the first stage of experimentation and pilot implementation, we need to consider its availability as a training tool for all and to foresee that promotion and demonstration actions are addressed (Laopodis, 1996):

- local and community level administration authorities, by demonstrating the potential of information society;

- civic and societal associations and groups, by giving them the opportunity to initiate and control open discussions and debates;
- citizens, by providing an open discussion forum available 24-hours a day;
- specific social groups, such as women, young voters, and citizens with special needs (e.g., the elderly and the disabled), by increasing the opportunities for participation;
- decision-makers at different policy levels (local, regional, national, etc.), by giving them a holistic approach, for full coverage of the election process life cycle.

METHODOLOGICAL APPROACH

Changes towards more direct forms of democracy have to be approached very gradually. It has to be made clear that experiments with electronic forms of democracy are primarily *a way to participate in the discussion, not in the actual decision-making*. This is to prevent the risk of an increasing gap between citizens and government with no satisfaction of expectations raised. Direct public participation in decision-making will only be possible when its legal status is introduced.

Methodologically, an experiment, bringing people behind the electronic steering wheel (keyboard, voice recognition, etc.) should be implemented in a number of distinct stages: envisioning, designing, creating, transforming, exploiting, and finally managing.

- *envisioning* - creating belief in the new direction and vision. Envisioning is not only about opening people's minds to change, it is also about creating a vision to which the whole idea can work. The vision should identify priorities for the operations and the objectives.
- *designing* - formulating the new processes and technological background. An analysis of the existing operation is essential to the project. Such an analysis provides an accurate base line against which any desired changes in processes and technology can be measured. It ensures that the vision is practicable given the context of the local communities, and helps to prioritize the changes proposed.
- *creating* - exploring the vision and developing a practical and effective pilot that will deliver in use the new issues. The plans and designs created in the previous phase are used to build and implement the organization, procedures, information systems, and technology that will transform the local society.
- *transforming* - implementing the required organizational changes and promote the new issues through an awareness campaign and pilot usage. Heavy emphasis is placed on change management activities to smooth the transition from old to new operations. Coordination between enablers is as important as ever to synchronize the people, process, and technology aspects of the change. This phase focuses on supporting proven citizens' participatory methods and techniques such as the European Awareness Scenario Workshops.
- *exploiting* - the exploiting phase, therefore, has no clear end point. However, several activities are essential to reap the full benefits of the launch effort. The first one is aimed at securing the benefits identified during the project and is

related to providing a framework for the effort to continue improving. The second activity is tuning the local society for further use since, after any major change, a period of confusion is undergone as new relationships are forged, and system bugs are rectified. A third set of activities relates to synergy with ongoing activities and/or launching complementary activities at regional, national, and European levels.

- *managing* - to ensure the efficient time, resource and financial management of the project.

BUILDING UPON THE EUROPEAN AWARENESS SCENARIO WORKSHOPS

The European Awareness Scenario Workshops (EASW) initiative launched in 1994 in the framework of the EC VALUE II Interfaces programme (presently Innovation) is the result of number of interrelated activities undertaken at European level to enhance the interface between Science-Technology-Society (European Commission, 1994, 1996d; Interfaces, 1994, 1995).

It is based on the *scenario workshop* methodology developed in Denmark (DBT, 1993; Bilderbeek, *et. al.*, 1994) to deal with the problem of formulating visions and recommendations for attaining *sustainable urban living in the coming decades* in different cities. This methodology revisited served as a platform for facilitating the participation of societal groups in information society-related development (Andersen, *et al.*, 1995; Laopodis and Fernandez, 1995, 1996).

This approach allows for the participation of all interested members of the public organized into four role-groups of participants: *local policy-makers*, *technology experts* in the field, *residents* and groups of citizens, selected after advertisement in local radios and press, *private sector/investors* representatives in the local or regional business community so that they can conduct an ideological debate within and between groups, in the early stages of the development of technology. The skills and experience of participants allow for contributions but the process does not privilege knowledge as an instrument of control. This way participants carry out assessments and develop visions and proposals for technological needs and possibilities. Through this process, the general public or appropriate public interest groups can have an influence on the direction or application of technology and ensures that policy-makers and research and technology development managers are aware of new demands from technology.

With the support of a facilitator (national monitors and several project advisers were added to the European version), the debate is organized around *four alternative scenarios* for the development, representing ideologically very different paths. The result of the process is a set of recommendations and a *vision* statement describing a commonly agreed path of sustainable development for the community, and a (or even *the*) means for successfully achieving that goal.

Laopodis and Fernandez and others have further developed this discussion on the role of citizens in the global information society (Andersen, *et al.*, 1995; Laopodis and Fernandez, 1996) by exploring case studies/scenarios on provision of ICT services for citizens in the local community, flexibility and integration of working and family life through teleworking and, finally, quality of life for elderly people in the information society.

This model of awareness raising for citizens in the global information society could be successfully used for experimenting with the introduction of electronic democracy in different communities. Several pilot projects emanating from research and technology development programmes such as Esprit have already demonstrated their potential value at a European level. Systems such as Municipality Voyager-Iperbole, Citycard, Web for groups, and so on (Omega Generation, 1996), are considered to include characteristics of the DEMOS proposal and are being adapted to local requirements.

THE DEMOS MODEL

Democratic Evaluation of Multiple Options in Society (DEMOS) is a proposal for a model improving direct electronic democracy. It relies on the simple concept of integrating publicly available information, local governments, and citizens in an interactive system with simple rules that offer transparency. Information and data regarding decisions to be taken can be generated for, by, and communicated to and from:

i) individual citizens (and citizens' groups) in the form of requests, expression of needs, discussions, opinions, preferences, amendments and, finally, acceptance through a voting mechanism;
ii) government structures of any kind, i.e., local, peripheral (region, county, city) and central (national, supranational) in the form of both informal and formal invitations to express opinions, preferences, as well as proposals, announcements of intentions, alternative options and major choices, as well as dissemination of public information and decisions;
iii) representative structures such as municipal, regional, national, supranational parliaments with decision-making power or, in the future, with a facilitator of the process role.

Reflecting the above structure, the DEMOS model consists of the following components (Figure 1, Figure 2).

Central Information Repository

This repository, which has to be operated under the responsibility of the formal institution itself (government, parliament, etc.), must contain up-to-date information on every institutional initiative or decision made, in non-bureaucratic language that is easy to understand for ordinary citizens, and is made accessible through telecommunications means and networks such as the Internet. However, in addition to other facilities, basic services have to be assured as a minimum by a normal phone (though a help desk) to unconnected citizens, and special care should be taken about informing elderly and disabled people by providing adapted means (voice, text, etc.).

Basic Information Highway

An Internet-based facility with full email, browsing capabilities, etc., constitutes the communications carrier.

Fig. 1 : The DEMOS Model

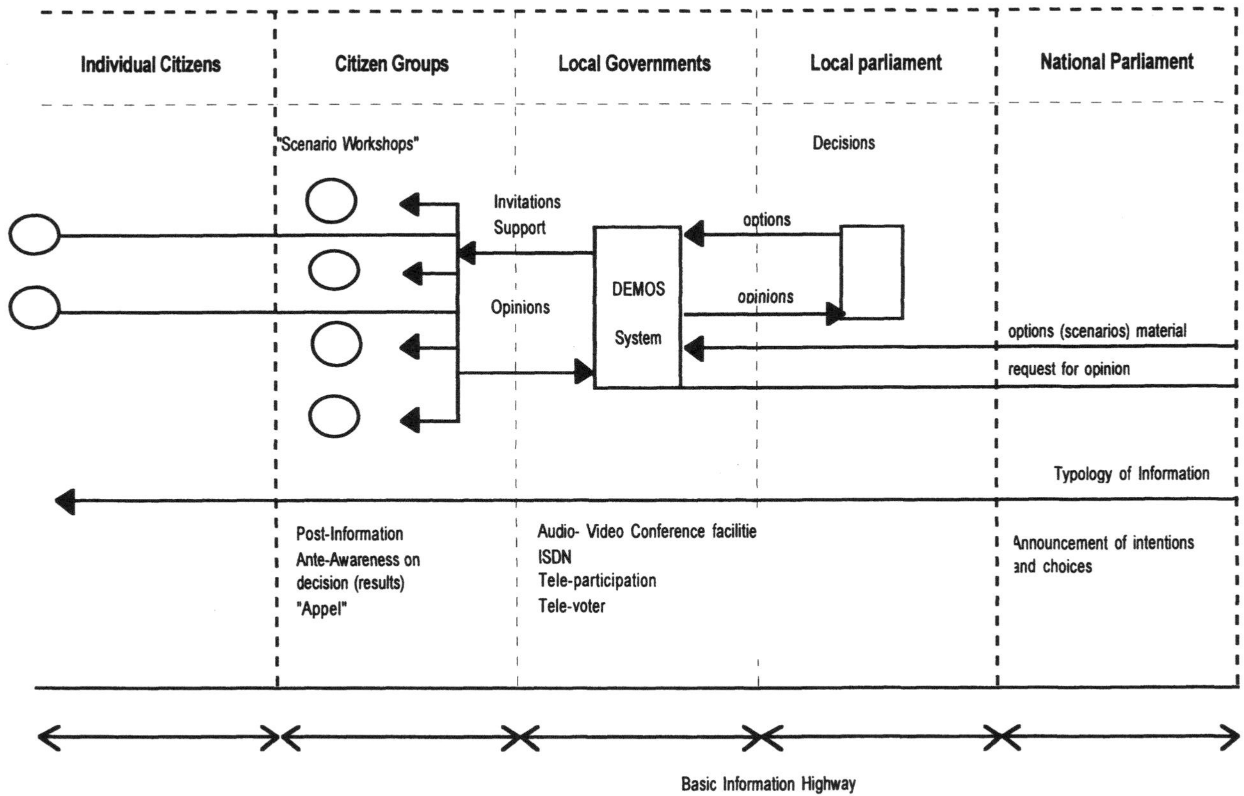

Workshop Function

This function consists of a number of support services, electronic or human-based, such as the following facilities which are primarily community-operated and inspired by the European Awareness Scenario Workshops initiative.

Audio and video-conference facilities
These facilities allow the organization and setting-up of virtual citizens' assemblies of any kind, according to their needs, using traditional and advanced telecommunications technology.

Awareness Scenario Workshops Module

- scenario development project teams;
- scenario teleworkshops;
- awareness raising.

  This module is the human heart of the system playing a multiple role:
- Scenario development project team: a multidisciplinary team of experts who develop scenarios for multiple options for society voluntarily or on request on hot issues involving political or technological options.
- Organizers of real and virtual scenario workshops: they develop the material, tools etc., to organize the debate, so that it is not restricted to selected groups but allows the teleparticipation of every aware citizen.
- Promotion/awareness and training: promotes the concept to citizens and decision-makers to allow for larger acceptance.

Citizens' Help Desk
A 24-hour, electronically accessible, help desk to answer any queries related to the basics and the use of the system.

Information/Data Typology
Classification and categorization of documents and standardized messages to allow secure and unambiguous circulation of virtual and real documents.

The EASW can be used as a tool both for promoting the concept and for improving citizens' participation in this democratic debate. This methodology offers a discussion forum where citizens, technological experts, local authorities, and the private sector can confront ideas and launch a discussion which can be followed by electronically-supported stages to avoid physically mobilizing many people. In addition, a scenario development mechanism should be established to offer governments, parliamentarians, and citizens' groups the possibility of disseminating controversial aspects of the same issue and trigger citizens' reactions. For both these activities a *teleworkshop support function* is needed using videoconference facilities in different places.

This mechanism should be composed of a citizens' knowledge database as part of a more substantial information kiosk for electronic democracy where all decisions are adequately registered and can be easily accessed by interested people.

Fig. 2 : The DEMOS Model : Internal Structure

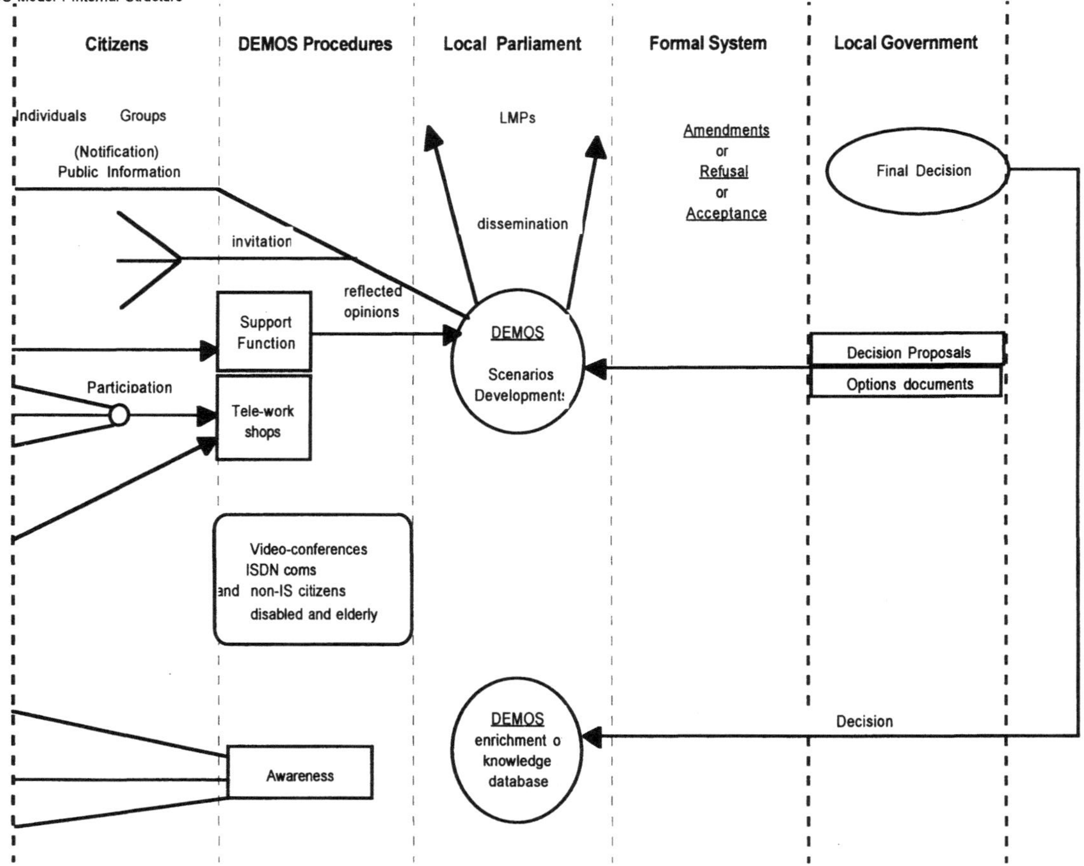

CONCLUSIONS

Enhancing citizens' participation in democratic decision-making in all matters of everyday life is a necessity but also a challenge especially in view of a global information society.

Initiatives such as the European Awareness Scenario Workshops (EASW) of the European Commission (DG XIII.D) have been launched during the last years to promote the concept of citizens' participation in a democratic debate for evaluation of options in relation with technological developments involving local communities and active citizens' groups. On the other hand, several experiments are being developed that aim at new forms of citizens' involvement using ICT (Omega Generation, 1996).

The model DEMOS proposed in this paper explores a means of offering the global information society so as to move this reflection towards a higher step, i.e., the gradual promotion of a direct electronic democratic system allowing societies to be governed by the people as a whole and not by isolated representatives' schemes quite apart from the citizens.

DEMOS uses the EASW methodology and its tools for awareness purposes and proposes a number of functions at the service of citizens at the local level in order to express their views, formulate proposals, forward opinions, and accept or reject governmental initiatives through an electronically-based system of expression of opinion and voting.

On the other hand, DEMOS allows governments at different levels to inform citizens about initiatives and proposals, to establish an interactive dialogue and, finally, to make decisions with (almost) all citizens involved. In such a system, representatives change their roles to arbitrators and guarantors of the process.

The DEMOS Model is under further study leading to an experimental implementation involving a consortium of citizens' groups, local governments, ICT companies, and universities.

REFERENCES

Andersen I., Bilderbeek R., Danielsen O., and Kluver L., *Feasibility Study on New Awareness Initiatives*, DTT(DBT-TNO), VALUE II Interfaces Project Report (Final) February 1995.

Bilderbeek R., *et al.*, *Testing the Feasibility of Scenario Workshops on Sustainable Urban Living*, VALUE II Interfaces project report, TNO-STB/UNECIA, 1994.

(DBT) Danish Board of Technology, *Project Publications* issue, 1993.

Dutton W., *The political implications of information technology: Challenge to power* in the *Information Society; Evolving Landscapes*, J. Berleur *et al.* (editors), Springer-Verlag, 1990.

European Commission, *VALUE II Interfaces Documentation (Brochure and Summary of Results, DG XIII.D)*, Luxembourg, 1994.

European Commission, Green Paper COM (96)389, *Living and Working in the Information Society*, 1996a

European Commission, *Networks for people and their communities; Making the most of the Information Society in the European Union*, Forum IS, June 1996, (URL:http:\www.ispo.cec.beinfoforum\pub.html), 1996b.

European Commission, Communication COM (96)395, *Information Society: From Corfu to Dublin*, 1996c.

European Commission, DG XIII.D, *Innovation project on local initiatives*, 1996d

Interfaces, *Proceedings of Interfaces '94 Conference*, December 1994, DG XIII.D Luxembourg, 1994.

Interfaces, *Proceedings of Interfaces '95 Conference*, December 1995, DG XIII.D Luxembourg, 1995.

Laopodis V., *Developing Standards for Inter-operability in the Global Information Society*, ICT Standardization and Disability in Europe, European Policy Workshop, Amsterdam, April 1996.

Laopodis V., and Fernandez F., *Enhancing citizens participation in the Information Society*, Proceedings of the 5th Informatics Conference Greek Computer Society, Athens, December 1995.

Laopodis V., and Fernandez F., *Awareness raising for citizens in the Global Information Society*, HUSITA 4 Conference proceedings, Rovaniemi, Finland, June 1996.

Omega Generation, *Municipality Voyager MV-Iperbole*, documentation, 1996.

28

Historical and topographical amnesia on the information highway: Metaphors and tacit knowledge

Leif Bloch Rasmussen and Gertrud Krarup
ProjectCentre CESAR, Copenhagen Business School,
Copenhagen Science Park Symbion, DK-2100 Copenhagen Ø,
Phone: + 45 39 17 98 66, Fax: + 45 39 17 98 63
Email: iqlbr@cbs.dk, iqgk@cbs.dk

Abstract

The information highway and the information age are two concepts loaded with metaphorical connotations. They seem to imply the possibility for orientation in space and connection in history as the tacit knowledge of how people could and should be able to cope with the future.

A cognitive semantic exploration of the 'directive' metaphor of being *on* the information highway and the 'container' metaphor of being *in* the information age, however, both point to a tacit acceptance of a very limited knowledge of time and space. They indicate the cultural and democratic risks of creating topographical and historical amnesia.

As a movement away from the dangerous implications of using these metaphors, we search for orientation in space and connection in history from two great historical figures: Kierkegaard on historical understanding through choices in our personal life using his *Stages on The Way of Life*, and Goethe on spatial understanding in the eye using his colour theory (*Farbenlehre*).

INTRODUCTION[1]

During the past few years, we have seen many reports on national information and communication technology (ICT) strategies from all over the world. They all seem to be alike and created from the same viewpoint and fundamental values: change is ongoing, it is global, it is fast and we all have to obey, participate, accept, and try to keep apace.

An Ethical Global Information Society J. Berleur & D. Whitehouse (Eds.)

It may be argued that these strategies are only examples of political decisions, without much impact on reality because the speed of technological development in the so-called free market is so fast that no one can and need control it. 'Remove the obstacles and don't brake' seems to be the credo for the industrialists and free riders in reengineering nations.

In this article, this credo will initially be confronted by departing from some speculations on our ability, or even inclination, to create the ultimate perception machine - the Perceptron - as envisioned by the French philosopher, Paul Virilio, and the American system philosopher, Charles West Churchman. Both Virilio and Churchman argue that, physically and mentally, we are losing some of our most fundamental categories and perceptions: *time and space.*

These two philosophers will set the scene for the metaphorical exploration of some of the national ICT strategies.

TOPOGRAPHICAL AND HISTORICAL AMNESIA - PHYSICALLY

In *La Machine de Vision*, Paul Virilio (1987) investigates how using computers may develop topographical and historical amnesia. One of the most important physical characteristics of this amnesia is the weakening of peripheral vision in favour of focal vision without context. This may in turn lead to 'lazy eyes' and, finally, blindness. Virilio sees this as a movement towards the giving up of human perception faculties in favour of the vision machine - the ultimate robot in the human being - the Perceptron. He states his main hypothesis this way:

> 'With the industrial proliferation of vision and audio-visual prostheses, with the excessive use of these means to instant transport of images from their tender beginning we will witness an ever increasing artificial coding of mental images with an ever decreasing time horizon to fix the images without much benefit afterwards - a fast collapsing of the mnemotechnical consolidation.
>
> This seems natural if you, on the other hand, remember that sight and its spatio-temporal organization comes before movement, speech and their coordination. It does this through recognition and making recognizable and the ability to create mental images: thoughts and cognitive functions, which do not know passivity[2]' (Virilio, 1989, p. 22. Our translation from the Danish version).

By not consolidating images, our consciousness simply refuses to create and sustain the image. We lose our faculty for creating images and space orientation through the eyes.

Similarly, Churchman (1976) has warned against the ultimate stress put on the future in systems design (SD). He argues that, as systems designers, by the use of global computer-modelling and global computer networks, we forget and abandon the past and put too much belief in a computerized future. As he puts it:

> 'One often hears these days that global-systems simulations are only "first approximations," crude and wrong in many ways. But both Descartes and Paul realized that if you believe you have a "first approximation," then you also have an idea about the second, the third, and the "limit," else your "first" is not an "approximation" at all: "Now we see through a glass darkly, but then face to face. Now I know in part: then I shall understand fully..." To Paul, the

"basic" aspects of mankind's progress lie in faith, hope and love. To Descartes, they lie in the proof of the existence of a benign Supreme Being. Most global simulators do not care to resort to such reactions to our past and indeed ignore them completely and without reflection. None of them seem to wish to forecast what society would be like in the year 2020 if mankind's faith, hope and love with respect to God were restored, although this may be the most important forecast of all. The philosophical point is that none of us who concern ourselves with SD have a sound basis for choosing between Paul and an MIT simulator' (Churchman, 1974, p. 460 - 461).

Both Virilio and Churchman point to the probability of the collapse of our physical understanding of the categories of time and space as we try to install computerized prostheses instead of our sense apparatus.

TOPOGRAPHICAL AND HISTORICAL AMNESIA - MENTALLY

However, this possibility of *physical* reduction, or even extermination of our senses, may be compensated through *mental* explorations and expansions or, literally speaking, through bigger brains and bigger minds. The information society and the so-called knowledge-based society may be compensating as we develop more abilities to use ICT without limits - spatially as well as temporally. This, at least, is the promise in what we have called the 'national' ICT strategies that we use as illustrations in this article.

Is there any indication in these strategies which may compensate for the physical deterioration of time and space? Or do they also accept and even provoke this deterioration conceptually?[3]

WAYS IN METAPHORICAL ANALYSIS

In Rasmussen (1994, 1995, 1996), Holm-Pedersen and Rasmussen (1995), Krarup and Rasmussen (1996), eight different ways of designing inquiring systems based on eight world views (in German, *Weltanschauung*) have been identified, described, and documented. Churchman's term, inquiring system, is used as it is a more generic and well-founded epistemological term than information systems or even knowledge-based systems. This work is especially based on Jantsch (1975, 1979), Churchman (1971, 1982) and Singer (1924, 1948, 1959).

These world views are the foundation for design methodologies; each methodology seems to make use of its own special metaphors and tacit knowledge. They are all related to the very different ways in which we imagine the information society: the way we are going to live and work on the information highway and in the information age.

The eight world views, design methodologies, and most frequently used metaphors in organizational design, are depicted in Table 1.

It is our contention that there will be much benefit from a more thorough investigation of the metaphors used in these world views and design methodologies and national reports, as this kind of investigation may reveal the hidden tacit knowledge we have to live and work by on the information highway and in the information age, if there is any at all. However, to our knowledge, there has been no such attempt to analyze the metaphors in the political manifestos of the information society (Krarup, 1994; Krarup and Rasmussen, 1996).

The attempt in this article is, however, much more modest. We aim to explore some of the possibilities in performing a thorough metaphorical analysis in finding the tacit knowledge behind three of the national strategies for creating the information society (those of the European Union, the United States, as well as the report from the European Round Table of Industrialists).

The hypothesis is that, even though such strategic manifestos seem to imply design for social and cultural benefits, they only make use of the first two of the eight world views and design methodologies: they are non-theoretical and/or positivistic in their world views and use trial-and error-doing and/or structured design in their design methodologies.

The hermeneutic 'proof' of this hypothetical pudding is not straightforward as the words used in the texts cannot be taken at their positive social and cultural face value. The tacit knowledge must be revealed. One way of doing this is through metaphorical analysis.

METHODS IN METAPHORICAL ANALYSIS

The importance of metaphors - and tacit knowledge - has primarily been discussed in linguistics, hermeneutics, and psychology. In these three disciplines, it has been acknowledged that metaphors and tacit knowledge play an important part of our daily, practical life. Lately, this knowledge seems to be part of a growing awareness of theories on language, communication, science, and society. At least four methods may be identified in metaphorical analysis:

The traditional method of metaphorical analysis parses the text for those words that, as metaphors, are an alternative and richer means of expression than the word in its literal use. *Metaphor* thus means transference from one domain to another. Typically, this transference takes the form of a figure of speech which replaces the real matter. In systems design and organizational theory (especially in literature and theories on organizational culture), systems design and futures research, some researchers have begun this kind of study (Morgan, 1986; Kendall and Kendall, 1993; Judge, 1993). This method is used in columns 2, 3 and 4 of Table 1.

The second method, cognitive semantics, challenges the above-mentioned method of analysis as based on the traditional western way of thinking. It accuses the method of being based on disembodied and abstract categories. Cognitive semantics confronts this view and looks for metaphors and image schemata which are embodied and concrete. Our perception is thus taken to be grounded in our body. The method may reveal tacit knowledge and hidden world views. This method is in accordance with Virilio, and is used in column 5 in Table 1.

The third method is based on theories of poetry and literature or, more generally speaking, philosophical theories of language and aesthetics. In its most radical form, the Danish philosopher K.E. Løgstrup claims that a metaphor may very well be defined as bringing two different words from different domains together, but that such a bringing together must bring some kind of radicalism and inventiveness along with it, or else it will turn out to be a pale and flat decoration.

Table 1. World views, design methodologies, and most frequently used metaphors in organizational design.*

World View	**Design Methodology**	**Metaphor** (Organizational Design based on Morgan, 1986)	**Metaphor (National Reports)**	**Image Schemata (National Reports)**
non-theory	practical trial-and-error doing	brain	market place, game, war, stake, power game	container (exterior-interior-border)
positivism	structured methods	machine	mechanism, geometry, globe, universe, ever-expansion, speed, highway, age, chemistry	directive (source-path-goal)
hermeneutic	socio-technical, prototyping	organism	adaptation, foster, embryonic, handicap, biology	centre-periphery
dialectic materialism	political power based	domination	revolution, radical	up-down
critical theory	dialectical spiral	politics, history		
teleology	pragmatic	flux, progress	destiny, spirit	
a-teleology, anti-teleology	none	psychic prison, existence		
feminology	value based	myth, life		

* The metaphors in column 3 are taken from Morgan (1986). The metaphors, history, progress, existence, myth, and life are our own stipulations. For reasons of brevity, metaphors and image schemata in the national reports are shown in the table; the explanation is contained in the text. It should be noted that the empirical research behind these explorations as presented here most probably would not stand up to trial in a positivistic court of scientific law. However, they are not intended to since they stem from the hermeneutic world view.

This method has been tried in the metaphorical analysis of the national strategies, but ended with only one possible metaphor: the American skyway. It is therefore not included in Table 1 as was originally intended.

Finally, the fourth method is political. It tells us that metaphors are political power instruments and that we are ruled by the political power idea: overrule and make obsolete a dead metaphor, and design a better one. Because metaphors are poetic speech, people will understand them (within their body), and obey. This hypothesis from the old theories of rhetoric is not used in the analysis even though, ironically enough, it is its main argument.

METHOD ONE: TRADITIONAL WESTERN WORLD VIEW AND NATIONAL ICT STRATEGIES

The traditional western world view seems to hold that reason may be depicted as follows:

> 'Reason is the mechanical manipulation of abstract symbols which are meaningless in themselves, but can be given meaning by virtue of their capacity to refer to things either in the actual world or in possible states of the world' (Lakoff, 1987, p. 7).

With the advent of the digital computer - and maybe even more so with the coming of neural networks - the hypothesis of reason and meaning as manipulation of strings of meaningless symbols seems to many computer scientists and system designers (through circular reasoning) to be the final proof that the mind works like a computer. This mind-as-computer idea is, of course, a metaphor, and it may be a dangerous one. It even elevates the brain to the equal of the mind.

Furthermore, it rests on the idea that there is a symbol-to-object correspondence independent of the human mind and body. The definition of meaning from these kinds of abstract symbols must therefore also be independent of the human mind and body.

The metaphors in column 2, 3 and 4 of Table 1 represent this method of metaphorical analysis of the three national strategies. Quite simply, we have identified all the words in these texts that communicate something other than their literal meanings.

Most of the metaphors are identified in the first three world views, and only 'revolution, radical' and 'destiny, spirit' belong to other world views. This is, of course, is not surprising. One would expect this on the political scene where the reports are written.

But, according to cognitive semantics, there may be tacit knowledge and hidden world views in the texts.

METHOD TWO: COGNITIVE SEMANTICS' WORLD VIEW - IMAGE SCHEMATA

Lakoff confronts the traditional western view:

> 'To question the classical view of categories in a fundamental way is thus to question the view of reason as disembodied symbol manipulation and

correspondingly to question the most popular version of the mind-as-computer metaphor. Contemporary prototype theory does just that - through detailed empirical research in anthropology, linguistics, and psychology. The approach to prototype theory that we will be presenting here suggests that human categorization is essentially a matter of both human experience and imagination - of perception, motor activity, and culture on the one hand, and of metaphor, metonymy, and mental imaginary on the other. As a consequence, human reason crucially depends on the same factors, and therefore cannot be characterized merely in terms of the manipulation of abstract symbols' (Lakoff, 1987, p. 8).

Of course, some part of human reasoning may be abstract symbol manipulation, but this kind of argument from the cognitive sciences suggests that this is a very limited view and that we should see it as a special case of a much more general theory of cognitive models. But to change the very concept of categorization is to change our concept of the mind and our understanding of the world.

Lakoff's evidence suggests:

'... a shift from classical categories to prototype based categories defined by cognitive models. It is a change that implies other changes: changes in the concepts of truth, knowledge, meaning, rationality - even grammar.

Some of the ideas that will fall are:

- Meaning is based on truth and reference; it concerns the relationship between symbols and things in the world.
- Biological species are natural kinds, defined by common essential properties.
- The mind is separate from, and independent of, the body.
- Emotion has no conceptual content.
- Grammar is a matter of pure form.
- Reason is transcendental, in that it transcends - goes beyond - the way human beings, or any other kind of beings, happen to think. It concerns the inferential relationships among all possible concepts in this universe or any other. Mathematics is a form of transcendental reason.
- There is a correct, God's eye view of the world - a single correct way of understanding what is and is not true.
- All people think using the same conceptual system.

These ideas have been part of the superstructure of Western intellectual life for two thousand years. They are tied, in one way or another, to the classical concept of a category. When that concept is left behind, the others will be too. They need to be replaced by ideas that are not only more accurate, but more humane' (Lakoff, 1987, p. 11).

It is Lakoff's hypothesis that 'Image schemata structure both our conceptions and our rich mental images' (Lakoff, 1987, p. 453).

The fundamental position in cognitive semantics, as part of Lakoff's kind of cognitive science, is that meanings are in the head. In other words, in cognitive semantics it is held that all human knowledge, knowledge handling, perception, and action are based on the conceptual system (Johnson, 1987; Lakoff, 1987). One of the basic principles is that meaning is often represented as geometric or spatial constructions. Major examples of these are the so-called image schemata proposed by Lakoff (1987) and Johnson (1987). Image schemata are simple, well-defined, and well structured images that are used over and over again to conceptualize structures in action, reflection, experience, and 'reality'. To take an example: the 'container schema' consists of the structural elements such as: interior-exterior-border. Other typical examples of image schemata are: centre-periphery, up-down, directive (source-path-goal). Both Lakoff (1987) and Johnson (1987) contend that the image schemata are kinesthetic because they all are related to the human body and basic types of bodily action.

The image schemata thus reflect - in terms of schematic structures - that human experience and cognition are organized across different domains, i.e., they are a kind of depth semantics. One way of detecting which image schemata underlie a statement is to analyze the metaphor which is used.

The scientific research question is, however: does knowledge based on *no*-body information support or suppress knowledge of body information and vice versa?

With Virilio in mind, we may rephrase this question: does our fundamental use of *no*-body information suppress the development of our body and its senses and replace them with prostheses?

The value of opening up a path of this kind of cognitive semantic inquiry can only be shown through detailed case studies of phenomena that reveal something about the nature of human reason. Of course, we see the national ICT strategies as one such phenomenon.

The implication for the analysis of the effect of information and communication technology on society is that one should look for the image schemata *re*-presenting those metaphors that are central to the texts and to the political decisions and national strategies.

This method has been used to identify and count all the image schemata in the texts. The idea of a percentage of image schemata in the text as potential 'proof' of amnesia may be ill warranted. It is based purely on the intuitive knowledge that what is in the text is also in your mind and in your action.

Our first attempt at this investigation is depicted in column 5 in Table 1. The image schemata of 'container' and 'directive' accounts for approximately 80% of the metaphors. We thus stipulate that most of the image schemata point to the tacit acceptance of the two first world views. And this only stresses the very strong limitations of sight (potential topographical amnesia), and of an only one way ahead scenario (potential historical amnesia).

This would not be so dangerous, if there were creative metaphors in the texts, as may be imagined from the third method of metaphorical analysis.

METHOD THREE: METAPHORS IN AESTHETICS - LØGSTRUP'S THEORY

Løgstrup states:

> 'Just because you replace a pale expression with a more lucid or graphical/pictorial, an abstract with a concrete, it is not said that you have a metaphor' (Løgstrup, 1976, p. 74. Our translation).

His reasoning behind this notion of metaphors is based on a theory of metaphors by Max Black (1954-55). He sees three different theories of metaphors:

1. Substitution theory, which states that the metaphorical expression is equivalent to what is literally meant. Using a metaphor is for stylistic reasons. The metaphor is a decoration. A metaphor in this theory may also be necessary when no literal equivalent can be found which for example is the case for a triangle's 'legs'.
2. Comparison theory, where the metaphor presents an understood or implied analogy or equality, which is left to the reader or listener herself to realize in order to bring the metaphorical expression back to its literal equivalent. The metaphor is a concise parable. Black mentions Schopenhauer's statement that a mathematical proof is a 'mouse trap'. The implied meaning is that both a mathematical proof and a mouse trap offer a reward which is an illusion, and that seduces the victim and presents it with an unpleasant surprise.
3. The interaction theory, where the word, which is the focal point of our awareness, gets a new meaning by being put into a framework that is different from where it belongs. This new meaning is also different from the one it has in the domain where it belongs. Both the framework and the domains are given a different meaning. Furthermore, the new framework expands the meaning of the word in a way that cannot be substituted by a literal meaning.
4. As an example, a person may be described as being as wily as a fox, as sly as a snake or as gentle as a dove. This does not mean the fox is inherently wily, the snake is sly or the dove is gentle. But we want to pinpoint a person's wiliness, slyness and gentleness and we use the way a fox walks, the snake's slithering movement, and the looks of a dove as a pictorial expression of the person. In the jump from one domain to another, and one framework to another, the metaphorically used word gets a meaning it did not have before.

While the substitution and comparison metaphors can be translated into a non-metaphorical expression, the interaction metaphor cannot. We may therefore conclude with Løgstrup that bringing two different words from two different domains together, in itself, does not make a metaphor.

Løgstrup goes even further and suggests that in order to have a metaphor:

- there must be strangeness between the two words and the two domains used
- the words must come from domains as far away from each other as possible
- the words must be as strange to each other as possible
- the words must create excitement in the expression
- the metaphors must create creativeness in the listener/reader
- the metaphor must be inexplicable, hiding its real meaning from direct translation.

For this third method of metaphorical analysis, we have derived two lessons from Løgstrup's way of looking at metaphors:

1. Find all those metaphors which fulfil Løgstrup's requirements. They must be there otherwise the texts on the information highway and information age are empty of feelings, meanings, and horizons. (This is the analysis preferred by Løgstrup.)
2. Find the tacit knowledge in the texts. (This is precisely what Lakoff's and Johnson's work on image schemata is all about) (Lakoff and Johnson, 1976).

Sadly enough we could only find 'skyway' in the American National Information Infrastructure (NII) report as a possible candidate for a metaphor in

Løgstrup's sense. It is even questionable whether it is a metaphor in the American language, even though it seems so for a Dane trying to understand American.

INSPIRATION OR AMNESIA BY METAPHORS

Use of metaphors may thus create energy as well as stability in design. It may create potentials for the way we live and work. But it may certainly create very strong limits to our design of the way we may come to live and work on the information highway and in the information age.

Bani Shorter (1987, p. 118) puts it razor sharply:

> 'Human beings do not get their psychic energy from a model, but from myth, dream, and parable, which is the same as accepting, that man's most fundamental point of reference is something mystic, archetypal, and religious, more than it is something intellectual. Our intellect is very limited by our being human and by our human senses. Our lives do not have the goal of finding out how to be better men or women; they aim to be *imitatio dei*, and through initiation be invited to take part in the potential of the original myth.
>
> Contrary to this models are created by humans which can be designed by what we already know and have seen. There are no metaphorical models; metaphor and myth are joined together with the mystical. It always contains something inexpressible and ineffable in precise terms; it remains unfinished, descriptive and familiar, but nevertheless unclear.'

This means that we need to use metaphors in Løgstrup's sense in order to get any psychic energy at all for our design. Metaphors are in fact also a gift, in the sense that they may fill the gaps which are always present in our communication and our rational design processes.

The lesson for theoreticians and practitioners in systems design may sound like this: stop building a surplus of Perceptrons, models and empirical data; imagine, create, and use inspiring metaphors.

At the same time, we have to admit that we will never be able to understand fully how system design really works, no matter how sophisticated our models may be. This insight was in fact put forward by Gödel, Wittgenstein, and Wiener more than fifty years ago, but the time may have come to bring this insight into our theories.

As mentioned above, there is only one metaphor in the texts which meet Løgstrup's requirements: skyway mentioned in the American NII report, p.23: 'Freeing up spectrum to create "skyways".' Whether this is really a conscious use of a metaphor is hard to say. It is hidden a long way back in the report. So we have to look at other spaces and at other times.

AGES PAST AND WAYS OUT

If our use of Lakoff's and Løgstrup's analysis is correct, we must look for better metaphors than the information highways in order to create visions for democracy, culture, and society in the information age. Global western amnesia is the problem, not globalization. The credo for sustainable development: *Think Globally - Act*

Locally may come to have a new meaning if acting locally is guided by a literally narrow point of view and an extermination of our sense-apparatus.

We need better metaphors to live and work by if democracy, culture, and society are to be revolutionized in a radical fashion. But can metaphors be designed? No, not directly, but indirectly.

If the fundamental problem in democracy, culture, and society as a result of ICT strategies is the destruction of our fundamental categories and facilities to grasp them, we need to recover these categories and facilities from the only possible source we have in our hands, heads, and hearts: the power of aesthetics, ethics, epistemology, and religion embedded in a firm belief in spontaneity.

In our search for the design of better metaphors, we might look at the present, to the future or to the past. As we seem to have forgotten much of the past and as we seem to be blinded to the future by the present we can only turn to the forgotten, still not used, past. To our minds, two original candidates seem ready at hand as signposts from the past: Goethe and Kierkegaard. They both lost on their own battleground at that point in history. The time may have come for ICT people to look back in order to envision the future. We will just sketch our visions for our own recovery.

RECOVERING FROM TOPOGRAPHICAL AMNESIA ON THE INFORMATION HIGHWAY

Goethe was very interested in one of the areas of spatial-temporal interest for a new revolutionary look at ICT: our senses and our perceptions of colours.

Goethe's main idea is directly opposed to the Newtonian colour theory used in all national ICT strategies. Goethe's colour theory creates a very close relationship between the eye, the human body, and colours. He expressed this relation in an aphoristic form in 1805-06:

'The eye is the last and highest result of light in the organic body
The eye as creator of light creates all that which light may create by itself
The light renders all visible to the eye; the eye renders everything to the human being
The ear is speechless, the mouth is deaf, but the eye senses and speaks. In that it mirrors the world from outside, the human being from inside
The totality of inner and outer is completed through the eye.'
(Our translation from Goethe, *Färgläre*, Swedish edition, 1976.)

When Goethe says that colour is a child of light and dark, he complements natural science thinking with a philosophical and poetic dimension. Light is symbolic for Goethe. He considers light as the most simple and most homogenous phenomenon in the world. It cannot be divided, split or refracted.

Newton analyzes and experiments until he reaches measurable light [particles] splitting and refracting. He represents the objective, measuring, natural science way of thinking - positivism.

Goethe's interest is in describing immeasurable light (the homogenous - the indivisible - the pure - the symbolic light). He thinks holistically. He expands natural science thinking to encompass the investigation of the physiology of senses

- how human beings experience colours. Outer observations leads to inner observations. Goethe's view leads to psychology.

That we have to act with qualitatively different ways of looking at the world is illustrated by the following citations from a conversation between Eckermann and Goethe. Goethe says:

> 'I disagreed with Newton's theory of light and colour, when I realized that it was a delusion. I experienced the light in its purity and truth and I had it as a vocation to fight for. But the other side strives in all seriousness to darken the light, as they postulated that shadow is part of light. It sounds meaningless when I say it this way, but the case is like this: They said that colours are something thoroughly shadowed and shadowy. They are the light itself, they are light beams, which are refracted in different ways.
>
> "I'm sorry for many a good student," Goethe said, "it can be completely indifferent to me as my colour theory is as old as the world and it will survive and cannot be denied and pushed aside in the long run."
>
> For Newton and natural science thinking, light is an intellectual, craftsmanlike challenge. For Goethe it is in addition a deep mental and spiritual matter.'
>
> (Our translation from Schmidt, 1993 and Eckermann, 1963.)

We have two colour theories: Newton's and Goethe's. However, the only one used so far on the information highway and in the information age is Newton's. Should this also be the only colour theory used in the future? If so, we will not only get rid of purple and crimson, the highest red colours, which curiously enough do not show up when Newton's light is refracted, but we will also get rid of our eyes as sadly envisioned by Virilio. The study and use of Goethe's colour theory is necessary on our way to recovering from topographical amnesia[4].

RECOVERING FROM HISTORICAL AMNESIA

The Danish philosopher, Søren Kierkegaard, on the other hand, has perhaps taken the most radical view on human choice and existence in history in his search for a way of personal Christian life in coexistence with other human beings and nature.

We live in stages in existence and coexistence, Kierkegaard tells us in *Stages on the Way to Life*. And we make pauses in what he calls *confinie*. He envisioned the following potential stages[5] and confinie in a person's historical existence:

- spontaneous stage; erotic, sensualism, *love*
- curiosity as confinie; the heroic mood
- aesthetic stage; beauty and pleasure, the individual, courage to act, *philia*
- irony confinie; distance to the world and oneself, purification
- ethical stage; good, the collective, *agape*
- humour confinie; hope for our finite life
- religious stage; belief, the mythic, the mystic, *caritas*
- clarity as confinie; hope for our infinite life
- epistemology; truth, *wisdom*

But Kierkegaard also tells us that we cannot communicate on serious matters in a direct way. We must also use an indirect message. And we cannot separate the message from the messenger. He insists that the only possibility is to let every man speak for himself, make his own choices, and formulate his own existence and coexistence. His work is perhaps the most generic and fully developed theory of communication between humans across different world views and cultures.

However, *on* the information highway and *in* the information age, it seems that personal choice and communication must be fixed at the first two stages and the first confinie in order for us all to be entertained and kept as prisoner without any personal historical development possible. The national strategies as well as the credos of the information highway and information age do not allow for personal collective choices to wander beyond the aesthetic stage of pleasure.

Imagine working and living in all these stages and confinies! Wouldn't it be marvellous, even if you have to choose once in a while.

CONCLUSION

Our way of writing has been like meandering or like a debate in the agora. However, any meandering and any debate must come to a pause, and ask: was it worthwhile or just a waste of time? We do not yet know exactly.

There is still much to said, heard, seen, and experienced in the globalization of the world. Maybe we are part of it, maybe not. Maybe globalization in itself is just another means of domination. Or as expressed by Janis Joplin a long time ago: 'Freedom [in the Global World] is just another word for nothing left to lose'.

In the words of Churchman at the end of his *The Design of Inquiring Systems*, the Latin *concludere* means 'to shut up together'. And yet - setting the agora for the next debate:

Topos and *ingegno* are, for Aristotle, those parts of rhetoric which are about proofs and inventiveness. *Topos* is based on so-called *enthymemes*, which are differentiated from strict scientific proofs by building on implicit understanding, assumptions (*doxai*), conjectures, probabilities, and everything that is more or less commonly recognized as part of the public debate. When a speaker must convince an audience on the righteousness of a decision of a political and juridical nature it does not help to use arguments and viewpoints which are unfamiliar or unknown to the audience. On the contrary, the speaker must build the arguments on ideas on which most people agree - what is clever policy, what is suitable morality, and what is a correct line of action. Aristotle calls such assumptions *topoi* which means places, namely those places which the rhetorical argumentation may take as starting points. The Romans called them *loci commune* (common places), and it is exactly such common places that we have to find in order to exist democratically and to coexist across values, opinions, cultures, regions, and life-forms. But *ingegno* (in Latin, *ingenium*) is the creative part of rhetoric. It brings new insights and new combinations to the debate and it is based on a poetic, unconscious, artistic creativity.

A very conscious poetic and political choice of metaphors might have been behind the terms information highway and information age.

REFERENCES

The National Information Infrastructure - Agenda for Action, 1993.

European Round Table of Industrialists: Building The Information Highways to Reengineer Europe - A Message from Industrial Users, 1994.

Europe and the Global Information Society - Recommendations to the European Council, 1994.

Berleur, J. (this volume) Culture and democracy revisited in the global information society: Summary of a position paper.

Berleur, J. and Whitehouse, D. (this volume) Recommendation: From sand, through silver, to gold plates.

Black, M.: Metaphor, *Proceedings of the Aristotelian Society*, Vol. LV, 1954-55.

Churchman, C.W.: Philosophical Speculations on Systems Design, *Omega*, Vol. 2, no. 4, 1976.

Churchman, C.W.: *The Design of Inquiring Systems*, Basic Books, 1971.

Churchman, C.W.: *The Systems Approach and Its Enemies*, Basic Books, 1982.

Eckermann, J.P.: *Samtaler med Goethe*, Gyldendal, 1963 (in Danish, org. German: Gespräche mit Goethe in den letzen Jahren seines Lebens, 1836-1848).

Goethe, J.W.: *Goethes Färgläre*, Kosmos Förlag, Järna, 1976 (in Swedish, org. German 1791 - 1832).

Holm-Pedersen, J. and Rasmussen, L.B.: Geographical Information Systems for Sustainable Development, paper presented to *Conference on GIS in Business*, Madrid, 1995.

Jantsch, E.: *The Design for Evolution*, Brazillier, 1975.

Jantsch, E.: *Self-Organizing Universe*, Addison-Wesley, 1979.

Johnson, M.: *The Body in the Mind*, University of Chicago Press, 1987.

Judge, A. J.: Metaphors in Concepts of the Future, *Futures*, Vol. 25, December 1993.

Kendall, J. E. and Kendall, K. E.: Metaphors and Methodologies: Living Beyond the Systems Machine, *MIS Quarterly*, Vol. 17, no.2, June 1993.

Kierkegaard, S.: *Stages on The Way of Life*, Copenhagen, 1962 (in Danish, org. 1846).

Krarup, G.: Cognitive Aspects as Design Criteria for Human-Computer Interface, Paper presented to Human Factors in Organizational Design and Management - *IV ODAM Conference*, Stockholm, 1994.

Krarup, G. and Rasmussen, L.B.: *Curriculum for Sustainable Development*, Paper presented to the TC-3/TC-9 Conference on ICT in Education, Israel, 1996.

Lakoff, G. and Johnson, M.: *Metaphors We Live By*, Chicago University Press, 1976.

Lakoff, G.: *Women, Fire, and Dangerous Things*, Chicago, 1987.

Løgstrup, K.E.: *Vidde og Prægnans*, Copenhagen, 1976 (in Danish).

Morgan, G.: *Images of Organizations*, SAGE publ., 1986.

Rasmussen, L.B.: Political Choice of Metaphors in Organizational Design, Paper presented to Human Factors in Organizational Design and Management - *IV ODAM Conference*, Stockholm, 1994.

Rasmussen, L.B.: *Alternative World Views in Systems Design*, Working Paper, Inst. of Informatics and Management Accounting, Copenhagen Business School, 1995 (in Danish).

Rasmussen, L.B.: *Alternative Models for Project Management*, Working Paper, Folkuniversitetet, Malmø, 1996 (in Danish).

Schmidt, L.: *Farven og Lyset - Studier i Goethes Farvelære*, Klematis, Aalborg 1993 (in Danish).

Shorter, B.: *An Image Darkly Forming*, Routledge, Kegan, Paul, 1987.

Singer, E. A.: *Mind as Behavior*, R.G.Adams & Co., 1924.

Singer, E. A.: *In Search of a Way of Life*, Columbia University Press, 1948.

Singer, E. A.: *Experience and Reflection*, Columbia University Press, 1959 (ed.: C.W. Churchman).

Virilio, P.: *La Machine de Vision*, Éditions Galilée, 1988. (Danish edition: Synsmaskinen, København, 1989).

---

[1] We emphasize that this article is exploratory and conjectural in order to provoke discussion as intended by the call for papers (Berleur, this volume). We hope it is a sand paper in the sense of being able to suggest further topics, and erasing those taken to be unfruitful (Berleur and Whitehouse, this volume). We wish to thank the referees for very useful comments.

[2] Jules Romains: *La vision extra-rétinnienne et le sens paroptique*, Paris, 1920. This future-oriented

book was revised in 1964: 'Experiments with that vision which is situated outside the retina, show us, that some kind of damage in the eye (*strabismus*, for example) provokes in the person a refusal from the consciousness of the image even though the eye has retained its abilities: the image is created, but consciousness refuses it with ever increasing eagerness, even to the point of blindness' (cited from Virilio, Danish version).

3 It is our hypothesis that this kind of investigation must be carried out in an indirect manner as we cannot grasp what is happening to our fundamental categories in a direct way. The explanation for this hypothesis will, hopefully, be obvious through the discussion, especially through cognitive semantics.

4 Anyone studying colours and colour theory must know the implications of the question: what created colours, the eye or the colours? The debate is there, but not in the creation of colours through as many pixels as possible. Quantity in itself will never catch up with quality.

5 The term 'stages' must not be taken as one step after the other. Stages are rather potential standpoints or world views through which we may exist and coexist.

The role of the Internet both as an ancient agora and a French café for the humanities

Dimitrios Theotokis and Georgios Gyftodimos
University of Athens, Department of Informatics
Panepistimiopolis, Ilissia 157 71, Athens Greece
Email:{dtheo, geogyf}@di.uoa.gr

Abstract

The role of the Internet in today's information world can be considered as one of an agora, a French pre-revolution café, or simply an unlimited source of information available to everyone on request. The beneficiaries of this information availability are many. Academic issues as well as everyday discussions may make use of the world wide web to promote debates, raise issues of interest, put forward concepts and ideas, and generally contribute to the proliferation of knowledge even at the most remote location on the globe either as a blue ribbon medium or as a moderated discussion forum. This increasing information availability, on the one hand, and demand, on the other, pose a very important question: what should computer scientists do to make this worldwide spread of information not only available, but also and most importantly, useful to its recipients?

INTRODUCTION

The Internet's rapid evolution has challenged, among other issues, many of the traditional approaches regarding the proliferation of knowledge, the availability of up-to-date information as well as the means for expressing one's own personal views and actively participating in an exchange of both information and knowledge. Frontiers are being bypassed and information is becoming available to everyone to seek and acquire.

Current technologies make it possible to transform the availability of such information and its subsequent ease of manipulation into a learning process[1]. A learning process that encounters no barriers, physical or logical, is available on

An Ethical Global Information Society J. Berleur & D. Whitehouse (Eds.)

request whenever and wherever such a need arises, can be tailored to meet its recipients needs and, above all, is subject to critical thinking for evaluation.

The Internet, by eliminating distance and physical frontiers, tends to become the forum where ideas are exchanged, cultures are viewed from different perspectives, issues are debated, and new concepts are promoted but, most importantly, people are brought together to form a multinational, frontier-less society that shares a common ideal: information exchange and knowledge proliferation.

The Internet's exclusive role in the 1980s, that of a scientific forum, is rapidly being overtaken by a wider, holistic and multiple perspective that renders its role to one of a means to an end rather than an end in itself. The end is the delivery of information, and its consequent proliferation around the world, that enables end users to become easily updated on developments in their field of study or interest.

Viewed from this perspective, the Internet leads to a number of important issues that require thorough thinking when addressed, such as:

- what security issues arise that need to be addressed?
- how can the validity of information be guaranteed?
- what are the social and political agendas that need to be addressed?
- how are controversial issues dealt with?
- how can this information flood be transformed into a knowledge acquisition mechanism that would not only further the epistemic aspects of the domains it addresses but will also reach people who are at present unable to obtain a broad perspective on their area of interest?
- how can technological developments, present and future, contribute in the better use of existing information pools?
- to what degree will this emerging technology change one's own contribution to society and, as a result, change society itself?

This analysis addresses the proliferation of knowledge and information that stems from existing information sources over the world wide web as well as the roles that the participants of this forum can play in the generation, formation, and exchange of such information and with respect to the humanities. The term humanities encapsulates a wide number of disciplines and aspects of human life. The authors, however, focus on the aspects of human culture, with particular reference to literature, language, history, and philosophy, areas where the Internet can play a very important role yet to be explored.

POSSIBLE ROLES OF THE INTERNET

So far, the Internet has been considered as the computer people medium for information exchange, a notion very well nursed by the obscurity of Internet access utilities such as ftp and ftam and the painstaking efforts that users had to make in using the Internet. The technological boom and, in particular, that associated with the world wide web, as currently experienced, diffuses this perspective in light of the user-oriented but not necessarily expert-oriented philosophy that has been adopted. Strange and confusing procedures are substituted by friendly graphical network browsers where information is presented in a polymorphic manner by means of video, sound, text, and iconic forms. Its users are no longer expected to be computer literate gurus in order to make use of this new born, yet rapidly evolving service. Instead, anyone with the bare minimum of technology can be part of this international forum of communication[2].

What is, however, the implication of more and more people having access to the same information, being able to communicate among themselves, exchanging their views and ideas, debating key issues, expressing beliefs and, in general, participating in this new found, frontier-less society? One must pause for an instance and draw two analogies of what the Internet can be perceived to be: an agora, on the one hand, and a French café, on the other.

INTERNET: THE WORLDWIDE AGORA

In the ancient state of Athens, the agora was the place where philosophical discussions, debates, and teaching took place. It was where Socrates and Plato, Demosthenes and Solon, among others, in their broad thinking, fought for their ideas, advanced philosophy, presented their views, and set the foundations for the humanities as we know them today.

In a similar way, today's agora, the electronic one, is not surrounded by pillars that overlook the Acropolis of Athens but is instead located in one's office, home, or workplace where it brings together people from all over the world, giving them the opportunity to participate in an open forum of thought exchange. Ideas ranging from poetry to archaeology and from sociology to pure science all, under the umbrella of the electronic agora, the world wide web, become available to anyone to acquire. Consequently, what used to be the privilege of the few is now available to everyone, for everyone to enjoy, contribute to, and obtain.

Web browsers, the medium through which the agora is realized, provide the means for both listeners and speakers to express their views, opinions, and concerns regarding current affairs and other matters.

Under this perspective, the Internet becomes an utterance for free speech and opinion proliferation, ensuring full freedom of expression for the speaker. For the listener, it provides capabilities of unrestricted and unrestrained searching so that she can choose the source of information she requires, form opinions by processing the information, and possibly become a speaker for or against that information.

The role of the participant as a speaker or listener may change in the web realization of the agora, in the same way it did in the ancient agora. This dynamic adaptation of a participant's role within the context of the agora is what makes the difference between the speaker and listener in broadcasting, and author and reader in journals and newspapers (where these roles depend on limitations imposed by the mediums themselves as well as by political and financial implications). Hereafter, the term speaker is used to refer to the person who addresses world wide web users, while the term listener refers to the recipients of the speaker's communication.

Listeners can dynamically locate, choose, and evaluate the information they require. They can even devote the amount of time they consider appropriate in doing so. In this way, they can process the information they receive, manage it, and even particularize it to the extent they consider useful. Their participation can lead them to reform current opinions and beliefs regarding a matter that has been debated. This is a significant perspective when taking into account the amount of information available and its diversity both in content and context.

Through the use of world wide web browsers listeners can, if considered appropriate, follow the interconnections related to the information currently observed whether provided by the speaker or not. As a result, listeners form their own criteria for evaluating the information provided by the speaker.

Browsers also support the user's role as a speaker. The Internet's immediacy brings together the speaker with her audience through their common interests, without the need for complex and expensive media. Users' interest and participation in such a communication may be fundamentally different. In its simplest form, this communication is a thorough observation of what is taking place around the world, like reading a worldwide newspaper that provides immediate and uncensored information. The information found in this newspaper can be traced to its author who can be reached and her views debated at either a public or a private level. At its highest level of complexity, it can be considered as participation in an interactive process where the listener aims to learn from knowledgeable speakers in terms of questions and observations. In this sense, the speaker's address to her audience is not in vain, like a television programme. On the contrary, it must be seen as feedback that originates from the listeners.

The provision of knowledge or opinion that the knowledgeable person has may or may not be filtered, censored or red taped. It is up to the end user, the listener, to decide what to do, when the validity of information is of extreme importance and needs to be examined by experts (for example, conferences on the world wide web, listservers) or in cases where the information provided generates an overflow which in turn results in misinformation.

Although any domain of human interest can be served by the Internet's role as an agora, there is a strong justification for focusing on the field of the humanities because of their relationship to everyone's life. Moreover, the humanities have a lot to gain from the use of the Internet as an agora podium:

- Local information. Even if it were possible to obtain it from all over the world, it would generate mountains of non-accessible data due to its volume, hence rendering it worthless.
- Truths and facts. These fundamental parts of a listener's life may deliberately or not be omitted or infringed. If this is the case listeners, by becoming speakers, can inform the world of such omissions and infringements. Moreover, the feedback generated is useful for the speaker who can use it to motivate other listeners to participate.

Specific issues that rely heavily on the Internet's role as an agora are:

- Presentation by the speaker of particular topics with specific interest that concern, among other things, ethnological and folklore issues. Some listeners may be aware of unknown details and sides that they can contribute to with their experience. Consequently, listeners become a source of reliable and cross-referenced information. Such information becomes more important if placed in a broader frame of collected elements which the listener can abstract or compose.
- The performance of local music by local people who have the feel and knowledge of local instruments, not due to some specific training but through the deep and undetermined knowledge obtained by close and continuous interaction with their environment (family or community). Such knowledge

would be impossible to formalize in the narrow space that general study provides. Such presentations could, in relation to the specific events when they are used or via the emotions they carry, provide insight to hidden aspects of a way of life.

- Description of historical facts, like archaeological findings from the area where a person lives. Consequently, the individual possesses a broader knowledge regarding these facts even if that knowledge is contained in tales passed down from father to son. Such elements are too small to be studied or, in some cases, are unknown and are lost forever as time passes.
- Minorities, local, national or international can promote their positions and make audiences aware of and, at the same time, sensitive to the facts that concern them more easily than by taking an official protest through the proper channels to which they may not even have access. The availability of such information is of great value since, on the one hand, it becomes the vehicle that transports worldwide problems and, on the other hand, it helps listeners to review or to reform their attitudes, philosophical positions, viewpoints, morals, and emotions by raising problems that exist outside the listener's prejudiced world.

From this perspective, the Internet can be seen as the place where speakers with different opinions regarding the same matter may address an audience whose role can be altered flexibly so as to adopt eventually that of a speaker. The Internet's characteristics range from its simple role as a source of information from which users make a selection based on what interests them and where, at the same time, they are free to manipulate this information to the degree they wish, to the socially and particularly complex manner in which they can actively and consciously participate in a society. Thus, the agora can play a significant role in the evolution of society. Such knowledge is particularly useful in the humanities due to both the importance that the area gains through this frontier-less concept and the discharge of priorities that stem from estimations of national importance that adulterate the information.

Listeners' active participation differentiates their role from the classic one in broadcasting, where no answers can be given or remarks made to the speaker and where the conversation time is strictly limited to that of the speaker. It also differs from the newspaper readers' role, since the latter can only interact with the medium via its editor.

The learning capability that such a forum provides changes fundamentally the notion of learning itself: listeners can form their own understandings and opinions in an unguided manner. At the same time, it provides the necessary guarantees that it does not follow the established standards of a particular learning centre which estimates what has value as knowledge, to whom such knowledge is addressed or what gains one can have from it. Subsequently, the danger of binding the information provider to criteria that specific persons set is eliminated. The multimedia dimension that the Internet supports should not be considered lightly, particularly since it appeals to an ever-increasing audience. This aspect allows the speaker to provide information that directly appeals to the listeners' aesthetics and feelings, like artistic pictures, musical sound, and images of current events that raise emotions. The listener can receive this information at the pace her perception /understanding allows.

INTERNET: THE WORLDWIDE CAFÉ FOR THE HUMANITIES

From a different viewpoint, the Internet can be seen as a café. This is a subtle role, one that associates the world wide web with the cafés in the French pre-revolution era. The cafés at that period were the place where the foundations of the French revolution were set. It was the fruitful debates and controversial issues of day-to-day life that were nursed to become the driving force behind a sequence of events that so dramatically altered the course of a nation.

In the case of the Internet, there are no country borders. The country is the world as a whole. The network becomes the place that nurses a new kind of revolution, one that is not limited to information technology but could address issues such as environmental policies, human rights, etc. The freedom to express one's views and *Weltanschauung*[3] [1] in a forum as wide as the Internet is bound to meet controversy and to raise issues that may lead to an uncontrollable boom of this newly found worldwide newspaper. In such a case, it is not beyond the imagination to force a new state of affairs. The role of this service may well prove to be one that could eventually instigate a sociological change.

In any case, whatever the course of things may be, one thing is certain: the face of information technology will dramatically change, changing along the way the manner in which people think and respond to important issues.

The concept of a café, although it has a lot in common with that of the agora, is significantly different. In this case, users do not observe or demonstrate significant and documented views under whatever criteria. Their participation is not considered as that of a simple listener or as a step towards the podium but is one that is continuously involved in debates. Even if users possess unformed opinions, they will form a clearer picture regarding the matter they discuss, they will assign their opinions the appropriate importance, will identify their significance within the broader framework, and will correct misconceptions so that they can convince others or even themselves.

Although the agora and café roles of the Internet can be thought of as very similar, in the context of the former, the speaker is considered to possess the knowledge regarding the topic under discussion. Subsequently, it is up to the speakers' discretion either to involve her audience in the discussion in a dialectic manner, like Socrates did, or simply to express her views in an attempt to convince them, as Demosthenes did. In both cases, the audience's role is a rather passive one, altered only by the speaker's interventions or when a member of the audience who believes can act as a speaker. In the latter, the café role of the Internet, speaker and audience interchange roles as circumstances occur. There is no one who is considered knowledgeable. Instead, everyone contributes to the discussion. Agreements or disagreements may occur and through them it is possible for personal opinions to be modified and widely accepted manifestos to be formed. The difference between a café and an agora can be shown when we consider Socrates' sentencing to death and Louis XVI's decapitation. Socrates persuaded his audience that to escape from prison would violate the philosophy and ethics of his teaching. The decapitation of Louis XVI was based on a decision formed as a result of common agreement among the parties involved in the French Revolution.

Despite the fact that this aspect of the Internet's role appears to be a less important one, it is as substantial as the former since it gradually leads listeners to realize that they participate in a group, they act according to the group's charter which by the way they can evaluate and criticize, they can obtain a philosophical consciousness not in the passive way of adopting the social norms of the society they live in but through their active participation in the formation of such opinions and the establishment of the personal role they can or must play.

The significance of the conversations in the café is very much like those that take place in everyday life enhanced by the fact that they are not restricted to a particular neighborhood that is influenced by local matters, norms or the preferences of particular people.

Like the cafés in pre-revolution Paris, which were the places where small groups gathered to express opinions and views of what was possible and larger groups were formed as opinions were clarified and defended, so the Internet can play the role of a meeting place for groups of people, irrespective of frontiers and local dependencies, where opinions broad enough to cover matters of world importance can be moulded.

The importance of such discussions for humanity is very high. Through the simple and narrowed range of interventions that occur as a result of the various debates, a holistic and gradually reformed perception regarding any matter will emerge; while, at the same time, misconceptions may arise either by embracing rumours or by distracting reality, present or past, on purpose. Such discussions will enable the formation, and subsequent evaluation, of opinions that are established either because it was not possible to review them or due to lack of debate.

As far as art is concerned and, in particular, local art, through the use of multimedia-enabled communications, the Internet becomes the vehicle that makes such information available worldwide. The identification of its value comes through the exchange of ideas. Seen as an aggregation, it is possible to provide the foreigner with a clearer picture of local, aesthetic characteristics and to provide the local person with the capability of objectively and critically evaluating her personal views on the matter.

INFORMATIONAL FREEDOM: WHAT DO WE DO WITH IT?

The freedom that the massive information availability could provide with respect to the social, political, and economic aspects of humanity could well lead to chaotic situations. If such a situation occurs, the information provided may become a vehicle for misconceptions and inconsistencies. Furthermore, locating this information may become a difficult and, in some cases, futile exercise for the end user. Even if mechanisms for accurate information location are devised, another issue that arises even under normal conditions is that of information abundance (which can lead to confusing and contradicting knowledge acquisition). Consequently, instead of the user's role being one of exploration of knowledge, this role becomes a struggle to keep up with the information flood.

With respect to the humanities, this can have devastating effects on a person's work, particularly when this work revolves around research and educational matters. Clearly, it is of fundamental importance to ensure the orderly flow of information by providing the appropriate infrastructure and frameworks.

Such infrastructure and its underlying frameworks must ensure both the use of existing technologies and platforms and, at the same time, lay the foundations for technological development to come [2]. The former is of immense importance, even though some of the technologies currently used are becoming obsolete, such as email services that do not provide multimedia capabilities. Firstly, users who are accustomed to using a particular service, find it difficult in many cases to keep up and at the same time keep track of the ever-emerging latest releases of software and hardware. Secondly, since the area of interest of these users is not in sheer computer science but the role of computers as a means to an end, it is of no value to these users to be constantly on the edge of the technology. Thirdly, investing time and money in technologies that are old within the space of six months to a year is pointless, particularly when one considers latest developments such as the network computer.

The freedom provided by the Internet has been often criticized by the press, with particular focus on the influence it exercises on small children as well as for penetrating one's home. Regarding the latter, one can assert that nothing reaches the user unless the user seeks for it on purpose. Unlike the publicity communicated through television, information available through the Internet cannot in general affect its recipients unless, of course, this is done consciously. Although sinister influences may result, this will happen in cases where people fail to evaluate critically the information they receive.

Consequently, such actions are performed using the user's own judgement and responsibility to a much greater extent than is required when shuffling through a magazine on a bookstand. As far as children are concerned, access to the Internet is only possible if they are given the appropriate means, means provided by the adults responsible for them. Such means are more closely controlled than the currently available yellow press or the danger of being influenced by everyday life events.

The Internet's proper or improper use is very much like the selection of a good or bad movie in the cinema or on television. In truth, it depends on one's culture. Even in this aspect, the Internet can cater for participation and discussion and hence cultural development, a capability that does not provide the unilateral communiqué between the so-called media and the listener. The listener's pseudo- participation in television programmes, like 'call us' programmes, has little to do with the truly in-depth expression of a person's opinion. In such television programmes, the subject is always closed and pre-selected, the reasons for it range from pure advertisement to subtle message-passing, the available time is minimal and, in any case, concerns only a small sample of the audience. If the dangers occurring from the Internet, where children are faced with questions regarding ethics or personal life, are compared to the ones that occur from toy advertising, synthetic food, pink telephone numbers or even those coming from directed information, the criticism that the Internet is faced with can only be moderately explained as impression-generating reporting.

The same holds for the humanities except that, in this case, under the pretense of epistemy, nationalistic factors that look on the spread of new ideas as serving particular interests become a serious factor of influence. More often than not such attempts regarding history, cultural heritage or the uniformity and aggregation of nations stem, for the uninformed listener, from dark sources and come to challenge historical validity. The Hellenic world is particularly sensitive to this matter since it has already, and is still, experiencing such attempts that unfortunately do not only originate from nationalistic trends in neighbouring countries but also from conscious economic and political policies of foreign countries that are only interested in succeeding in their foreign policy.

The answer in all cases is the same. Inhibition is not the solution to the problem since, despite being ineffective, it can lead to underground sources of information control. By contrast, through uncensored information and juxtaposition of the real facts, the truth will eventually emerge.

The participation of the offended person or group in the agora free-forum and the epistemic objective position are the means that will provide uninformed people with the ability to check, evaluate, and to conclude. Their participation in a café will enable them to debate objectively so that they can form the proper and uninfluenced opinions, make the interconnections between facts and other opinions, and assign the appropriate significance to matters. Such opinions will eventually affect and influence the place where decisions that inhibit historical facts take place.

CONCLUSIONS

The use of the Internet as an agora and as a French pre-revolution café can play an important role in the humanities due to its frontier-less opening in either expressing or observing opinions. The use of the podium as an additional facility, in a virtual interactive book providing insights to a specific knowledge domain which deals with problems concerning the actual world, will enable the user to learn about the subject she wants in a way that guarantees participation and discussion.

Exchange of ideas through the Internet, exploiting different resources in a frontier-less way, permits people to feel as though they are participating in a global village, disposing of the unlimited resources of digital libraries where information is sustained in real-time intervals.

Pupils can participate in that village for peer learning as well as follow important courses and, thus, access for all schools may be assured. This access, however, cannot guarantee participation: participation may be assured by the application of the appropriate didactic methodology, allowing pupils to investigate knowledge by participating in debates, expressing opinions, and undertaking actions according to their own estimations.

The Internet by itself is a digital city. Search and communication is allowed, strongly supported when the person is able to identify her interests. However, there is always a need for supporting person-to-person communication: the huge amount of available information that can be reached leads to a rather impersonal aspect; it may be complemented by the expression of personal opinions, and such opinions cannot be interchanged unless a specific domain for each subject kernel is constructed and made public. So, the agora may be considered rather as a requisite. On the other hand, the café allows the user to participate freely in a community, and thus this is a must rather than a simple possibility.

Both roles that the Internet can play have significant importance in the large-scale proliferation of opinions, resolution, and the rectification of misunderstandings regarding historical, ethnic, and linguistic issues.

In any case, as Sun's ex-Chief Technical Officer, Dr. Schmidt said: 'The Internet was the first technology that we as humans had built that we truly did not understand. We are only beginning to discover its uses. Each time it starts to make sense, it changes. For instance, in that old corporate business model, there was an Intranet - representing the insiders or good guys - and the Internet - representing the outside or bad guys. Those two should be together. There should be no division ...'

REFERENCES

1. Checkland P. B.: The use of the term Weltanschauung in Soft Systems Methodology. *Journal of Applied Systems Analysis*, Vol. 13, 1986.
2. Theotokis D., Gyftodimos G., and Georgiadis P. Atoms: A Methodology for Component Object Oriented Software Development Applied in the Educational Context. In the *Proceedings of the 3rd International Conference on Object Oriented Information Systems*, D. Patel, Y. Sun and S. Patel (Eds.), Springer, 1996, pp. 226-242.

---

[1] Learning is considered here within its broader meaning, including that of traditional subject learning.

[2] The term communication is used here within its broader meaning of addressing issues of thought exchange and proliferation.

[3] The term *Weltanschauung* refers to one's point of view regarding a situation of concern.

30

A self-regulated Internet community

Dimitrios Vogiatzis and Symeon Retalis
National Technical University of Athens,
Department of Electrical and Computer Engineering,
157 80 Zographou Campus, Athens, Greece
Email: dimitrv@central.ntua.gr, retal@softlab.ntua.gr

INTRODUCTION

It would be a commonplace remark to note that the Internet is growing fast; nevertheless, we feel compelled to report that the Internet doubles in size every 12-15 months. There were roughly 12 million hosts in July, 1996 [1]. Whereas it is difficult to tell the exact number of actual users, we know that they are scattered worldwide.

In a sense, the Internet is a community. But, unlike a traditional community, it cannot be located on the map unless we consider cyberspace as its natural site. This community only produces and consumes information. The old questions about politics emerge again seeking a new context on the Internet. In particular, who is in charge? Why should it be that way? How is power exercised? How are vague ideas about the state of things to be consolidated in rules, ethics, or laws? We shall attempt to answer these queries in the context of the current and prospective state of the Internet.

At a rather abstract level, the central idea we are trying to convey is that of freedom of expression, which has been an essential ingredient of democratic countries. That is, being free to publish in various forms (via text, sound, video, etc.) any idea, irrespective of the cultural make-up of the potential recipients. We are also advocating tolerance, one of the fundamental ideas of the Declaration of Human Rights of the French Revolution of 1789. Furthermore, we stand unfavourably against unfair advantage gained by plagiarism. In the next paragraphs, we will mention a particular way in which these ideas can be consolidated. In any case, we will be talking about netizens (citizens on the network) and their political rights within the Internet community. The following terms will be used interchangeably: the net and the Internet.

An Ethical Global Information Society J. Berleur & D. Whitehouse (Eds.)

There are currently societies and consortiums that deal with different aspects of the Internet. The W3C consortium [2] mostly deals with the standardization of the world wide web, but also has a societal component which strives to preserve freedom of expression on the Internet. The purposes of the Internet Society [3] range from hardware to assisting developing countries maintain and evolve their Internet structure. On the other hand, the Web Society [4] is concerned with political, legal, and societal issues as well as with tools to make information retrieval easier.

We are not proposing a novel community, but rather a set of principles in the light of which existing or future societies can be evaluated as far as the free flow of information is concerned. Thus, we will not discuss hardware or related protocols.

Figure : Internet growth (source: Network Wizards http://www.nw.com)

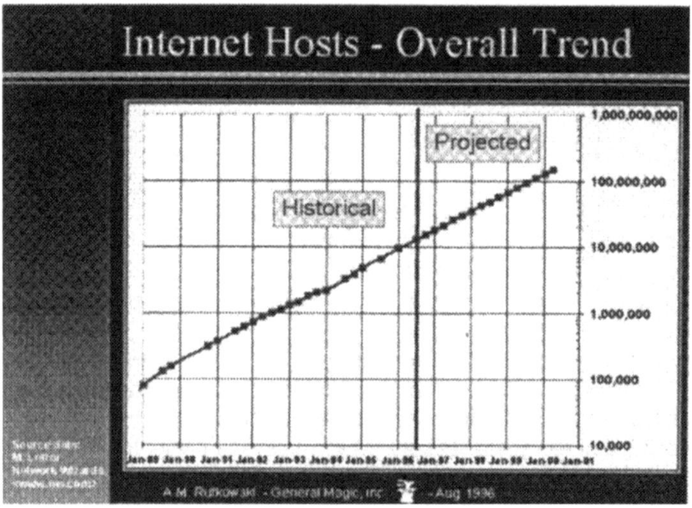

THE CURRENT STATE OF POLITICS ON THE INTERNET

The Internet is interesting not only as a massive global network but also as an example of something that continuously evolves with no apparent designer in charge. At the beginning, the Internet was used mostly by academics for information retrieval and exchange of information resources (hypertext documents). Nowadays, it is used not only for collaboration, exchange of know how, expertise and experiences (such as ftp, email, newsgroups, and conferencing systems) but for instruction delivery (open and distance learning programmes), for commercial reasons (shopping, advertisements of products) as well as for entertainment (real-time audio, video, multimedia games, and so on). So when we say that the Internet is changing, we not only mean that it is growing - nobody knows the number of netizens - but also that its use has changed and the software applications that increase its potential are constantly being developed.

We will try to depict, through a few specific cases, some of the issues that have arisen on the Internet lately, with the purpose of attesting that we have not yet understood how to live in the Internet community. Mostly, we are feeling our way into it, blundering about. As a result, topics, discussion cases, and questions arise, such as computer crime (hackers, violation of national security), protection of intellectual property (copyright issues), and freedom of expression.

In December 1995, CompuServe (a worldwide Internet service provider) banned access (although temporarily) to certain newsgroups following the orders of the German authorities about obscene material. CompuServe followed a decision of only local importance and applied it to its servers worldwide for technical reasons.

In January 1996, the German phone company, Deutsche Telecom, blocked users of its network from accessing the email address of Ernst Zuendel in Canada because of the neo-Nazi context of his web pages. Soon mirror sites were created which enabled the outflanking of the restrictions imposed.

China is following a rather strict policy as far as the Internet is concerned. From now on in China, all computer networks are subject to the authority of the State Council. The ministry of posts and telecommunications will provide approved communication channels for Internet access. The purpose of this policy is to impose censorship on material of a political or a pornographic nature. However, this target can be achieved without compromising the free expression of ideas. There is software which can scan and censor unwanted words that can be employed by netizens according to their own values and ethics [5].

The aforementioned cases also bring to light certain issues. First, there is a confusion between Internet service providers and content providers as the case of CompuServe and Zuendel demonstrates. Second, it seems that in times of globalization, we still face certain issues at a local level. Third, it appears that occasionally the restriction of pornography is a pretext for political control as the new legislation in China shows. Last but not least, netizens are nowhere to be found. Most, if not all, of the policies applied so far have been decided by governmental agencies, organizations or Internet service providers. It is clear that netizens are not represented on any of these bodies.

THE BUILDING BLOCKS OF DEMOCRACY ON THE INTERNET

Netizens are the active members of the Internet, in the sense that they receive and disseminate information by means of various Internet services like email, newsgroups, web pages, Internet Relay Chat (IRC) etc. Thus, it is only natural for netizens to participate in decision-making as far as the net is concerned. But, before going any further, we have to discuss briefly the identity of netizens. Currently, there are individual users, and there are various conglomerations ranging from enterprises and educational establishments to governmental agencies. Ideally, netizens should be the only body to run the net. In other words, we are talking about a community that is self-regulated. This has been largely the case so far, but this status has to be preserved in an era of big changes.

At this point, we should be more specific about the identity of netizens. In ordinary societies, it is the adults - practically those aged at least 18 years old - who have political rights. The question is not whether there should be the same age threshold on the net, but whether there should be an age limit in principle. We believe that there should be a hierarchy of presuppositions for participation in the three bodies proposed below, through which power is exercised, otherwise the whole process is reduced to ridicule. Age should be one of the criteria for participating in decision-making; for instance, it would certainly be awkward for children to decide on the infringement of a particular code of ethics on the net. On the other hand, traditional societies do not put much faith in adolescents; however, teenagers tend to be much more computer literate than grown-ups. Therefore, adolescents cannot and should not be excluded from participating in some of these bodies. After all, computer literacy is one of presuppositions, the other is a level of political maturity.

Another subject of concern is the difference in political rights within the net, between individual users and corporations, educational establishments, or societies of various sorts, like the W3C Consortium or the Internet Society. We believe that such societies should only act as consultative committees to executive, legislative or judiciary bodies. Their role is most valuable because of the experience these societies have accumulated.

Netizens exercise power directly on all matters of concern. That is, they participate voluntarily in debates and they finally reach a consensus. In order to clarify the way political issues are handled, we will examine them in the light of these three political bodies which also draw the distinction among the political powers in democratic societies.

Executive body

The net is conceived as an autonomous community. The most important decisions concerning the affairs of the net are to be taken within the net and by all members who qualify as netizens. The word executive is somewhat illusive. In the real world, a government does not execute orders; on the contrary, it is the primary source of power. Therefore, this is probably the most influential body on the net. The members vote on all subjects that concern the net, irrespective of their exact geographical location. Normally, we would expect the existence of many executive bodies, each dealing with a specific subject.

We are already experiencing a limited form of executive power. The creation of a novel newsgroup involves voting. A more evident example is the display of a blue banner on black web pages; this has expressed the grievances of netizens in relation to the United States' Communications Decency Act. However, we have also witnessed the dark side of authority by system administrators who may cast many votes.

Legislative body

Netizens are to create a Bill of Rights, that is, some form of constitution for the net which will regulate information flow and form the basis of the law-making process. The rights and the responsibilities of netizens are the core activity of this body. Normally, we endorse the principle of free information access and free expression within the net. Obviously, totally unregulated free access to any source of information might not prove to serve the basic function of the net. For instance, invasion of privacy or access and disclosure of corporate data are not considered as cases of free access.

We have witnessed many cases where the rights of netizens are clearly compromised. For instance, free access to North Korean databases is forbidden for South Koreans [6]. Thus, a definite bill of rights will help us towards setting a framework for the activities of the netizen.

There have been many excellent propositions that have defined a scheme for the state of things on the net. We could cite the Electronic Rights and Ethics [7] or the aims of the Web Society [4]. The task of a legislative body would be to debate new acts of law and finally to vote for or against them.

Judiciary body

Traditionally, the role of courts of law has been to detect infringement of the resolutions of the legislative body. The judiciary is usually staffed by professionals (judges, for instance). On the net, the first issue to be addressed is the make-up of the members of this body. We endorse the participation of every netizen in this body. However, as the network becomes more and more complex, with the adoption of business acts, certain issues might become too complicated and therefore demand a certain professionalism. That is, it might prove that netizens without special training might not be able to handle appropriately certain matters.

Let us see some of the issues that might arise, for which the judiciary body is responsible: copyright infringement, unauthorized access to confidential information (by hackers, for instance), and invasion of privacy are some of the issues that are dealt with in ordinary courts outside the net. It is not commonplace to talk about such subjects on the net, much less in the context of a formal body, and yet these subjects mainly concern the net.

A precise definition of the responsibilities of this body is somewhat problematic. An ordinary court of law pronounces sentences; we can hardly foretell the nature of those sentences within the net. Perhaps, they could range from a simple recommendation to expulsion from the net for a certain period.

The three bodies through which power is exercised (executive, judiciary, legislative) are mentioned in Aristotle's works, and were reinvented by Montesquieu to become the core of the first French constitution after the revolution of 1789. However liberal these bodies may seem, one might consider them as a barrier towards free expression especially if we take into account the present anarchistic nature of the Internet; but this is illusory. Every netizen is allowed to participate in this three-ply structure; that is, nobody is excluded from power. Second, we advocate direct involvement, that is, without representatives. Third, we have already mentioned that the Internet is changing. Commercial interests and governmental agencies are influencing the net profoundly. There is no time available to be uninterested in the process of forming the future state of the Internet. Whether these structures will preserve the free exchange of information on the Internet depends on netizens getting involved. Incidentally, it is interesting to cite an ancient historian:

> '... and our ordinary citizens, though occupied with the pursuits of industry, are still fair judges of public matters; for, unlike any other nation, regarding him who takes no part in these duties not as unambiguous but as useless ...' Thucydides, *The History of the Peloponnesian War, Funeral Oration of Pericles,* circa 431 BC.

There are also certain issues that have be dealt with from a practical point of view. Of particular importance is the subject of netizen authentication and privacy when voting. Fortunately, the technology is ripe enough to meet the aforementioned demands; for example a public key cryptography like RSA [8] can fulfil our needs.

Naturally, there must be a means of communication between the netizens when exercising their political powers. Newsgroups or mailing lists can play such a role; nevertheless a major problem lies in the sheer volume of information that is communicated. For instance, a major subject that concerns the legislative body might involve reading a great number of electronic messages. After all, membership of the legislative body might be in the order of hundreds or even thousand of netizens. Obviously, we cannot expect an individual to be able to consume that amount of information. Some form of computer aid is required which would summarize the information involved, thus vastly reducing the information overload.

We have mentioned that all netizens are eligible to participate in the executive, legislative, judiciary and executive bodies. However, it is undesirable or even unfeasible for all of them to participate unconditionally in the exercise of power. The purpose of the self-regulated Internet community would be best served by large committees which would staff the three bodies for a limited time span. For instance, when there is a breach of a particular law, a court could be formed to deal with it, then the court could vanish into thin air [9]. Thus, the limited time span committees serve a two-fold purpose: they entice netizens to behave in a responsible manner and the very fact of their limited time span facilitates the participation of most netizens.

Furthermore, we might not totally exclude the concept of electing representatives especially for domains of minor importance demanding a certain level of know how. For example, an elected consultative committee for the judiciary body would be very helpful.

CONCLUDING REMARKS

Netizens will encounter more and more often a confrontation between their desire to be autonomous, in the sense of self-governed, and some of the governments around the world. However, we believe that netizens constitute a very influential lobby on a worldwide basis. In fact, just as certain rights are (or should be) given to each netizen, each one should be held accountable for his or her actions. Each netizen, as a member of the Internet community, is responsible or obliged to all other netizens to respect and value the rights of privacy of all; to recognize and respect the diversity of the population and opinion in the community; to comply with legal restrictions regarding the use of information resources; to recognize that all members share information and technology resources; and to refrain from acts that waste resources or prevent others from using them.

The problems of running the net for the benefit of its netizens have not been solved here. In this paper, we have tried to propose a set of principles for evaluating the levels of democracy in the Internet community. We believe that it is up to the netizens to be more active in finding such an answer.

REFERENCES

[1] Net Wizards, http://www.nw.com/zone/WWW-9607/report.html

[2] http://www.w3.org/pub/WWW/

[3] http://info.isoc.org/

[4] http://aace.virgina.edu/aace/websoc/

[5] Bhorn M, Chen Y, Y: The World-Wide Market: Living with the Realities of Censorship on the Internet. *First World Conference of the Web Society*. San Francisco, CA, October 1996.

[6] Fox R., News Track, *Communications of the ACM*, September 1996, 96.

[7] Electronic Rights and Ethics, http://www.zip.com.au/~pete/ere.html

[8] Rivest, R.L., A. Shamir, and L. Adleman. A Method for Obtaining Digital Signatures and Public-Key Cryptosystems. *Communications of the ACM*. February 1978, 120-126.

[9] Ethics and Law on the Electronic Frontier, http://www-swiss.ai.mit.edu/6095/index.html

PART SIX

Recommendations

31

Recommendations: From sand, through silver, to gold plates

Jacques Berleur and Diane Whitehouse, Editors,
with the help of all the advocates and devil's advocates

IFIP-WG9.2/9.5 Corfu International Conference Gold Plate (May 8-10, 1997)

The information and communication technology society is potentially extremely inclusive, but in practice it is very exclusive, elitist, and sectarian.

To empower people we need universal service and equity of access that provide meaningful, quality information via diverse channels. We want to create 'free spirits'. To promote in the long term a real democracy presupposes an information society where citizens are able to participate in the decision-making process. Civic experiments are therefore needed in the short term which are controlled by all reactive, anticipatory and, above all, participatory means. In others words, we need a critical mass which in turn is also a mass that is critical.

IFIP-WG9.2/9.5 Corfu conference advocates at the highest level an 'action plan' for an ethical global information society that supports:

- people-centered development and public advocacy, i.e., promoting discussion and participation,
- cultural diversity,
- universal low cost access,
- local civic networks,
- development of a framework of rights and responsibilities for a global information society favouring a responsible citizenship.

'Thales of Miletus in the first half of the 6th century was a member of a group of Greek philosophers who combined wisdom and intellectual inventiveness to find solutions to social problems. The group developed a process of philosophical analysis; first thoughts were written conceptually in sand and discussed; some were wiped away to be replaced by others. Those judged best by consensus were

An Ethical Global Information Society J. Berleur & D. Whitehouse (Eds.)

transcribed onto ten silver plates, then the best of the silver were transcribed onto a single gold platter; this quintessence of wisdom was carried to the place of public pronouncements, the agora.'[1]

Our conference was based on this process of refinement, as suggested by Thales of Miletus. Ideas were debated, distilled, and crafted. Entirely new ideas were also added to plates. The conference concluded with the public advocacy and debate of gold plates (the final distillation of the sand and silver plates). A public choice of the most popular ideas displayed on a gold plate was made during the final session of the conference.

Sand plates were transcribed as written personally by different participants at the end of the first day; silver plates were already the 'product' of working group discussions, as well as the 'gold plates' which were advocated in the agora.

THE PROCESS

The whole process of developing sand, silver, and gold plates means progressing from *ideas* (written on sand plates), to *challenges* (on silver plates), and finally to *actions* (gold plates).

Day 1: Sand day

The role of the first day's papers was to stimulate conference attendees to think about their best *ideas* in terms of promoting culture and democracy in the global information society. At the end of the first day, every conference attendee was invited to write in one or two sentences on a 'sand plate' his/her best idea about culture and democracy in the information society.

These 'sand ideas' are given in annex 1 of this chapter.

Day 2: Silver day

The creation of the silver plates took place on the second day within working groups. Out of the synthesis of groups' thoughts on the sand plates, each working group was invited to produce four or five silver plates.

These silver plates had to emphasize the main cultural and democratic *challenges* to the global information society as they appeared on the sand plates, and in the two first days of conference papers. At least one silver plate was supposed to include a creative metaphor.

The silver plates are also given in annex 2 of this chapter.

Day 3: Gold day

First session: From silver plates to gold plate

All the silver plates were mixed up, and divided into three stacks which were provided to three working groups.

As the final process of refinement, the job of each working group was to produce a single gold plate. It was asked that the potential gold plates should each demonstrate a proposal for *action.*

Each group had to decide which of their members would act as the advocate for the gold plate and also designate a 'devil's advocate'. The groups then accompanied their advocates and their plate to the agora.

Final session: the agora

In the agora, the plenary audience heard the arguments for and against each gold plate from all the advocates and devil's advocates. A vote to award the winning gold plate followed. The proposal put forward on the winning gold plate is included in the box at the head of this chapter.

SAND AND SILVER PLATES: MAIN TRENDS

... in terms of ideas

Globalization is not *per se* viewed as determined by technology. But specific metaphors, such as 'global village', 'information highway', 'information society' may be policy instruments for hidden goals which are purely linked to economic or political interests.

Repeatedly, the participants argued that people must be empowered, and that people and communities must be the driving forces for technological innovation. With the Internet in mind, they advocated easy access for all as well as 'universal service'. The diversity of voices is the guarantee of true democracy. Culture is seen as the way of empowering people, through awareness campaigns, training of the public, local experiments, participatory design, introduction of specific skills for analyzing the social implications in professional practices, etc. But information overflow is also seen as an ethical and political problem which could lead to disempowerment.

'Virtuality' was also considered an ideological concept: virtual community, virtual democracy, etc. Therefore, it seems rather urgent to investigate, much more than has been done so far, the consequences and influences - positive and negative, of the 'virtual worlds (or words?)' on real personalities, real cultures, and real democracies, and to involve many more segments of society in the process. From another point of view, we are far from really understanding all the risks of the Internet which was developed without the minimum guarantee of reliable and secure functionality.

Democracy seemed to be the focus of the majority of the conference participants: deregulation, exclusion, elitism, and sectarianism were seen as the main threats of the so-called global information society. The old problem of information poor and information rich is re-appearing dramatically on the scene. The international distribution of labour and cheap intellectual labour bought in the developing nations are affected through new means such as the Internet. Elitism, nationalism, and other ideologies serve the most sectarian interests of the global information society. Participation and solidarity expressed through local communities could prevent us from being passively led where we do not want to go. Is it a utopia to think about an information society redesigned from the grassroots level? Can the Internet become a real agora? The round table on the subject, in this volume, may help to outline some of the issues at stake.

The global information society project must be revisited, so that we look at it from the point of view of the users and the usees ('the people affected or effected by the spreading of the new technologies', as they are now referred in the IFIP-TC9 circles)[2]. There is a strong advocacy for providing a more effective and more motivating role for citizens to monitor and influence what is going on.

Daedalus or Icarus? Technology is open to misuse!

.... in terms of challenges

The challenges are clearly expressed in the silver plates. They are addressed to governments, institutions, and corporations, as well as to the members of professional societies or to non-government organizations. The challenges are to:

- provide, at the global and local levels, complete, understandable, transparent and quality information to all citizens so that they will be able to participate in the decision-making processes,
- provide technical means, free or low cost access to the communication channels (the Internet or others to come), in public spaces and at home,
- allow free expression,
- respect diversity of cultures as opposed to the current trend towards homogenization,
- commit the public and ICT professionals to a process of education for the common shaping of a real democratic information society,
- include social implications and ethics in the learning and training of professionals,
- develop local civic networks.

As requested by the organizers of the conference, one group created a metaphor. Moreover, the group accompanied the metaphor with a drawing! Their challenge is 'to make the best use of the river of information ...' Both the metaphor and the drawing are included at the end of annex 2 of the present chapter.

ARGUMENTS AND RATIONALES FOR ACTION: TOWARDS THE WINNING GOLD PLATE

In the agora, three groups presented their gold plates. Each group nominated an advocate and a devil's advocate to argue for and against the gold plate. Each set of ideas was presented in order. There was much commentary from the floor. Public debate came fast and furious.

Some attendees argued for the need for harmony and synthesis; others for dialectic, discussion, and debate. Some welcomed the advocates' views, others the standpoints of the devil's advocates.

One spokesperson wanted the plenary group to search for any missing information that had not been presented, X-information, such as a public awareness campaign that would focus on the information society or the river of information that flows along to all users. Yet another recognized that it was the very diversity of ideas that had been discussed in the agora that was important for there were a million or more ideas the plenary group had failed to discuss. It is this kind of debate, she argued, that should continue both in the information systems profession and in society at large.

Quickly, there came a suggestion for a vote on the three gold plates. But at least one attendee was suspicious of free voting, whether in everyday life or on the Internet. Another preferred that any final decision should be taken by an executive of wise persons. Many of the participants in the agora did not wish to have to vote in favour of a single gold plate: they liked all three of the ideas.

Here, we outline in order the arguments put forward in the agora by each of the three groups through their advocates and devil's advocates.

Advocate 1 (Jan Holvast)

Presuppositions:
The information and communication society is potentially extremely inclusive (98%), but in practice it is very exclusive, elitist, and sectarian (2%).
Access to information is power.
Action Programme:
Long term: Empowerment of the people. Democracy is power (crátos: strength, power) of the people (dèmos: land inhabited by people, citizens, people)
Middle term: To create an information society which provides relevant, complete and transparent information to make citizens able to participate in decision-making processes
Short term: (Local) experiments with civic networks in order to facilitate people:

- to get the information they need,
- to make a free choice about the way they want to use the information,
- to make clear that information can be dangerous and wrong,
- to decide to be inclusive or exclusive (defined by themselves),
- to stimulate self-determinism.

This process needs to be designed, implemented and controlled by means of anticipation (WG9.2, 'usees'), legislation and participation ('usees') in order to secure diversity.
We need a critical mass as well as a mass that is critical.

Devil's Advocate 1 (Leif Bloch Rasmussen)

Citizens!
I have had some trouble in finding out how to look like a devil. Should I be the devil, his advocate, Mr Bangemann, a 'Sophocrat', his mother, or someone else other than the devil? Or should I just take any look at all? In fact, the devil's mother must be Sophia - the wife of God in the Bible. Sophia is wisdom, so this might be a good way of being the devil. However I have found that the devil might be myself, plain as I am, and that the devil might be in all of us.

So: Dear fellow devils! Two things are important in democracy and civilization and in my group's proposal for the empowerment of people: information and administration (control).

But they neglect two opposite concepts: 'X-information' and 'ministration', which are much more important for the empowerment of people.

'X-information' is all that knowledge that is left out in our rationalization towards getting data and information. It is forgotten, embodied, tacit knowledge. It is myth, legend, story-telling, metaphors, and rhetoric in their best sense. This is what is guiding our actions, thoughts, and feelings. We need local and global diversified 'X-information systems', not uniform, global (0-1) information systems.

Similar notions hold for 'ministration'. This means the ministering to people for their personal, unique, feeling and needs. Administration means most often control of people. Against a uniform way of looking at people and the world, we need ministering, not administrative systems.

So I say: think again. Do not act according to this gold plate. Create 'X-information' and 'ministering' before you try to design any information system or administrative system for the empowerment of people. Otherwise the technology - the computer - may turn into being the master.

Hope it's not too late!

Advocates 2 (Diane Whitehouse and Julie Cameron)

Today's reality is about an enormous number of people who are excluded from access to information and communication technologies (ICT), what the group referred to as usees: for example, anyone who uses a technology directly or indirectly but who has no influence on the rules for its use, its development, or those who control it; or anyone who has no knowledge of the technology itself or who does not understand the implications of using it. Some practical examples can include anyone who is not a business person or a professional person; anyone who does not have a substantial income; anyone who is neither young nor male; those who live in either in non-urban areas or in areas of urban decay; and those who live in developing countries.

On the other hand, the group also felt strongly that individuals may want to be or may decide to be excluded: and this is their right too. Nevertheless, the group hoped that, by encouraging access to ICT, people will be able to take charge of the technological aspect of their lives.

A minimum set of services provided to all citizens at an affordable price to be defined within individual nation-states is one prequisite to access. The other prerequisites are access to skills for using ICT and an understanding of how to use cyberspace, what are its strengths and weaknesses, and what is its source and credibility. The group saw this as similar to the recent set proposals developed by the Commission of European Communities: 'a defined set of services of specified quality which is available to all users independent of their geographic location and, in the light of specific national conditions, at an affordable price'.

Equity of access refers to both physical and mental ability to access information. Citizens need to know how to access the information provided in cyberspace. Educators need to ensure equity of knowledge, and communities need especially to ensure equity for disadvantaged groups.

Developing individual citizens with spirits that are as free as possible – 'free spirits' – ensuring a diversity of culture and thought expressed in open debate and in a free flow of information, not simply on the Internet but in everyday life too was thought to be extremely important.

The group was comprehensive in the range of individuals and groups it wanted to include in this process of empowerment: citizens, educators, designers, librarians, information providers, ICT providers, and information service providers. The group looked forward to 'people power' shaping new technologies through the work of groups, cooperatives, and collaborative initiatives.

The group was concerned about the overwhelming influence of multinational software and hardware providers in their dominance of ICT provision, and there was some hope that the United Nations and professional associations like the International Federation for Information Processing (IFIP) might play some role in diminishing this monopoly. This role would involve informing decision-makers developing policy positions, and ensuring that ICT professionals act with awareness and in accordance with appropriate ethical guidance from charters, codes of ethics, and codes of practice within informed legal frameworks. No single organization – multinational or government – should control either information infrastructure or its content.

The group was aware of today's proliferation of 'stupefying entertainment, needless gadgets, and useless services'. The group was concerned about the abundance of pseudo-information, information that has not been validated, and data that are neither safe nor secure. Users have a responsibility to ensure that information is accurate and meaningful. The sheer volume of unrefereed material 'published' means that some is dubious. Users need to be aware of the need to query the source of data and its quality, they need to ensure that the data they maintain and provide meet quality standards, and they should also monitor the data provided to them by others. As solutions which draw from theory, the group saw the need for more effective application of communication theory, redundant channels, and of feedback loops.

After much deliberation, the group decided it was most important to sum up its thoughts in a clear, succinct statement which it outlined as:

'To empower people, we need universal service and equity of access that provide meaningful, quality information via diverse channels. We want to create free spirits!'

Devil's Advocate 2 (Niklas Damiris)

First, a comment concerning the way I would like the following to be read. I take it that the role of the devil's advocate is not to try to demolish the position put forward by the group. Rather, by pointing out omissions and by questioning self-evident assumptions of the gold plate statement, he is in fact strengthening the position of the group through constructive critique! In my role as devil's advocate, I would like to make three points which the gold plate does not take into account.

First, I find it rather arrogant and presumptuous to talk about and think of people as in need of empowerment and in need of being freed through information technologies. Expressing matters this way implies that most humans are either victimized or 'wimpy'. I see, instead, individuals as already force-full and powerful. This means I see people from the start as naturally full of potential that is afforded them in lieu of their being embodied and embedded in the world. People become free by recognizing their freedoms as indissociable from their powers and responsibilities. So there is no need to create free spirits. Then the problem becomes explicitly ethological/ethical: namely, how the various powers expressed by and through individuals and groups can be coupled and combined without frustrating and damaging each other. That means conflict; but *agon*, as the ancient Greeks and ethological studies of animal conduct confirm, engenders democracy (now literally the power of people!).

This brings me to my second point. Because we live in a mass society, conflicts between groups are becoming the rule not the exception. That conflict is the issue; giving people access to more and more information is not the point.

Finally, I want to point to an omission. No reference has been made to economic matters. The desire to provide meaningful information and respect cultural diversity is pure wishful thinking if it is articulated independently from financial considerations. Economics indeed has a very complex relation to the aforementioned desire. My point here is not merely to raise the issue of who will and how we will pay for the costs of universal access. More provocatively, I want to use the occasion to question the role and function of economic variables in a mass society.

Advocates 3 (Karin Geiselhart and Marc van Lieshout)

That was very good info-entertainment but let's change channels. We know that we are in agreement with the other channels. How can we all act politically?

Our basic point is to state that our conference is a working conference, and that we are expected to produce outputs that could be used to carry forward the work of the group in other forums.

We want IFIP to advocate at the very highest level of action. We want to propose a plan that is based on a people-centered development, public advocacy, that

- illustrates cultural diversity,
- provides low cost access,
- local civic networks,
- within a framework of rights and responsibilities for a global information society.

We want 'information for independent people'. We want to promote the work of the United Nations, the European Community, the G7 and others, work that is enshrined at every possible social level. This is the motivation behind our group's gold plate: to create a statement of intention that can be proposed to international institutions, for debate and, hopefully, eventual commitment to a set of principles that all could strive for in various ways. The *Action Plan* to be formulated should be the result of activities within IFIP itself, entailing the aspects as formulated in the message.

We want people to know that their privacy and their individuality is at stake in the information society.

The group came to this message following an inventory of the most promising silver plates. The inventory showed the following aspects:

- Diversity was formulated as a basic need of society; not as a situation that either exists or not, but as essential for a society to be existent;

- It is not only essential that information is offered to people, it should also be the other way around: people should be enabled to offer information they consider to be important to others. Local communities were considered to be important places for the organization of the democratic process. The conscious reader will have noticed that in our statement it is presupposed that democracy does not simply surface but it must be organized;
- Important aspects within a global information society are the possibilities to increase public advocacy and awareness; not as something to be imposed, but as objectives to be realized by creating stimulating conditions;
- Low cost universal access was seen as one of the conditions *sine qua non* for realizing an equitable and ethical global information society that enables all people to become part of it;
- Empowerment of the people presupposes a community. Though the globalization enables global communication patterns, it was seen as essential to have a focus on local (existing) communities.

The principle challenge for a group of high-minded idealists, which we all seem to be, is how to progress with such a 'normative' agenda in the real world. It seems like we are the good ones at that task!

Devil's Advocate 3 (Richard S. Rosenberg)

Get real. A group of Europeans with North Americans and Australians, under the auspices of IFIP, have asked (who?) for a more equitable world - access to the Internet for all, a responsive democratic process, and more. Why should anyone pay attention? Will the global communications and information corporations suddenly recognize their responsibilities and reduce profits to make the world a better place? Will such governments as the United States realize that a wired world is a better world and that they have an obligation to help people everywhere to connect? I think not.

It is irresponsible to suggest that 'feel good' messages or gold plates will have a real impact. If it is our goal to produce mandates and resolutions with all the right sentiments, then we have probably succeeded. If we wish to participate actively in changing the world by employing the Internet as a necessary tool, then we have a long way to go. Understanding, analysis, synthesis, and dissemination are obvious precursors to direct advocacy but they are not enough. Another statement to the world by well-meaning intellectuals is just that, another demonstration of good intentions.

So what am I for? Simply put, action. Let me preface the following comments with a cautionary note about the word advocacy. There is a common misunderstanding about the nature of public advocacy or activism. It does not and should not mean a self-appointed group of supposedly wise men telling people what it is in their self-interest to demand or to do. Rather, advocacy in the present context is the exercise of a professional's responsibility in informing the public of some of the implications of an evolving technology. The following words of the political scientist, C.B. MacPherson, in discussing the views of John Dewey with respect to the nature of a liberal democracy, are quite relevant:

> The root difficulty lay not in any defects in the machinery of government but in the fact that the democratic public was 'still largely inchoate and unorganized,'

and unable to see what forces of was no tinkering with the political machinery: the prior problem was 'that of discovering the means by which a scattered, mobile, and manifold public may so recognize itself as to define and express its interests.' The public's present incompetence to do this was traced to its failure to understand the technological and scientific forces which had made it so helpless.[3]

It is our job to help the public to understand, and it is its job to demand its rights, which include those that have been articulated in the gold plates produced at this workshop.

THEN, WE VOTED

Eventually, the session did end with a vote. It was a vote in favour of all three gold plate ideas being expressed in a single location, included 'on a single plate' (though not merged or amalgamated) (for: 27; against, 11). The result is the expression of all three gold plates outlined in the box at the beginning of this chapter.

It was decided to leave up to the editors to present them in a consistent way and to prepare a file to address the final gold plate to organizations, institutions, authorities which are preparing our future throughout the world: associations, civic networks, groups of people which are working or sometimes fighting for the reappropriation by the people of what must remain our tools and techniques.

This final plate cannot be read without glancing at all the other plates, either sand or silver, which prepared it. Even if the literary, rhetorical style of the agora, with its advocates and devil's advocates, makes the arguments sometimes funny, dubious or artificially contentious, they have to be considered because they also contain their part of truth!

The issues at stake are multiple: technological, economic, social, political, global, etc. But they are also ethical. The round table on ethics which gathered all the people who contributed to the first part of this volume, identified the main ethical issues. Sometimes ethical issues, such as privacy, computer crime, copyright, censorship, and so on are covered by the law. But new problems appear more explicitly such as equity of access, respect for the diversity of cultures, equitable distribution of benefits, ownership of data when considered as a resource (for development, for instance) as opposed to a commodity, global governance, etc. We need to delineate clearly ethical/social or ethical/political questions, without confining ethics to the domain of individual responsibility. Ethics also refers to the way we act together, socially and, today, worldwidely.

We revisited the project of a global information society which, for the Europeans at least, was presented and adopted by the European Council in Corfu (June 24-25, 1994)[4]. Visitors came from nearly twenty countries, and from four continents. Africa was absent!

We did not revisit thoroughly the official documents prepared by all our countries. They informed our thinking but they were intensely criticized, and they were not considered as top-down messages but instruments which people can use themselves to critique, evaluate, and assess the rhetoric of the global information society.

Maybe we could dare to say metaphorically: From Corfu 1994 to Corfu 1997.

IFIP-WG9.2/9.5 Corfu International Conference Gold Plate (May 8-10, 1997)

The information and communication technology society is potentially extremely inclusive, but in practice it is very exclusive, elitist, and sectarian.

To empower people we need universal service and equity of access that provide meaningful, quality information via diverse channels. We want to create 'free spirits'. To promote in the long term a real democracy presupposes an information society where citizens are able to participate in the decision-making process. Civic experiments are therefore needed in the short term which are controlled by all reactive, anticipatory and, above all, participatory means. In others words, we need a critical mass which in turn is also a mass that is critical.

IFIP-WG9.2/9.5 Corfu conference advocates at the highest level an 'action plan' for an ethical global information society that supports:

- people-centered development and public advocacy, i.e., promoting discussion and participation,
- cultural diversity,
- universal low cost access,
- local civic networks,
- development of a framework of rights and responsibilities for a global information society favouring a responsible citizenship.

Annex 1

Sand Plates

We give here the sand plates as they were written by the participants, but also as regrouped by the editors according to 'generic ideas'.

A. Globalization - Information Society - Metaphors

- What type of social ties characterizes the information society (IS)?
  What could be a possible definition of 'community' in the IS?
  What could be an artistic activity-practice in the framework of the IS?
- Information technology (IT) is not the driving force, it is driven by ideologies like 'deregulation', 'economic globalization', and 'decentralization'. Attempts at influence should address those ideological practices.
- Metaphors like the information highway and IS are important political instruments which are used by technologists, economists and politicians - in short 'digitalists' - in order to control and organize public opinion, and thereby secure hidden political goals of growth and competitiveness in the market.
  Counter-metaphors would be designed, and this can be done using the knowledge of rhetoric from the past. Knowledge and ethics of metaphors and rhetoric must be mandatory for information and communication technology (ICT) professionals.
- In a time of radical social changes (globalization and cultural extinction, market dominance, and threats to democracy), it is essential that we find out where we want to go, and how to use technology to get there. (Rather than leaping backwards into the future, it is time for all of us to look before we leap.)
- We are moving into a world without rules, without speed limits and without boundaries. We need to develop community standards to live in this environment.
- To counter the threats of the ideological forces of 'deregulation', 'economic globalization' and 'decentralization' that largely determine the use of IT, we need structural, institutional, and cultural changes, providing a more effective and more motivating role for citizens to monitor and influence what is going on.
- Threats. Space and time are shrinking with great speed in the global information society (GIS). Consequences: international distribution of labour will be affected; cheap intellectual labour may be purchased via the Internet from universities in economically deprived countries. Creation of elitist, nationalist, and other ideologically biased concerns; combination of such networks will promise sectarian interest versus those of the GIS.
- IS *is not - should not be* - a matter by itself,* but only one topic which intervenes in the evolution of complex matters which have priority such as democracy, education policy, privacy, consumer protection, ...
  (* except for economic - and political - forces which have to sell IT!)

B. Empowerment of people

- The IS represents a new opportunity to design our world from the grassroots. From the people to the people.
- Usenet and the Internet are important new means of mass communication. They grew up from the marriage of computing and communication technology and the hard work of many Netizens to create a way for people to have a voice and to communicate. There is a need to protect and support and make them available to all.
- How do we, IT professionals, make society feel that they really are/should be the stakeholders in influencing IT for the positive evolution of society? Should we?
- Regardless of how we define culture, democracy or the IS, we need to consider the issues related to users of the technology and to 'usees' - those affected by it. Those issues are universal.
- We must think about culture and democracy as *processes* and not in terms of their *products*.
- The key elements for promoting democracy in the GIS are to:
  - raise awareness through participatory methods concerning decision-making at the local level,
  - train citizens through pilot experiments in relation with local authorities.

C. Culture - Virtual worlds

- The most important task of the GIS *is not* to create virtual personalities, virtual cultures, virtual democracies; *but to facilitate an understanding* of real personalities, real culture, real democracies. How do we guarantee this?
- Culture and democracy in the GIS are endangered, because of losing the feeling for reality while using the Internet.
- Culture = People's means of self-expression and community development.
- Even though the Internet community creates cultural interchange, however, there still remains cultural aspects of that social context.
- A virtual agora for the poor and excluded may be wishful thinking because the risk of demagogy is too great.
- We need to be both optimistic and critical in assessing the contribution of new ICT to strengthen virtual democracy and citizens' participation.
- There is no new virtual culture. Virtual culture is our culture put on the 'net'.

D. Democracy

- The 'net' gives us the opportunity to reconsider our ideas about politics. In particular, we can question the system of elected representatives. We can consider the option of a referendum. Thus Usenet could be a boost towards direct democracy.
- It is imperative that new models of democracy be developed for an IS which applies to organizations as well as nations.
- It is clear that technologies by themselves will not create democratic or social improvement or cultural creativity.
  Citizens and organizations have to transform themselves through participation and solidarity showing the way in order to be fully acquainted with the use of ICT.
- Community is the best protection against abuse of privacy.
- Getting the laws from a stranger? Benefits and disadvantages.
- In what ways (give examples) could the IS enhance democratic participation of the ordinary citizen and reduce the democratic deficit which is felt by major layers of societies nowadays (expressed, for example, by abstention from voting)?
- *Aware* of the fact that the Internet was developed without minimum guarantee of reliable and secure functionality, *recognizing* that essential actors governing Internet development are following goals and plans which do not include sufficiently improved safety and security, *observing* the growing amount of malicious, illegal and criminal use of the Internet, as well as *understanding* inherent limitations of assessing the quality of stored or communicated information, the following *agenda* should be enacted:
  - a public *information campaign* should be stated to inform people about serious basic risks of the Internet,
  - *equal, safe and secure use of the Internet* should be enforced by legal and technical means in the next generation of systems,
  - and *projects for democratic applications* should be *rigidly analyzed* for their constitutional and legal acceptability.
- To consider ICT as an instrument for long-term equity and sustainability is the only 'ethical' attitude.
- Privacy enhancing technologies and international harmonization of privacy legislation.
- The only challenge of IT is a political one: How to give power (crátos) to the people (dèmos)?
- Achieving authentic democracy will require re-*doing* technology and democracy as we currently practice them.
- The Internet reaches about 1% of the world population today and is unlikely to reach more than 20%.
- 'Including people in'. Or, in other words, virtual happiness in a teledemocratic society which only excludes people not able to be 'in': Is that the choice?

E. Miscellaneous

- It is important to understand what is new about the computer-mediated communication (CMC) / ICT and try to go ahead in promoting and protecting the medium for that new contribution. The old has its place. The new should need help.

- There is too much information on the web which cannot be identified. A first step in reducing information overflow would be to 'rate' it and to indicate author, producer, status (draft, final), date, duration of validity, etc. A summary should accompany the material on disposal.
- Please apply both
  (a) structural and procedural methods and
  (b) mutual communication for creating shared meaning to solve a problem.
  Please try to guarantee that (a) and (b) are both taken into account and applied in a balanced way.
- Address the shadow! (The unsaid and unthought in what is said about the IS.)
- Daedalus or Icarus?

Annex 2

Silver Plates

Group 1

1. *Empowerment of the People*
   A challenge to government, institutions, companies and members of society. To make available free or very low cost access to the 'net' (in public spaces and homes) and to make the possibility and capability available for everyone to be able to communicate and express their views. Also, the people themselves need to be part of developing the present and future communication systems.
2. ICT Society is potentially extremely inclusive, but in practice it could be also very exclusive, elitist, and sectarian.
   The challenge for true democracy is to create an IS which provides relevant, complete and transparent information to make citizens able to participate in decision-making processes which enrich their own lives. An active citizenship for all presupposes shared information which is socially validated through cross-examination mechanisms. Problem-solving must result in efficiency which benefits all.
   Taken at the global level, this democratic challenge must be implemented through a managerial articulation between the global and local levels.
3. Information providers should respond particularly to the needs of the public, especially with respect to that information that is needed for the democratic process. This information should be accessible and comprehensible to the public and the quality of information should be made explicit.

Group 2

4. 'Society is a thin film bordering on chaos' ... technology, apocalypse, Frankenstein ...
5. We need to engage diverse perspectives in the design and control of ICT systems (i.e., the perspectives of those who use them, who are and will be affected by them, of different disciplines, cultures, gender ...).
6. Both the education of ICT professionals and the active involvement of the general public are necessary precursors to the shaping of a democratic information society.
7. To avoid becoming prisoners we need to be vigilant, to ensure those who wish to be included can be and those who do not wish to use ICT have that choice as well.

Group 3

8. The IT community should wash their words - preserve the diversity of languages!
9. a. *The challenge we see for global democracy*: Involve the participation of both people using IT and the participation of people who do not have access to it. Against the risk of homogenization the challenge is for cultural diversity to be maintained and promoted in the emerging information society.
   b. To attain this, the expression of different cultures has to cope with the extension of democratic participation on a world scale.

10. *Challenge*: To include social implications and ethics in the learning process of professionals. To avoid narrowsightedness, non-IT professionals, including concerned and affected people, ought to be integrated into this learning experience.
11. Local civic networks should be designed, implemented, and managed to secure diversity.
12. *Escher - Recurrence*
    The challenge is: To make the best use of the river of information - see drawing!
    Objective: sustainable relation between the river and the communities profiting from the river.
    Core functions: irrigation - damming - driving - washing - purifying - power: constant negotiation.
    Coordinated use of control mechanisms: dams - dikes - directions.
    Attention to data-fishing, free access, bridges to join communities, early warning systems for freezing or drying up downstream pollution.

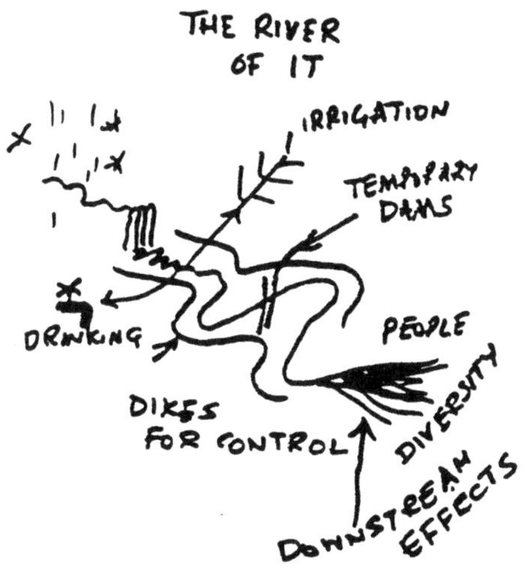

---

1 *Can Information Technology Result in Benevolent Bureaucracies?* T. R. H. Sizer, L. Yngström, J. Berleur and R. Laufer, Eds., Proceedings of the IFIP-WG9.2 Namur Working Conference, North-Holland, 1985, Chapter 1.

2 See: Discussion and Conclusion, in: *Information Technology Assessment* , Jacques Berleur and John Drumm, Eds., Proceedings of the Fourth IFIP-TC9 International Conference on Human Choice and Computers, Dublin, July 8-12, 1990, Elsevier Science Publishers (North-Holland), 1991, p. 388.

3 C.B. MacPherson, *The Life and Times of Liberal Democracy*, Oxford, England: Oxford University Press, 1980, p. 73.

4 Commission of the European Community, *Europe and the Global Information Society - Recommendations to the European Council - The Bangemann Report*, 26 May 1994, CD-84-94-290-EN-C. See also: *Europe's Way to the Information Society. An Action Plan*, Communication from the Commission to the Council and the European Parliament, and the Economic and Social Committee and the Committee of Regions, Brussels, COM(94) 347 final, July 19, 1994. And: *Europe's Rolling Action Plan for Information Society*, COM(96) 607 final, Brussels, November 27, 1996. These documents are worth being compared to other ones such as for instance: National Telecommunications and Information Administration (NTIA), *National Information Infrastructure : Agenda for Action*, Washington, DC, Department of Commerce, September 1993.

INDEX OF CONTRIBUTORS

MIX
Papier aus verantwortungsvollen Quellen
Paper from responsible sources
FSC® C105338

If you have any concerns about our products,
you can contact us on
ProductSafety@springernature.com

In case Publisher is established outside the EU,
the EU authorized representative is:
Springer Nature Customer Service Center GmbH
Europaplatz 3, 69115 Heidelberg, Germany

Printed by Libri Plureos GmbH
in Hamburg, Germany